A History of Sub-Saharan Africa

In a trawl through the entire sweep of sub-Saharan history, the authors, both teachers of African history and experienced travelers to the region, have written an accessible and comprehensive introduction for students and general readers. The opening chapter on geography and climate frames the discussion, demonstrating how the environment has shaped the societies and cultures of those living in the region. Thereafter they describe the rise of states and empires in the classical period, the slave trade within Africa and beyond to the Americas, and the European conquest. The concluding section focuses on Africa in the twentieth century as it gains independence and searches for a new identity beyond colonialism. While the authors mull over the debates which have shaped the study of African history over the last decade, at the center of this story are the tragedies, triumphs and resilience of the African people. The book is illustrated with photographs, maps and sidebars which feature the salient points on either side of a debate, and lists of further reading for those who want to delve deeper.

ROBERT O. COLLINS is Emeritus Professor of History at the University of California, Santa Barbara. His most recent books are *The Nile* (2002), and, with Millard Burr, *Revolutionary Sudan: Hasan al-Turabi and the Islamist State, 1989–2000* (2003) and *Alms for Jihad: Charity and Terrorism in the Islamic World* (2006).

JAMES M. BURNS is Associate Professor of History at Clemson University. He has written *Flickering Shadows: Cinema and Identity in Colonial Zimbabwe* (2002) and co-edited, with Robert O. Collins, *Problems in African History* (1997).

A History of Sub-Saharan Africa

ROBERT O. COLLINS
University of California, Santa Barbara

and

JAMES M. BURNS
Clemson University

CAMBRIDGE
UNIVERSITY PRESS

CAMBRIDGE UNIVERSITY PRESS
Cambridge, New York, Melbourne, Madrid, Cape Town, Singapore, São Paulo

Cambridge University Press
The Edinburgh Building, Cambridge CB2 2RU, UK

Published in the United States of America by Cambridge University Press, New York

www.cambridge.org
Information on this title: www.cambridge.org/9780521687089

First published 2007

Printed in the United Kingdom at the University Press, Cambridge

A catalogue record for this publication is available from the British Library

ISBN-13 978-0-521-86746-7 hardback
ISBN-10 0-521-86746-0 hardback

ISBN-13 978-0-521-68708-9 paperback
ISBN-10 0-521-68708-X paperback

Contents

Illustrations

Maps

Boxes

Tables

Preface

The following *History of Sub-Saharan Africa* was born after decades of gestation. It is the work of two historians who, between them, have been teaching Africa's history to American undergraduates for the better part of four decades. As any honest professor of history will ruefully admit, those lecture notes become yellowed with age when not continually revised to incorporate new information and interpretations. This is particularly the case for the dynamic historiography of Africa. In the 1960s the efforts of African historians were focused on such questions as "Where did the Bantu come from?" "Did Africans resist, or collaborate with, European imperialists?" "Did colonial rule bring ruthless exploitation or beneficent development?" During the subsequent half-century these and myriad other questions have been addressed by historians, their compatriots in the social sciences, and even many scholars from the physical sciences in a never-ending search for the African past. Today new questions engage the attention of Africa's scholars, who explore such issues as identity, popular culture, and the environment, to name but a few. This volume aspires to synthesize the work of the vast army of scholars, young and old, who continue to revise and broaden our understanding of the continent's past.

We wish to give special thanks to Marigold Acland, the Senior Editor for the Middle East and Africa at Cambridge University Press, to Mary Starkey for her splendid copyediting, and to Steve Brown of UCSB, a talented cartographer (and a good friend), who produced this volume's superb maps.

Robert O. Collins
Santa Barbara, California

James M. Burns
Clemson, South Carolina

Conversion table

1 mile = 1.61 kilometer
1 foot = 0.3 metre
1 inch = 2.54 centimeter

1 pound = 0.45 kilogram
1 ounce = 28.35 gram

100 degrees Fahrenheit = 37.78 degrees Celsius

Introduction

The purpose of this book is to provide for the general reader, teacher, and student a one-volume *History of Sub-Saharan Africa* that relates the vibrant story of the African past as it is understood by contemporary scholars. There have been three concerns that have guided us in this enterprise – accuracy, clarity, and style. We have sought to introduce the reader to the central themes of African history and to clarify the debates by historians about the African past with a zest that will seduce the reader to turn the next page and reach the next chapter.

This book and text is the product of many decades of lecturing, writing, and teaching African history to American undergraduates and graduate students. The dedication "To our students" should not be interpreted as a gift to them, but rather an acknowledgment of the interactions with our students, undergraduates and graduates, by which we developed and decided that the approach to present the African past that flows through the following volume is the most efficacious to understand the history of the African people. Historians seldom inform their readers about their qualifications except for a brief blurb on the dust jacket. We are two professors of the history of Africa who have lived, lectured, researched, and traveled in the continent during the last half-century in order to publish many books, articles, and essays pertaining to the African past. More germane to this particular volume is the fact that both of us together have cumulatively taught African history at five American colleges and universities and lectured in universities in Africa, Europe, and the Middle East for more than fifty years to thousands of students, colleagues, and the general public. Through a long process of trial and error, this experience has earned us some insight into the challenges of presenting Africa's history to people who know little about the subject, and whose views of Africa are most often influenced by adventure films, sensational media reporting, and racial stereotypes which are usually pejorative in content and presentation.

In writing a history of Africa for those who previously knew little of the continent and its peoples, scholars in the past have engaged in a delicate balance between the exotic and the mundane. Possessing a myriad of distinctive cultures, which has bestowed upon its peoples a rich and fascinating past, Africa is unique among the continents, but an overemphasis on the romantic features of its history, on the one hand, runs the risk of depicting Africa as exceptional, exotic, and perhaps outside the mainstream of human history. On the other hand, to compare the past of the African peoples with those on other continents by focusing on monumental architecture, literature, expansive states and empires, technological achievements, and other patterns familiar to scholars of world civilizations runs the risk of missing the distinctive genius that makes Africa special.

Our text begins with the premise that African history, like all human history, has been shaped by the environment. Africa's geography, geology, topography, climate, disease, soil, fauna, and flora have combined to create a unique environment that confronted men and women with specific opportunities and challenges. This constellation of nature contributed to the evolution of the first human beings. It also militated against the widespread urbanization that has characterized societies on other continents. The environment of the African continent discouraged the development of densely populated, literate, urban societies, but that same environment shaped African societies to value human relationships, in all their complexity, over material wealth and more participatory governance over autocracy.

We are not, of course, the first scholars to confront these issues or attempt to translate them for a general audience. During the 1960s, the decade of the independence of Africa, there was a scholarly explosion in the search for the African past that continues unabated to this day. By the 1970s and 1980s historians began to seek generalizations from the massive mountain of new information in books, journals, and conferences in order to give greater clarity to the African past, not only for students in their classrooms, but for the curious general reader who simply wanted to know about Africa. During the past twenty years there have been several excellent introductory volumes about African history. These texts fall into two general categories. The first are comprehensive accounts, emphasizing details and narrative but neglecting the larger themes of the continent's history. Although such texts are excellent sources of hitherto unknown knowledge, they expose students to a bewildering amount of information while often leaving them no wiser about the fundamental dynamics of the African past. The second category takes a much broader approach, which characterizes our own volume, that emphasizes the larger themes that have shaped and continue to shape the continent's history. Although there is considerable merit in this approach, these grandiose sweeps of interpretation, which have influenced our own volume, often leave students and the general reader with the impression that African history consists of impersonal, mechanistic, and predetermined forces which permit the Africans little if any control over their own destiny. We, therefore, begin with the assumption that, while African history has been shaped by its unique environment, it has been made by the African people. Their personalities, their inspirations, their accomplishments, their innovations all become blurred as scholars expand the search of larger themes. Our text aspires to identify these important themes that have shaped African history, while keeping a focus on the lives and activities of the people who made those themes possible, by exploring representative examples, rather than providing a catalogue of facts and figures.

A further challenge to writing such a text is the inevitable bias in favor of written sources. History is a discipline dominated by texts, and most African communities did not possess writing systems until the modern era. Thus, the historians of Africa have been largely dependent on the writings of outside observers, but the dearth of the written record also forced them to utilize other academic disciplines from the scientific and social sciences – archaeology, anthropology, ethnography, linguistics, sociology – in their search for the African past. Consequently, those African societies that have left little evidence of their activities have often been marginalized in the presentation of African history. Thus, the role of hunter-gatherer bands or stateless societies is generally of less interest to the historian, if not entirely ignored. In this respect African history is much like the story of the man who came upon an elderly woman one evening on her hands and knees under a street-lamp searching for something. The man asked her if he could help, and she told him she had lost her car keys and was trying to find them. "Where did you drop them?" the man asked as he began to scour the ground. "Down the street," replied the old woman. "Why then," asked the man incredulously, "are you looking here?" "Because," she replied, "the light is better!"

This dearth of sources has meant that much of African history has been presented in very general terms that some students find refreshing and others find exasperating. The willingness of the academic scholar to admit his limitations may be rare in most disciplines, but in African history and in this text it is not unusual. The gaps in our sources are matched by dramatic academic controversies about the interpretations of those sources we do possess. Rather than ignore the deficiencies in our knowledge and the debates over the interpretations of what is known, we have chosen to highlight these areas of speculation and disagreement in a series of sidebars rather than clutter the text with vehement arguments for and against that will only confuse and frustrate the reader seeking definitive answers. Instead, we seek to give readers an opportunity to consider the arguments and evidence in these debates, thereby giving them a better sense of the rich and stimulating intellectual world of the historian of Africa and allowing them to reach their own conclusions about the African past.

Attentive readers will have observed that the title has confined the text to the history of Africa below the vast Sahara Desert. This requires some explanation. We recognize the inescapable fact that every historical work inevitably concentrates on some regional, cultural, chronological, or political community. Thus, by concentrating on Africa south of the Sahara we affirm that this region has a history peculiar to itself. It also implies an important difference between those neighboring regions – North Africa or the Atlantic and the Indian Ocean worlds – and sub-Saharan Africa. However, the important links between Africans south of the Sahara and the regions beyond cannot be denied, and where appropriate our narrative illuminates these ties. Ideas, peoples, technologies, and commodities all crossed the deserts of North Africa and the sea lanes of the Atlantic and Indian Oceans in both directions. Our focus on sub-Saharan Africa has been influenced not only by space, but by the internal integrity of Africa south of the Sahara. Anyone who has taught African history in a college or university lecture hall has experienced the anguish of editing important stories out of their narratives. Our concentration on sub-Saharan Africa is inspired by our desire to devote as much attention as possible to the relevant aspects of this story that would have been seriously diluted by the pages required to elucidate the intricately complex history of northern Africa in the Mediterranean, Asia and the Indian Ocean, and the Americas across the Atlantic. Having defined our geographic perimeters, we have in places taken the liberty in the text to use the simple term *Africa* to replace the stylistically awkward *sub-Saharan Africa* when referring to Africa south of the Sahara.

Contrary to common misconceptions, Africa is not a country but a vast continent with a cultural and geographic diversity unequaled by most other regions of the world. To relate every relevant known fact about the continent would be to burst the boundaries we have set for ourselves and bury the reader in a blizzard of blinding detail. Our book therefore is constructed around several consistent themes that are the framework for the narrative that enables us to tell a coherent story to prepare students and the general reader for greater exploration of specific topics that have attracted their attention and curiosity or larger fields of African studies that we have not addressed. Finally, this book has been composed in such a way as to give the reader more than just themes and a narrative of events. Maps, illustrations, and primary documents are included to help readers to better understand the themes and narrative in the text. Too many history texts adopt an omniscient tone and construct narratives that present history as revealed truth. We would prefer to have our readers evaluate pieces of evidence and to construct their own opinions about African history from the contents of this volume.

PART I

Foundations

1   The historical geography of Africa

So Geographers in *Africa*-Maps
With Savage-Pictures fill their Gaps;
And o'er unhabitable Downs
Place Elephants for want of Towns.

Jonathan Swift, "On Poetry: A Rapsody"[1]

The history of Africa cannot be understood without knowledge of its geography. The natural features of the continent – its deserts, sahel, savanna, swamps, rainforests, plateaus, mountains, rivers, and lakes – have shaped the evolution of mankind in the geologic past and the historical development of African societies in the last several millennia. The pattern of rainfall has determined the growth and enormous diversity of the fauna and flora of Africa. The diverse geologic, geographical, and natural history of Africa has defined the history of the African peoples. Africa is an enormous landmass, 12 million square miles, larger than North America and four times the size of the United States. It is also the oldest continent, from which Europe, Asia, and the Americas floated away on tectonic plates many millions of years ago. They left behind Africa the ancestral continent, a solid, vast, uplifted flat plateau 2,000 to 4,000 feet above sea level, which slept in its geological continuity. Its rocks and sediments remained horizontal throughout millions of years, undisturbed by the gigantic metamorphic upheavals of the Himalayas, European Alps, and the American and Andean cordillera on the new continents.

Africa, however, was not immune to millions of years of geologic activity that shaped the earth as we know it today. There were three stable rock cores in the earth's crust below its oldest continent that thrust upward when the primal mass of the mobile surface of the earth began to cool. They are known as cratons and are found today in West Africa, the Congo, and southern Africa, suggesting that the continent was remarkably stable throughout geologic time while the rest of the world was in motion. These cratonic masses were huge, but as the earth cooled, its heated core would burst upward in volcanic eruptions, carrying its magma and rich minerals from the oldest rocks of the mantle through pipes into Africa – gold, diamonds, platinum, copper, nickel, tin, chrome – and rare metals – ruthenium, iridium, and osmium. These dramatic

---

[1] Jonathan Swift, "On Poetry: A Rapsody," in *The Poems of Jonathan Swift*, ed. Harold Williams, Oxford: Clarendon Press, 1937, vol. II, pp. 245–246.

intrusions did not define the African landmass, which was accomplished by the uplift of the earth's crust into the original continent penetrated by these cratons and volcanic intrusions. Thereafter, this great landmass was governed by temperature and rainfall which controlled the growth of its vegetation and the evolution of *Homo sapiens*.

Africa is the only continent that is equally divided by the equator and consequently does not experience wide fluctuations of temperature. Elevation, wind, and the oceans, east and west, have defined the wide variety of environments in Africa: 40 percent of Africa is desert; the tropical rainforest only 8 percent; the rest is a vast expanse of sahel, savanna, and wooded grasslands between desert and jungle. When there is not a dramatic change in temperature, bacteria and their insect-bearing hosts flourish to breed diseases that in temperate climes are destroyed by frost. Moreover, the consistent high temperatures rapidly decompose vegetable matter, eliminate the nutrients, and leave the African soil impoverished, deficient in the humus and fertile topsoil necessary for productive agriculture. Africa is thus a stable continent resting on its cratons and a granitic shield whose soils are starved of nutrients·over 90 percent of its continental surface.

Although the soils of Africa are poor, its vegetation is rich and varied, having evolved to take the greatest advantage of those nutrients available and the amount of rainfall. Where there is the greatest rainfall, there is the greatest luxuriance and variation of plant life. Although there are exceptions depending on elevation and soil, those regions of Africa that receive less than sixteen inches of rainfall are the open sahel and savanna. The more fortunate areas that receive between sixteen and fifty-six inches of rain are thick with grass and woodlands. Those regions, the basin of the Congo for instance, that have an average annual rainfall of eighty inches created the tropical rainforest, the jungle. The increase in rainfall changes the cycle of vegetation from annual to perennial. The grass of the savanna is seasonal, and by recycling its nutrients annually it can provide greater forage to support a larger animal population than the rainforest. Trees are taller and live longer, some for hundreds of years. They recycle the nutrients from the soil so slowly that the forest can sustain fewer animals than the savanna, as those that live there must climb trees and subsist on leaves and fruit, for there is no nutritious grass.

The great herds of animals that roam the savanna of Africa in past and present contribute to their own fecundity. Although the grasslands derive their nutrients from the soil, those that are grazed by gazelles, hartebeests, and other four-footed mammals produce twice as much forage as plant species that are not annually cropped. The more one eats the grass, *Kyllina nervosa* or *Andripogon greenwayi*, for example, the more it will produce as its evolutionary response to the greed of the herbivores. Like the mammals the vegetation of Africa evolved to meet the optimum conditions of soil and rainfall to produce proteins and carbohydrates. The soil nutrients determine the quality of the plants, the rainfall its quantity. When the soil is poor, the plant may grow large with little

Figure 1.1 *The East African savanna.*

Figure 1.2 *Savanna land surrounding Mount Kenya.*

nourishment that requires the animals to consume large amounts of "fast food" to meet their metabolic needs. Elephants and buffaloes eat huge amounts of deficient forage, which their digestive tracts have evolved to absorb, where soils are poor in nutrients and the rainfall is more than sufficient. The other herbivores prefer the rich grasslands at the bottom of the Great Rift Valleys of East and Central Africa.

The Great Rift Valleys

During the division of the continents Africa also experienced the fracture of its tectonic plate. The more stable African plateau was bisected by two deep rift valleys from south to north. The rifts are huge trenches formed as if God had sliced the continent with a great cleaver. In fact, the great African Rift Valley begins in the Mozambique Channel and moves relentlessly up the Zambezi River Valley where it divides into two branches, the Eastern and Western Rift Valleys. The Eastern, or Great Rift, is a trench some forty miles wide whose floor goes up and down from 1,200 to 3,200 feet with escarpments on either side rising 2,000 feet. It cuts northeast from the Zambezi through the Tanzanian Plateau and Kenya to Lake Turkana, the Omo Valley, through the Ethiopian highlands to the Danakil Depression, the Red Sea, Gulf of Aqaba, Dead Sea, and the River Jordan to end at Mount Hermon in southern Lebanon. The bottom of this great ditch collects the waters that form a chain of lakes in Kenya famous for their prolific bird life – Natron, Mayara, Navasha, Elmenteita, Nakuru, and Turkana. The Turkana Basin is the site of dozens of hominid remains from between two-and-a-half to one million years ago where early man struck flakes from lava flows to help them scavenge the carcasses of animals killed by carnivores.

The Western Rift bifurcates from the Zambezi Valley to cut north through Central Africa to disappear in the great swamps of the Upper Nile in the Sudan, known as the Sudd, the Arabic word for barrier. Like the Eastern Rift the bottom of the western branch is a chain of lakes – Malawi, Tanganyika, Kivu, Edward, George, and Albert. Unlike the Eastern Rift, however, the bottom of its trench differs dramatically. The surface of Lake Tanganyika languishes at 2,500 feet above sea level, but it is the world's deepest lake, nearly a mile, 4,708 feet. Further north in the rift Lake Edward, called the bird lake for its profusion of pelicans, egrets, gulls, and Nile geese, is shallow before its waters flow down the tumultuous cascades of the Semliki River to Lake Albert. Known as the Luta Nzige, "the brightness of light that kills the locusts," Lake Albert is an elongated and shallow saucer, only160 feet deep, from which treacherous waves surge along the surface when the north winds of winter blow down the funnel of the rift. Lake Albert spills its water into the Sudd, the lugubrious swamps of the Nile, some 35,000 square miles covered by aquatic plants, lagoons, and a few people, into which the grand escarpment of the Western Rift and its waters disappear.

The rifts represent the geologic splitting of the African tectonic plate, but they later became the paths of migration where water and grass were plentiful for man and beast from northeast Africa and the Upper Nile. There was fertile soil for cultivation in the bottom land. The steep escarpments of the rifts made the passage east and west across them more difficult, but never impossible, to Lake Victoria, lying on the plateau 2,000 feet above the two rift valleys on either side and 4,000 feet above the Mediterranean. It is the third-largest inland sea after Lake Superior and the Caspian (which is salty, and a shallow saucer no more than 260 feet deep). Its vast water surface, 26,000 square miles contained by the geological configuration of its shores, creates its own climate divorced from the land that surrounds it. Located on the equator, the high temperature of its surface water, 79° F, produces a rapid rate of evaporation which in summer creates violent thunderstorms and dangerous waves for the fishermen who make their way through the papyrus and water hyacinth near the shore to open water.

The two other historical African lakes are Chad, lying in its great basin between the Niger and the Nile Rivers, and Tana and its islands of antiquity sheltered by the surrounding mountains of Ethiopia. In geologic time Lake Chad was an inland sea that became in historical times the sixth-largest lake in the world, covering some 8,000 square miles. Today drought and the diversion of its waters have reduced its surface to less than 1,000 miles, mostly marsh and shallow open water near the mouth of the Chari River and its major tributary the Lagone. Historically, the lake has been surrounded by cultivators growing sorghum, millet, and rice, and pulling fish from its waters. The herdsmen brought their cattle, sheep, and goats to drink from its waters. Their combined resources sustained the Sudanic kingdom of Kanem-Bornu for a thousand years (1068–1846 CE).

Lake Tana was quite different. Like many lakes, it is a saucer, 1,200 square miles, lying in the heart of the Ethiopian highlands at 6,000 feet. Its narrow shores are flat with palms and giant *warka* fig trees. There is cultivation and fishing, but surrounding its blue-green waters are the tombs of the emperors of Ethiopia and on its islands the ancient monasteries of Ethiopian Christianity. Its southern shore is the peninsula of Giorgia where the Blue Nile is born at Bahr Dar to flow to the Mediterranean. The father of this mighty river is the highland massif of Ethiopia. The mother is the rain carried on the wind. Without the clouds coming out of the South Atlantic across Africa, there would be no rain, and without the wind to propel them, there would be no water for the rivers of Ethiopia or the Blue Nile.

Highlands and mountains

During the geologic rise of the horizontal African plateau and the parting of the Rift Valleys there was a great deal of volcanic activity from the

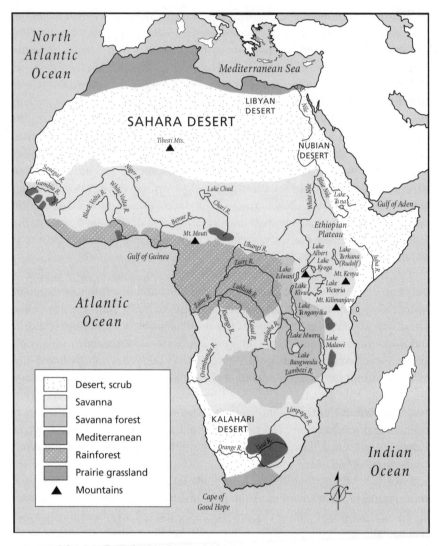

Map 1.1 *Topographical map of Africa.*

earth's mantle that thrust up highlands and isolated volcanic peaks. There are the mountain massifs in the Sahara – the Ahaggar, Aïr, Fezzan, Tibesti, Ennedi – and the more modest uplifts in the Futa Jalon of Guinea and the Adamawa and Jos Plateaus in Nigeria, but the most populous are the highlands of uplifted Ethiopia in northeast Africa. The Ethiopian Plateau is over half a million square miles, the size of Western Europe, with an elevation from 6,000 to 13,000 feet. It tilts to the west where most of its drainage flows into the Nile Basin. Formed in the Tertiary Age, the plateau has been sliced by the rains crossing Africa from the South Atlantic that have scarred the highlands into many thousands of gullies and ravines amidst the lava flows to create dramatic landscapes. These streams, rivers, and tributaries culminate in the great gorge of the Blue Nile, known to the Ethiopians as the Great Abbai, a gorge as deep and broad as the Grand Canyon of the Colorado.

The isolated peaks thrusting up from the African savanna were taller and more dramatic than the plateaus. The most famous is Mount Kilimanjaro, rising 19,317 feet above the plains of Tanzania to its "illimitable" snows. Further north is Mount Kenya, 17,040 feet and far to the west overlooking the Gulf of Guinea rises Mount Cameroon to 13,353 feet. Volcanoes, however, are not always isolated. During the breaking apart of the Western Rift Valley a range of eight volcanoes over 10,000 feet rose in close formation to block the rift from west to east. They are the Virunga Mountains, known also as the Mfumbiro, "the Mountains that Cook," for on Mount Nyirangongo the magma bubbles at 10,000 degrees Fahrenheit while on its lower slopes the mountain gorilla makes its home.

Not all the mountains of Africa are volcanic in origin. The most dramatic range is the granitic Ruwenzori that defends the eastern escarpment of the Western Rift Valley overlooking the Semliki River between Lakes Edward and Albert. The range is short, less than a hundred miles in which, however, several peaks tower above the equator over 16,000 feet whose icy crags, glaciers, and swirling mists rise into stormy skies in the heart of Africa. They were well known to the ancient Greeks, who called them the *Lunas Montes*, the Mountains of the Moon. No sensible person can believe there are mountain glaciers on the equator, and certainly not Victorian geographers. The Africans, of course, had the more sublime answer, for everyone knows that these great peaks draw down the moonlight which envelops their summits. They are enshrouded in rainclouds 300 days of the year. Here in the Ruwenzori earthworms will grow to three feet, canaries five feet from beak to tail, all dominated by gigantic flowering trees of great age. Melting ice water hurtling over cliffs into space does not reach the ground, blown away by the wind. It is Africa in all its immensity. In 1889 the Anglo-American explorer Henry Morton Stanley (1841–1904), on his third and final African expedition, saw the peaks and sensibly gave them the Ankole word for the Ruwenzori, "Rainmaker."

Further south Africa created a more modest but historically more important range: the Drakensberg, which is the dramatic part of the Great Escarpment that separates the high plateau of the interior of central and southern Africa from the East African coast of the Indian Ocean. Its wall of mountains extends from Mount Drakensberg (11,400 feet) 700 miles northeast along the Indian Ocean shore of southern Africa to Cathedral Peak. In Lesotho the steep escarpment is broken by basalt pinnacles from 10,000 to 11,000 feet, snowcapped in winter, and a steep scarp known to the Zulu as Izintaba Zokhahlamba, "barrier of pointed spears." Below the escarpment are sandstone terraces cut by deep valleys to the coastal plain and the sea. Further north the steep Drakensberg escarpment gives way to gentle slopes punctuated by rugged peaks of 7,600 feet before the range integrates itself into the interior plateau.

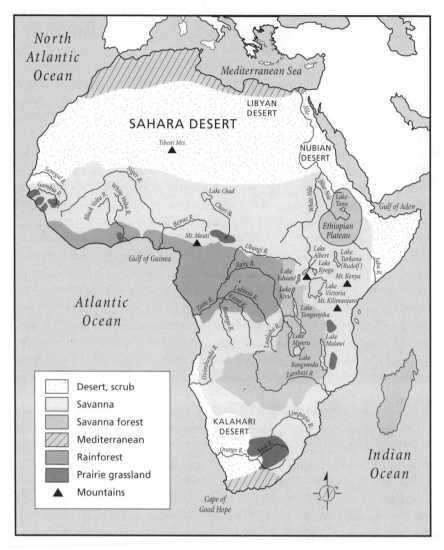

Map 1.2 *Vegetation regimes of Africa.*

The rainforests

Every year in the spring the monsoon comes billowing majestically out of the South Atlantic to drop its huge amounts of water diagonally across Africa from the West African coast and the Congo River Basin to the Upper Nile where it rises to expire on the Ethiopian Plateau, some years leaving great quantities of water, others less. This annual event is controlled by the larger pattern of global climate determined by the vast ocean masses of the Pacific, Atlantic, and Indian Oceans. They generate the rainfall that makes possible the tropical rainforests of the West African coast, the great basin of the Congo, and the more temperate climate on the Ethiopian Plateau whose streams and rivers create the Great Abbai, the Blue Nile, that has carved its own grand canyon through the highlands to the plains of the Sudan.

The African rainforest stretches along the West African coast a hundred miles deep from the Senegambia, to curve around to the Niger Delta, Cameroon, and Gabon to the mouth of the River Congo. The great basin of the Congo, a million square miles, the size of the United States east of the Mississippi, is the great tropical rainforest of Africa, known in popular culture as "the jungle." It is in fact a complex ecosystem dominated by a vast expanse of forest with towering trees whose canopy admits only slivers of sunlight to the decaying undergrowth below. During the day it is a silent, closed world, but it comes alive after dark. No other ecosystem in the world is more diverse. Over four hundred different species of trees can be found in just one square mile – not including the thousands of multiple vines, shrubs, and plants on the ground and in the trees. Like Lake Victoria the tropical rainforest makes its own weather from the moisture rising from the forest into dark, massive clouds whose water descends to continue the regeneration of the vegetation below. Some estimate that the South Atlantic monsoon provides only a third of the water for the rainforest, but it is the origin for its biomass. The rains that spawn the great rainforest of the Congo blow out of the South Atlantic between April and October, and peak in July and September. The monsoon is controlled by the Inter-Tropical Convergence Zone (ITCZ) which runs from west to east and is moved north and south by the larger dynamics of global climate to provide the rainy season in summer and the dry months of winter. The average annual rainfall in the Congo rainforest is about 80 inches, but some regions of the coast of Cameroon, which receives the brunt of the southwest monsoon, can receive over 200 inches annually. The slopes of Mount Cameroon absorb more than 300 inches.

Compared to the arid regions of Africa, the Sahara and Kalahari, the temperatures in the rainforest are not severely hot, averaging about 80°F, but the climate and the environment are dominated by the intense humidity, over 90 percent, which determines life in the rainforest. Trees are the kings of the rainforest. They have lived for hundreds of years and with ruthless efficiency have denuded the soil of its nutrients, which must be taken from the air, the rain, and the decaying vegetation below, the compost that feeds the living plants on the ground. Although the tropical rainforest is more vulnerable to climatic or geologic change than other habitats, more of the landmass of Africa has been covered by tropical rainforest than any other continent. The forests have played a significant role in the evolution of the primates, the ancestors of man, and are rich in animal life. Hundreds of feet above the ground squirrels fly through the treetops. Myriads of birds feed on the wealth of fruits, nuts, and leaves in the canopy. On the ground are huge herds of small animals, insects, and reptiles, but also large antelopes, hogs, and cats.

The immensity of the rainforest, however, can be intimidating with its silent massive power, disconcerting and disorienting to those who have marched through it. Even from the vantage of the rivers through the rainforest the explorers and travelers of the last hundred and fifty years gazed in awe at the massive, seemingly impenetrable wall of extravagant vegetation. Joseph Conrad (1857–1924) wrote in his *Heart of Darkness*: "Going up that river [Congo] was like travelling back to the earliest beginnings of the world, when vegetation rioted on the earth and the big trees were kings . . . Trees, trees, millions of trees, massive, immense, running up high."[2] The whole of the great basin of the Congo is laced by hundreds of rivers that coalesce to form the mighty Congo which is the recipient of its major tributaries – the Ubangi, Kasai, and Lualaba – to flow out of central Africa from Kisangani to Malebo Pool at Kinshasa, 1,000 miles. Its tributaries constitute a vast network of paths through the rainforest. Down these rivers the humans made their way through the rainforest, where they fished and cultivated the fertile enclaves along the river banks to pass through the silent world of the trees to the open African savanna to the south and east.

Sahel and savanna

The great savanna of Africa curls around the tropical rainforest of the West African coast, the tropical rainforest of the Congo, to become the high veld (Afrikaans, "field") of central and southern Africa. The savanna is the grassland plains, but as in Asia, Europe, and North America it is interrupted by sporadic woodlands and forests. The northern savanna grasslands extend across Africa from Senegal on the Atlantic to the Red Sea, the area the medieval Arab geographers called the *bilad al-sudan* ("land of the blacks"), and then continues down the coast of East Africa. Between the Sahara Desert and the savanna lies a fringe of arid land known as the Sahel (Arabic, *sahil*, "shore") undoubtedly so described by early travelers emerging from the hostile desert to see in the distance a line of green vegetation like mariners approaching land from a cruel sea. The Sahel is a band of scrub, bush, thorns, sandy soils, and solitary trees that supports limited numbers of herdsmen and marginal agriculture characterized by erratic rainfall, ten to fifteen inches, from the South Atlantic monsoon. On the great grasslands south of the Sahel the more reliable rainfall, some twenty-five inches, permits more intensive cultivation and larger herds. The savanna is broken by woodlands and ancient trees like the broad-brim acacias, tamarind, and the majestic baobabs (*Adansonia digitata*) whose giant trunks are water towers in times of drought. Its fruit, monkey bread, is consumed. Its bark becomes cloth and rope, and its leaves are medicinal.

The southern savanna on the plateau of central and southern Africa, known as the veld, is much like that of the northern savanna, with grasslands, thorn bushes, trees, and woodlands. Like the desert the veld is not uniform but consists of a great variety of plants, depending upon elevation and rainfall.

[2] Joseph Conrad, *Heart of Darkness*, London: Penguin Books, 1995, pp. 59, 61.

There is the high veld, comprising most of the plateau country of southern Africa between 4,000 and 6,000 feet above sea level, contained on the east by the Great Escarpment of the Drakensberg. These flat plains are dissected by deeply carved valleys and punctuated by isolated steep-sided hills called *kopjes* or *koppies* (Afrikaans, "small hill"). In the western region of the high veld are shallow saline salt pans or lakes. There is also a middle and low veld. The middle veld lies between 2,000 and 4,000 feet above sea level in the Transvaal, the Cape, and Namibia into which the cratons have intruded with their wealth of minerals. The low veld savanna, 500 to 2,000 feet, lies on the eastern plateau just above the Great Escarpment, but whose soils, carried from the more elevated land to the west, are more fertile in Swaziland and KwaZulu-Natal.

The coasts of Africa

Surrounding the whole of the African continent is a narrow coastal plain beginning at Cape Verde, and the site of the port of Dakar, capital of Senegal. From there the coast curls around the protrusion of West Africa along its surf-bound shore to the Niger Delta, the mouth of the Ogoué River, the Congo, to the Cape of Good Hope. From there the coast stretches up the northeastern shores of the Indian Ocean to Cape Guardafui at the Horn of Africa in the Arabian Gulf. This coastal plain ranges from a few miles to a hundred before reaching the escarpment of the African plateau. Its soils are fertile having been deposited by the rivers falling off the plateau. Unlike other continents, however, there are few natural harbors for the African coastline has not been uplifted in geologic time to enable the power of erosion to carve inlets for deep-water anchorage. Throughout 12,000 miles of the African coastline there are less than a dozen natural harbors – Dakar, Freetown, Calabar, Luanda, Saldanha Bay, Cape Town, the Island of Mozambique in Mossuril Bay, Dar es-Salaam, Mombasa, Zanzibar. The dearth of African harbors was not to be compensated by its great rivers, whose estuaries are shallow and striated compared to other continents whose estuaries provide deep and safe anchorage.

Rivers

Africa's dramatic and evocative rivers captured the imagination of the European explorers who first encountered them. The Congo of Conrad is the third largest river in length, 2,914 miles, whose massive discharge surges out a hundred miles into the Atlantic. The Nile of the Victorians is the longest river, 4,238 miles, spanning thirty-five degrees of latitude. The Niger is the great river highway of the Western Sudan; its 2,542 miles end in its expansive delta whose many rivers spill into the Atlantic at the Bight of Benin and the Gulf of

Figure 1.3 *Victoria Falls, Zimbabwe. Most of Africa's rivers drop precipitously before flowing into the ocean.*

Guinea. The Zambezi of the Portuguese and David Livingstone (1813–73), the first European to see its Victoria Falls, flows 1,675 miles out of central Africa into the Indian Ocean. Unlike the other great rivers of the world – Amazon, Euphrates, Ganges, Mississippi, Rhine, Volga – the rivers of Africa have never been waterways into the interior of the continent. They rise on the interior plateau of Africa and are navigable for long stretches until suddenly they fall off the escarpment in a series of impassable rapids to the narrow coastal plain and the sea. The Niger and the Nile have formidable deltas before the cataracts upstream. There are numerous other rivers – Juba, Limpopo, Orange, Ogoué, Rovuma, Rufiji, Tugela, Volta – but they are short, crossing the foreshore of the coastal plain and often with insufficient volume to be navigable. Only the Gambia River of West Africa has proved a navigable passage, 175 miles into the interior. The neighboring Senegal River, rising in the Futa Jalon Plateau of

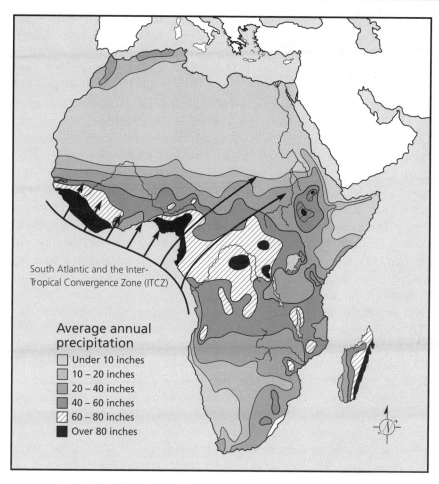

Map 1.3 *Precipitation and flow of rainfall across Africa.*

Guinea, flows 1,020 miles west to the Atlantic Ocean in the winter dry season, where its mouth fans out into a delta, whose passage is obstructed by sandbars. Throughout history this geological configuration of the continent and its rivers prevented outsiders from venturing into the heartland of Africa.

Deserts

Although once green with lakes, rivers, abundant fauna and flora, and man, the Sahara completed its desiccation some 5,000 years ago at the end of the long gradual climatic change of the Pleistocene. The Sahara (Arabic, *sahra'*, "desert"; plural *sahara*) is a huge landmass of some 3,320,000 square miles, 3,000 miles from east to west and between 800 and 1,200 miles from north to south that rests on the horizontal strata of the ancient African continent. There is much mythology, geographic as well as romantic, about the Sahara. Deserts are usually regarded as seas of sand dunes, but only about 25 percent of the Sahara is sand. The rest is gravel (*serir*s and *reg*s), rock, plateaus (*hammada*s), and mountains, Aïr, Fezzan, Tibesti with the highest peak in the Sahara, Mount Koussi (11,204 feet), the Ahaggar Massif, the size of Germany and France, and the Southern Atlas mountains in Morocco that guard the northern fringe of the great desert. Here in the canyons of mountains and plateaus water can be found in the wadis to cultivate crops. The Sahara also has deep depressions, the Qattara of Egypt lies 436 feet below sea level. The real deserts, the sand seas, are the great ergs, huge shifting sand dunes. The Great Eastern Erg is to be found in the Libyan Desert and the Great Western Erg in the Ténéré Desert of Niger which even the Tuaregs, lords of the desert, avoid. The great dunes come in all sizes. There are those formed in the lee of hills. Some are parabolic blowout dunes. There are the crescent *barchan*s, transverse dunes. Some pyramidal dunes will rise 500 feet while the *draa*, the ridges that dominate the ergs, will be over 1,000 feet. The desert sands of the dunes also can sing in a booming voice on the wind that remains a mystery.

There are thousands of oases dotting the gravel and sands of the Sahara, but most are uninhabitable, a single palm and a well filled with saline water and sand occupying an acre or less. The great oases, however, are large habitable regions of naturally watered or irrigated land – Agades, Bilma, Dakhla, Ghat, Kharga, Kufra, Siwa, Taghaza – that derive their water from deep sandstone aquifers to produce forests of date palms, citrus fruits, vegetables, and the cultivation of cereals such as wheat, barley and millet. Like the rainforest, however, the Sahara has always been inhabited, even after it dried up. And like the rivers of the rainforest the paths across the Sahara were well-defined tracks from one oasis to another and known to the Toubou and Tuareg, the guides of the great trans-Saharan caravans that passed from the savanna kingdoms of the *bilad al-sudan* to the ports of the Mediterranean.

Far to the south there is another desert in Africa, the Kalahari in Namibia and Botswana. It is a dry basin of 190,000 square miles in southwest Africa, mostly sand and gravel with few hills or plateaus. Its rainfall is negligible, at most five to ten inches annually. Without the oases of the Sahara it has been inhabited to this day by small parties of hunting and gathering peoples. In the north the Kalahari swallows the waters of the Okavango (Kubango) River in its delta. Rising just south of the Vila Nova in central Angola on the Bié Plateau (5,840 feet), it flows southeast through Angola to Namibia and on to Botswana where it spreads into a triangular, swampy delta rich in wildlife for 150 miles before dying in the sands and gravel of the Kalahari.

Islands

Unlike the Pacific, Atlantic, and Indian Oceans Africa does not have elongated archipelagoes. It has offshore islands that appear isolated, but which have been an integral part of the history of the African continent. The nine islands of the Azores lie a thousand miles from the northwestern African shore, active volcanic peaks rising from the turbulent waters of the Atlantic. Further south is Cape Verde, the westernmost point of the continent, a triangle of volcanic islands jutting into the Atlantic with their peaks enveloped by cloud and mist. There are no further eruptions along the austere and dramatic coast of West Africa until the Gulf of Guinea. Here in the Bight of Biafra off the coast of southern Nigeria volcanic eruptions produced the islands of São Tomé, Príncipe, and Fernando Po, known today as Bioko. Each has its steep volcanic peaks rising to 6,000 and 10,000 feet that collect well over 200 inches of rainfall from the South Atlantic monsoon in the rainy season. All of these volcanic pimples on the ocean are less than 1,000 square miles and are not repeated along the uninterrupted coast of western Africa to the Cape of Good Hope.

The islands of the Indian Ocean have a different origin, dominated by the world's fourth-largest island, Madagascar, lying off the southeast coast of southern Africa. It appears a lonely appendage to the African continent, separated from the mainland by 250 miles of the Mozambique Channel, but at nearly 1,000 miles long and 300 wide, the island is of Africa rather than in it. A central plateau rising between 2,500 and 4,500 feet dominates Madagascar and covers more than half the island. On its eastern escarpment short, torrential rivers plunge into a narrow, fertile coastal plain to drain into 400 miles of interconnected lagoons and deep harbors protected by coral beaches. The western slopes of Madagascar are much different than those facing the Indian Ocean, for the plateau slopes gently through low hills to the Mozambique Channel.

To the northwest lies the small chain of the Comoros, islands in the Mozambique Channel attached more to Madagascar than to the islands that dot the East Africa coast from Kilwa in the south to Lamu in the north. These islands were a scattered rather than a comprehensive archipelago geographically dominated by Zanzibar (Unguja) and Pemba surrounded by smaller islets. Thirty miles from the coast they were formed in geologic times by streams flowing out of the landmass of Africa, and are consequently characterized by ridges parallel to the coast, below which are lowlands and mangrove swamps along the shore, broken by coral inlets. The islands receive some seventy inches of rain a year between March and May and October and December.

Conclusion

Africa is a large and diverse continent punctuated by every geographical and geologic feature from high mountains to arid deserts. The configuration of its rivers, lakes, plateaus, sahel, and savanna has created throughout time the natural resources, plants, and animals that enabled humans to survive in the distant past and to proliferate in the last two millennia. Geography shaped the history of the African peoples who adjusted their way of living and their societies to the demands of the land, whether rainforest or savanna. Like peoples everywhere the Africans were ultimately dependent upon the environment wherever they lived.

Further reading

Since this chapter is principally concerned with physical geography, the reader seeking additional information should consult W. M. Adams, A. S. Goudie, and A. R. Orme (eds.), *The Physical Geography of Africa*, Oxford: Oxford University Press, 1996. Also the reader will find it very useful for this and all subsequent chapters to consult a historical atlas, the best being the magnificent J. F. Ade Ajayi and Michael Crowder (general eds.), *Historical Atlas of Africa*, Cambridge and New York: Cambridge University Press, 1985, which can be found in most major libraries, but the reader should consider the more handy inexpensive paperback Colin McEvedy (ed.), *The Penguin Atlas of African History*, New York: Penguin Books, 1995.

2   Kingdoms on the Nile

Dynastic Egypt and the Nile

The Nile Valley is the home to Africa's earliest literate cultures, and it is thus where we begin our story. Though early humans evolved in Africa approximately 2 million years ago, the first African whom we know by name is the Egyptian king Narmer, who lived a scant 5,000 years ago. It was the unique geography of the Nile Valley that gave rise to the first literate civilizations on the continent.

Egypt in history is an African desert where rain seldom falls. It would be a land of sand and rock and wind without the Nile bringing water and nutrients that bind Egypt to the equatorial lakes of East Africa and the highlands of Ethiopia. The implacable Egyptian desert lies on either bank of the river, but in the Pleistocene (1,600,000–10,000 BCE) the Sahara was green with grasslands, forests, and animals in profusion, which drank from its lakes and flowing rivers. Semi-nomadic herdsmen had domesticated cattle around 9000 BCE. They built monolithic tombs with ritual cattle burials and standing stone structures aligned with the sun to calculate the change of seasons. Five thousand years ago the Pleistocene gradually came to an end and the relentless desiccation of the Sahara began. Hunters, gatherers, and herdsmen who had roamed its savanna and forests and had established settlements now had to follow the water, without which they could not survive, to congregate by the banks of the Nile. Here they encountered and settled with people who had experimented with agriculture by cultivating the rich Nile loam, living in villages, and developing new social and political relationships. It was in coming together in this limited space by the banks of the Nile that hunting camps became villages and villages became towns dependent upon agriculture, first domesticated in Mesopotamia about 9000 BCE, which reached Egypt, very slowly, about 5500 BCE. Wheat, barley, and millet were cultivated, fish were caught, and domesticated cattle, sheep, and goats foraged on the grasslands by the river, while geese and chickens pecked their way through the farmyards. The abundance in the fields and the evolution of political and social organizations enabled the Egyptians to build pyramids, temples, and urban communities whose continuity transcended 3,000 years, longer than any civilization in Asia or the West.

The long history of dynastic Egypt, 3100 to 332 BCE, was totally dependent upon the Nile (Iteru, "the river"). The rise and fall of the Nile determines its

Figure 2.1 *Great Pyramid of Cheops.*

regimen, then and today. Every year the waters from the South Atlantic are carried across Africa by the winds controlled by global climate determined by the vast surface of the oceans. This monsoon arrives on the coast of western Africa in the spring and proceeds northeast across the continent to the highlands of Ethiopia where the clouds are forced to rise and deliver their remaining rains on the plateau and steep ravines. Thousands of streams become major tributaries that flow into the grand canyon of the Blue Nile to carry the water and the nutrients from Ethiopian soil to Egypt at Aswan, the First Cataract of the Nile, and thence downstream to the Delta and the Mediterranean Sea. By August and September the Nile and its tributaries from Ethiopia are in full flood, which in the past and today accounts for 86 percent of the total flow of the river. Then the Nile slowly falls as the rains diminish in Ethiopia, leaving behind *kmt* (the black land) – dark, fertile soil that gave the Egyptians the name for their homeland and their civilization. After the fall of the Blue Nile flood Egypt became dependent upon the steady but sluggish flow of the White Nile from the great lakes of equatorial Africa to provide the farmers with water for the winter harvest. Until the completion of the first Aswan Dam in 1902, the rulers and their subjects feared throughout 5,000 years of history that nature and the Nile would give too little or too much. If the waters of the Nile did not flow, the people of Egypt perished. If the river rose in flood, the enormous power of moving water destroyed their villages, towns, and temples.

During the rise of the Nile from June to September, the season of inundation, *akhet*, the abundant waters loaded with Ethiopian nutrients spilled into the basins beyond the banks of the river. When the flood receded, seeds of grains were planted in the season of growing, *peret*, to sprout like magic from the rich moisture and abundant alluvium to be harvested in February and March. The annual cycle was consummated in April and May by the *shemu*, the months when the floodplain hardened under an unremitting sun until the Nile waters returned to be celebrated in July by the "Opening of the Year," *wen renpet*.

The combination of water, land, and labor provided the resources for the pharaohs to rule the state, build pyramids, and erect temples for 3,000 years. Egypt later became the granary for Greece, imperial Rome, and the Arabs and Turks during the last millennium. The economic foundation of dynastic Egypt was its agriculture, but its 3,000 years of monumental edifices could not have been achieved without the means to mobilize the powers of the state. The pharaohs and their officials had to establish a bureaucracy to tax and to move its grain, stone, and people up and down the 800 miles from the First Cataract of the Nile and the end of continuous navigation at Aswan to the Mediterranean Sea. During the winter months from October to April, a wind both dry and steady blows out of central Asia across the Mediterranean up the funnel of the Nile, enabling the Egyptians from time immemorial to hoist their large rectangular sails to the masts of their feluccas and move majestically upriver only to float down on the current. From April to October the winds from the South Atlantic made the passage downstream quicker for the vessels carrying the large stones for pyramids, palaces, and temples from the quarries near Aswan, as well as goods in great demand from the south – gems, gold, diorite, ebony, ivory, spices, and slaves.

Dynastic Egypt embraced three millennia with centuries of prosperity and depression, but throughout its long history the characteristics of the good times and the bad remained constant. The remarkable long-term stability of the state, a thousand years longer than Western civilization, began when King Narmer (known as Menes, the last sovereign of pre-dynastic and the first king of dynastic Egypt) in 3100 BCE joined Upper and Lower Egypt into a single kingdom. He became the "Lord of the Two Lands" – Ta-mehu (the north) and Ta-shema (the south). Thirty dynasties and a hundred generations later Alexander the Great of Macedonia (356–323 BCE) conquered Egypt in 332 BCE to end dynastic Egypt, but his Greek, Roman, Byzantine, Arab, and Turkish successors maintained the stability of the state created by the first pharaohs. This stability was made possible by the conservatism of Egyptian society, inspired and insured by the mighty defenses of formidable deserts on either side of the Nile. The Egyptians remained self-contained in the fertile band of soil along the banks of the river. Their rulers, the pharaohs, followed one another by primogeniture which insured continuity, preserved the dynasty, and limited disputes over succession, which were so destructive to many African states. This insular society enabled the pharaohs to mobilize the material resources of the kingdom and to organize their subjects to erect levees, dig irrigation canals, build pyramids and tombs, and to construct temples. They used flint, copper, bronze, the wheel, and the *shaduf*, a pole on a fulcrum with counterweight on one end and a water-bucket on the other, to raise water into the fields. They had cattle to milk and oxen to pull the plows and the ubiquitous sheep and goats to provide meat, and ritual sacrifice. They lived on cereals, onions, melons, cucumbers, lentils, and their favorite white radish supplemented by figs and dates, washed down with beer. When not otherwise preoccupied, they wove fine linen from flax.

Egypt has always been a narrow sliver of green fertility over 600 miles from Aswan to modern Cairo at the apex of the Nile Delta. A fan of abundance spreading outward to the Mediterranean 150 miles wide and over 100 miles deep, the Delta, known to the ancient Egyptians as Ta-meha, is choked with Ethiopian silt. The southern frontier of Egypt was at the First Cataract, Aswan, and the residence of the powerful governor of Upper Egypt, the Keeper of the Door to the South. He controlled the insatiable demands by the pharaohs for gold, diorite, ivory, and slaves from the south. During 500 years of the New Kingdom (1570–1070 BCE) Egyptian trading forts were constructed beyond the First Cataract to defend Egyptian colonization in Lower Nubia. The most powerful pharaoh of the New Kingdom, Ramses II (r. 1279–1212 BCE), established a more permanent Egyptian presence in Nubia, but later pharaohs confined their Egyptian adventures south of Aswan to raids, negotiations, and trade. The population of dynastic Egypt, like its government, was also stable, estimated throughout 3,000 years at between 2 and 4 million Egyptians, ruled by their pharaoh. He was the high priest, the god-king on earth, protected by the falcon-headed god, Horus. He was the link between the gods and man, the living symbol of the sun-god, Amun-Re, and Osiris, god of the underworld, who gave religious stability by his spiritual authority over the priests who administered to the people from their temples. The early pharaohs were regarded as infallible, and although the nature of Egyptian kingship experienced various permutations during the millennia, the pharaoh as the territorial incarnation of the sun-god was the ideological cement that held the state together. He was the principal administrator of the kingdom and the center of administration whose officials were the bureaucrats of his royal court. He was the supreme soldier, the inspiration if not leader of his armies.

The pharaohs, and their monuments, temples, and tombs, are the legacy of ancient Egyptian civilization which the arid deserts have preserved throughout the millennia. The resources that made these structures possible came from the farmers, the peasants, free men, who tilled the soil, grew the grain, paid the taxes, and supplied the labor and skills to divert the Nile waters, and build the monuments. Slaves from Nubia filled the ranks of the army. Although there were many free Egyptian soldiers, the pharaohs had no incentive to reduce the number of the prodigious cultivators by drafting them into an unproductive military establishment. There were also priests. Not surprisingly, the Egyptians loved life on earth so much that they and their rulers sought to continue it in an afterlife. Consequently, the life of the pharaohs, peasants, and priests was devoted to the world after death that produced the massive pyramids of the Old Kingdom during the fourth, fifth and sixth dynasties (*c.* 2600–2200 BCE), the elegant tombs of the New Kingdom in the Valleys of the Kings and Queens across the river from the magnificent temples at Thebes (Luxor), and the thousands of other monuments, temples, and tombs on either bank of the Nile from Aswan to the Delta. Pyramids and mortuary temples were for pharaohs and high officials of the state. The tombs of the local officials and farmers were earthen burials in which were placed grain and implements to sustain them in the afterlife. The humble household shrines for the veneration of ancestors were characteristic of later African societies.

The long history of dynastic Egypt and its conservative, self-contained culture has, not surprisingly, obscured its relations with Africa south of the Sahara and the Mediterranean world to the north. But Egypt is in Africa, and of Africa. The Egyptians wrote and spoke a language of the Afro-Asiatic linguistic family, whose modern members include Arabic, Berber, Amharic, Hebrew, Somali, and Tuareg, and the hieroglyphs on thousands of tomb walls portray them with pigmentation from light to dark. Egypt, a river in the desert, evolved a very distinct culture in Africa to which different Africans further up from the First Cataract of the Nile at Aswan into the kingdom of Kush, the Sudan, and Africa made significant contributions.

Dynastic Egypt and the Kerma culture of Nubia

The earliest written records for Africa south of Aswan are to be found in Nubia from Egyptian inscriptions in 2900 BCE. Known to the Egyptians as Ta-seti (the land of the bowmen), Nubia during the Old Kingdom (2755–2255 BCE) was peripheral and uncertain, a place to raid and to trade, but not to acquire colonies. Nubia was the land of the Nile extending from Aswan to the Batn al-Hajar (the Belly of Stones) below the Second Cataract which even in high Nile constituted a formidable obstacle to navigation, and thence over four more cataracts around the great S-bend of the river 1,163 miles to the confluence of the Blue and White Niles at Khartoum, the modern capital of the Sudan. In 2250 BCE Harkhuf, the governor of Upper Egypt, traveled overland deep into Nubia along the Oasis Road to the Fourth Cataract and returned with descriptions of a well-populated and prosperous land. During the next 2,000 years relations between dynastic Egypt and Nubia varied from peaceful commerce to warfare and colonization. When imperial Egypt was strong, during the Old, Middle, and New Kingdoms, the

Box 2.1 The debate over African origins and influence in Egypt

Cheikh Anta Diop, in *The African Origin of Civilization: Myth or Reality* and other works, has set forth the challenging thesis that the origins of ancient civilizations can be divided into two basic divisions: the Southerners (or Negro–Africans), and the Aryans (a category covering all Caucasians, including Semites, and Indo-European groups, and American Indians). Each grouping has a cultural outlook based upon their response to conditions of climate, with the basic difference being that the Aryans have a harsher climate. Diop's thesis (similar to that of W. E. DuBois) also holds that the ancient pharaonic Egyptian civilization was a Negro civilization, arguing that if the ancient Egyptians were Negroes, then European civilization is but a derivation of African achievement. This excerpt, in Diop's words, summarizes his thesis:

> The ancient Egyptians were Negroes. The moral fruit of their civilization is to be counted among the assets of the Black world. Instead of presenting itself to history as an insolvent debtor, that Black world is the very initiator of the "western" civilization flaunted before our eyes today. Pythagorean mathematics, the theory of the four elements of Thales of Miletus, the Epicurian materialism, Platonic idealism, Judaism, Islam, and modern science are rooted in Egyptian cosmogony and science. One needs only to meditate on Osiris, the redeemer-god, who sacrifices himself, dies, and is resurrected to save mankind, a figure essentially indentifiable with Christ. A visitor to Thebes in the Valley of the Kings can view the Moslem inferno in detail (in the tomb of Seti I, of the Nineteenth Dynasty), 1700 years before the Koran. Osiris at the tribunal of the dead is indeed the "lord" of revealed religions, sitting enthroned on Judgment Day, and we know that certain Biblical passages are practically copies of Egyptian moral texts ... It is simply a matter of providing a few landmarks to persuade the incredulous Black African reader to bring himself to verify this.
>
> Cheikh Anta Diop, *The African Origin of Civilization: Myth or Reality*, translated from the French by Mercer Cook, Chicago: Lawrence Hill & Company, 1974, pp. xiv–xv (abridged)

Martin Bernal, in *Black Athena*, has furthered Diop's revisionist thesis, arguing that Greek civilization and even much of the Greek language rest on cultural borrowings from Egypt and the Levant from about 2100 to 1100 BCE.

> The scheme I propose is that while there seems to have been more or less continuous Near Eastern influence on the Aegean over this millennium, its intensity varied considerably at different periods. The first "peak" of which we have any trace was the 21st century. It was then that Egypt recovered from the breakdown of the First Intermediate Period, and the so-called Middle Kingdom was established by the new 11th dynasty. This not only reunited Egypt but attacked the Levant and is known from archaeological evidence to have had wide-ranging contacts further afield, certainly including Crete and possibly the mainland ... It is generally agreed that the Greek language was formed during the 17th and 16th centuries BC. Its Indo-European structure and basic lexicon

Box 2.1 (continued)

are combined with a non-Indo-European vocabulary of sophistication . . . I discuss some of the equations made between specific Greek and Egyptian divinities and rituals, and the general belief that the Egyptian were the earlier forms and that Egyptian religion was the original one.
Martin Bernal, *Black Athena*, London: Rutgers University Press, 1987, vol. 1, pp. 17–23 (abridged)

Mary R. Lefkowitz and Guy Maclean Rogers, professors of classics at Wellesley College, have edited a 500-page volume, *Black Athena Revisited*, in which twenty-four scholars provide their reaction to Bernal's controversial theories. The following is an excerpt from Guy Maclean Rogers' summarizing of the discussion:

No expert in the field doubts that there was a Greek cultural debt to the ancient Near East. The real questions are: How large was the debt? Was it massive, as Bernal claims? Was it limited to the Egyptians and the Phoenicians? . . . All of the contributors agree that the early Greeks got their alphabet from the Phoenicians; but little else. Indeed, in terms of language, the evidence that Bernal has presented thus far for the influence of Egyptian or Phoenician on ancient Greek has failed to meet any of the standard tests which are required for the proof of extensive influence . . . Similarly, in the area of religion, Egyptian and Canaanite deities were never worshipped on Greek soil in their indigenous forms . . . Archaeologists, linguists, historians, and literary critics have the gravest reservations about the scholarly methods used in *Black Athena* . . . What may have happened in the past is certainly not the same thing as what probably happened, as best we can reconstruct it, based upon careful, thorough, contextualized evaluation of all the evidence.
Guy MacLean Rogers, *Black Athena Revisited*, Chapel Hill: University of North Carolina Press, 1986, pp. 449–452 (abridged)

pharaohs sent their military expeditions into Nubia for gold, semi-precious stones, diorite for royal tombs, and slaves for the army, fields, and households. When imperial Egypt was weak from internal strife or threatened by Asian invaders, the Nubians, whose numbers were a few hundred thousand, traded on amicable terms at Aswan, the gateway to the south for dynastic Egypt. This hostile and peaceful interaction over thousands of years led to an ever-increasing influence upon the art, culture, and religion of dynastic Egypt that came from the south through Nubia.

After 900 years the Old Kingdom disintegrated into political and social chaos – the First Intermediate Period, or Dark Ages (*c.* 2255–2134 BCE). During these two centuries a new wave of immigrants entered Nubia from the southwest, the modern Sudan and Chad, speaking a Nilo-Saharan language far different from the Afro-Asiatic language of dynastic Egypt. Driven to the river by the increasing desiccation of the Sahara, they settled along the Nubian Nile south of Aswan where they assimilated the indigenous peoples without opposition from an Egypt rendered impotent by internal dissension. During these centuries the new Nubians developed their own distinctive culture with its crafts, architecture, social structure, and language (modern Nubian is part of the Eastern Sudanic branch of Chari-Nile sub-group of the Nilo-Saharan language family). They were the Nubian predecessors of Kush with their capital at Kerma, upstream from the Third Cataract on the east bank of the Nile and 500 miles from Aswan. Known as the "Land of Yam" to the Egyptians, Kerma lay in a well-watered basin where the Ethiopian nutrients deposited by the Nile supported the agricultural resources of the kingdom. They were rich in cattle for domestic use, sacrifice, and exported large numbers to Egypt. Prosperous and powerful, the kings of Kerma built a sprawling city with a white temple (*deffufa*) fortified by mud-brick walls and rectangular towers astride the ancient routes of trade from south to north and east to west. Their craftsmen produced exquisite black-topped pottery. The indigenous burials of their kings pre-date any Egyptian influence and were accompanied by ritual human and animal sacrifice. One Kerma royal tumulus records the slaughter of 4,000 cattle for the deceased.

During the Middle Kingdom (*c.* 2134–1786 BCE) the Egyptians once again embarked upon imperial adventures south of Aswan for diorite, gold, ivory, and slaves. The Nubians resisted. They were formidable warriors and famous archers, many of whom had served in Egyptian armies. To control the trade, and to plunder, enslave, and defend its southern frontier the powerful pharaohs of the Middle Kingdom constructed forts along the Nile between Aswan and the Second Cataract. During the later dynasties of the Middle Kingdom a steady stream of Asiatic immigrants settled in the Nile Delta of Lower Egypt. Many were servile, but others became integrated into Egyptian society. They were the *Hikau khasut* (the Hyksos), and were concentrated in the eastern Delta around their center at Avaris (Tell ed-Daba) from which they invaded Upper Egypt. Their skilled archers, superior bronze weapons, and war-chariots drawn by horses, hitherto unknown in Egypt, enabled them to seize the capital, Memphis, about 1650 BCE. They ruled lower Egypt for another hundred years through a combination of economic, political, and military power that plunged dynastic Egypt into the Second Intermediate Period (*c.* 1786–1570 BCE), a dark age of political chaos that divided Egypt once again into two lands and civil strife. When the central authority of Egypt collapsed before the invasion and encroachment by the Hyksos (*c.* 1750–1650 BCE), the Nubian kings of Kerma grasped the opportunity to seize the Egyptian forts at the Second Cataract, occupied the Nile to the gates of Aswan, and opened diplomatic relations with the Hyksos. Having defeated the Hyksos and reunified Egypt Amosis (*c.* 1570–1546 BCE) and the powerful warrior pharaohs of the eighteenth dynasty were determined to seek revenge. By 1502 BCE they had crushed the power of the Nubians and destroyed Kerma. The kingdom disappeared into political obscurity, but not its culture.

Relations between Egypt and Nubia changed dramatically with the revival of Egypt under the New Kingdom (*c.* 1570–1070 BCE). The military expeditions

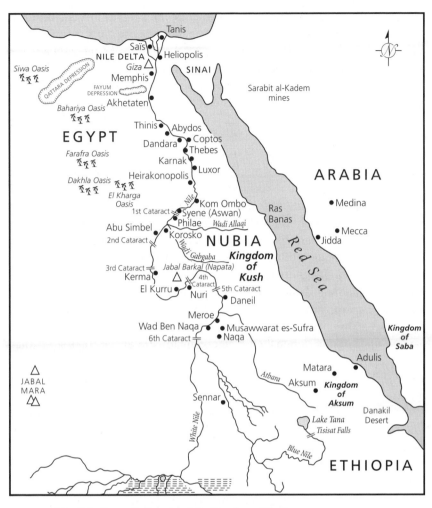

Map 2.1 *Dynastic Egypt and the kingdom of Kush.*

of the Old Kingdom and the raids from Nile forts south of Aswan during the Middle Kingdom were replaced by 500 years of colonization so that the New Kingdom could secure its southern frontier and exploit the Nubians by incorporating them into imperial Egypt. Unlike the trading forts of the Middle Kingdom at the Second Cataract, Egyptian settlements were built in Nubia at strategic locations along the Nile over 600 river miles south of Aswan. The New Kingdom pharaohs established military garrisons, a bureaucracy to collect taxes, and settlers to consolidate the Egyptian presence in their colonies. They built forts and constructed temples as far south as the Fourth Cataract, where the great temple of Amun lies below Jabal Barkal. The Nubian elite were deeply influenced by the Egyptians during these five centuries of New Kingdom colonization. The sons of Nubian chieftains were educated in Egypt and adopted Egyptian customs and clothes, but they represented an imperial veneer as official agents for their Egyptian rulers. Most Nubians labored in the fields and the gold mines, served as mercenaries in the Egyptian army, maintained the temples, and were servants of the nobility, but they spoke their own language and maintained their distinct customs and culture. Those in Lower Nubia were more easily assimilated into Egyptian culture, but the large majority of Nubians retained their distinct identity.

At the end of the eleventh century BCE the New Kingdom slipped into decline. Like their predecessors in the Old and Middle Kingdoms the pharaohs of the New saw their authority dissolve with the diminution of the Nile flood and consequently their resources. Powerful provincial governors challenged the weakened authority of the central government at Thebes, forming political factions as rival warlords with their own independent armies and dynasties. Threatened in the Nile Delta by Asiatics from the east and Libyans from the west the later pharaohs of the New Kingdom concentrated their forces in the north, leaving the historic capital of Thebes in Upper Egypt to the priests of Amun. The unity of Upper and Lower Egypt, established by King Narmer in 3100 BCE, disintegrated. From its Delta ports Lower Egypt became increasingly involved in the cosmopolitan world of the eastern Mediterranean. Upper Egypt disintegrated into banditry, wanton destruction, and civil war and the end of Egyptian domination of the Nubian Nile about 1000 BCE. After the departure of the Egyptians the indigenous Nubian political, economic, and social structure recovered to dominate the land south of Aswan. By the ninth century BCE "Egyptian" viceroys in Nubia came from the local hereditary ruling families who no longer had ethnic or political ties with Egypt, one of whom established himself as the ruler of the kingdom of Kush between 890 and 840 BCE.

The kingdom of Kush, 806 BCE–350 CE

Little is known of Kush until 760 BCE when Kashta (c. 760–747 BCE) and his army crossed the southern frontier of Egypt at Aswan to enter Thebes, where he established himself as the first Nubian pharaoh to receive from Amun the divine mandate to rule. He even intimidated the high priestess of Amun into adopting his daughter as her successor. In order to give legitimacy to his rule in Egypt, and perhaps to enhance his prestige, he worshiped Amun in his temple at Jabal Barkal in Nubia. His successor, Piye (c. 747–716 BCE), firmly settled Kushite control over Upper Egypt, paying scrupulous honor to Amun and other Egyptian gods on his march north. His brother, Shabaqo (c. 716–702 BCE), completed the conquest of Egypt to rule an empire extending over 2,000 miles along the Nile from the Fourth Cataract in Nubia to the Mediterranean Sea in alliance with the powerful Amun priesthood. He moved the capital of Kush to Thebes, and is regarded as the founder of the twenty-fifth Egyptian dynasty (c. 767–656 BCE).

Figure 2.2 *Meroitic pyramids, modern Sudan.*

Unfortunately for the Kushites their conquest of Egypt coincided with the expansion of a new Asiatic power, the Assyrians. At first the pharaoh Taharqo (*c.* 690–664 BCE) was able to defend his northeastern frontier from his capital at Tanis in the Nile Delta, but in 671 BCE the Assyrian king Esarhaddon (680–669 BCE) launched his formidable army into Egypt from his capital at Babylon on the east bank of the Euphrates River. Taharqo and his forces were defeated. Memphis was captured, and Lower Egypt occupied by the Assyrians. Taharqo rallied his Nubians to retake Memphis in 669 BCE and marched to the Delta, but the Assyrians returned under King Ashurbanipal (668–627 BCE) in 663 BCE. He occupied Memphis and sacked Thebes and Karnak, the holy cities of Upper Egypt. The last Nubian pharaoh, Tanwetamani (664–656 BCE), abandoned Egypt to return to the sanctuary of the kingdom of Kush in Nubia at his capital, Napata, whose temples and palaces lay at the foot of Jabal Barkal by the Fourth Cataract. Here the kings of Kush were protected by the desert and the rocks of the Batn al-Hajar, which enabled them to rule over this corridor virtually undisturbed for another thousand years. By language and culture they were linked to Africa beyond Aswan more than were the Egyptians, who were drawn increasingly into the Mediterranean world of Mesopotamia, Persia, Greece, and Rome. Nevertheless, the commercial, cultural, and political interaction between Nubia and its kingdom of Kush, constructed over two millennia, continued to bind two peoples and their cultures together.

The rulers of the kingdom of Kush were mostly male, but the queen was invariably portrayed next to the king and had great influence in the affairs of state. In the reign of King Natakamani (mid-first century CE), Queen Amanitore was an equal, co-ruler. There is evidence that queens occasionally ruled independently. The priesthood usually determined the successor upon the death of the king, but there were instances when the army intervened in the decision, presumably to select the most able from the sons of the queen. The king, queen, and their court were distinguished by a large number of royal insignia, crowns, jewelry, and elaborate hairstyles for the queens. The coronation of a new king was a great event that began in the hypostyle hall built by Taharqo to enhance the temple of Amun. Having sworn his obedience to Amun, the king then set out on his coronation journey through the kingdom, culminating in the crossing of the Bayuda Desert from Napata at the Fourth Cataract to Meroe, 156 river miles north of the confluence of the Blue and White Niles at modern-day Khartoum. Although the earliest capital was at Napata, and it remained the religious center of the kingdom, Meroe became the political center after the retreat from Egypt around 500 BCE and continued to represent the historic continuum of the unified kingdom. The kings of Kush were inclined to be peripatetic, the court residing at one of the imperial palaces scattered about the kingdom. The kings and queens were great builders – of temples as the guardians of state religion, palaces for their pleasure, and tombs for their souls. The temples at Jabal Barkal, Musawwarat es-Sufra, and Naqa complement the royal palaces at Napata and Meroe, insuring that there was no separation of state and religion, as confirmed by the pyramids constructed for the afterlife at El Kurru and Nurri at Napata and those at Meroe.

The kings of Kush administered the state by a large bureaucracy whose administrative details are obscure, but whose officials are known. The provinces, which usually coincided with the river banks between the cataracts, were each administered by a *pesto* (governor) directly responsible to the king. They were normally royal incumbents or well connected at court. The middle tier of officials was concerned with the administration of palaces and temples, and would include the priesthood. The minor civil servants were responsible for local affairs in the settlements scattered along the Nile. Although the structure of the administration of state remained surprisingly stable throughout the centuries, the authority of its officials varied widely depending upon personality, family, ability, and connections at court.

The civil service administered the state, but the army secured its integrity by defending its frontiers, securing internal peace, and protecting the king, whose legitimacy was derived from the gods but who was dependent on the army for the power of his authority. The king was the commander-in-chief, and some kings – Taharqo, for example – led the Kushite army before succeeding to the throne. The Nubians were famous for their courage and fighting abilities, earned as slave troops or mercenaries in every Egyptian army from the first-dynasty pharaoh Djer (*c.* 2900 BCE) to the Egyptian army today. The troops were equipped with shield, axe, pike, and sword, but they (and the Nubians after the fall of Kush) were most feared as archers whose skills have been recorded throughout the centuries. Elephants played a central role in the temple cult at Musawwarat es-Sufra, and were certainly used by the army.

Although the Egyptian cult of Amun had been introduced by earlier dynasties, the worship of Amun only became established in the temples of Kush during the colonization of the New Kingdom (c. 1570–1070) with his temple at Jabal Barkal. The Nubian elite thought it prudent to accept the religion of their conquerors, but their enthusiasm soon died after the decline of the New Kingdom, only to be revived by Egyptian priests after the Kushite conquest of Egypt by the twenty-fifth dynasty (c. 767–656 BCE). The worship of Amun, however, was very eclectic, for he appears in many forms of local origin, often side by side with the Egyptian Amun. The established religion of Egyptian gods at court and temple enhanced by Egyptian sacred architecture was a veneer that obscured the religious reality of the traditional Nubian gods worshiped by the people of Kush, particularly Apedamak, the Lion of the South. He was a war god with bows and arrows, "one who sends forth a flaming breath against his enemies in this his name Great of Power, who slays the rebels with his strength."[1] Apedamak took the place in Kush of the Egyptian Osiris as the consort of Isis, who was herself personified as "the mistress of Kush" in a kingdom where queens as mothers and rulers were revered, a custom common throughout Africa. There were other local gods, Sebiumeker and Arensnuphis, who were venerated in the countryside and to whom the Nubians appealed in graffiti on temples and rock outcrops. Ariten, Amanete, Harendotes, and Makedeke were all local gods unknown in the Egyptian religious pantheon. There were also many popular religious customs of the ordinary people – funerary banquets on the tops of hills, for instance – which were of Nubian origin.

Burying the dead was the most important end to life in both dynastic Egypt and Nubia, but their graves are distinct: the Nubian deceased were buried in a fetal position, unlike the extended position in Egypt, and placed underground or beside their pyramids of unique construction. The Egyptian pyramids of the Old Kingdom at Giza outside Cairo are 700 feet high. The numerous pyramids at El Kurru near Napata and those at the second capital, Meroe, are only a hundred feet, but their narrow base gives them a point that belies their height. Unlike in Egypt there is no internal burial chamber, the mummy being interned in a separate chamber below or at Meroe in a mortuary chapel on the eastern face of the pyramid. The temples of Kush reflect the Egyptian influence adapted to the diverse spiritual needs and environmental realities of Nubia, resolved by filling the pyramid's core with rubble behind a stone or brick façade. Their traditions of human and animal sacrifices throughout the centuries were not of Egyptian origin. Nubian burials, pottery, and pictographs confirm the cultural independence of African Nubia from African Egypt. The construction of temples followed the same diversity as pyramids. The great

[1] F. Hintze, *Die Inschriften des Löwentempels von Musawwarat es Sufra*, Berlin: Akademie-Verlag, 1962, p. 28.

temple of Amun at Jabal Barkal was Egyptian in design, but those in the south – at Meroe, Naqa, Wad Ben Naqa, Musawwarat es-Sufra, and the great temple at Daneil discovered in 2001 – exhibit Egyptian influence but not an architecture found in Egypt.

The kings, the elite, the bureaucracy, and the army depended upon the farmers, herdsmen, and tradesmen of Kush to supply the resources that sustained them. Above the Second Cataract the high banks of the Nile limited cultivation except in the Letti and Kerma Basins into which the waters could flow. On the Butana Plain between the Nile and the Atbara Rivers, known as the Island of Meroe, summer showers and thunderstorms provided sufficient rainfall whose runoff would collect in the wadis where the moistened soil permitted extensive farming for rain-fed agriculture. Large herds of cattle, sheep, and goats grazed on the rain-fed pastures, enabling the evolution of a mixed farming that has been characteristic of the savanna in sub-Saharan Africa throughout history. There was forage for elephants, and the center of their cult was located at the great temple complex of Musawwarat es-Sufra. Wells and *hafirs* (excavations or walled enclosures to collect water) were common and of local design and construction. The staple foodstuffs were grains – sorghum and barley – and vegetables – beans, lentils, and onions – long cultivated in Egypt. Cotton was grown for cloth; wine was pressed for thirst. The Nile was rich in fish, an important part of the Nubian diet.

Kush also owed its resources to gold, and to control of the commercial routes from Egypt to the Red Sea and Asia to the east and Africa to the south. Trade came from India and Arabia to Egypt through Nubia. Nubian gold was mined in the Wadi Allaqi and the Wadi Cabgaba east of the Nile. Diorite to construct the sarcophagi of the pharaohs was cut from quarries beyond Tushka west of the Nile. Ivory and slaves came from the Upper Nile in the south. The Nubian artisans were skilled goldsmiths and intricate carvers of ivory. Pottery, in shape and design, was mostly crafted by hand for domestic use, but the potter's wheel and the finely decorated wares they produced were unique, different from those in Egypt, and their designs have changed little throughout the millennia. Their red-and-black pottery, as thin as eggshell, was used for the finest clay vessels ever made in Africa. The kings and queens wore long gowns with a pleated sash over the right shoulder. Women of the upper and middle class were bare-breasted with elaborate pleated skirts. Men wore loincloths – richly fashioned for the elite, simple for the peasants. Both men and women of the elite and commoners wore jewelry – necklaces, bangles, and anklets crafted in a distinctly Kushitic fashion from gold, copper, beads, and ostrich eggshells. Women wore their hair short with a topknot but were fastidious about painting their nails with henna (a reddish cosmetic dye), and the royal ladies were particularly fond of very long fingernails.

The difference in language between dynastic Egypt and Kush can be found in Meroitic, the official script of the kingdom. Meroitic owes its origins to the borrowing of Egyptian hieroglyphics by the priesthood. The elite used

Egyptian, an Afro-Asiatic language, for religious and secular purposes, but Meroitic (Nubian) is not an Afro-Asiatic language in structure and grammar; it is a member of the Nilo-Saharan languages, whose linguistic descendants today extend from Nubia through the Sudan and Chad to Uganda, Kenya, and Tanzania. When the capital of Kush was moved from Napata to Meroe about 500 BCE, their scribes borrowed signs from Egyptian demotic to create a syllabic alphabet in which twenty-three Egyptian symbols are represented in a cursive script to spell the Meroitic language. The first Meroitic inscriptions date from 200 BCE. Unfortunately, the language it transcribes has yet to be deciphered and remains unknown except for titles and king lists. This cursive alphabet does not appear to be an evolution from old Egyptian, but rather a more practical means to communicate on papyrus and skins that was widely used during the later centuries of the kingdom of Kush.

During the thousand years of the kingdom of Kush the Butana Plain was covered with forests that supplied the fuel to smelt the ample deposits of iron ore whose locations have yet to be discovered. The Kushites had learned the advantage of iron weapons and tools from their defeats by the Assyrians in the seventh century BCE, and large armies could now be equipped with metal weapons more cheaply. After the move of the capital from Napata and Jabal Barkal to Meroe a flourishing iron industry developed that produced axes to cut timber for charcoal to forge iron for hoes to clear the land, turn the soil for planting, and make weapons for the army. The slag from their domed furnaces was deposited in huge heaps that today lie like slumbering mounds of the past outside the ruins of the capital, tombstones of the environmental degradation of the Butana. After 2,000 years of climatic change, deforestation, and desiccation the Island of Meroe is today an arid hinterland.

The conquest of Egypt by Alexander the Great in 332 BCE terminated the extraordinary civilization of dynastic Egypt, but the kingdom of Kush south of Aswan remained secure against Greek and Roman military expeditions. Both the Ptolemies and the Roman rulers of Egypt, like the pharaohs, periodically launched brief raids into Nubia, the most famous of which was led by Petronius, the Roman prefect of Egypt, in 23 BCE. The Ptolemies and Romans, however, were more interested in geography and trade south of Aswan than in imperial acquisitions, which to them were of little value; this left the Nubians to continue undisturbed the long evolution of their own distinctive culture. The kingdom of Kush at Meroe reached its zenith at the beginning of the Christian era under King Natakamani and his queen, Amanitore. During the following centuries the authority of the state dwindled into disintegration by 350 CE. After the withdrawal of the Roman frontier in Nubia to the First Cataract at Aswan, the Kushites sent an embassy to the Roman emperor Constantine in 336 CE, but there is no record of the reason or its return. The demise of Kush remains a mystery. There were no natural disasters, no massive movements of its people, but the Christian Byzantine historians in the sixth century, three hundred years later, describe a Nubia that was no longer the kingdom of Kush.

Environmental degradation in the Island of Meroe, the collapse of international trade with Asia, the concentration of Rome in the Mediterranean, and the corrosive disruption by nomadic raiders, Blemmyes from the Red Sea Hills in the east and Ballana from the west, combined to erode the authority of the kingdom. From the first to the fourth centuries royal pyramids diminished in size and were constructed more with mud brick than cut stone, an indication of the declining resources of the state. A powerful aristocracy challenged the authority of the monarchy. The kingdom of Kush slowly collapsed into local chiefdoms, defined between the cataracts of the Nile, which encouraged parochial independence instead of the unity that the kings of Kush had imposed on the Nile south of Aswan for a thousand years. In lower Nubia these Ballana chiefs continued to be buried with great splendor – no longer in pyramids, but in extensive tombs accompanied by their worldly possessions as well as their slaves to attend to their needs in the afterlife.

Despite the boast on his stele erected in 350 CE that he, Ezana, the Christian Ethiopian king of Aksum (325–350 CE), had conquered the kingdom of Meroe, Kush had already dissolved into petty principalities. The power of the kings was no longer recorded. Ezana retired to the salubrious climate of the Ethiopian highlands, leaving behind the Nubians with their historic mission as the cultural bridge between Egypt and Africa below the Sahara. The presence of dynastic Egypt south of Aswan had disappeared six centuries before the end of the kingdom of Kush, but Kerma and Kush had been closely intertwined with it for two millennia without abandoning their distinctive culture or losing their identity. Throughout those twenty centuries Nubia had remained the crucial link – the kingdom of Kush – between Egypt and sub-Saharan Africa.

Further reading

Dynastic Egypt

The volume of material readily available concerning dynastic Egypt is enormous. The reader is best advised to consult one of the following general works and then consult their excellent bibliographies for more specific subjects.

Aldred, Cyril, *The Egyptians*, 3rd ed., London and New York: Thames & Hudson, 1998
Assmann, Jan, *The Mind of Egypt: History and Meaning in the Time of the Pharaohs*, trans. Andrew Jenkins, Cambridge, MA: Harvard University Press, 2003
Kemp, Barry, *Ancient Egypt: The Anatomy of a Civilization*, London: Routledge, 1989
Reeves, Nicholas, *Ancient Egypt: The Great Discoveries*, London and New York: Thames & Hudson, 2000 (lavishly illustrated and describes the major discoveries year-by-year since Napoleonic times for a general audience)
Shaw, Ian (ed.), *The Oxford History of Ancient Egypt*, Oxford: Oxford University Press, 2000

The kingdom of Kush

Edwards, David N., *The Nubian Past: An Archaeology of the Sudan*, London: Routledge, 2004

The Kingdom of Kush: Handbook of the Napatan-Meroitic Civilization (Handbook of Oriental Studies/Handbuch der Orientalistik), Leiden: Brill Adademic Publishers, 1998

O'Connor, David, *Ancient Nubia: Egypt's Rival in Africa*, Philadelphia: University of Pennsylvania Press, 1994

Welsby, Derek A., *The Kingdom of Kush: The Napatan and Meroitic Empires*, Princeton: Markus Wiener, 1998

3   The peoples of sub-Saharan Africa: society, culture, language

Europeans and Americans imagine Africans to be rural, unsophisticated people who have, until relatively recently, lived in a pristine, unchanging state of nature. Such images are the stock in trade of a century of Hollywood movies. They continue to permeate Western media, from credit-card commercials to tourist advertisements. Nineteenth-century imperialists relied on these stereotypes to justify their conquest of the continent. More recently, many in the West have turned the stereotypes on their head, idealizing Africans as more spiritual, and less materialistic and wasteful, than themselves. There are grains of truth to this oversimplification. Throughout their history, Africans have been less likely to live in cities than their contemporaries in Europe or Asia. There are profound continuities in African history that have at times acted as a brake on dramatic change. And over the past millennium, African economies have not matched regions such as Europe and Asia in their output of manufactured goods. But this monolithic view of Africans, whether held by neo-imperialists or critics of globalization, is very much a stereotype, whose oversimplification hides the remarkable diversity that characterizes the peoples of the continent.

Perhaps the most important thing to understand when comparing African societies to those of other regions of the world is that historically speaking, the continent has the lowest population density of any of the major continents. This crucial fact has shaped all aspects of African life. At the beginning of the twenty-first century the population of the African continent is approximately 750 million, which gives it a density about the same as the United States, roughly 65 persons per square mile, compared to Great Britain with 585 people per square mile. However, throughout its history Africa has been underpopulated in terms of its vast landmass. At the beginning of the Christian era the population of China has been estimated at 57 million people, the Roman Empire 54 million, and Africa only 20 million, half of whom resided in North Africa and the Nile Valley, provinces included in the census of the Roman Empire. There were thus only 10 million Africans living south of the Sahara Desert. Fifteen hundred years later the world population had grown to over 300 million while the peoples of Africa south of the Sahara had only increased to some 47 million. Five hundred years later, in 1900, the population of sub-Saharan Africa had soared to 129 million, but during the same centuries the world population had risen from 500 million to over 2 billion. Then in the twentieth century the population of sub-Saharan Africa, now under colonial rule, grew from 142 million in 1920 to 200 million in 1948, and 300 million at the African year of independence, 1960. Since then the population of Africa has more than doubled in the last forty years, and will double again by the year 2025.

Where have the Africans lived? The Sahara and Kalahari Deserts have obviously been the home of very few Africans, as are the tropical rainforests of the eastern Congo. The Africans, historically and today, live in six main geographical regions and average 130 inhabitants per square mile. The Mediterranean coast of North Africa has long been heavily populated along its littoral. The Nile Valley in Egypt from Aswan to the Mediterranean, only 800 miles, was able to sustain some 4 million people in the three millennia of dynastic Egypt (3000–332 BCE) where today there are some 70 million. Further south there has always been a considerable concentration of population around the fertile shores of the equatorial lakes of eastern Africa as well as along the Indian Ocean coast from Somalia to the tip of southern Africa. The greatest density of population, however, has always been along the West African coast between the Senegambia, Nigeria, and Cameroon.

Africa is still an agricultural and pastoral continent. These historical vocations have changed in the twentieth century – and, most dramatically, since 1940 – by the movement of rural people to the cities. There are areas of heavy urbanization in Egypt, South Africa, Nigeria, and in the cities of the Mediterranean littoral of North Africa that have been major trading ports throughout the millennia. Over 70 percent of Africans, however, still till the soil as subsistence farmers or tend their herds of sheep, goats, cattle, and camels. To any farmer land is the essential commodity, but in Africa ownership of the land was traditionally not by freehold but by usage, and was not the property of any individual but of the community. So long as you cultivated the soil you *owned* it. When you did not, the land was free to those who would. Pastoral herdsmen established their rights to the pasture by tradition and use rather than any deed of ownership. This did not prevent disputes and violence over grass and water, particularly in times of drought, but every goatherd and cattleman knew precisely their traditional rights to pasture and water for their animals.

Do Africans live in tribes? *Tribe* was the word invented by the Europeans to distinguish between different Africans with whom they came in contact. They were trying to make sense out of the very complex and enormous diversity of the African peoples. They sought to learn about the Africans out of curiosity, but also to exploit and rule them. They could not administer a colony without a classification of its subjects, and consequently tribes were defined by administrators and anthropologists with a vigor that has been accepted by many Africans with equanimity but regarded by others, because of its association with colonial rule, as a pejorative term. More troubling to scholars is the term's lack of precision. Colonial rulers believed tribes to be unchanging, clearly defined communities. Historians have recognized that African identities are in constant states of flux. Today many scholars have substituted the term "ethnicity" for "tribe." Though this has done away with much of the colonial baggage of the earlier term, it has failed to bring clarity to the enormous diversity of the African peoples.

Studies of societies across the continent reveal widely practiced social institutions, many of which have deep historical roots. The following sketch of some common practices does not hold for every society, or throughout all history. But it does provide an introduction to the social institutions that have guided the lives of many Africans for millennia. In the history of Africa, kinship, determined by one's ancestors and descent, has been the most binding social institution. There are two basic definitions of descent, the most common being the progeny of the father and his male ancestor – patrilineal descent. Others will identify with the male relatives of the mother – matrilineal descent. Whether patrilineal or matrilineal, descent was the cement of African society, for it gave identity to the child, terms of marriage for an adult, and inheritance as an elder. The ancestors comprise the lineage that establishes legitimacy for the living, and in many a lineage loyalty to a common ancestor, the founder. Kinship, however, can also be solidified by marriage, for it is the traditional social institution to reproduce children without whom the society cannot survive. But marriage is more than the conceiving of offspring. It has been in every culture the bonding of two extended families, not just that of a man and woman. The social importance of marriage was unquestioned in all African cultures, and had to be arranged by the family elders. It was a community affair consummated after negotiations by the family of the groom to transfer property – bride-wealth – to seal the union of two lineages. Bride-wealth was the social contract of African societies. It was an acknowledgment by the family of the groom of the worth of the bride. It compensated her family for the loss of her presence and labor. It guaranteed that inheritance would pass to the family of the groom in patrilineal societies from the children of the bride. It strengthened relationships between families and lineages that often were rivals in the fields, the pasture, and the marketplace.

Marriage in Africa has historically been characterized by polygyny, one husband and two or more wives, a practice accepted in the Hebrew Bible, the Old Testament of the Christians, and in Islamic law. Historically, the high mortality rate among African men encouraged the acceptance by society of women sharing a common husband. Economically, polygyny was essential for an agrarian or pastoral lineage. Cultivating fields and tending cattle are labor-intensive activities that require many hands to produce crops and look after the herds. Large families were the solution, and could be best accomplished by men having more than one wife. Large families enjoyed greater opportunities for prosperity, accumulating wealth and social prestige for the family head and his lineage. This was particularly compelling because of the high rate of infant mortality from tropical disease, and the need for children as "social security" insurance against drought, disease, and old age. Customarily when a married man died his brother would accept his wife as another spouse and responsibility for her children. Polygyny was also encouraged by the historical custom in most African societies that prohibited sexual intercourse between the husband and wife after birth until the infant was weaned, usually a period of two to three years. During the interim it was expected that the husband would take a second wife.

Kinship was not confined to lineage. In many African societies the individual was also given identity through membership in the age-grade social organization which drew members from many families and lineages. An age-grade is composed of age-sets, those males and sometimes females of similar age from different lineages and villages who upon puberty are initiated into adulthood with instruction of their cultural history, its traditions, and their responsibilities to the ethnic group symbolized by the rite of circumcision. Bonded together by a common experience the members of the age-grade remained a fraternal body throughout their lives, advancing from being the young enforcers of society, the warriors, then to marriage, and later to becoming the senior governors who in old age were honored with revered status as elders. The age-grade ceremonies took place every fourth or fifth year, not unlike the graduation ceremonies at an American university whose students become loyal alumni. The young warriors of the age-grade protected the land, and the bond of combat remained throughout their lives. Upon marriage and maturity the members of the age-grade settled disputes over land and cattle. In old age they would gather as the judicial elders who would settle more contentious matters of land, bride-wealth, and perform their primary function as keepers of the traditional religions. They maintained the sacred shrines, and as mediums presided over spiritual functions that accompanied the change of seasons.

There are three religious traditions that historically have provided spiritual sustenance to African peoples: Islam, Christianity, and the traditional religions that pre-date these foreign imports. Many African religions have a pantheon of gods, though most recognize one deity as more powerful than the others. All religions recognize and distinguish between good and evil, and the Africans, like the ancient Greeks, have good gods and bad gods. The ancestors of the lineage are the intermediaries between the gods and man with whom the venerated elders communicate by meditation and sacrifices to propitiate the gods who control the rain, crops, cows, pestilence, fertility, childbirth, and social order. There are, of course, spirits who are the conveyors of good and evil from the gods. Evil was almost universally associated with human greed expressed by malevolence in an infinite number of manifestations, both imagined and real. There were in all African societies the ritual experts, the diviners. They were the priests, elders, or other members of society with knowledge of the rituals that could prevent disasters and promote the prosperity of the community. There were those, however, who were malevolent practitioners of witchcraft – the cult leaders of misfortune in an unpredictable

world. African traditional religions, whatever the rituals, served the same purpose as the monotheistic religions – Judaism, Christianity, and Islam – seeking to define the relationship of man and woman to that which neither could
explain.

To the casual observer, African communities appear to be divided into hundreds of distinct ethnic groups, creating an apparently incomprehensible maze
of peoples. What methodology best provides a road map through this labyrinth
to reduce chaos to comprehension, to give clarity to obscurity? In the nineteenth
and early twentieth centuries some ethnologists sought to establish human relationships one to another by physical characteristics: height, weight, and size
of skull. Others sought to classify by pigmentation of the skin. In the latter
half of the twentieth century the government of South Africa sought to classify
its people by race without ever resolving the problem of how to do so. However, scholars have demonstrated that the cultural diversity of Africa is best
understood by the common denominator of language. Language remains the
ultimate marker whose basic structure endures despite changes in culture and
society.

Languages can change very rapidly, and have done so in the history of
Africa. There is slang, street-talk, colloquialisms, regional peculiarities, but in
fact the core structure of a language changes very slowly. It is one of the most
inflexible aspects of human culture and consequently the key to its classification, whether in Asia, Europe, the Americas, or Africa. The understanding
of these linguistic relationships in Africa provides the framework, the structure that reveals the historical relationship of those Africans who speak over
800 different languages and innumerable dialects. We owe our understanding
of African linguistic classification to Professor Joseph H. Greenberg (1915–
2001). He defined rational rules that established the correlation between the
multiplicities of African languages. One can reconstruct historical relationships among Africans by the commonality of the structure of their languages,
even if they are mutually unintelligible.

Greenberg has defined four principal linguistic families in Africa: Niger-
Congo, Afro-Asiatic, Nilo-Saharan, and Khoisan. The great Niger-Congo
family has six major branches and hundreds of sub-branches. West Atlantic
includes the populous Wolof and Fulbe (Fulani) originally from the coast of
Senegambia. In the interior of the western Sudan are the Mande speakers –
Malinke, Bambara, Soninke – and the Gur languages of the peoples in the Sahel
north of the West African coast, the Dogon, Mamprusi, and Mossi. Along the
tropical coast of West Africa live those who speak languages of the Kwa linguistic family – Akan, Kru, Yoruba, and Igbo – while those speaking languages
of the Adamawa-Eastern branch form a corridor of languages across Africa
from the Niger to the Nile. The largest branch of the Niger-Congo linguistic
family is Benue-Congo, which includes the Bantu group, which originated on
the Cameroon–Nigerian frontier and expanded to fill the southern half of the
African continent.

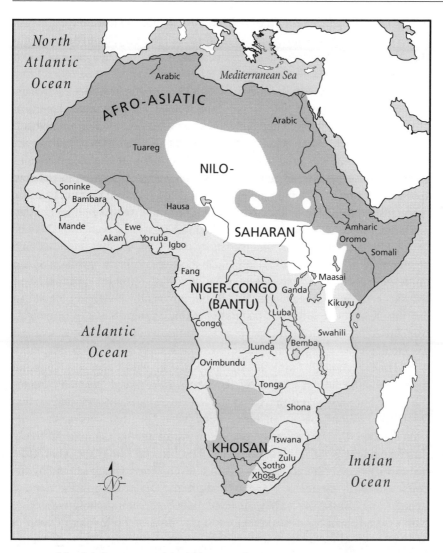

Map 3.1 *Languages of the African peoples.*

The other great linguistic family of Africa is Afro-Asiatic, whose speakers account for nearly a third of the languages of Africa. Where this great language family originated has been a matter of considerable debate among linguists, but current scholarship identifies its birth in the highlands of modern Ethiopia. Today its speakers are found in North Africa, the Sahara, the Nile Valley, the Middle East, and Arabia. Afro-Asiatic includes the Semitic languages Arabic and Hebrew, but also the language of the dynastic Egyptians as well as the far-flung Berber and Tuareg of northern Africa. One of the major branches of Afro-Asiatic is Cushitic, whose five sub-branches penetrate deep into northeast Africa to include the languages spoken in Sudan, Ethiopia, and Somalia as well as the Hausa language of northern Nigeria. It remains unclear how the Hausa of the Western Sudan, whose origins are Cushitic, migrated far to the west, but Hausa, an Afro-Asiatic language, has become the trading language of much of western and central Sudanic Africa.

The third language family of Africa, Nilo-Saharan, is as distinct as Niger-Congo and Afro-Asiatic, but its speakers account for only some 5 percent of sub-Saharan Africans. They are found today in West Africa, the Sahara, the Chad and Nile Basins, and in the great funnel of the Rift Valley in East Africa. The Nilo-Saharan-speaking Songhai live along the banks of the Niger River and once ruled a far-flung empire in the western Sudan. Nilo-Saharan speakers include the Toubou, the traditional guides of the desert, and further to the east on the Chad–Sudan frontier the Fur, who established the kingdom of Darfur in the seventeenth century. The most important branch of this linguistic family is Chari-Nile, which contains those who speak Eastern Sudanic languages in the Nile Basin. They include the Nubians in the northern Sudan on the Nile south of Aswan and the populous Nilotic peoples – Dinka, Nuer, Anuak, and Shilluk in the Upper Nile Basin. Beyond the borders of the Sudan and into Kenya live a host of peoples speaking Eastern Sudanic languages, from the Acholi of northern Uganda to the Turkana and Maasai of Kenya and Tanzania.

The fourth linguistic family of Africa is Khoisan, whose speakers are found today predominantly in south and southwest Africa, though isolated communities of Khoisan speakers in East Africa and the Congo rainforest suggest that this language family once blanketed the continent. Their numbers are insignificant compared to the rest of the peoples of Africa and include two culturally different southern African communities. The first, known as the Khoi, have historically been pastoralists, and were known by early Dutch settlers by the pejorative term "Hottentot." The second are the San, known in the popular literature as "Bushmen." They are hunters and gatherers whose dwindling numbers and small bands still roam the arid regions of the Kalahari Desert in the southwest. Both the Khoi and the San belong to the same language family with its distinctive click sounds, which have been adopted by their immediate neighboring Bantu speakers of the Niger-Congo language family in South Africa, the Xhosa. The modern media have often portrayed them as the noble savages of the eighteenth-century European Enlightenment. In reality they were hunters and gatherers who once ranged widely over most of the African continent but whose space was steadily reduced throughout two millennia by farmers and herdsmen. Their linguistic descendants today are clusters of San in East and Central Africa, the Sandewe and Hatsa, and the Khoisan-speaking people of Southwest Africa.

The classification of languages illuminates the great diversity of the African peoples and the relationship of one cultural group to another. To the north in a great arc are the Afro-Asiatic speakers; below them are those of the Nilo-Saharan family and the Khoisan of southern Africa. These families contain

Box 3.1 Bantu and Africa

The oldest question in African studies remains one of the most contentious: how did the majority of people living in Africa below the equator come to converse in languages descended from one distant, extinct parent language known as *Bantu*? All the Bantu speakers, who comprise over 400 ethnic groups, use the root *ntu* for the word man, the plural of which is *ba* – hence the name Bantu for all these languages with a common ancestor. This riddle intrigued the first European explorers of the continent, and it continues to engage linguistic scholars in controversy and debate as to its origins, spread, and relationship of one Bantu language to another. In the nineteenth century imperialists, such as the Englishman Sir Harry Johnston, interpreted the wide dispersal of languages with similar grammar, morphology, and vocabulary as evidence for an invasion during which superior warrior migrants drove out or conquered more primitive peoples. Johnston was writing in an age in which social Darwinism influenced virtually every discussion about race and identity, so that Victorians believed that race and language were an inseparable part of human biology. Thus, the spread of the Bantu was understood to be similar to the spread of the English "race" in North America, Australia, and southern Africa.

Such ideas concerning the integration of race and language came to be discredited after the Second World War when a new generation of scholars began to examine the question of Bantu. Since the dispersal of the Bantu languages began several thousand years ago, and there are no written texts to act as guides, study of their dissemination was dominated by linguists and archaeologists. Working in concert, specialists from these two disciplines developed a consensus, supported by archaeological and linguistic evidence, that removed the racial overtones of Johnston theory but accepted its basic assertion that migrating groups of people speaking Bantu-related languages displaced less technologically sophisticated communities. Archaeology demonstrated continuities among ceramics at sites stretching from the East African highlands to South Africa. This pattern seemed to coincide with the assumed routes of the Bantu languages as they spread throughout Africa south of the equator. Thus, Bantu came to be understood not simply as a language, but as a package of economic and cultural traditions that created densely populated communities of Iron Age farmers who absorbed or supplanted indigenous peoples. Thus, the nineteenth-century invasion theory became peaceful migration in the twentieth, but the dynamics of the process have changed little since the days of Harry Johnston.

During the last decades of the twentieth century, however, this displacement theory came under increasing scrutiny by scholars who

Box 3.1 (continued)

argued that Bantu may have spread with very little movement of peoples. Critics of the migration hypothesis contend that migrants would have faced enormous challenges as they moved from one environment to another, from tropical rainforest to savanna. They have identified many inconsistencies in the archaeological record that link the spread of the language with ceramics and iron-working technology. Finally, they have argued that a relatively rapid, large-scale movement of peoples through a diverse and often inhospitable continent seems unlikely. Today most scholars recognize the spread of language as a complex process in which technological innovation, cultural interaction, and migration played significant roles in the passage of Bantu speakers into sub-Saharan Africa that hopefully will become clearer as archaeologists and linguists continue to explore the mysteries of Bantu.

many languages whose structures indicate a common source, and which continue to share some common words, which reflect their ancient relationship. From the Nigerian and Cameroon frontier to the Cape of Good Hope Africa was infiltrated by that member of the Niger-Congo family, Bantu, which today dominates most of eastern, central, and southern Africa. Its origins and dissemination throughout the continent remains a central theme in understanding pre-colonial African history.

When Europeans began to penetrate into the savanna of central and southern Africa they encountered peoples speaking languages that were mutually unintelligible but had discernible similarities in structure and vocabulary. The first European to record this phenomenon was Dr. Wilhelm Heinrich Immanuel Bleek (1827–1875) in his *Comparative Grammar of South African Languages* published in London between 1862 and 1869. Since then his observations have proven correct. This vast expanse of the African landmass from Cameroon to South Africa is Bantu Africa, whose 450 closely related languages constitute what linguists classify as the Benue-Congo branch. The term *Bantu* derives its name from a root, *ntu*, meaning *people*, that is common in all Benue-Congo languages. These languages are as closely related as English and German despite the fact that though speakers of Bantu languages share a common linguistic vocabulary and word structure, many of the languages are mutually unintelligible.

Recognizing the cohesiveness of Bantu Africa, scholars began to inquire as to its origins and the spread of the language. Where did it originate, and how did people speaking variants of the ancestral core languages populate the greater whole of sub-Saharan Africa? Unlike ancient Egyptian, the early Bantu languages did not have a script. Although Bantu-speaking communities have rich oral traditions, they seldom are more than a few hundred rather than

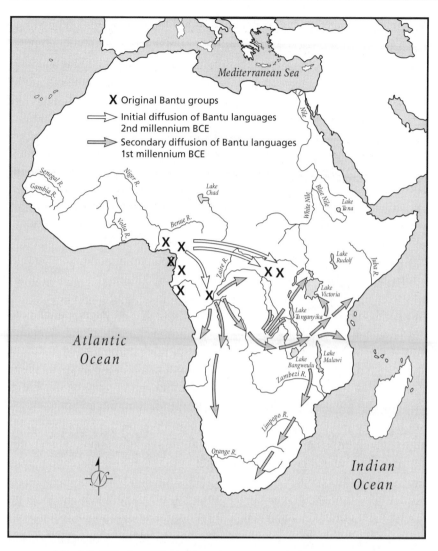

Map 3.2 *Diffusion of Bantu languages.*

a thousand years old. Compared to the Nile Valley, archaeology has supplied only limited evidence of human history in the enormous region of sub-Saharan Africa, but linguists have successfully applied the tools of their discipline to reveal the basic unity of this language family. Languages evolve by fission, constantly changing as a community of people speaking a common tongue separate and develop new words and sounds either under their own initiative or by accommodation with new people and borrowing parts of their language. People who have separated recently still share many common words and can understand one another. The British, Americans, and Australians have been disconnected for 200 years but, with some exceptions, understand one another. If, however, populations have been separated for a thousand years or more

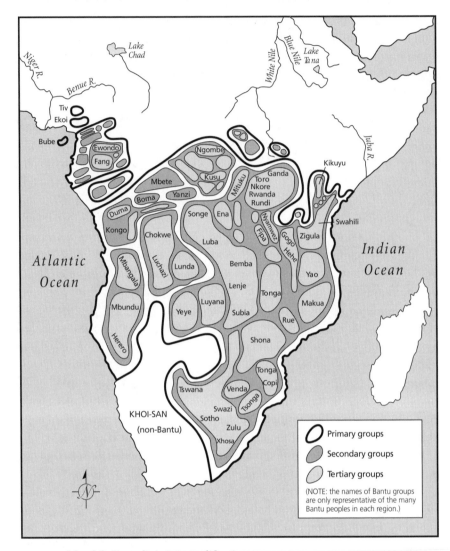

Map 3.3 *Bantu linguistic qualification.*

the understanding diminishes despite common words and morphology. By assembling the basic vocabulary shared by related societies the linguist can determine those cognates that are derived from the ancestral language. The higher the percentage of cognates the more closely related are the languages. Those with a very low percentage are obviously peoples speaking the same original languages who drifted apart long ago to evolve their own distinctive languages from nuclear Bantu. The work of the linguists has provided a methodology by which the historian can identify the origins of the Bantu language and track the process whereby it filled up the lower half of the African continent.

By comparing these cognitive relationships the Bantu homeland can be located with uncommon accuracy to an area on the borderlands between the Republics of Cameroon and Nigeria. In this upland region the original eight sub-groups of Bantu are to be found. Of the eight, three expanded beyond this homeland. Two percolated east along the northern edge of the equatorial rainforest to the interlacustrine regions of the great lakes of equatorial East Africa, the Congo, Uganda, Kenya, and Tanzania. The third Bantu language made its way through the rainforest to swing northeast to the East African coast and south to occupy the savanna of Central and southern Africa. As a result most of the Bantu languages of sub-Saharan Africa are very closely related since they derived from the one primary sub-group that came up the rivers of the Congo, the paths through the rainforest. The complex process whereby this language spread so widely, and among diverse environments and peoples, forms an important theme for the subsequent history of the continent.

Further Reading

Greenberg, Joseph, *The Languages of Africa*, Bloomington: Indiana University Press, 1970

4   Crops, cows, and iron

Although there is circumstantial evidence that the inhabitants of southern Africa and the Nile Valley sought to manipulate the growth of plants as early as 18,000 years ago, the systematic domestication of plants, or agriculture, evolved independently in the Middle East about 8000 BCE, and by 4000 BCE there were substantial agricultural settlements along the banks of the Nile and in its delta. There is still controversy as to whether the domestic cultivation of crops in the Nile Valley was borrowed from the nearby Fertile Crescent or evolved locally in the rich soil deposited on the banks of the river; it was probably a bit of both. Whatever its origins, this agricultural revolution made possible the evolution of settled communities. Hunting and gathering was an inefficient means of survival, let alone procreation. Hunting was dangerous, limited to small animals or, for the hominids, scavenging the remains left by more powerful carnivores. Gathering, though more mundane, could be an unreliable and often arduous enterprise. There are 200,000 species of wild plants, but most are indigestible, poisonous, without nutrition, hard to gather, or difficult to prepare. Only a very few, no more than a dozen, were edible and available for *Homo sapiens*. One acre of any one of them cultivated by farmers could support a hundred times the number of hunter-gatherers, who have consequently been overwhelmed over the last two millennia by the slow but steadily increasing numbers of Africans practicing agriculture.

The agricultural revolution

Agricultural food production cannot be dissociated from the pastoral revolution. Indeed, the breeding of animals into livestock was similar to, complemented, and paralleled the domestication of plants. Africa has a large number of animal species, but only six became of any value to modern humans in Africa – and all of them were of Asian origin: camels, cattle, goats, sheep, pigs, and the horse. Like the farmer displacing the hunter-gatherer, these domestic animals replaced wild game as the principal source of protein, providing both meat and milk. The great variety, splendor, and awesome herds of wild African animals were largely irrelevant to the history of modern humans in the continent, for the African farmer was dependent on domestic mammals for his survival and prosperity. Since domesticated animals before being slaughtered had a longer life than wild game, their milk provided a continuous supply of protein. They increased the yield of crop production by their manure, the ancient reliable fertilizer and a dependable source of fuel for the fire. The larger domestic mammals, the cow (oxen), horse, and camel dramatically expanded the area of food production by pulling the plow. The cow, the horse, and particularly the camel became a means of transportation far more efficient than the bipedal hominid. Wool was sheared from the skins of sheep and goats; leather tanned from the hides of cattle. The domestication of agriculture and a few animals, large and small, were complementary and their evolution symmetrical.

The domestication of plants and animals has produced profound changes in the cultural, political, and social life of modern humans that differentiates them from their hunter and gatherer ancestors. Farming requires a sedentary lifestyle that in turn creates a more dense population, not simply by having to live in a permanent place near the fields, but by providing the means and incentive to raise more children. Always on the move, the hunter-gatherer mother could carry just one child at a time, so abstinence or some form of birth control would have limited the number of births. The farmer had no such restraints, and in a labor-intensive occupation there was every incentive to have children to tend the sheep and goats, and adolescent boys and girls to work the fields and milk the cows. A settled existence also enabled the cultivator, unlike the hunter-gatherer, to store surplus food. The storage of food provided a reliable supply during the lean months after the harvest, and if the rains failed and the crops shriveled in the sun, there hopefully would remain a sufficient surplus stored from the previous year to forestall famine. The size of the stockpile was like cash in the bank. The more industrious and successful farmer became a member of the social and political elite by gaining control of food production. They became the "big men," who no longer had to labor in the fields but used their leisure time for politics, the arts, and war. Indeed, the organization required by cultivation and animal husbandry demanded the cooperation and leadership that produced the village headman, chief, king, and pharaoh.

The earliest domesticated plants were derived from wild varieties, and the place of their identification as a crop is usually indicative of their origin. The subsequent spread of a domesticated plant can then be determined by the locations where it next appears unless it was domesticated independently rather than transplanted. The earliest domestication of plants – wheat, barley, chickpeas, lentils – occurred in the Fertile Crescent of southwest Asia, the modern Middle East, between 8500 and 8000 BCE. The Fertile Crescent may have been the original region for agriculture, but seeds from indigenous wild plants, different from those in southwest Asia, were gathered and systematically planted in China, the Americas, and Africa. The oldest known cereal grains in the Nile

Valley were independently cultivated in the Fayum between 4500 and 4200 BCE, but there were undoubtedly older settlements independently cultivating local grains. Further west indigenous sorghum, millet, and rice were domesticated in the sahel and savanna of western Sudanic Africa by 5000 BCE. In the tropical rainforests of the West African coast yams were cultivated and palm oil tapped by 3000 BCE. In the highlands of northeast Africa, the Ethiopians were the first to grow coffee, teff (*Eragrostis tef*), a cereal, and the indigenous tuber banana (*Musa ensete*) hundreds of years before the Christian era.

There was borrowing as well as independent domestication of local wild plants. Egypt, comfortably situated in the fertile Nile Valley, easily adopted wheat, barley, and peas from the Fertile Crescent about 4000 BCE, 4,000 years after they were staples in the Middle East, to add to their indigenous cultivation of sycamore fig and a vegetable known as *chufa*. One wonders why the passage of such nutritious crops took so long to reach the banks of the Nile just across the isthmus of Suez and Sinai. The southwest Asian crops also reached Ethiopia, but much later through the kingdom of Saba in southern Arabia (the modern Yemen), where wheat, barley, and millet flourished in the Ethiopian highlands to supplement the indigenous coffee, teff, and the banana. The domestication of wild plants in Egypt and Ethiopia created a sedentary, agricultural society that prospered with the arrival of cereals, goats, and sheep from southwest Asia. The hunter-gatherers who had roamed the savanna, sahel, and woodlands of Africa for so many millennia had to make the choice whether to become sedentary or to move on. During the desiccation of the Sahara some settled by the Nile to become farmers, while others regarded themselves as better off hunting and gathering by following the wild animals and plants southward into the heart of Africa.

The domestication of wild plants, whether in the Fertile Crescent, Egypt, West Africa, Ethiopia or elsewhere, was probably more accidental than conscious. The gatherers would obviously collect those berries, nuts, and peas of the largest size whose seeds, cast off during consumption, reproduced plants over many generations whose fruits were larger, more edible, and more nutritious. The modern *Homo sapiens* could not help but recognize the difference between the seeds that came from a sturdy progenitor and the lesser wild ones in the bush. Through the millennia modern humans, not surprisingly, began to select those seeds that would produce the best size, oil, and fiber. The ancient farmer learned from trial and error over many generations that those seeds that were watered and weeded produced higher yields. A few wild plants had been domesticated, but some were more easily tamed than others. The nutritious wild cereals and peas of the Fertile Crescent or the sorghums and millets of West Africa were edible, their seeds easily sown, and grew quickly – in a few months – to be harvested by those deciding between hunting-gathering and sedentary village life. The sorghum, rice, and finger millet of Africa and the emmer wheat, barley, and lentils from the Fertile Crescent grown in Egypt and Ethiopia were low in protein but high in carbohydrates and yields. More than half the calories consumed daily by humans in the twenty-first century come from cereals – wheat, corn, barley, rice, and sorghum. The ancient Africans probably ate more carbohydrates than the moderns, but like them found their protein in the meat and milk from domesticated animals and fish, as well as plants such as peas that have abundant protein. In the tropical regions of Africa where cereals could not be grown, the need for carbohydrates was supplied by the cultivation of the ubiquitous tubers of the African yam.

The wheat, barley, and peas of the Fertile Crescent and the sorghum and millet of western Africa were annuals that die in the dry season of both regions. With only one year to live the annual cereals expended their energy on producing large seeds for regeneration rather than the wood or fibers of perennial plants such as bushes and trees. Humans could collect and eat their big seeds, store them in gourds, beat them into flour, bake them in the fire, ferment them into beer, and preserve them to plant in the next rainy season. The cereals were also prolific, growing like weeds, with substantial protein, so that even hunter-gatherers 10,000 years ago could collect hundreds of pounds of food energy per acre with little effort. The advantage of a steady food supply, whether in the Fertile Crescent, China, Egypt, Ethiopia, or western Africa, persuaded the wanderers to settle in permanent locations that became villages, gathering the wild grains whose ritual led to their domestication – planting, weeding, and harvesting in the fields: the beginning of agriculture. Not everyone adopted new crops and livestock. Some Africans were more innovative than others in the development of agriculture and the domestication of animals that gave them an advantage in food production, procreation, and consequently survival and well-being.

The pastoral revolution

There are very few wild plants edible by humans. There are even fewer wild animals that *Homo sapiens* was able to domesticate for human use. Africa has 70 percent of the world's large mammal species weighing over 100 pounds, none of which has proved possible to domesticate for meat or milk.[1] Africa is, geologically, the parent continent, but Asia and Europe – Eurasia – form the greatest landmass and are ecologically the most diverse. Sub-Saharan Africa has fifty-one species of large mammals, compared to seventy-two scattered across Eurasia. Africa has the barrier of the Sahara Desert and the great tropical rainforest of the Congo. Its savanna and sahel, which sustain the large mammals, cannot compare to the great plains that stretch from the North Sea to the Siberian Pacific Ocean, which contained a few species ready to become the domestic servants of modern humans. The domestication of big animals

[1] Jared Diamond, *Guns, Germs, and Steel: The Fates of Societies*, New York: Norton, 1997, p. 162.

was crucial to the evolution of agriculture and the farmers. They provided meat, milk, fertilizer, transportation, hides, and pulled the plow in the fields; but they were few. Only fourteen animal species out of many thousands have submitted to human control, and only six – camels, cows (the ox), goats, pigs, sheep, and the horse – supply the needs of modern humans. The camel and the donkey have long been used in northern and northeast Africa for meat, milk, and transport, but not in Africa south of the Sahara. The other big domesticated mammals – the Bactrian camel of Central Asia, llama, reindeer, water buffalo, and yak – are unknown to Africa.[2]

The big, wild African animals remained resistant to human domestication. The African elephant was tamed as a tank for the armies of Hannibal but never bred in captivity. A zebra was harnessed to the coach of Lord Walter Rothschild in London, but the species refused to reproduce in England. Humans selected those mammals that could be most easily transformed for their needs. Selective breeding produced those best suited to the human environment to supply their demands for carbohydrates, protein, and taste. As the modern humans in Africa began to select larger seeds for greater yield, they began to select and breed their domesticated sheep, goats, pigs, and cows. The selection was designed to provide greater yields in meat, milk, hair, and hides than those in the wild. Domesticated animals in Africa became more efficient but smaller than their wild ancestors by feeding and breeding that made them more productive and more docile. Sheep, goats, and cows were bred for their meat and milk. They came from southwest Asia into Africa.

The sheep today is the descendant of its wild ancestor the Asiatic mouflon sheep (*Ovis orientalis*) from the steppes of Central Asia. This specie was domesticated in the Fertile Crescent about 8000 BCE along with the goat. Domestic goats in Africa and elsewhere were descended from *Capra aegagrus*, the scimitar-horned goat of Central Asia, which made its way, like sheep, on four feet into the verdant Holocene Sahara by 6000 BCE. During the subsequent millennia sheep and goats adapted to the progressive semi-arid conditions of the African sahel and savanna, evolving a digestive system to devour almost anything that grows in order to sustain their survival in Africa as they became a source of meat, milk, and ritual slaughter. Goats and sheep are environmentally destructive. They consume forage before it has a chance to recover on marginal lands. They have been in the long historical past and still are today a pest best controlled by domestication rather than roaming free to devour the stalks and seeds from cereals to be harvested. Their offspring were captured, reared to maturity, and taught to behave. But the mutual needs of sheep, goats, and humans forged an important symbiotic relationship in African cultures.

Sheep and goats were the first domesticated species to arrive in Africa, about 6000 BCE, and they spread throughout the continent and have thrived ever since.

[2] Ibid., p. 160.

Domestic cattle were different, not only because of size and productivity of meat and milk, but in the cultural importance that many African societies attached to their cattle. Cattle today in Africa and throughout the world are descended from the wild aurochs, *Bos primigenius*, a huge beast from Eurasia, seven feet high (2.3 metres) at the shoulder and with long curved horns, that migrated into northern Africa a million years ago. The hunters killed aurochs in the Nile Valley 19,000 years ago, but it was not until 6000 BCE that humans were herding their descendants in the Sahara. There is still controversy regarding the evolution of the huge, ferocious auroch to the mild, docile bovine provider to modern humans. All mammals require salt and water, without which they will perish in a matter of days. By setting out salt and water, as does today's farmer, *Homo sapiens* may have accustomed the free-ranging aurochs to human habitations where in return for salt and water they would, throughout hundreds of generations, be tamed. The earliest known remains of domesticated cattle, as old as 8000 BCE, were found at Çatal Hüyük in Turkey. Their horns appear to have been ritual symbols of fertility. Two thousand years later in Mesopotamia and the Nile Valley the aurochs had become a cow that provided meat, milk, and hides. Milk became butter, cheese, and yogurt that could be stored or traded for cereals. About 6000 BCE the dairy industry in Africa had begun.

Cows' milk can replace that of the human mother and sustain the adult. It consists of calcium, carbohydrates, proteins, and vitamins in a combination that no plant or legume can provide. Milk contains lactose, a sugar, from which the human intestine absorbs calcium, which hardens the soft bones of a newborn infant. Dependency on milk did not stop with the weaning of the child. African adults consumed milk and dairy products to supplement the inadequacies of their cultivated cereals, which are high in carbohydrates but low in calcium and iron. Without calcium the human mother suffered from malnutrition and gave birth to deformed children with stunted legs, collapsed chests, and twisted pelvises. Milk from sheep, goats, and the domesticated auroch, the cow, provided the minerals lacking in cereals and enabled the population of the modern humans to increase. This discovery was not brought about by a dramatic revelation, but was accomplished over many thousands of years of experience by trial and error whereby milch pastoralism evolved to be integrated with agriculture.

The domestication of sheep, goats, and cattle was common by 6000 BCE throughout the vast expanse of a well-watered Sahara from the Atlantic to the Red Sea. Bones and pots above and below the ground give ample evidence of their domestication. Hundreds of rock paintings on cave walls depict scenes of milking from the enlarged udders of cows with their calves. The human population increased and spread throughout the verdant Sahara from about 7000 BCE until its increasing desiccation at the end of the Holocene Wet Phase about 3000 BCE. Desertification sent the cultivators and herders south to the sahel and savanna and into the Nile Valley. The sahel is the marginal arid

Figure 4.1 *Maasai men herding their cattle, modern Kenya.*

lands between desert and grasslands; the savanna are the plains and woodlands extending in a great arc across Africa 3,700 miles from the Atlantic to the Red Sea to curve through the Upper Nile Valley and the highlands of Ethiopia to the grasslands of eastern and southern Africa. The limits of these rich grazing lands were determined, however, by the presence of the tsetse fly. The tsetse fly carries the virus *trypanosomiasis*, fatal to domestic animals and humans, which causes an illness known as *nagana* in cattle and sleeping sickness in people. The fly inhabits the deep bush along streams and rivers and requires at least twenty-five inches of annual rainfall. Consequently, the tsetse-fly belt in Africa has advanced and retreated throughout the millennia with the earth's fluctuations in climate. At the end of the Holocene Wet Phase, about 3000 BCE, when the Sahara was becoming the vast desert of sand, rock, and wind of today, the tsetse-fly belt had moved 200 miles south, opening up the grasslands of sahel and savanna for the pastoral peoples to follow with their cattle, sheep, and goats to displace the hunter-gatherers.

The advance of the herdsmen was not entirely at the expense of the hunter-gatherers. The landmass of Africa is immense. There was ample room for both economic activities to exist before the encroachment of the cultivators, and there appears to have been a symbiotic relationship between them. The hunter-gatherers harvested wild foods, nuts, seeds, berries, and tubers. The pastoral people needed more than just milk and undoubtedly gathered as well, fished in the rivers and lakes, and may have begun cursory cultivation of sorghum. They seem to have exchanged milk for meat with hunter-gatherers or perhaps learned from them the skills of the hunter to obtain wild meat if their herds were decimated by disease or reduced by theft. The pastoral revolution in Africa by Cushitic speakers of the Afro-Asiatic family from Ethiopia and the Nilotes from the Upper Nile Valley speaking Nilo-Saharan languages appears to have reached its southward limit on the Serengeti plains in modern Tanzania about 2000 BCE, the savanna where *Homo sapiens* had first appeared 200,000 years before. Here they interacted with the indigenous hunter-gatherers speaking the click languages of the Khoisan linguistic family. Later their way of life would be transformed by the arrival of people from the west, cultivators speaking languages of the Niger-Congo linguistic family.

The Iron Age

The iron revolution transformed agriculture and warfare in Africa by means of the hoe and the spear. Although the red earth of Africa, produced by iron oxides, covers much of the laterite crust of the ancient continent, iron ore also occurs as hematite, the primary ore for iron, sometimes found on the surface but usually dug from shallow deposits. Magnetite, a black iron oxide, can also be found in alluvial sand and the gravel of rivers. Limonite is a yellowish-brown iron oxide common in African swamps and lakes. At Télénougar in central Chad shafts were dug deep enough to provide lateral galleries to extract the ore. The problem of iron ore was not its extraction, but its smelting. The conversion of iron ore into a useable metal was complex, and although there is evidence from East and West Africa of the independent development of iron-working, the process was probably imported, like plants and animals, from southwest Asia. The earliest confirmed site for smelting iron, dated to 1500 BCE, was found in Anatolia in Turkey. The Hittites of Anatolia were able to dominate Mesopotamia with their iron weapons whose forging they sought to keep a state secret.

Hitherto early metal-working in southwest Asia, the Middle East, and particularly in the Sinai Peninsula had been confined to copper, which was easily mined or even collected as rock which when heated separated the metal from the ore. When cooled the copper could be hammered into shape for ornamentation, tools, currency for trade, or weapons. Copper, however, is a soft metal, and to reinforce it early modern humans learned, about 4000 BCE, to mix the ore with tin that when heated produced a much harder metal known as bronze. Sub-Saharan Africa had no bronze age. Since there are few deposits of tin in sub-Saharan Africa, the Africans combined copper with zinc to produce brass. Copper and gold, another pliable metal mined in Nubia, were the favorites of the dynastic Egyptians. During the New Kingdom of ancient Egypt (1570–1070 BCE) the use of bronze spread west along the Mediterranean shore of North Africa to the Maghrib of northwestern Africa, from where copper smelting was transferred across the desert to the Saharan oases between 1000 and 500 BCE to exploit the desert's rich copper deposits.

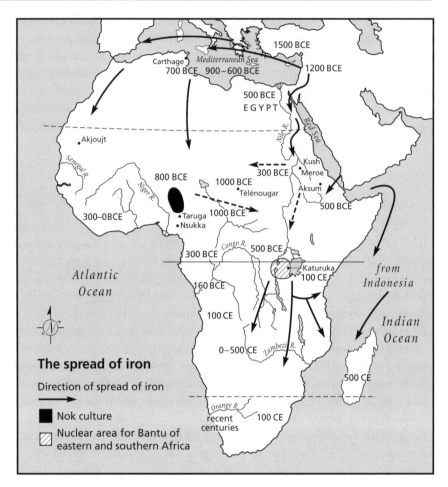

Map 4.1 *The Iron Age in Africa.*

Iron was different. It can only be extracted from the impurities in the ore, the slag, under greater heat than copper, tin, or zinc. This required a furnace, rather than just a fire, to hold the heat in order to produce a chemical reaction by placing the ore between layers of prepared charcoal into which oxygen (air) was pumped into the base of the fire to produce sufficient heat to melt the ore. Sometimes a flux, lime extracted from seashells for instance, was added to accelerate the smelting process. Ancient furnace technology in Africa consisted of a trench or bowl, a method that was later replaced by a kiln of beehive shape or a more efficient shaft of cylindrical construction. The oxygen was then forced into the furnace by pot or leather bellows through clay pipes (tuyères) whose oxygen could raise the heat to 2,200° F. After several hours, sometimes as many as twelve, the smelting was completed. The furnace would then be broken open. The purified lump of iron, known as bloom, was extracted and reheated to remove any remaining impurities, then forged by hammering into jewelry, hoes, tools, and weapons. The quality of the finished product varied widely from one African furnace to another depending on the iron content of the ore, the type of furnace, temperature and its control during the smelting, and the skill of the Master of the Fire, the possessor of a special but ambivalent status involving secret rituals to placate supernatural powers. In some societies this position was very prestigious, but in others – Ethiopia and the *bilad al-sudan*, for instance – the master smith was despised for his servile status while at the same time greatly feared for his supernatural powers.

Properly smelted and forged iron is a hard metal that can be shaped to a cutting edge whether for the hoe or the sword. Its advantages over copper and bronze were obvious to the Nubian and Egyptian troops of Taharqo, the king of Kush, when they were overwhelmed in crushing defeats by the Assyrians wielding iron weapons and led by Esarhaddon and Ashurbanipal in the seventh century BCE. Having retreated from Egypt, the Nubian pharaohs of the kingdom of Kush needed no more lessons from the Assyrians before developing their own iron industry at Meroe. Here below the pyramids of the kings and queens of Kush lie today the great slag heaps from their iron furnaces. Although iron ore was plentiful in Africa, the means to smelt it were not always available. Furnaces can be constructed, but the charcoal cannot. It must come from timber on the land. There was only a limited supply of acacias and sycamores in Egypt. The pharaohs had to import cedars from Lebanon to build their royal barges, and iron from Kush. In the kingdom of Kush the Butana Plain between the Atbara River and the Nile was methodically deforested, its trees cut to produce charcoal for the iron smelters of Meroe. It has been estimated that one ton of timber needed to be cut to produce the charcoal necessary to fire a furnace for one iron smelt. The size of the slag heaps at Meroe seems to confirm that its furnaces consumed 56,000 cubic feet of wood every year for 300 years or annually 100 trees sixty-five feet high.

Kush paid a heavy price, as environmental deforestation most certainly contributed to the collapse of the kingdom in the fourth century of the Christian era. The iron works at Meroe, however, have left from their heaps of slag a curious anomaly. One would have thought that this important city of iron working would have been the center for the dissemination of its technology throughout sub-Saharan Africa, but there is no convincing evidence for this apparently obvious conclusion. Paintings of iron working have been found in rock shelters west of the Nile in Chad, but that appears to be as far as the iron industry of Meroe spread into Africa.

Despite Hittite efforts to keep the secret of iron working, new technologies have always been vulnerable to those who want to know. Many scholars believe that the secret of iron smelting eventually came to Africa with Phoenician merchants. The Phoenicians living in Lebanon on the eastern shores of the Mediterranean were smelting iron by 1000 BCE. They were a seafaring people whose square-rigged ships sailed along the North African coast where they established settlements that became colonies. The most famous was Carthage in modern Tunisa, founded about 800 BCE, but other settlements were scattered along the Mediterranean littoral and the Atlantic coast of Africa as far south as Cerne near Cape Blanc in Mauritania. The indigenous peoples of North Africa who surrounded these Phoenician colonies were Berbers who cultivated wheat, barley, and millet on the rich coastal lowlands between their pastures for sheep, goats, and cattle. The Phoenicians were traders as well as sailors who exchanged iron implements and the technology to make them in return for the cereals and livestock of the Berbers. By 600 BCE Carthage had become a wealthy and powerful city-state in the western Mediterranean whose commerce depended on goods brought across the Sahara by the pastoral, nomadic Berbers of the interior who controlled the early trans-Saharan routes. Two thousands years later these routes were to become great arteries of trade between Africa and the Mediterranean world. In 500 BCE, however, they were paths used from time to time to connect the chain of Saharan oases inhabited by Berbers who since great antiquity had maintained the line of communications and contacts between the sahel and savanna of Africa south of the Sahara Desert and the Mediterranean coast north of it. The paintings in the rock shelters of the Sahara graphically depict the two-wheeled horse-drawn chariots, most probably for war, but also able to transport African gold, ivory, and slaves taken in raids in return for salt, cloth, beads, and iron from North Africa.

Not all scholars believe that iron entered Africa exclusively through the Phoenicians and their Berber trading partners. Some argue that it is more likely that its diffusion occurred in a wide arc stretching from Morocco to Yemen. Others believe that Africans developed iron-smelting technology independently of the Phoenicians, perhaps even separately in East and West Africa, and there is evidence to support this view.

Regardless of where the technology originated, by the middle of the first millennium BCE iron furnaces were in use in central Niger, the inland delta of the Niger River in Mali, and in central Nigeria at Taruga on the Jos Plateau. Taruga is near the site of the Nok culture, known for its exquisitely fashioned terracotta figurines of clay baked in furnaces adaptable to iron technology. Slag has been found in thirteen furnaces in the Taruga area, the oldest dating to 400 BCE. The beehive and cylindrical furnaces of West Africa were quite different from those in North Africa and Mesopotamia and were indicative of innovations in, if not the invention of, iron-smelting technology that were unique to Africa.

Whether imported or independently developed, iron technology was dispersed widely and rapidly throughout western Africa. Equipped with iron tools and weapons the Africans could now assault the natural and political obstacles to their expansion. The land could be cleared, the forest penetrated, and large wild animals more easily killed. Iron tools made possible more intensive and productive farming that required a distinct division of labor in societies where everyone had hitherto been completely involved in growing only a sufficient amount of food for subsistence. This division of labor created not only a ruling class, but groups of artisans, craftsmen, and commercial traders, all of whom no longer tilled the soil.

The spread of iron smelting in equatorial, eastern, and southern Africa is less clear despite the fact that iron ore is found throughout tropical Africa. The quality of the ore varied greatly from as little as 25 to over 75 percent iron. Most ore was simply excavated from surface deposits, but shaft mines were dug in southeastern Nigeria, southern Ghana, Chad, and the Transvaal in South Africa. Mining and smelting required labor organized under the supervision of a Master of the Fire.

Linguists have observed that the dates for early iron working in West Africa correspond roughly with the beginning of the dispersal of the Bantu languages out of their homeland, but similar dates alone are insufficient evidence to conclude that the spread of iron technology and Bantu linguistics were in some way related. The assumption by early historians of Africa that a Bantu invasion or migration throughout the continent was precipitated and made possible by the discovery of iron technologies can no longer be sustained as the simple solution to a historical movement that was, in reality, extremely complex and whose dynamics remain obscure. Today, there is no agreement among scholars as to whether the early Bantu-speaking Africans possessed iron-working techniques, but few would deny that their rapid dissemination was instrumental in the dramatic expansion of the Bantu languages throughout the continent.

5 Northeast Africa in the age of Aksum

Towering above the vast Sudanic plain to the west and the Horn of Africa to the east are the massive highlands of Ethiopia, which have captured the imagination of foreigners for more than 2,000 years. The ancient kingdom of Ethiopia was celebrated by the Hebrews in the Bible. In Islamic traditions and history Ethiopia has been regarded as special and unique, for the Prophet Muhammad requested asylum for his followers from the Christian *negus* (king) al-Asham of al-Habasha (the Abyssinians) who enthusiastically agreed to give them sanctuary in the first *hijra* (Arabic, "migration": flight of the Prophet's adherents from Mecca) in order to celebrate their beliefs free from the persecution they had experienced in Mecca.[1] Medieval Europeans and Crusaders knew of a Christian kingdom in the Ethiopian highlands, which they hoped to enlist against their Muslim enemies, but its isolation prevented the consummation of any grand alliance. In the sixteenth century Portuguese mercenaries arrived to prevent the kingdom from being overwhelmed by the Muslims from the plains of Somalia. Thereafter, European interest in Ethiopia waned until the resurgence of the empire in the nineteenth century, which precipitated the invasion by a British expeditionary force to rescue the British ambassador incarcerated by the emperor Tewodros (Theodore) II (1818–1868). The British stormed the capital at Magdala on April 13, 1868 and secured the release of the ambassador; Tewodros took his own life and the British withdrew. The cult of Ethiopia, however, continued well into the twentieth century, as the descendants of freed slaves in Jamaica revered the historic kingdom as the birthplace of their divine leader, the emperor Haile Selassie, and it was no coincidence that Addis Ababa was selected as the site of the new Organization of African Unity (OAU) in May 1963. As the only African nation that had not succumbed to European colonial rule, Ethiopia holds a special place in independent Africa, and throughout the African diaspora.

---

[1] Although the term "Ethiopian" was used by the ancients and lingered into the Christian era, it had nothing to do with the Ethiopians of the highlands; it was a generic term, often with pejorative connotations, for all black Africans. Throughout history the people of Ethiopia have been known as Abyssinians (Arabic, Habasha), and Abyssinia was the name for the highlands until the twentieth century when Emperor Haile Selassie in his efforts to modernize insisted that "Ethiopia" and "Ethiopians" replace "Abyssinia" and "Abyssinians." By the mid-twentieth century Abyssinia had ceased to be used, and is regarded by Ethiopians as a derisory term.

The great Eastern African Rift Valley slices through East Africa and Ethiopia, to become the trench for the Red Sea, Gulf of Aqaba, Dead Sea, and the River Jordan, and ends its declivity at Mount Hebron in the Lebanon. In Ethiopia the western escarpment of the Rift rises dramatically as the buttress to its highlands only forty miles from the shores of the Red Sea and the ruins of the ancient port of Adulis, not far from modern Massawa. On the plateau above the torrid Danakil Desert at the bottom of the rift the highlands are transformed into green pastures and cultivated fields, well watered by some forty-five inches of rainfall per year with an average temperature of 60° F. The Ethiopian Plateau rises 6,000 and 10,000 feet just north of the equator, and the altitude creates a mild temperature that prevented the spread of the deadly diseases from the lands below – malaria, bilharzia, and the tsetse fly that carries the trypanosomes for sleeping sickness in humans and the fatal *nagana* in cattle. This huge volcanic uplift, the size of Western Europe, dramatically demonstrates the power of geography in shaping the African past. These lofty highlands trap the rainclouds rolling across Africa from the South Atlantic and the moist winds from the Indian Ocean, which rise above the escarpment to drop their rainfall – often in violent thunderstorms.

The rugged escarpments that force the rainclouds to rise were also the battlements of a great natural fortress. They defied invaders from the plains below, while deserts and arid grasslands discouraged invasion from the south. These natural barriers produced a dramatic landscape of gorges, ravines, and canyons, that of the Blue Nile as deep as the Grand Canyon. They also enabled the evolution of an ecosystem unique in Africa and a people who developed their own distinctive culture from it. The Ethiopian highlands contain mammals, birds, and plants found nowhere else in Africa. Coffee was first domesticated in Ethiopia, as was the ensete (*Ensete edulis*), a banana, that was for long the staple foodstuff in the southern regions of the Ethiopian Plateau, and noog, an oil plant. Finger millet (*Eleusine coracana*) originated in Ethiopia, and there were Ethiopian varieties of wheat, barley, and sorghum, but the cereal unique to Ethiopia was teff.

Teff (*Eragrostis tef*) was first cultivated in northern Ethiopia as early as the eighth century BCE to become the staple cereal of the kingdom of Aksum before the Christian era and of Ethiopia today. Wheat and barley were brought from South Arabia by Sabaean immigrants but could not compete with the indigenous teff, which flourished after long adaptation to the distinctive environment of northern Ethiopia. It is a prolific plant that produces an abundance of very small grains containing, however, more carbohydrates, protein, and amino acid than the seeds of larger cereals. Teff may yield less per acre than barley, wheat, or sorghum, but it will ripen with little rain when other grains wither, so it remains today the most valued crop of subsistence farmers in Ethiopia.

Adulis, the port that was the gateway to the highlands, lay only seventeen miles from the shores of the Arabian Peninsula across the straits of the Bab al-Mandab, connecting the Arabian and Red Seas: its eastern shore is the westernmost tip of Asia; the western shore is Africa. The shallow straits, dotted with many islands, were more a bridge than a barrier to the inhabitants of the coastal towns, and settlers from Asia easily crossed the straits to establish their roots in the dramatically different environment of the temperate, well-watered highlands. Although this environmental and geographical distinction gradually produced a unique civilization 2,000 years ago, the two regions, Asia and Africa, would have recognized themselves as a part of a unitary Red Sea world with economic ties with the Mediterranean in a far-flung commercial nexus.

The origins of highland urbanization owe a great deal to southern Arabia, where archaeology suggests that the earliest kingdoms date from 1300 BCE, culminating in the kingdom of Saba in the tenth century BCE. Sabaea was a sophisticated civilization whose economic and technological achievements rival those of the great *poleis* of Greece, which were its contemporaries. Among the engineering marvels of the Sabaean civilization was the enormous Marib Dam, which boasted walls 15 feet high and 25 feet thick, built to store water for irrigation on fertile, terraced hillsides. Water, cultivable land, and the plow dramatically increased the productivity by those farmers whose surplus enabled the stratification of society into craftsmen and rulers. Sometime between the eighth and third centuries BCE Sabaean colonists crossed the straits from Arabia to Adulis and Africa. They did not linger in the heat of the coastal plain but made their way up the escarpment to the cool, fertile highlands. There they encountered several groups, practicing a variety of economic activities, and speaking an array of Afro-Asiatic languages, and there is persuasive evidence that this great language family, which includes modern Arabic and Hebrew, originated in northeast Africa. In the highlands farmers cultivated indigenous crops, such as noog and teff, while pastoralists maintained cattle and small livestock in the drier regions. From the intermixing of these peoples, and the sharing of their economic and technological accomplishments, emerged the origins of the kingdom of Aksum.

Aksum

The Sabaeans brought with them specific techniques for irrigation, terracing, and, most significantly for the historian, an alphabet. The Sabaean script was boustrophedon (Greek, "as the ox plows the field"), which reads on alternate lines from left to right and right to left. As the centuries passed, the people of the highlands were connected to Adulis and the Red Sea trading complex only by narrow trails leading down the escarpment that over time steadily restricted contact with their Sabean ancestors. In their ecological isolation the Cushitic inhabitants transformed the imported Sabaean script and its

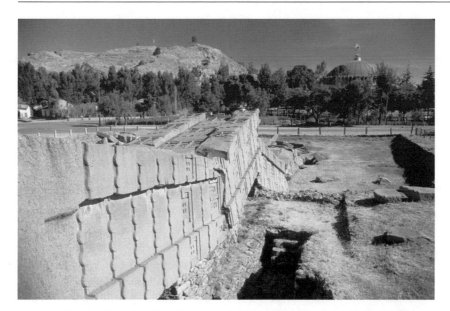

Figure 5.1 *Stelae of the kingdom of Aksum. Built during the third and fourth centuries* CE, *the monoliths of Aksum are among the largest stone carvings ever made.*

vocabulary. The boustrophedon style was abandoned. A new vocabulary was adopted to describe the conditions and culture of the highlands, and the calligraphy distinctive to the kingdom of Aksum developed into Ge'ez, the ancestral writing of modern Ethiopia. Between the plow and the pen Aksum emerged as an indigenous state supported by its rich resources on a fertile plateau and the vital (though often tenuous) link through Adulis with the larger commercial network of the Red Sea, the Gulf of Arabia, the Mediterranean Sea, and the Indian Ocean. Aksum in its highland fortress was able to select those foreign innovations most advantageous to its people without eroding their indigenous civilization and represented the beginnings of literate, agricultural, and commercial states in northeast Africa over 2,000 years ago.

The kingdom took advantage of its strategic location – protected by the mountain walls of the highlands, yet close to the shores of the Red Sea – to exploit the trade that now prospered from the growth of Greek and later Roman mercantile technology. The combination of its agriculture – irrigated, terraced, and tilled by the plow – literacy for the social elite, and commerce through the port of Adulis enabled the chiefs and then kings of Aksum to build a powerful state. By the third century BCE kings of Aksum ruled from urban centers. Temples of limestone were constructed at Yeha, Haoulti, and Mantara for a pantheon of gods, and craftsmen fashioned bronze and iron axes, swords, sickles, rings, and jewelry, which bore strong resemblances to those of their relations in southern Arabia.

The kingdom exported ivory, the horn of the rhinoceros (worth a fortune in Asia as an aphrodisiac), hippopotamus hides, gold dust, frankincense, spices, and even live elephants. The fresh, aromatic frankincense of Ethiopia was highly prized in dynastic Egypt, democratic Athens, and imperial Rome as a source of spiritual and physical well-being that became less attractive to austere Christians who, in no small way, contributed to the economic decline of Aksum. All of these goods were exchanged for cattle and salt from the Danakil Desert, the most precious commodity in sub-Saharan Africa. Equally desired by the elite of Aksum was the merchandise – cloth, beads, porcelain, and ironware – brought to Adulis by merchants from the Mediterranean, the Black Sea, India, and China, and carried for eight days up the escarpment to Aksum. In the fifth century Aksum reached the height of its development and prosperity. The capital, Aksum, was well known throughout the Roman and Persian empires and as far as China in the east. Over 20,000 Aksumites inhabited the city whose elite spent their wealth from agriculture and commerce on elaborate houses and conspicuous consumption – fabrics from India and China, glassware and ceramics from Persia, spices, wine, and hardware from the eastern Mediterranean. In death the rulers and the elite were buried in stone tombs and erected tall obelisks of finely cut granite carved with decorative relief to represent a multi-storied building, each taller than its predecessor. More than 140 stelae have been found in Aksum, but only a few remain upright. One still standing is 69 feet tall, but the largest stele, exceeding 108 feet and weighing over 700 tons, cut from a granite quarry two-and-a-half miles west of Aksum, has fallen. The chiseling of these monuments with stone and fragile iron tools most certainly required artistic and technological skill, political stability, social organization, and leadership. The rapid decline of the carving and erection of obelisks, not surprisingly, coincided with the arrival of Christianity, which demanded the worship of Christ in his Church rather than using the resources of the state to commemorate kings by means of stelae.

The arrival of Christianity in the Ethiopian highlands was a watershed in the region's history. Ethiopian traditions maintain that in the fourth century CE King Ezana of Aksum (325–350) was converted to Christianity by two brothers, Frumentius and Aedesius, Christian traders returning from India who were shipwrecked on the Red Sea coast. Taken from Adulis to the court of Aksum they converted King Ezana and his court to Christianity and assisted in the administration of the kingdom. Aedesius returned to Syria, but Frumentius traveled to Alexandria where he was installed by the patriarch Athanasius (297–373) as a bishop of the Egyptian Coptic Church and sent back to Ethiopia as the *abuna* (Ge'ez, "bishop"), about 333.

Armenia had become Christian in 301, Rome in 312. Twenty years later in Aksum the *abuna salama* Frumentius established the beginnings of Ethiopian Christianity and was the first of 111 Egyptian monks to be appointed by the patriarchs of Alexandria as the *abuna* or head of the Ethiopian Church for the next sixteen centuries until 1951. This link was to remain vital to the Ethiopian Church and the monarchy for nearly two millennia. After the rise of Islam it was their intellectual, religious, and psychological channel to the outside world. The authority of the patriarch in Alexandria gave the Ethiopian Church its legitimacy and a confirmation of the apostolic succession and hence the link with the Christianity of the Eastern Church.

At the Council of Chalcedon in Syria in 451 the Christian Church was deeply divided over the nature of Jesus Christ. The majority, who claimed orthodoxy, argued that Christ's manhood and Godhood constituted two separate natures, human and divine. Those who adhered to the minority Monophysite doctrine believed that these two separate natures were fused into one in which his divinity superseded his humanity. The Orthodox–Monophysite struggle has been long and bitter, and remains today one of the principal schisms in the Christian Church, but at the end of the Council of Chalcedon priests supporting the Monophysite doctrine fled from persecution, nine of whom (known as the Nine Saints) reached Ethiopia. Here the traditions recognize them as the founders of the Ethiopian Orthodox Church, who translated the scriptures into Ge'ez and established monasticism, which became the historic institution for the continuity of Ethiopian Christianity. The Nine Saints are deeply revered today. They are credited with establishing the Ethiopian Church in the fifth century, and are believed to have preserved that vital connection with the Mediterranean world through the Monophysite Coptic patriarch in Alexandria and in Jerusalem where Ethiopian monks established their hospice after the collapse of the Roman Empire. The institution of the Egyptian *abuna* survived until the twentieth century because it benefited both the Coptic and Ethiopian Churches. When Christian Copts were persecuted by Muslims in Egypt, the patriarch threatened to appeal to his Christian brethren in Ethiopia to obstruct the waters of the Nile. When Muslims sought to isolate Ethiopia, the Egyptian Coptic Church was their link with Christendom and the institutional support for the monarchy, whose kings were crowned by the *abuna*. The solidification of Church and state in Ethiopia has been the principal reason for its longevity as an independent kingdom and state to the present day.

Although King Ezana was converted to Christianity in the fourth century, the traditional independence of the highlanders discouraged their rapid conversion. Moreover, when they did convert, it was to a unique version of Christianity that introduced significant indigenous beliefs and traditions into the faith, most enduring of which was the deep belief by Ethiopian Christians in the Solomonic tradition inherited from the Queen of Sheba who, legend insists, traveled from her kingdom of Saba to King Solomon in Jerusalem between 950 and 930 BCE. She bore him a son who became king of Aksum, Menelik I, who returned to Jerusalem, stole the Ark of the Covenant, and brought it to Aksum. The Ark was a wooden box lined with gold containing the two tablets on which God had written the Ten Commandments. This is legend, but belief can be more powerful than historical fact as it has been and still is in Ethiopia. Replicas of the Ark, known as *tabot*s, are found in 20,000 churches as the symbol of the religious legitimacy of Ethiopian Christianity, and the *tabot* has remained ever since the center of faith in every religious festival of the Ethiopian Orthodox Church. The mythical activities of Solomon, the Queen of Sheba, and her son Menelik I took place centuries before the foundation of the kingdom of Aksum, but they became the spiritual confirmation that the rulers of Ethiopia were descended from Menelik I who was the first in the long line of the Solomonic dynasty of Ethiopia whose kings, according to the traditions, have ruled Ethiopia throughout the centuries until the dynasty ended with the assassination of the last emperor, Haile Selassie, in 1975.

After reaching the zenith of its prosperity and power in the fourth and fifth centuries Aksum slipped into decline because of environmental degradation, the collapse of the Roman Empire and its Mediterranean and Red Sea commercial network, and changes in global climate. Rain from the South Atlantic would normally reach Aksum in northern Ethiopia in April and May and continue until September, enabling farmers to plant twice and harvest two crops each year in soils of marginal nutrients. Terracing, irrigation, the plow, and manure made possible food for the Aksumites and its deciduous forests the energy for smelting iron and manufacturing glass, brick, and pottery for the marketplace, charcoal for the kitchen stove, and timber for the house. Like the kingdom of Kush, where the Island of Meroe was denuded of its woodlands for charcoal and iron smelting, northern Ethiopia was stripped of its trees from the fourth to seventh centuries; and archaeologists believe that as much as 87 percent of the highlands may have once been forested. Today only 2.4 percent of the Ethiopian highlands are covered with trees. There was the need for more intensified cultivation to supply a growing population who consumed ever larger amounts of timber for charcoal and industry, exposing the land to fatal erosion as the rains now washed the hillsides bare.

Aksum grew from its agricultural resources but prospered from the Mediterranean, Red Sea, and Indian Ocean trade. This came to an end with the dissolution of the Roman Empire in the Mediterranean and the conquest of southern Arabia by the Persians, who now controlled the trade routes to the Persian Gulf and India. No longer able to barter the wealth of Africa through Adulis, which was destroyed in the eighth century by the Arabs, Aksum was confined to its degraded highlands at a time of global climatic change. Beginning in the eighth century the annual rainfall became limited to just the spring rains, restricting the farmers to only one annual crop of teff, a cereal that could pollinate without regular rainfall. By the ninth century the kingdom of Aksum had been reduced to a few monasteries and villages. Aksum left behind its stelae, both erect and fallen, a place of pilgrimage, and the symbiotic relationship between Church and state in Ethiopia. The decline of Aksum has been memorably described by the eighteenth-century English historian Edward Gibbon, who wrote: "Encompassed by the enemies of their religion, the Ethiopians slept for near a thousand years, forgetful of the world by whom they were forgotten."[2] Yet Gibbon's eloquent assessment betrays an ignorance of the subsequent history of Ethiopia. To be sure Abyssinia, now Ethiopia, was indeed isolated from the mainstream of the European Christian world, but it did not sleep. It developed its own unique religious and architectural traditions with little or no external influences; nor was the country forgotten by its Christian brethren. The unique monolithic churches of Lalibela, carved from solid blocks of rock in the thirteenth century by the legendary Zagwe emperor Lalibela, remain an enduring monument of traditional Ethiopian architecture with their striking exteriors and the refinement of their interior designs.

Christian states of Nubia

Just as geography had conditioned the history of Aksum so too did it determine life in the Nile Valley, a thin sliver of fertile soil sharply confined by desert sands whose topography has shaped the history of its Christian states. The disintegration of the kingdom of Kush and its symbolic termination by Ezana, the Christian king of Aksum in 350 CE, was followed by 200 years of rule in Lower Nubia by the Ballana, who came from the southwest to settle by the Nile. In the fifth century they established three kingdoms – Nobatia, Makouria, and Alwa – from Lower Nubia upstream from the First Cataract at Aswan to the confluence of the Blue and White Niles. As absolute rulers the Ballana kings sought legitimacy by adopting Kushitic symbols of monarchy. Nobatia was soon absorbed by Makouria to dominate Lower Nubia from Aswan to the Fifth Cataract, while the smaller kingdom of Alwa ruled the Nile from Meroe to its capital at Soba near the confluence at modern Khartoum. Little is known of the history of Nubia during the reigns of the Ballana kings, who were buried with their crowns and all the accoutrements for their afterlife – wine, cups, cooking utensils, lamps, jewels, weapons, and slaves ritually sacrificed. The burials were in monumental tombs, rather than pyramids, but they are reminiscent of dynastic Egypt and the kingdom of Kush, and could not have been constructed without the central organization of the state to mobilize the human, material, and religious resources to build them.

Between 543 and 580 CE the Nubians discarded their old gods and the idols of pharaonic Egypt to embrace with religious enthusiasm the new Monophysite Christian faith, which became the state religion of the Christian kingdoms of the Sudan. The evangelization of Nubia had been undertaken by missionaries sent by the great Byzantine emperor Justinian (527–565 CE) or, more likely, his empress, Theodora, who was an outspoken advocate of the Monophysite persuasion. Justinian converted the great temple of Isis at Philae near Aswan

---

[2] Edward Gibbon, *Decline and Fall of the Roman Empire*, Philadelphia: J. B. Lippincott, 1887, p. 135.

Figure 5.2 *Ethiopian Orthodox church at Lalibela. Under the Zagwe dynasty in the thirteenth century CE Ethiopian Christians carved several of these churches out of solid rock.*

into the church of St. Stephen, and in 543 the missionary Julian traveled up the Nile to convert the Nubians of the kingdom of Nobatia. His success was assured by the conversion of the king, which was followed by a spate of church building on the remains of old temples. He was succeeded in 569 by Longinus, who until 575 continued the conversion of Nubian rulers and their subjects by expanding the Christianity of the Monophysite doctrine into the kingdoms of Makouria and Alwa. The new religion was adopted with a spiritual passion that produced an astonishing ideological transformation. The great symbols of dynastic Egypt and Kush – tombs, temples, statuary, and divine kingship – soon disappeared, to be replaced by the strict observance of one God, the faith in whom inspired Nubian Christian churches, art, and literature.

The acceptance of one omnipotent King in heaven superseded the concept of divine kings on earth. The Christian kings of Makouria and Alwa, mere mortals, acknowledged the spiritual supremacy of the Coptic patriarch of Alexandria and his appointed bishops in Nubia in return for his support of their secular rule. Although the Monophysite Christianity of medieval Nubia was regarded

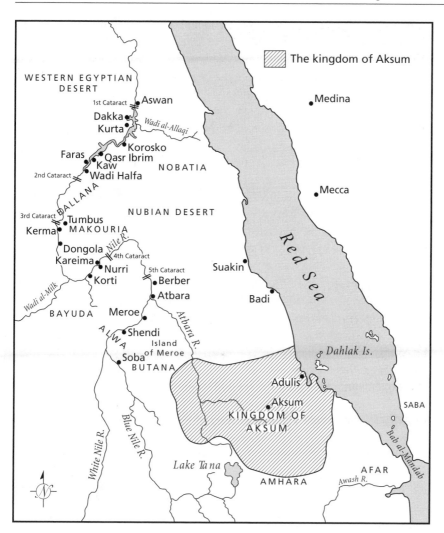

Map 5.1 *Aksum and the Christian kingdoms of Nubia.*

as heretical by both the Western Church in Rome and the Eastern Church at Constantinople, the arrival of Christianity restored the historical ties of Nubia with the Mediterranean world and renewed its cultural relationship with Egypt. It gave an identity to the peoples of the Nubian Nile by preserving their past culture in a Christian context that enabled them to resist for another 500 years the later challenge from Islam.

The Nubian kings embraced the new religion with the same fervor as their subjects, but their interests were as much political as spiritual. A religious alliance with the Coptic patriarch of Egypt and the Byzantine emperor would strengthen their isolated rule in Nubia. The excitement and acceptance with which Monophysite Christianity was received by the rulers and the ruled, however, cannot be explained solely by secular considerations. The old symbols of the kingdom of Kush had ceased to have meaning, and even the popular cult of Isis no longer gave legitimacy to the Ballana kings. Christianity was a new message, easily understood in the oneness of God, fulfilling a spiritual need that the Egyptian and Kushitic gods of the past could no longer satisfy. Even if regarded by other Christians as heretics, the Christian Nubian kings and their subjects became part of the larger world that embraced the new dynamic ideology and faith of Christianity.

We do not know the details of this rapid and remarkable conversion. Was it the charisma and rhetoric of a wandering mendicant, the fiery missionary, perhaps Julian, who could captivate the populace? Or were these early missionaries more ambassadors than evangelists who began at the court of an absolute Ballana monarch whose baptism would be quickly imitated by his courtiers and soon followed by that of his subjects? The rapid and complete acceptance of Christianity in Nubia by the end of the sixth century was probably a bit of both. The appeal for a new ideology coincided with royal decrees to adopt the new faith. The first Christian church was a remodeling in the latter half of the sixth century from the brick temple of Taharqo at Qasr Ibrim, built a thousand years before. The bricks and stones from palaces and temples scattered along the Nubian Nile could easily be converted to the naves of Christian churches. The average Nubian church was the size of a modern-day chapel, but there were large churches, cathedrals, at Old Dongola, Faras, and Qasr Ibrim.

Unlike Aksum, however, the institution of monasticism never developed in Makouria and Alwa. The monasteries of Ethiopia were the repositories of its history, literature, and language (Ge'ez), and the bastions against Muslim invasion. The failure to establish a monastic tradition in Nubia was perhaps more geographical than ideological. Unlike the highland plateau of Ethiopia, the Nubian Nile is a thin band of green by the river where there was only room for the church and not the expansive Ethiopian estates required to support a monastery. Moreover, the Monophysite missionaries in Nubia were concerned with conversion, which required their presence at court and preaching in the villages rather than retiring into the Nubian Desert to contemplate the nature of Christ in a wasteland that could not support even the most ascetic monks.

Moreover, the Nubian Church never established the ecclesiastical unity of the Ethiopian Orthodox Church. The primate of the Ethiopian Church was the *abuna* appointed by the patriarch of the Egyptian Coptic Church. Although he was an Egyptian monk, the primacy of the *abuna* was accepted by every Ethiopian emperor, noble, and peasant as the symbol of the centrality and continuity of the Church. Unity in the Nubian Church could never be achieved when each of its thirteen bishops was consecrated separately by the patriarch of Alexandria and they answered to him individually. There was no *abuna* and consequently no single individual to unify the Nubian Church under the control of rival bishops, who were one in doctrine and spirit but who were determined to defend their bishoprics against all rivals by appeals to their spiritual authority and as patrons of art and literature.

After the death of the Prophet Muhammad in 632, Muslim Arabs erupted from the desert steppes of Arabia to conquer the lands to the east and west. By 641 they had occupied Egypt, where the Egyptian Coptic Church had to accept its position as a minority religion, but Arab control of Upper Egypt on the borders of Christian Nubia was precarious and characterized by frontier raiding between Arab invaders and Nubian defenders. In 651–652 the Arab governor of Egypt, Abdallah ibn Sa'd Abi Sarh, led a well-equipped expedition to subdue the Nubians of Makouria. The Arabs marched as far as Dongola and laid siege to the town, but suffered heavy casualties from the skilled Nubian archers and were obliged to make peace, the *Baqt*. The *Baqt* is one of the most famous documents of medieval times; it defined the terms of peace on the frontier between Christian Nubia and the Islamic world for another six centuries (652–1257), a record in the history of international relations. It was originally regarded as a truce, not a treaty, and its longevity was more the result of reality and the benefits therefrom than an immutable convenant of ambiguous jurisprudence. The *Baqt* was an agreement of accommodation that regularized trade and was unique in the Muslim world, for it recognized that Christian Nubia was sovereign and exempt, not only from the *dar al-islam* (land of the faithful), but also from the *dar al-harb* (land of the enemy). This anomalous distinction recognized the invincibility of the Nubian army and the accuracy of its famous archers more than the erudition of Islamic jurists. The *Baqt* established peace and regulated commerce between Christian Nubia and Islamic Egypt. According to the terms of the agreement

> Each year you [Nubians] are to deliver 360 slaves, whom you will pay to the Imam of the Muslims from the finest slaves of your country, in whom there is no defect. [They are to be] both male and female. Among them [is to be] no decrepit old man or any child who has not reached puberty. You are to deliver them to the Wali of Aswan.[3]

In exchange, the Nubians were provided with foodstuffs from the Nile Valley.

The coming of Islam to Egypt and the Nile limited and ultimately ended the contact of both Ethiopia and Nubia with the Mediterranean world. This isolation forged on the anvil of Islam disrupted the commercial relationships with their Red Sea trading partners facilitated by the Egyptian Coptic Church, but the Muslim rulers were never sufficiently strong to conquer either of these two Christian states of northeast Africa. The Ethiopians were protected by their highlands, the Nubians by the rocks of the Nile cataracts and the burning sands of their deserts.

When Muslim Turkish mercenaries, the Tulunids, took control of Lower Egypt in the ninth century, they sought to rid themselves of the unruly Bedouin

---

[3] W. Y. Adams, *Nubia: Corridor to Africa*, Princeton: Princeton University Press, 1977, p. 451.

Arabs in Upper Egypt by encouraging them to roam into Nubia. The desert, which the Nubians avoided, was the home of the nominally Muslim Bedouin Arabs who rode out of the desert to raid the Christian settlements by the Nile, and once again the Christian Nubians of Makouria defended their kingdom against Islam for another 300 years until the Mamluk sultans established their rule over Egypt in the second half of the thirteenth century. The Mamluks perceived their principal duty as protecting the *dar al-islam* from infidels – Mongols, Crusaders, and Christian Nubians. Sultan Baybars (1260–1277) and his successor, Qalawun (1279–1290), sent military expeditions south of Aswan to pillage the Nubian Nile and return to Egypt without ever occupying Makouria. By the thirteenth century the Christian kingdoms of the Sudan were collapsing. During the centuries of the *Baqt* the authority of the monarchy had gradually been eroded by the hierarchy of the Church, whose bishops allied with the feudal nobility to undermine the Crown, which was beset by the incipient intrusions of Bedouin Arabs from Upper Egypt. These were far more corrosive to the Christian kingdoms than the challenge from the Mamluk sultans. When the last Mamluk expedition was sent to Nubia in 1366, the kingdom of Makouria had disintegrated into petty chiefdoms into which the Bedouins had settled. During these undocumented times trade disappeared, as did the *Baqt*, the Church, and the nobility, which imploded upon its own impotence. Christianity was no longer a threat on the frontier of Islam at Aswan. The vacuum was filled by the arrival of the Muslim *fuqura* (Arabic, "holy men," sg. *faqir*) practicing sufism, Islamic mysticism, in fraternal brotherhoods, the *turuq* (sg. *tariqa*), who brought Islam to the Sudan. They were neither warriors nor traders but religious teachers who spread Islam among the rustic Arab nomads and Nubian farmers just as Julian and Longinus had converted the Nubians to Christianity six centuries before.

By the fifteenth century Nubia was open to Arab immigration, particularly after the Juhayna of Upper Egypt learned that the grasslands beyond the hostile Aswan Reach could support their herds, and there was no longer any political authority with the power to obstruct their advance. They occupied Lower Nubia, where they intermarried with the locals and introduced Arabic and Islam to Nubian Christians. Inheritance among the Arabs is through the male, while among the Nubians it was passed through the female line. Intermarriage consequently resulted in Nubian economic and political inheritance passing from Nubian women to Arab sons and thereafter down the patrilineal line. The Juhayna and other Arab nomads wandered both east and west from the Nile with their cattle, camels, sheep, and goats. Some settled in Nubian villages by the Nile to become farmers. In Upper Nubia the kingdom of Alwa remained the last indigenous Christian barrier to Arab infiltration of the Sudan.

Medieval Arabic writers called the northern frontier of Alwa *al-abwab* ("the gates"), a term that still applies to the regions from al-Kabushiyya south of the confluence of the Atbara River with the Nile, to Sennar on the Blue Nile. Alwa appears to have been more prosperous than Makouria. It preserved the iron-working techniques of Kush, and its capital at Soba near Khartoum on the north bank of the Nile impressed Arab visitors with its buildings, churches, and gardens. Alwa was able to maintain its integrity so long as the Arab nomads failed to combine against it, but the collapse of the kingdom of Makouria resulted in a steady infiltration of Arab herdsmen. Alwa disappeared into unrecorded history. By the sixteenth century an Arab confederation led by the Islamic folk-hero Abdallah Jamma, "the Gatherer," destroyed Soba, leaving the Christian remains of the kingdom of Alwa to the mysterious Funj.

Further reading

Aksum, 200–700 CE

Kobishchano, U. M., *Aksum*, trans. L. T. Kapitanoff, ed. J. W. Michaels, University Park: Pennsylvania State University Press, 1979

Phillipson, David W., *Aksum: Its Antecedents and Successors*, London: British Museum Press, 1998

Sergew, H. S., *Ancient and Medieval Ethiopian History to 1270*, Addis Ababa: United Printers, 1972

Christian states of Nubia

Adams. W. Y., *Nubia: Corridor to Africa*, Princeton: Princeton University Press, 1977

6   Empires of the plains

In the eleventh century reports circulated in the bazaars of North Africa of a powerful African monarch who reigned far to the south, beyond the expanse of the Sahara Desert. His empire sent gold and slaves across to the Maghrib, where they percolated into the economy of the burgeoning Islamic world. This mysterious ruler, known as "the *ghana*," was reputed to be the most powerful king in all of Africa. His wealth, and that of his successors, became legendary.

The *ghana* was not a myth, but the ruler of an African kingdom called Wagadu, whose capital, Koumbi Saleh, lay on the desert's edge in modern Mauritania. From there the rulers of Wagadu dominated a vast commercial empire that stretched from the Niger River in the south to the desert's edge in the north, and from the Senegal Valley in the west to the inland Niger Delta in the east. Later it would be eclipsed by an even larger empire, Mali, which in time would itself be supplanted by the still larger empire of Songhai. Between and around the borders of these empires mushroomed an array of cities and states, all connected in a commercial web that stretched north to the Atlantic, and south to the tropical forests of Central Africa.

The first accounts of the states of the Western Sudan appear in Arab writings of the eighth century. Ghana probably emerged as a small state around 300 CE, and had grown into a thriving empire approximately 600 years later. Archaeological evidence indicates that several lesser-known complex societies appeared on the sahel and savanna at roughly the same time, including Takrur on the Senegal River, Dhar Tichitt on the sahel to the west of Koumbi Saleh, and, most ancient of all, at the town of Jenne-Jenoe, on the flood-plain of the inland Niger Delta, where urban settlements developed during the first millenium BCE.

Environment shaped the history of these states. The plains of West Africa, called the *bilad al-sudan* ("land of the blacks") by Arab merchants, are divided by environment and climate into a series of roughly parallel zones that run across the continent from east to west. In the farthest north is the semi-arid grassland known as the Sahel (Arabic, "shore") with the same root for the East African coastal language, Swahili. The Sahel measures only a few hundred miles from north to south, but stretches east–west across the continent from the Atlantic to the Red Sea. Gradually as one moves south beyond the Sahel the sparse savanna grasses thicken, and become punctuated by shrubs and small

Figure 6.1 *Dogon village, modern Mali.*

trees, in an environment called woodland savanna. As one continues south the solitary trees of the woodland savanna become groves, and gradually forests. Eventually this wooded grassland becomes the great tropical rainforest that stretches from Liberia in the west, through the southern fringes of Ivory Coast, Ghana, and Nigeria, and, further east, into southern Cameroon, northern Gabon and the Republic of Congo, and the vast Congo River Basin of the Democratic Republic of Congo.

The Western Sudan's great highway is the River Niger, which begins in the highlands of modern Ivory Coast, Mali, and Guinea. Though the river rises less than 200 miles east of the Atlantic coast, it flows in a great northeastern arc into the plains of the savanna in modern Mali, reaching its northernmost point near the fabled city of Timbuktu in the Sahel, before turning southwest. There in the forests of Nigeria its waters are joined by the Benue River, and from there it continues due south through modern Nigeria, where it fans out into the great Niger Delta, and flows into the Atlantic Ocean.

The broad flat expanse of the Western Sudan enables the placid Niger to meander in its sweeping arc from west to east, making the river ideally suited to human navigation. This topography has also allowed for the easy movement of peoples, languages, animals, crops, arts, and ideas. The dramatic diversity of temperature and climate that separates these broad strips of territory has encouraged economic specialization within each region. Pastoralists living on the edge of the desert in the Sahelian city of Timbuktu are only 125 miles north of the fertile floodplain of the Niger River. Farmers on the savanna below the Niger are in turn only a few hundred kilometers from the edge of the great equatorial rainforest. Throughout the long history of the Western Sudan the close proximity of these disparate zones has made trade crucial to the prosperity of settled communities. Protein-deficient farmers of the savanna needed meat from their pastoral neighbors, and salt from desert nomads. Nomadic herders of the Sahel needed the cereals produced by the farmers, and exchanged them for the meat and hides of their livestock. Forest dwellers traded meat and skins from animals they hunted, as well as food-stuffs from forest crops. Fishermen of the Niger sent their protein-rich catches in all directions. This regional interdependence encouraged commerce, economic specialization, and in strategic locations the creation of towns, cities, and states. These trading relationships were forged centuries before Arab writers ever heard of the wealth of the *ghana*.

However, until recent times most scholars attributed the rise of Sudanic states to the introduction of the camel into the Sahara some time around the fourth century CE. Camels brought the first Arab travelers to the previously unknown empires of the Sudan, thereby providing historians with the earliest written evidence of their existence. Armed with these documents, they assumed that the cities of the Sudan had emerged in response to the needs of Arab and Berber desert traders. Before the appearance of the rare and exotic goods supplied by the trade, scholars reasoned, rulers lacked the leverage they needed to elevate themselves in the eyes of their followers. Such an interpretation argued against common sense, as it is unlikely that merchants would chance the arduous trip across the desert if there were no urban markets to attract them, but it was supported by the few written sources available, all of which were produced by literate outsiders who traveled into the region after the advent of camel commerce.

Recent archaeological excavations have revealed that the Western Sudan had thriving urban centers before the first camels made their way across the desert. Indeed, at Jenne on the Middle Niger, archaeologists have uncovered a sprawl-ing urban settlement that lacks the monumental architecture, elaborate tombs, and memorials to powerful individuals that are associated with contemporary Near Eastern and Nile Valley remains. Instead, the settlement pattern suggests a diffusion of political power and a remarkable degree of social and economic equality. Although some archaeologists question whether or not such settle-ments constitute true urbanization, others see in Jenne a remarkable example of social complexification without state-sponsored coercion.

Although there can be no doubt that complex societies emerged in the West-ern Sudan before the advent of camel-borne commerce, the integration of the camel into the trans-Saharan caravan trade stimulated political expansion in the region. The quickening pace of economic activity spurred urbanization and encouraged economic specialization, which in turn demanded greater political authority to safeguard the merchants and the indigenous elite who participated in the trade. Merchants at both the northern and southern markets required secu-rity, without which commerce could not continue, let alone flourish. Leaders who could monopolize exotic trade goods possessed wealth, and therefore political power, that went far beyond what they could achieve from the agricultural and pastoral tribute provided by farmers and herders. These rulers protected the merchants, and monopolized the luxury goods – cloth, hardware, horses, and books – that were previously unknown in the Western Sudan and now in great demand.

The trans-Saharan trade was conducted and controlled by Muslim Berbers and Arabs. After a hazardous journey of two months these desert merchants arrived exhausted in the commercial emporiums of the Sahel, where they sold their goods to local traders. From there the goods would be taken south on donkeys, or put on boats on the Niger and shipped downstream to commercial ports. A merchant class known as the Wangara dominated the trade within the empire of Ghana. They established commercial links that stretched from the edge of the desert to the gold-producing forests in the south. In the later empire of Mali this commercial class was known as Dyula, a name that retains currency in the Western Sudan today. The Dyula were Mande speaking, as opposed to the Arab and Berber traders who controlled the cross-desert trade. Their dealings with Berber and Arab merchants were usually accompanied by their acceptance of Islam, which made them among the first Muslim converts in West Africa, and their commercial transactions brought them into contact with the diverse ethnic communities of the Western Sudan. The Dyula forged their connections, with Muslims and non-Muslims alike, through intermarriage, observance of local customs, respect for traditional religions, and a willingness to do business with pagan elites.

The Dyula handled all aspects of the trade below the desert. They brought the gold from the mines on the Upper Niger to the commercial centers downstream where it was exchanged for goods from the Mediterranean world. They also brought the cola nut that grows on the *Cola nitida* tree in the forests of West Africa. It contains caffeine and is widely used and accepted by Muslims as a mild stimulant that invariably accompanies social occasions throughout West Africa, the Sahara, and the Maghrib. Through their political connections, and with the resources necessary to undertake long-distance trade, they traveled widely in their commercial enterprises throughout West Africa.

Many African political authorities who desired wealth from the goods of the Maghrib sought to enhance their power and legitimacy by embracing a religion that would transcend the parochial traditional rituals and bind them to peoples far beyond the Western Sudan. In the empires of the plains Islam thus became a court religion, the result of the relationship between Muslim merchants of the trans-Saharan trade and the ruling African elite with whom they had to negotiate their commercial transactions. Not surprisingly, the monarch and his nobles became by custom, wealth, and religion increasingly isolated from the countryside and villages where the cultivators and herdsmen of the Western Sudan were quite content to worship with all the traditional ritual and ceremony, to demonstrate respect for the ancestors, and to placate the gods to insure individual and social prosperity.

Ghana

Ghana was first briefly mentioned by the Muslim astronomer Ibrahim al-Fazari (d. 777) in the eighth century as the "land of gold." The origins of the *ghana* are enshrouded in the mythology of ancient kings known as *kaya-magha* ("the king of gold"), who ruled west of the Niger and north of the Senegal Rivers. By the ninth century the *ghana* controlled the region, known as Wagadu, and prospered from his royal monopoly on the trade in gold and slaves that passed through the city of Awadaghast up the Walata Road to the Maghrib. The most authoritative account of the fabled gold trade of the *ghana* was written in the eleventh century by the Arab geographer Abu Ubayd al-Bakri (1040–1094), who learned of the *ghana* from the Berber merchants who visited Islamic Spain. He observed that although Muslim merchants were important in commerce and the administration of the state, the *ghana* and his subjects continued to practice their traditional religions.

> Their religion is paganism and the cult of idols. When the king dies they construct a large hut of wood over the place of burial. His body is brought on a scantily-furnished bier and placed in the hut. With it they put his eating and drinking utensils, food and drink, and those who used to serve him with these, and then the entrance is secured. They cover the hut with mats and clothing and all the assembled people pile earth over it until it resembles a considerable hill, then they dig a ditch around it allowing one means of access to the heap. They sacrifice victims to their dead and offer them fermented drinks.[1]

Archaeologists working at Koumbi Saleh have unearthed artifacts that confirm al-Bakri's account of the *ghana*'s burial.

The *ghana* ruled over an empire that was sharply divided between city and countryside. At Koumbi Saleh he was surrounded by merchants who paid taxes in salt and gold that supported court life and royal administration. Outside the city the *ghana*'s subjects were for the most part Soninke-speaking farmers, fishermen, and herdsmen. They were ruled by hereditary village chiefs who were virtually autonomous so long as they acknowledged the authority of the *ghana*, paid him tribute, and sent their sons as hostages to the royal court to insure their loyalty. In return the *ghana* was expected to protect his people from the raids of desert nomads by a militia summoned from chieftains in the countryside.

Ghana established a pattern of expansion that would become characteristic of the great states of the Western Sudan. Because their wealth came largely

---

[1] J. S. Trimingham, *History of Islam*, London: Oxford University Press, 1962, pp. 53–54, quoting Bakri.

from long-distance commerce, empires expanded along an east–west axis in a bid to monopolize the north–south trade routes. While ambitious rulers might attempt at times to project their power north into the desert, or south towards the goldfields, the easiest and most successful strategy was simply to establish control across the desert's edge, in the knowledge that all trade would eventually come through their territory. Representing this on a map can be deceptive, as Ghana, and its successor states Mali and Songhai, are frequently drawn as great, flat concentric circles. In reality it was the trading towns that connected these dots, not the vast spaces between them, that represented the wealth of the empire.

Ghana's influence waned after the eleventh century. Until relatively recently it was assumed that the proximate cause of its demise was an attack in 1076 of Berber Almoravids, who sacked the capital, Koumbi Saleh, and thereby dealt a terminal blow to the coherency of the empire. Today this invasion thesis is no longer widely accepted. What is clear is that during this era the empire dissolved into rival chieftaincies, political instability, and economic depression. It appears that a host of problems, not least of which was the diversion of the gold trade east, down the Niger and up the Taghaza Trail across the Sahara, rather than through Awadaghast, led to the decline of the empire. With a slackening of economic activity Koumbi Saleh, existing as it did on the marginal agricultural land of the sahel, could no longer feed its bloated population.

Mali

The eventual successor state to Ghana was Mali, which emerged during the early thirteenth century. Its origins are tied to the opening of the Bure goldfields on the Upper Niger. This was the land of the Mande-speaking peoples who long had close ties with the Soninke of the *ghana*. Like other savanna societies they were farmers with sheep, goats, and chickens. They acknowledged the authority of the *farma*, master of the land and chief of a *kafu*, a cluster of villages either on the savanna or in clearings of the forests.

The origins of Mali are remembered in the epic legend of Sundiata, the founding monarch of the dynasty. According to oral traditions the decline of Ghana provided the opportunity for the powerful sorcerer called Samaguru to build his own empire among the southern Soninke, known as the "Sosso," named for their homeland on the Upper Niger. In the epic Sundiata is portrayed as a powerful sorcerer in his own right, and the champion of the Mande peoples. In the climactic battle at Kirina, Sundiata and his Mande chiefs triumph over the armies of Samaguru, thus laying the foundations for the empire.

While his life is shrouded in legend, the ruler who came to be known as Sundiata, or "Lord Lion," was a real historical person, probably born not long after the turn of the thirteenth century CE. His clan, the Keita, would dominate the empire for over two centuries. Sundiata built his empire from the Mande *farma*s from the forest and the fertile Niger Valley, who joined him in his conquests east towards the great bend in the Niger, north to the shore of the Sahara, and west to the Atlantic. In the process he conquered the remnants of Ghana, building a much larger empire on its foundations.

Sundiata took the title of *mansa* of Mali and built his capital at Niani. As *mansa* Sundiata forged the religious and secular ideology of the Malinke to become master of the land and guardian of the ancestors, if not a divine king, whose power was increased and respected for his religious authority. To quote his epic, "Sundiata rests near Niani-Niani, but his spirit lives on and today the Keitas [princes of Mali] still come and bow before the stone under which lies the father of Mali."[2]

The advent of the Malian empire represents a turning-point in the history of Islam in the Western Sudan. Arab and Berber merchants had brought the religion to the court of the *ghana*, where it had become influential. But successive rulers had kept Muslims at arm's length. The core of the *ghana*'s political support was his Soninke subjects, who invested him with spiritual and ritual authority that was crucial to his legitimacy. Thus embracing Islam would invariably threaten his standing with his own countrymen. The ambivalence of the empire toward Muslims is reflected in the fact that the *ghana* established two towns at Koumbi Saleh, one of which served the Muslims of the empire.

Mali would be a larger, wealthier, and more cosmopolitan empire than its great predecessor. With this expansion came a greater interaction with the Islamic world beyond the desert, and more opportunities for literate Muslim administrators and merchants at the *mansa*'s court. Sundiata himself appears to have been uninfluenced by the religion, but his successors took a greater interest in the faith. Islam became the court religion under Sundiata's son Mansa Uli (1255–1270), who made the pilgrimage to Mecca and received diplomatic recognition from the Muslim world. Though other *mansa*s were to become devout Muslims, none could ignore the deities, rituals, and festivals that remained central to the lives of their Mande countrymen.

The administration of the empire of Mali was not unlike that of the *ghana*. The court observed Islam, and literate Muslims were secretaries and accountants. Beyond Niani, however, the traditional chiefs ruled the land according to custom so long as they paid their annual tribute to the *mansa*. The local priests continued to propitiate the ancestors and minister to their deities. The external security and internal enforcement by the state was the responsibility of the army, which consisted of a small elite corps of horsemen and foot soldiers with bows and arrows, commanded by officials from the royal court. When

---

[2] D. T. Niane, *Sundiata: An Epic of Old Mali*, trans. G. D. Pickett, London: Longman, 1965, p. 84.

faced with a serious threat, the *mansa* could call upon his tributaries to provide levies, but this was rare.

Despite the glamour and importance of the gold and salt trades, the economy of the empire was based on agriculture and pastoralism. Niani was situated in the rich alluvial soil of the Upper Niger tributaries from which its empire stretched east and west across the fertile plains of the savanna with sufficient rainfall to grow large quantities of sorghum, millet, and, in the delta of the Middle Niger, rice. On the empire's northern borders the sahel provided grazing for cattle, sheep, goats, and camels.

Mali achieved the limits of its expansion and power in the fourteenth century, symbolized by the famous pilgrimage (*hajj*) of Mansa Musa (1312–1337) to Mecca in 1324–1325, which attracted the attention of both the European and Muslim worlds. It was a pilgrimage in the grand manner. He crossed the Sahara and arrived in Cairo with a hundred camels carrying gold. His appearance created a good deal of consternation, envy, and respect, and his generous spending depressed the Cairo gold market for another decade. His munificence was the envy of Sultan al-Malik al-Nasir Muhammad ibn Qalawun (1299–1341) and the Mamluk elite. He established cultural and economic ties with the Arab world, and Arab scholars returned with him, one of whom, Ishal al-Tuedjin (al-Sahili), became the principal architect of the Western Sudan, building mosques at Gao, Timbuktu, and Niani.

The pilgrimage of Mansa Musa inspired European cartographers to produce imaginative maps, one in 1375 showing Musa on a throne holding a hefty nugget in his hand. The great days of Mansa Musa and his equally able nephew, Mansa Sulayman (1341–1360), could not be sustained. The wealth of the empire attracted the avarice of its neighbors. From the forest and grasslands in the south the Mossi people had been organized by a ruling aristocracy into a number of states whose horsemen began to raid and pillage along the empire's exposed southern frontier at the end of the fifteenth century. The predatory Tuareg nomads were more dangerous. Sundiata and the freed slave Sakura, who in 1285 had usurped the throne and declared himself the *mansa*, had driven the Tuareg from Timbuktu and rebuilt the decrepit city into a center of Muslim commerce and learning. The Tuareg, however, returned to harass the forces of Mali on their northern frontier and retake Timbuktu in 1433.

Pillage sapped the strength of the empire on its frontiers, but the decline and fall of Mali was more from internal decay than external enemies. The court was frequently torn by internecine strife among rivals seeking to influence the *mansa* while manuevering to succeed him. The court's hold over the non-Mande provinces of the empire was often precarious, and succession struggles offered opportunities for secession. This happened in the late fourteenth century when in the east the ancient commercial center of Gao freed itself from imperial rule. In the west the infiltration of the pastoral Fulbe (Fulani) into the Upper Senegal eroded Malinke authority, and in the fifteenth century the Fulbe founded an independent non-Muslim state in the Futa Toro

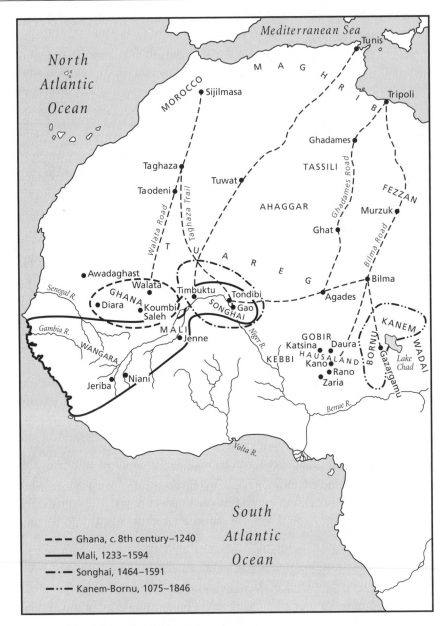

Map 6.1 *Empires of the plains.*

Plateau as a successor to the ancient kingdom of Takrur. In the Lower Senegal the Serer and Wolof peoples had abandoned their fragile allegiance to Mali a hundred years before. By the middle of the sixteenth century the disintegration of the empire of Mali was confirmed when the Songhai sacked the capital, Niani, in 1545–1546. After a futile attempt in 1599 by the *mansa* to reassert his authority over the commercial emporium of Jenne on the Middle Niger, the empire lost control of the Bambuk goldfields and disintegrated into petty chiefdoms.

The Songhai

The Songhai are unique in the history of the Western Sudan. They were descended from the Sorko fishermen of the Middle Niger whose canoes gave them mastery of the river and control of its trade across and along the great bend of the river, 1,200 miles west to east. As the camel was the mobile military vehicle of the desert, so the war canoe became the swift means to dominate the farmers and trading villages along this broad flowing reach of the Niger. The riverine world of the Songhai made them different from the farmers and herdsmen on the banks, as did their speech. Both the Soninke of Ghana and the Mande of Mali, not to mention the Fulbe, Mossi, Serer, Wolof, and other West African peoples, all spoke languages of the Niger-Congo linguistic family. Songhai was a language related, not to the peoples who surrounded them, but to the Nilo-Saharan family whose linguistic relatives lived in the Sahara, the Upper Nile, and East Africa. When, why, and how the Songhai became linguistically isolated on the Niger from other members of their language family far to the east remains unknown.

As early as the ninth century the Songhai by occupation and language had established their identity and state with a capital at Kukiya which in the twelfth century was moved upstream to the Muslim commercial center of Gao, the terminus on the river of the trans-Saharan Ghadames Road from Tripoli. The Songhai exchanged fish and food with the Muslim merchants for salt, cloth, and hardware. Many merchants became Muslims in the process. During the thirteenth and fourteenth centuries they remained tributaries of Mali. On his return from Mecca Mansa Musa visited Gao and built its great mosque. Upon the decline of Mali, however, the Songhai became increasingly independent, and a warrior king, Sunni Ali Ber (1464–1492), carved out an empire from Gao as far west as Jenne to embrace the whole of the Middle Niger. He captured Timbuktu in 1468, contained the Mossi in the south and pacified the Tuareg on his northern frontier.

Sunni Ali cared little for Islam and its Muslim scholars in Timbuktu, but he organized the agricultural development of the Niger Valley with slave labor, promoted peasant cultivation, and encouraged the commercial centers of Jenne and Timbuktu. Upon his death in 1492 he was succeeded by one of his generals, Muhammad Ture (1493–1528), who seized control of the state from the son and heir of Sunni Ali, founding a new dynasty known as the Askiya (1493–1592). Muhammad Ture consolidated the conquests and administration of Sunni Ali, but unlike him he was a devout Muslim. He understood the importance of the Muslim trans-Saharan trade and made the *hajj* to Mecca in 1496–1497, established a hostel for pilgrims from Mali, and accepted the title of caliph of the *bilad al-sudan* from the *sharif* of Mecca. Upon his return he reorganized the administration by appointing trusted servants or members of the royal family in the provinces to replace the traditional ethnic governors. His attempts to centralize the empire, however, were undermined by the historic problem of succession. Old and blind, he was deposed in 1528 after another internal struggle and exiled to an island in the Niger, where he died ten years later. Rivals competed for the title of *askiya* until the last son of Muhammad Ture, Dawud (1529–1582), seized the throne in 1549 and reasserted his authority over those chiefs who had ceased to pay tribute to the central government after the deposition of his father in 1528. He was a devout Muslim concerned with the construction of mosques and Quranic schools, but upon his death in 1582 after a long rule, his ineffectual successors could not contain the threat from the north.

Toward the end of the reign of Askiya Dawud the control of the trans-Saharan gold and salt trade was challenged by Mawlay Ahmad al-Mansur (1578–1603). The sixth sultan of the Saadian dynasty of Morocco, he was known as "the Victorious" after defeating the king of Portugal, Don Sebastian (1557–1578), and his large Crusader army at the battle of Wadi al-Makhazin (battle of Alcazarquivar or the battle of the Three Kings) on August 4, 1578. The Portuguese debacle ended the Crusader threat from Europe and enabled Ahmad al-Mansur to consolidate his rule in the Maghrib against Christians and Turks and to turn his ambitions to seize control of the Saharan salt mines, the trans-Saharan trade, and the Western Sudan. Sands he could cross and salt mines he could control, but he did not possess the gold of West Africa. At the height of his prosperity and power he therefore sent Judar Pasha (d. 1604), a Spanish eunuch, to lead a Moroccan expeditionary force of 4,000 troops equipped with cannons and muskets across the Sahara to conquer the Songhai empire. Leaving Marrakesh in November 1590, the Moroccan army crossed the desert after considerable difficulty and arrived five months later at Tondibi, thirty miles north of Gao, the Songhai capital. On March 12, 1591 Judar Pasha, his 2,500 musketeers, and 1,500 cavalry routed 20,000 spear- and swordsmen of the Songhai army of Askiya Ishaq II (1588–1591).

This was one of those decisive battles that change history. The age of empires on the plains of the Western Sudan was over. The sprawling states of the *ghana*, Mali, and Songhai that had dominated the *bilad al-sudan* for seven centuries had disintegrated before new technologies and foreign invaders from North Africa three centuries before more formidable imperialists were to arrive in the Western Sudan from Europe. Having achieved victory at Tondibi, the Moroccan officers and troops withdrew to Timbuktu where, isolated by the sands of the Sahara, their offspring, who came to be known as the Ruma, established personal fiefs as a military caste who became increasingly independent from the sultan of Morocco. By 1632 they ruled throughout the Middle Niger Valley by patronage and privilege, alienating the traditional Songhai elite. Petty states rose and declined from the economic depression that accompanied political instability. Agricultural settlements dispersed for security elsewhere, and famine and epidemics that accompany dearth became common. Fulbe cattlemen on the Futa Toro took advantage of the dissolution of government to encroach from the west. Bambara farmers sacked the once-great commercial center of Jenne. The Tuareg, ever predators, ravaged the Middle Niger, sacked Gao in 1680, and in 1737 the Ouilliminden Tuareg massacred the Ruma who had hired them as mercenaries. The Western Sudan, the *bilad al-sudan*, had to await an Islamic regeneration in the nineteenth century to rebuild its states at the time when the trans-Saharan trade and political and individual security moved eastwards to the central Sudan and the empire of Kanem-Bornu.

Kanem-Bornu

To the east of the great Niger river states lay the central Sudan. There flourishing empires capitalized on their closer proximity to Egypt and the Islamic heartlands. The largest of these empires came to be known as Kanem-Bornu. This cumbersome name is the result of an original state, called Kanem, which stood on the northeastern shore of Lake Chad (in the modern Republic of Chad), relocating its capital to the western side of the lake (which is in modern Nigeria). The Saifawa dynasty of Kanem-Bornu ruled the kingdom for 771 years, the longest reign in recorded history.

Where did Kanem-Bornu come from? The state appears to have been founded by a nomadic people known as the Zaghawa, who spoke a Nilo-Saharan language, and probably emerged from the central Sahara Desert. The region around Lake Chad had long been an attractive place for settlement. The lake provided fish and water for agriculture, and archaeology suggests that it had been home to farmers and fishermen as early as the middle of the first millennium BCE. Its northern edge lay relatively close to the desert oases of Kawar, which linked the central Sudan with key salt-producing centers of the Sahara, and the trade of the Fezzan in the north. Archaeologists speculate that the Zaghawa may have been among the first people in the central Sudan to acquire iron-working technology and horses from the Berbers of North Africa. If so, this may have allowed them to establish their authority over the stone-tool-using farmers and fishermen of the Lake Chad Basin. Like the empires of the Western Sudan, Kanem-Bornu grew wealthy by dominating the Sahelian trade routes connecting north and south. Unlike those empires, it had no gold-fields in its trading orbit. Instead it sent ivory, slaves, and animal skins north, in exchange for salt from the Sahara, and horses as well as manufactured goods from the Maghrib.

Less is known about the early history of Kanem-Bornu than of its great western neighbors. The kingdom is first mentioned by Arab chroniclers in the ninth century. Recorded history begins at the end of the eleventh century

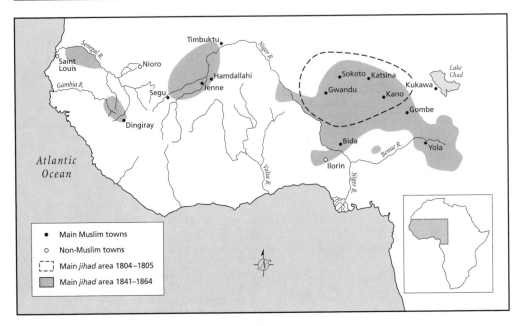

Map 6.2 *Islam in West Africa.*

when Humai ibn Salamna, founder of the Saifawa dynasty, is said to have driven out the Zaghawa clans and founded the kingdom of Kanem, establishing his capital at Nijimi, a site that has not yet been discovered. The Saifawa rulers of Kanem-Bornu claimed descent from a great ancestor named Saif ibn Dhi Yasan, who was originally from Yemen. The attribution of the empire's origins to a heroic Arab figure indicates the important role Islam has played in the legitimacy of the ruling dynasty. The immediate predecessors to the Saifawa had been Muslim converts, and under Saifawa rule the religion's influence expanded.

Kanem-Bornu reached its apogee of power under the reign of Mai (a royal title similar to *ghana* and *mansa*) Dunama Dabalemi ibn Salma (1221–1259). In his reign, according to Muslim chroniclers, the kingdom could put 40,000 mounted warriors on the field of battle. During the thirteenth century Islamic influence expanded at the Saifawa court. Mai Dunama's predecessor was the first ruler of Kanem-Bornu to make the *hajj* to Mecca. And Mai Dunama reputedly pressed his followers to abandon traditional religious practices in favor of Islam – most sensationally when he desecrated a religious artifact called the *mune* which was held as sacred to the kingdom's animists. It is unclear what the *mune* actually was, and some have speculated that it was an ancient statue of the Nile Valley god Amun. Regardless, it was a religious symbol of great significance, and by profaning it, Mai Dunama was said to have precipitated a rift between the Saifawa and the Bulala, a powerful clan of pastoralists. Conflict with the Bulala and other pastoral groups eventually drove the Saifawa to retreat west, across Lake Chad, sometime in the late fourteenth century. There they established a new capital, Birni Gazargamu, and a new kingdom, now known as Bornu.

The Saifawa were wracked by fratricidal struggles between rival claimants to the empire's throne. However, from time to time a strong leader emerged, such as Mai Ali Gaji ibn Dunama (*c.* 1476–1503), who defeated the Bulala and reinforced the dynasty's hold over Kanem. Throughout the sixteenth century Bornu expanded under a succession of able *mais*, the greatest of whom was Idris Alawma (*c.* 1571–1610), who consolidated the internal administration of the state, expanded the empire and its commerce, stabilized the turbulent Bulala frontier in the east, and encouraged the spread of Islam. The *mais* of Bornu established formidable armies, known for their large troops of cavalry. They were also the first African monarchs below the Sahara to import firearms, purchasing muskets from Arab merchants, and hiring Turkish mercenaries to train their armies and fight their wars.

The Saifawa faced growing threats during the seventeenth and eighteenth centuries. Internal rebellion and external pressure from nomadic pastoralists in the north, as well as the growing power of the Hausa states in the west, sapped the authority of the *mais*. These challenges to the kingdom of Bornu were made more dangerous by drought, famine, and the importation of firearms across the Sahara, which accelerated the ferocity of warfare on the plains of the *bilad al-sudan*. The dynasty clung to power until 1841, when its last ruler was pushed aside and nearly eight centuries of Saifawa rule in the central Sudan came to an end.

Over the course of a thousand years the empires of the plains each had its distinct characteristics, but they all had many more features in common. The fundamental resource of the state came from the crops and herds of farmers and herdsmen, but the trans-Saharan trade provided those specialized goods – salt and, later, firearms for gold and slaves – that enabled the social and political elite to establish a nobility to dominate and exploit the commoner. In order to encourage the trade the elite had to secure the safety of its merchants and their own interests by the regulation of commerce. This was accomplished in every case by a creation of a state that became an empire. This transformation could not have occurred, however, without the traditional African social structure of ethnic groups, clans, and lineages. The able ruler could command the allegiance of his courtiers, warriors, and merchants from his court at the capital, but his authority was based on his abilities, personality, and above all success at securing allegiance from the heads of many different clans and lineages by diplomacy or war.

In this manner a strong *ghana*, *mansa*, *askiya*, or *mai* could rapidly spread his authority over immense territories by accepting the submission by negotiation or surrender of leaders who became vassals, symbolized by the payment of tribute and services. In return the central ruler would leave local jurisdiction to the traditional authorities – chiefs, headmen, elders – who protected and supervised the laws, religion, and taxation of their own people. There is still debate as to whether this system of governing was not unlike feudal Europe, where the king was dependent on the nobility for tribute and troops, but it helps to explain how these empires of the plains could be formed quickly as well as how rapidly they could collapse. When kings were strong, the tributary chiefs paid their obligations to the ruler in kind and in services, usually military. When kings were weak, they did neither, becoming autonomous or independent until subdued and forced to acknowledge the return of a central authority. Expansion and consolidation of the empire was the task of diplomacy, military force, and religion over a host of tributaries. Thus, the far-flung empires were defined by the number and loyalty of the ethnic leaders and their followers who acknowledged the authority of the center so that the territorial extent of the empires expanded and contracted with that loyalty and consequently with greater fluidity than European states, which fought over fixed frontiers.

At the center of these accordion empires was the monarch and his court whose resources to rule came from tribute in the form of agricultural and pastoral produce and the profits from trade and the taxes levied upon it. Neither could be defined in terms of real estate, for the agricultural and pastoral tribute depended more upon the beneficence of nature passed from peasant to lord to monarch to provide the economic foundation of the state. The trans-Saharan and internal trade provided the necessary – and considerable – income to maintain the army, an impressive and symbolic court, and to reward faithful retainers. The rulers of the Western Sudan did not think of their empires as territories defined by boundaries inhabited by politically loyal subjects; they conceived of them as defined by nature, personal relationships, and trade rather than geography.

Ethnic and commercial structures defined the empire, but the army made possible its expansion. Until the thirteenth century the soldiers of Mali were infantry and bowmen, and warfare was characterized more by intimidation than slaughter. The introduction of the large war-horse for cavalry transformed the conduct of war in the *bilad al-sudan*. The horse had reached the sahel and savanna in the first century of the Christian era, but they were small ponies, ridden without the saddles and stirrups necessary to do battle. In the thirteenth century Mai Dunama Dabalemi of Kanem imported large numbers of cavalry horses from Mamluk Egypt, with which he had excellent commercial and diplomatic relations. Mali adopted hard-charging mobile cavalry in the fourteenth century, and Sunni Ali effectively used his horsemen in the expansion of Songhai in the fifteenth. By the sixteenth century the horse and its quilted armor became the striking force of the Yoruba army of Oyo, but here on the fringe of the rainforest the presence of the tsetse fly ended its southward expansion.

The horse was expensive, costing numerous slaves, but transformed its owners into an elite corps who took great pride in their skill as horsemen and in the bravado of their charge, brandishing sword and spear with contempt for the arrows and pikes of common infantry. The horseman was obviously a very superior person, symbolized by codes of honor and self-glorification, riding his extravagantly bedecked steed. The wealth and power of the horsemen made them military aristocrats in society, and perhaps explains their failure to adopt the muskets that began to arrive in the states of the Western Sudan from North Africa during the sixteenth century. Cavalry certainly contributed to the dependence of the state on slavery, for mobile horsemen could easily capture slaves to pay for an expensive horse. Slaves were needed to care for the horses of the cavalry, and even rode the horses of their masters on ceremonial occasions.

If the empires of the plains had common commercial, social, and military institutions that were their strength, they also had common problems that eroded the authority of the rulers. There was the perennial problem of succession. Descent and succession in African states, traditional or Muslim, has never been defined. In polygamous societies the heir to the ruler could be one of many brothers or sons from many wives or concubines, which stimulated internecine succession struggles or rebellion by members of the royal family anxious to assert their independence. Dynastic and internecine conflict not only weakened the state, which depended upon a strong ruler, but often resulted in the accession to the throne of a weak monarch who could easily be manipulated by a successful court faction.

Famine was more devastating to the people of the plains than strife over succession, and was the principal reason for the dearth of demographic growth and the need for slaves to labor when indigenous freemen had perished. The great famines were recorded in oral traditions and by Islamic scholars. There were many reasons for famine – torrential thunderstorms, locusts, the collapse of governance from internal struggles or external wars – but the principal cause in the *bilad al-sudan*, as elsewhere in the world, was drought. During the first millennium CE the rainfall in western Africa was consistent and sufficient, measured by the high levels of lakes and river flows. During the next 500 years the Western Sudan experienced much less rainfall, desiccation in the sahel, and drought in the savanna that produced the famines recorded by Muslim chroniclers. The rains returned in the sixteenth century. The rivers flowed, and Lake Chad reached a level it has never again achieved. Drought returned in the seventeenth and eighteenth centuries, and there was widespread famine from the Senegambia in the west to the Upper Nile in the east. Population growth was imperceptible, and throughout the centuries the empires of the plains were underpopulated.

All rulers of these Sudanic states were confronted by religious tensions and marauding nomads, both of which presented a continuous challenge to the central authority, more by erosion from the *razzia* than confrontation on the battlefield. There was sullen animosity between the rulers and nobles at court, practicing Islam and surrounded by a Muslim bureaucracy with Muslim merchants, and the leaders and peoples of the countryside, who firmly adhered to their traditional religious practices and resented the arrogance of the Muslim court aristocrats and their commercial courtiers. This religious antagonism ironically created dissension within the Muslim community between those who were strict observers of Islam and those Muslims who were quite prepared to recognize and participate in the traditional religious rituals and festivals.

The Saharan nomads were an external but constant threat to the stability of the state. The Tuareg controlled the oases of the Sahara and dominated the routes of the trans-Saharan trade. Through the centuries they relentlessly raided along the sahelian frontier. The *razzia* was a common occurrence as the Tuareg swept out from the desert to pillage. When the empires where weak, they even occupied the northern commercial centers, capturing Timbuktu in 1433. When the rulers were strong, they would drive the Tuareg back into their desert sanctuaries, as did Sunni Ali of Songhai who recaptured Timbuktu in 1468 and waged war against them in the southern Sahara throughout his reign. This contest for control on the frontiers of Islam in the *bilad al-sudan* continues to the present day throughout the volatile borderlands between Sahara and Sahel, disrupting contemporary African states as in the past it had destabilized the empires of the plains.

Further reading

Levtzion, Nehemia, *Islam in West Africa: Religion, Society, and Politics to 1800*, Brookfield, VT: Variorum, 1994

Levtzion, Nehemia and Jay Spaulding (eds.), *Medieval West Africa: Views from Arab Scholars and Merchants*, Princeton: Markus Wiener, 2003

Norris, H. T., *The Arab Conquest of the Western Sahara: Studies of the Historical Events, Religious Beliefs, and Social Customs Which Made the Remotest Sahara a Part of the Arab World*, Harlow: Longman, 1986

Trans-Saharan trade

Bovill, Edward W., *The Golden Trade of the Moors*, new introduction by Robert O. Collins, Princeton: Markus Wiener, 1995

Empires of the plains

Bjørkelo, Anders, *State and Society in Three Central Sudanic Kingdoms: Kanem-Bornu, Bagirmi, and Wadai*, Bergen: University of Norway Press, 1976

Connah, G., *Three Thousand Years in Africa: Man and his Environment in the Lake Chad Region of Nigeria*, London: Cambridge University Press, 1981

Levtzion, Nehemia, *Ancient Ghana and Mali*, New York: Africana Publishing Co., 1980

McIntosh, Roderick J., *Ancient Middle Niger: Urbanism and the Self-Organizing Landscape*, Cambridge: Cambridge University Press, 2005

McIntosh, Susan K., *Prehistoric Investigations in the Region of Jenne, Mali: A Study of Urbanism in the Sahel*, Oxford: BAR, 1980

McIntosh, Susan K. and Roderick J. McIntosh, "Cities without Citadels: Understanding Urban Origins along the Middle Niger," in *The Archaeology of Africa: Food, Metals, and Towns*, ed. Thurstan Shaw et al., London: Routledge, 1993, pp. 124–156

Palmer, Sir H. R., *The Bornu, Sahara and Sudan*, New York: Negro Universities Press, 1970

7   East Africa and the Indian Ocean world

In West Africa long-distance trade across the sands of the Sahara made possible the exchange of commodities from the Mediterranean world for those of Africa, which encouraged the expansion of states south of the desert. In East Africa long-distance trade over the waters of the Indian Ocean made possible the exchange of commodities from Asia for those of Africa, which cultivated the rise of commercial emporiums and city-states to promote them. There are striking similarities between Saharan and Indian Oceanic commerce. Both traversed great distances. The Bilma Trail (Garamantean Road) was the shortest route, 1,500 miles across the Sahara. The trade routes of the Indian Ocean were longer, thousands of miles of open water between the coast of East Africa to southern Arabia, the Persian Gulf, and the Indian subcontinent. Along these two great passages of economic, cultural, political, and religious intercourse the merchandise for trade in the great market towns were much the same – gold, ivory, perfumes, exotic woods, and slaves from East Africa in return for cloth, porcelain, salt, and hardware from Asia. There were accepted standards of exchange, tariffs, and a royal monopoly on special items such as gold and slaves and commercial agreements between rulers and merchants to promote their own and mutual interests.

The West African trans-Saharan trade developed with regularity after 1000 CE, but the East African trade was of greater antiquity. In 2450 BCE Pharaoh Sahure of the Old Kingdom (2755–2255 BCE) sent trading expeditions to the land of Punt, which stretched from the shores of the Red Sea through the straits of Bab al-Mandab and along the coast of northern Somalia to Cape Guardafui at the Horn of Africa. During the reign of Pepi II Neferkere (2566–2476 BCE) Harkuf, his governor and Lord of the Gate to the South at Elephantine (Aswan), boasted of having made eleven expeditions to Punt. A thousand years later during the reign of Queen Hatshepsut (1503–1483 BCE) five ships were dismantled, carried across the desert, and reassembled on the Red Sea coast, launched, and sailed to Punt. The Egyptian pharaohs were eager to trade cloth and hardware for myrrh, ebony, ivory, and tortoise shell, as well as pygmies to keep the wardrobe of the pharaohs in proper order. In dynastic Egyptian sources the only remaining references to Punt are found during the rule of the last great pharaoh, Ramses III (1182–1151 BCE). Thereafter the land of Punt and the East African coast remained undocumented until an official, either of imperial Rome or a Greek shipping agent in Alexandria, compiled a commercial handbook, *Periplus Maris Erythraei* (*Periplus of the Erythraean Sea*, or *Voyages to the Red Sea*), between 45 and 50 CE, 1,500 years after the expeditions of Queen Hatshepsut.

The *Periplus* was an extraordinary document, a guidebook for merchants trading with the ports and people of Punt and the East African coast during the first century of the Christian era. At that time the Greeks controlled the sea trade from the Mediterranean, the Red Sea, and beyond into the Indian Ocean and along the East African coast (known as Azania), where they had to compete with traders from southern Arabia, the Persian Gulf, and India. The *Periplus* records the names of ports, gives advice on how to comport oneself with local leaders, and describes the goods for trade. The Africans were tall and described as "red men" who fish, hunt, and herd cattle, sheep, and goats. These Azanians were most probably Cushitic speakers who had migrated into eastern Africa from Ethiopia, and were not the darker-complexioned inhabitants described by Muslim traders on the East African coast several centuries later. They had valuable items to trade – ivory, rhinoceros horn, tortoiseshell, spices, particularly cinnamon (*Cinnamomum zeylanicum*), the most profitable spice in the trade, and perfumes (frankincense, myrrh, and ambergris) – that were exchanged for iron, wheat, cloth, and porcelains.

The Greek merchants sailing the Red Sea to round Cape Guardafui and on to the East African coast were the western representatives of the larger international trading network of the Indian Ocean. Called the Sabaean Lane, after the kingdom of Saba in southern Arabia, the name has continued to be applied to the flow of trade in the great oceanic arc sweeping from East Africa to southern Arabia, the Persian Gulf, India, the Malabar coast, Ceylon, and Asia as far as China. This ancient, long-distance trade was made possible by wind and sea. Unlike the Atlantic and Pacific, the Indian Ocean is a relatively calm body of water, blessed by steady, predictable winds that propelled seafaring traders with little danger and considerable comfort. From November until March the monsoon winds of the Indian Ocean blow dry and steady from the northeast out of central Asia, assisted by the central Indian Ocean current (the Equatorial Current), which strikes Somalia and turns south to provide an automated seaway down the East African coast. Any sailor from India, the Persian Gulf, and southern Arabia simply had to raise the great lateen sail on the mast of his dhow and go with the flow of wind and sea. During the winter months the merchants brought goods out of Asia to exchange for those of Africa and enjoy the hospitality and company of the Azanians, who were eager to sell their merchandise.

In May the monsoon reverses its direction. Until October the winds blow moist and steady from the southwest, and the central Indian Ocean current now flows north with the wind, carrying a dhow out of East Africa to Asia in thirty days. When the wind and currents changed in May, the sailors would hoist their lateen sails and carry the produce of Africa back to Asia. This regimen of wind and sea was well known to the mariners of the Indian Ocean, who

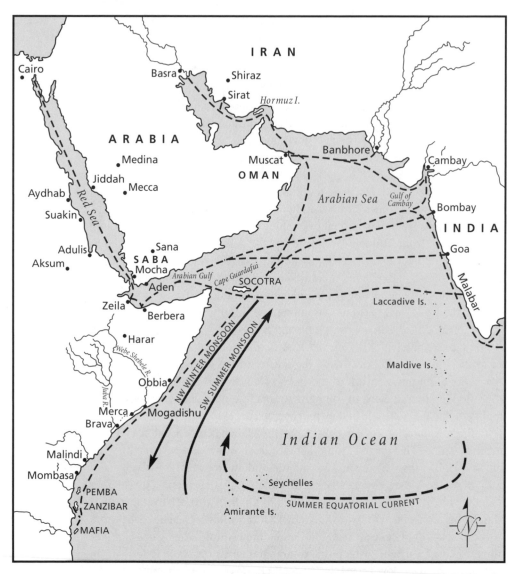

Map 7.1 *Indian Ocean, Red Sea, and the Sabaean Lane.*

adapted their lateen sails to capture its monsoon winds, like a spinnaker, and run before the wind on the fast-flowing current. Sweeping along the Sabaean Lane, navigation was by conspicuous headlands along the coast. Moreover, the dhows were sewn boats whose seams were tightly caulked, requiring no nails or brass screws. The ports of call were few, for East Africa has only a half dozen natural harbors, but there were hundreds of miles of smooth, sandy beaches punctuated by creeks and forests of mangrove. The captains would haul their shallow dhows onto the beach at high tide and wait for the tide to recede, leaving them high and dry near a market town. There their ships would be supplied by small-scale African traders, who brought goods and supplies in their catamarans from the many lagoons, creeks, and reefs to the ocean-going dhows. When the markets and the festivities that usually accompanied the mutual satisfactory exchange of goods were finished, the dhows would float away on the next incoming tide to new locations awaiting the southwest monsoon that would blow them back to Asia.

Who were these incomers from Asia? Some were Indonesians who settled in Madagascar between the second and fourth centuries. They left plants, such as the Asian banana, but only an ephemeral influence on the East African coast as they passed south to the great island. Some came from China as early as the seventh century, and between 1405 and 1433 Chinese merchant fleets under the command of Cheng Ho were conspicuous in the trade of the Indian Ocean. Official relations were established between the Ming court in Beijing and officials in the East African coastal ports of Mogadishu, Malindi, Mombasa, and Kilwa. Chinese charts from this period demonstrate the superiority of their ships and navigational skills compared to those from southern Arabia and the Persian Gulf. In 1415 a delegation from Malindi arrived in the Chinese capital with a magnificent giraffe for the Ming emperor. The giraffe was a sensation in the capital, but the later internal isolation of the Ming dynasty (1368–1644) ended the Chinese connection with East Africa. The Chinese had come to the Indian Ocean out of curiosity, and to trade for products such as ivory, rhino horn, and tortoise shell, but they left no discernible influence on the cultures of the East African coast.

There are records of Indian traders from the Deccan on the East African coast in the fifteenth century and cloth merchants from Cambay in the sixteenth, but the dominant Indian maritime traders until the end of the eighteenth century were Gujaratis. The most frequent visitors were Arabs from southern Arabia and Persians from their gulf. Arabs from the Yemen, Hadhramaut, and Oman had come to the East African coast centuries before the advent of Islam. Many Arab traders came regularly every year to the same locations on the coast, but they did not establish permanent settlements until the eighteenth century, when the Barayk family relocated from the Hadhramaut to Lamu and the Mazruis from Oman to Mombasa on the mainland, to be followed in the nineteenth century by the Busaidis from Muscat, who took up residence on the island of Zanzibar. The Persian influence originated, according to the mythology of the coast, in Shiraz in southwestern Persia. Most of the Arab and Persian settlers arrived in East Africa no earlier than the Puritans in North America in the seventeenth century.

Although the international commercial trade of the Sabaean Lane was ancient, in the seventh century the traders brought Islam, which had a powerful influence on the Africans of the coast. Sometime before the eighteenth century there emerged from these coastal populations a community known as Swahili, the "people of the coast," from the Arabic *sahil* (shore). Islam offered a common identity to the diverse peoples of the coastal communities. It gave literacy

Map 7.2 *The world of the Swahili.*

to their language, KiSwahili, whose traditions and poetry were written in Arabic script, the writing of the Quran, and the term "Swahili culture" became a reality when KiSwahili evolved as the commercial and cultural language of the East African coast. Islam linked its converts to this international world of

Arabs, Persians, Somalis, and the Muslims of India and Indonesia, with whom they carried on extensive trade.

Throughout history these "people of the coast" have been a cosmopolitan society who identified themselves as *waSwahili*. They were conscious of being different from the other coastal people living in the commercial enclaves and on the fertile ridge above the narrow coastal plain, who were not Muslims and known collectively as the Mijikenda, with whom they intermingled in the market and cooperated for mutual defense but seldom intermarried. Their language, KiSwahili, is an African language of the Benue-Congo (Bantu) branch of the larger Niger-Congo family that is distinguished from the other Bantu languages by grammar and loanwords from the Asian languages of the Indian Ocean world. The Swahili controlled the commerce of the Indian Ocean on the East African coast from which the merchants prospered and displayed their wealth by building grand houses of coral stone in which they dined on Swahili cuisine, dressed in sumptuous clothes, and in their leisure composed elaborate poetry. They built mosques, public baths, and harbors. Although they perceived themselves as belonging to a single society, a common culture, and civilization (*ustaarabu*), they remained fiercely independent in their trading towns, city-states whose commercial and political rivalries precluded a greater unified Swahili empire.

Although the Swahili have myths that claim an Asian origin, they are in fact an African people who have had commercial, social, and sexual intercourse with Asians for two millennia. Those who first came out of the interior of Africa to the coast in the distant past were hunters and gatherers whose descendants are still found today in small clusters. The first settlements on the coast were made before the Christian era by Cushitic-speaking pastoral peoples coming from Ethiopia and represented today by the Oromo of southern Ethiopia and the Somali. They are probably the "red men" described in the *Periplus*. Sometime between the second and fifth centuries Bantu-speaking cultivators settled on the coast. They established a symbiotic relationship with the herders, and firmly established the African foundations for the language of KiSwahili. The final ingredient in the Swahili mixture came from Asia.

The African underpinnings of Swahili culture are reflected in the civilization's architecture. As coastal settlements came to be influenced by Islamic architecture from Asia after the thirteenth century, the structures of coral stone were built with straight lines and right angles on top of indigenous settlements characterized by circular mud and wattle "huts" that had been used by the Bantu-speaking African inhabitants for centuries. Although much admired and regarded by the Swahili patricians and in the literature of the West as the epitome of Swahili civilization, stone buildings, particularly houses, represented only a small fraction of the houses in most Swahili urban settlements, the others consisting of circular huts of mud and thatch. Moreover, the pattern of settlement, even of the stone buildings, had often been adapted from the non-Swahili Mijikenda towns on the highland ridge beyond the coast.

Box 7.1 The African and Asian worlds of the Swahili

Scholars of East African history continue to debate the origins of the Swahili civilization of the East African coast. Some argue that Swahili society is fundamentally African; others that it was pervasively Asian. During the colonial era there was general agreement among scholars that the roots of Swahili culture emanated from Islamic Asia, as most of them were British and intimately acquainted with the Islamic civilizations of India, particularly the great Mughal (Mogul) empire (1526–1707) that introduced the Arabic alphabet and left behind world-renowned palaces, mosques, tombs, and fortifications. British colonial officials in East Africa also favored the interpretation of foreign, Asian origins for Swahili culture, to give legitimacy to Britain's own occupation and rule of the coast. As for the Swahili, most of them were convinced that their heritage came from the Islamic heartlands, the birthplace of the Prophet Muhammad. During the colonial era, many Swahili also perceived that those British subjects who were regarded as Asian were given preference over those recognized as African in the civil and commercial affairs of the East African coast.

Early excavations by British archaeologists employed by the colonial governments of Kenya and Tanganyika (now Tanzania) appeared to confirm the accepted belief that Swahili culture was a peripheral portion of the larger Islamic world rather than an extension of cultures and societies from the African interior. Obsessed by the stone and coral houses, mosques, palaces, and public places built by the wealthy Swahili commercial elite were the visible manifestation of the influence of Muslim merchants and rulers interpreted by the pioneering archaeologist Neville Chittick: "We should picture this civilization as a remote outpost of Islam, looking for its spiritual inspiration to the homeland of its religion."[1]

After Kenya and Tanzania became independent in the early 1960s, the relentless pendulum of inquiry oscillated toward an interpretation of the Swahili and their culture as fundamentally African in origin, not an Asian import, that had evolved through the centuries from a branch of Bantu-speaking coastal peoples who had expanded their influence from Kenya to Mozambique before the Indian Ocean commerce appeared to shape – significantly to be sure – their civilization.[2] These assertions are largely the result of a more sophisticated understanding of Swahili

[1] Neville Chittick, "The Coast of East Africa," in *The African Iron Age*, ed. P. L. Shinnie, Oxford: Clarendon Press, 1971, p. 137, quoted in Graham Connah, *African Civilizations: An Archaeological Perspective*, New York: Cambridge University Press, 2001, p. 182.

[2] Derek Nurse and Thomas Spear, *The Swahili: Reconstructing the History and Language of an African Society, 800–1500*, Philadelphia: University of Pennsylvania Press, 1985; John Middleton, *The World of the Swahili: An African Mercantile Civilization*, New Haven: Yale University Press, 1992.

Box 7.1 (continued)

linguistics, and a shift in the focus of archaeological investigations. After the 1960s in East Africa, as in much of the continent, archaeological interest imperceptibly shifted from the very visible monumental architecture left by the elite to the study of the material remains of the common folk. In the Nile Valley the search for the tombs of the pharaohs was replaced by investigations into the lives the laborers who built them. On the Swahili coast archaeological investigations of coral mosques and the palaces of the Muslim elite now became excavations of the less glamorous but far more numerous ancient circular houses that were constructed from African designs and local African building materials.

Politics, also, has played a role in this debate as to the origins and evolution of the Swahili. With the same enthusiasm as British archaeologists in the colonial era seeking proof of Asian influence, scholars in the post-independence years have sought to compensate for their bias by discovering evidence to confirm the indigenous African roots of Swahili civilization. Not surprisingly, politicians in Tanzania and Kenya readily embraced this belief that Swahili culture was indigenous to Africa. Julius Nyerere, the first president of Tanzania, eagerly sought to make Swahili the official language in preference to English and the language of instruction in Tanzania's public schools in order to cultivate the African roots of the nation as a unifying symbol of the diverse, polyglot country of Tanzania.

Although numerous rulers of Swahili city-states claimed that their origins were from Shiraz in southwestern Persia, their assertions are more myth than historical reality. The Persians had been the dominant commercial power in the Indian Ocean from the third to the seventh centuries, and their influence remains to the present day. One of the Swahili calendars is Persian, the Persian New Year festival is still celebrated by Swahili communities, and many technical sailing terms today are from Persian. Other Swahili have claimed origins from southern Arabia, particularly after the coming of Islam. The Arabs called the coast the "land of *zanj*" (Arabic, "blacks"), from which the island of Zanzibar (*bahr al-zanj*) derives its name. The term *zanj* was often used as a derogatory epithet for East African slaves, but also as a more beneficent name for Africans of the coast who were not sent to Asia as slaves. The third Asian influence came from the western coast of India. Though few Swahili recognize an Indian heritage, both Muslim and Hindu Indians from the region of Gujarat have settled in the Swahili trading cities for centuries. As the principal financiers of the Indian Ocean trade, known as Banyani, they provided the fiscal liquidity for commerce but were never considered to be Swahili.

The Swahili claim a homeland on the Somali coast in the pre-Islamic centuries from which they spread their identity after the first century of the

Christian era southward along the East African coast as far as Mozambique. The place of origin is known in the traditions as Shungwaya, and plays a central role in Swahili traditions and mythology. The location of Shungwaya may be near the mouth of the Tana River, but it is more a region from which Swahili culture expanded south under the influence of the Indian Ocean trade and Islam than a specific site. The Swahili archipelago of settlements scattered 1,500 miles along the coast was not the result of any mass migration from Shungwaya. Rather, the existing African coastal settlements in the south were transformed into Swahili trading ports by the ancient trade between Asian and African merchants who were ultimately forged into a new unified cultural society by Islam.

In the first century the Azanian coast of East Africa consisted of rustic trading posts as part of the larger Indian Ocean commercial world. Fifteen hundred years later the culture and society known as the Swahili had transformed some forty settlements into city-states whose foundations were those of the indigenous African peoples and whose structures were built on the prosperity of the Indian Ocean trade. The principal trading towns were Shanga, Pate, and Lamu in the north, Malindi and Mombasa on the central coast, and Kilwa in the south. Throughout the centuries Kilwa and Mombasa were the great trading emporiums, but all the Swahili towns were active in the African–Asian trade. The commercial success of the coastal enclaves was founded on the security for merchants provided by the patricians who controlled the ports, the organization by the Swahili of caravans that carried the gold, ivory, slaves, and the plethora of African commodities from the interior to the coast that enabled the patricians to acquire the coveted goods of Asia. Historically, the traditional terms of trade and the manner by which they should be conducted between Asian traders and Swahili merchants was determined by the natural laws of the seasonal monsoon that required Asian traders to reside on the coast from October to May before the southwest monsoon and the Indian Ocean current enabled them to make a quick return to Arabia, the Persian Gulf, and India. During these months both parties forged enduring relationships through mutual hospitality, stimulating bargaining, and social relationships. The hospitality of the Swahili patricians, elders, landlords, and merchants toward foreign traders was repaid by mutually satisfactory terms of trade, trust, and their return on the following autumnal northwest monsoon.

Although the local Swahili artisans fashioned pottery for their kitchens, the trading elite used porcelain from China for dinner and decoration in the house, mosque, and on tombs. Glassware from the Netherlands, the Levant, and southern Arabia was in great demand for the household, as was iron from India and copper from Persia for hardware, weapons, and jewelry. Cotton cloth, particularly blue in color from India, always found a profit in the market. Small beads – blue, green, and red – from India were eagerly solicited by the Africans of the interior. These precious imports were exchanged for elaborate furniture and handsome doors of inlaid ebony and ivory, and the more standard African commodities – ivory, slaves, ambergris, copal, spices, leopard skins, tortoise shell, pearls, and particularly gold. The gold came from the shallow mines of Great Zimbabwe in Central Africa and was carried to the coast at Sofala and then north by sea to Kilwa (*Kilwa Kisiwani*, "Kilwa on the Island"). In the past the gold trade had been organized by Swahili merchants from the Somali coast, but by 1200 the merchants of Kilwa, who dominated the coastal sea lanes to Sofala, had established control of the gold trade from Zimbabwe. They built mosques, stone houses of coral rock, public baths, and two harbors to accommodate the large ocean dhows seeking cargoes of gold, ivory, and slaves. The great medieval mosque at Kilwa had barrel vaults to support eighteen cupolas. There was the two-storied palace of the sultan, surrounded by a great wall to enclose his five acres. It was all very grand and described in 1331 by the great Muslim traveler Muhammad ibn Abdullah ibn Battuta (1304–1369):

> [Kilwa is] a great coastal city. Most of the people are Zunuj [*zanj*], extremely black . . . The city of Kilwa is amongst the most beautiful of cities and elegantly built. All of it is of wood, and the ceiling of its houses is of *al-dis* [reeds]. The rains there are great. They are the people devoted to the Holy War because they are on one continuous mainland with unbelieving Zunuj. Their upper most virtue is religion and righteousness and they are Shafi'i [the Muslim Sunni school of law in East Africa] in rite.[1]

Vasco da Gama (1460–1524) was the first recorded European to visit Kilwa, in 1502, and the chronicler of his famous second expedition (1501–1503) described the city 200 years after Ibn Battuta:

> The city [Kilwa] is large and is of good buildings of stone and mortar with terraces, and the houses have much wood works. The city comes down to the shore, and is entirely surrounded by a wall and towers, within which there may be 12,000 inhabitants. The country all round is very luxuriant with many trees and gardens of all sorts of vegetables, citrons, lemons, and the best sweet oranges that were ever seen, sugar-canes, figs, pomegranates, and a great abundance of flocks, especially sheep, which have fat in the tail, which is almost the size of the body, and very savory. The streets of the city are narrow, as the houses are very high, of three and four stories, and one can run along the tops of them upon the terraces, as the houses are very close together: and in the port there were many ships.[2]

Three years later the Portuguese returned with a well-armed fleet of eleven ships under the command of Francisco de Almeida (1450–1510), the Portuguese viceroy, determined to assert Portuguese control throughout the Indian Ocean. Although the Swahili city-states were historically engaged in fierce commercial rivalry, none of them possessed the means or the will to conquer

---

[1] *Ibn Battuta in Black Africa*, ed. Said Hamdun and Noël King, Princeton: Markus Wiener, 1994, p. 22.

[2] G. S. P. Freeman-Grenville, *The East African Coast: Select Documents from the First to the Earlier Nineteenth Century*, London: Collings, 1975, p. 66.

one another or to successfully repulse any concerted attack by the Portuguese, whose cannon destroyed their coral-stone walls and whose musketeers crushed the local Swahili militia. Kilwa was sacked, and never recovered its position as the preeminent Swahili city on the coast.

The sack of Kilwa symbolized the contrast and disparity between Swahili and Portuguese civilizations. Although the Swahili cultural life of Kilwa was different but comparable to, if not more refined than, that of Portugal in the fifteenth century, there were decisive distinctions in the marine technology of the Atlantic and that of the Indian Ocean. The Portuguese caravels were constructed of hardwood to withstand the tempestuous seas of the eastern Atlantic, and upon their decks could be mounted cannons capable of demolishing the walls of the lightly fortified coastal and island Swahili towns. Indian Ocean commerce had never been driven by conquest, for despite the intense commercial rivalry between the independent Swahili city-states there appears to have been general consensus that force was to be used to extract better terms of trade, not to lay waste a profitable trading partner. Moreover, the Indian Ocean captains had dozens of commercial enclaves from which to choose and, not surprisingly, preferred to conduct their business with placid, rather than hostile, competitors. These city-states had a long history of cultural and religious heterogeneity during which they had peacefully integrated new arrivals into their cosmopolitan communities. The Portuguese historical experience had been quite different. The kingdom of Portugal had been the creation of an implacable hostility toward Islam and deep suspicion of its powerful Christian neighbor, imperial Spain. As a nation the Portuguese were determined to defend the kingdom and the faith by a deep belief in their own incomparable, uncompromising mission, which had no place in the cosmopolitan world of the Swahili and the Indian Ocean.

Swahili society was highly stratified by those who controlled the wealth from the Indian Ocean trade and those who supplied the goods for export. The ruling class – anthropologists call them patricians – were the wealthy merchants. They were African Muslims who claimed Arab or Persian ancestry for religious and social legitimacy and convenience in commerce. They built ornate multi-roomed stone houses with baths and internal pit-toilets, and clad their women in silk and cotton robes bedecked with elaborate gold jewelry. They ate Swahili cuisine on porcelain dishes from China and Persia and were patrons of the arts, particularly Swahili poetry written in Arabic script and regarded as the epitome of aesthetic expression. The literacy of the Swahili elite was an essential instrument in commerce that to them confirmed their superiority over the non-literate, non-Muslim Mijikenda and slaves brought from the African interior. They owned large estates surrounding the towns where their slaves cultivated millet, cotton, fruits, and vegetables to supply local markets and the ocean-going dhows. The Swahili chronicles are filled with references to kings, sultans, and wazirs (high officials), but these are simply various titles for the "big man" in the city. The affairs of the

Figure 7.1 *Modern Zanzibar town. The architecture of Zanzibar reflects the island's African and Asian roots.*

community – internal order, Indian Ocean traders, and religious and legal matters – were the responsibility of the leading families whose officials were hereditary but from which the most talented were selected to preserve the influence and position of the family.

The construction of their remarkable stone buildings required sophisticated technology; outsiders – European scholars and imperialists – long assumed that it was imported by Muslim immigrants from Arabia and the Persian Gulf when in fact it was more an integration of indigenous materials and craftsmen with those of Asia than the imposition of an alien colonization. There are more than 173 settlements or towns (*mji*) spread over the length of the coast. Some settlements began as mud, wood, and thatch huts as early as the end of the first millennium of the Christian era – Kilwa (*c.* 800), Pate (*c.* 900), Mombasa (*c.* 1000) – and had by the twelfth century evolved into buildings in stone whose construction continued for the next 700 years. The great era of stonework at Kilwa – mosques, palaces, harbors, and public baths – was in the fifteenth and sixteenth centuries. These stone structures may have found their inspiration from wealthy Muslim merchants familiar with Arabia or Persia, but the architectural plans were indigenous to the coast, and those who came with the resources to build adopted local designs suitable to the environment of the East African shore.

The stone was coral readily cut from the reefs, which can be easily carved before it turns to hard stone in the African sun. Hard coral on land was quarried into large blocks for walls and foundations. The coral stone blocks would either be dressed or used as rubble and then cemented with a lime-mortar obtained by burning coral. Scaffolding required for the multi-storied structures was easily obtained from the prolific mangrove swamp forests. These same mangrove poles were often used as rafters for the roof, supported by walls or columns. More elaborate domed, vaulted ceilings were usually found in mosques. The entry way into the stone house is a seat-lined porch with elaborately carved doors into a room opening on to a courtyard. The rooms have high ceilings and are long and narrow, the width determined by the length of the mangrove rafter poles. Smaller rooms and inside toilets and washrooms are located off the courtyard. The walls were covered with a lime-based plaster. There were well-designed systems of drains to carry off the heavy rainwater to the streets and the sea. The Swahili stone house is a private place, the narrow windows more for ventilation than light, which comes from the courtyard. The main and private rooms are on the south side of the courtyard for living, eating, and sleeping with their toilets and bathrooms. The thick walls and high ceilings make the Swahili stone house cool and dry in a hot and humid climate, and the symbol of the social stability and economic wealth of the owner. Its plain outer walls and massive carved doors protect its inhabitants from the outer world, but inside the walls are richly decorated with rugs and tapestries and rows of niches to display elegant porcelains.

Among the Swahili marriage was a most vital institution in their social stability, pursuit of commerce, and the political domination by the patricians, which was characterized, however, by a great deal of diversity. The proper marriage (*ndoa*) was recognized by Islamic or customary law, but the clandestine or secret marriage and concubinage were also regarded as lawful. All other sexual unions were not, and even excessive polygyny was lawful but disapproved. Marriages were understood by all as instruments of corporate strategies concerned with the acquisition of rights in property and power determined by the marriage of the eldest daughter, usually shortly after puberty, constituting the renewal and perpetuation of the corporate lineage. Patrician marriages were invariably made between social equals (*kufu*) and arranged between paternal cousins to preserve the rights in lineage and property to which both spouses belonged. Marriage was one of the principal means for the orderly dispensation of property between groups of the same or different generations, and consequently arranged in very complex formal negotiations to insure the perpetuation of the four categories of property recognized by the Swahili within the lineage – immovable, reproductive, and personal property, and trade goods. Symbolic of property was the great stone house to which the first-born daughter was given the right by her father and which, theoretically, she could dispose of as she wished, but in fact it had to remain in the family by the marriage of her daughter to paternal cousins.

Commerce encouraged more flexible forms of marriage among the Swahili. For centuries coastal merchants arranged unions for their children with both Arab and Asian merchants from abroad and African traders from the hinterland who brought the slaves, ivory, and gold from the interior. These marriages symbolized the ties of "blood" that forged social relationships and created commercial interdependency. Marriage with foreigners outside the lineage produced tensions within Swahili society, as they could potentially link families that were perceived to be of unequal social rank. However, these relationships were crucial to the vitality of the Swahili commercial network, as they came to constitute, over time, powerful commercial corporations in which marriage was employed to establish complex social and mercantile ties with partners in the interior, along the Swahili coast, and the Sabaean Lane. In this Swahili merchants behaved not unlike their contemporaries, the capitalist merchants of early modern Europe – the English in Mogul India, and the Dutch in Indonesia – who similarly used marriage to cement relationships with important trading families in India and Southeast Asia.

The intricate rituals of marriage may have provided social stability and the patricians may have supplied the wealth, but the less prosperous Swahili built the towns. They were the Muslim craftsmen and artisans who constructed and decorated the stone houses of many rooms, vaulted mosques, and stone pillar tombs, or the minor officials who executed the administrative functions of the city-state and the pilots of catamarans who controlled the vigorous inter-coastal trade between the city-states. They were the Swahili who came from families that cultivated the fields outside the walls and supplied the sailors for ocean-going dhows. They were illiterate Muslims with no claim to Arab or Persian ancestry, but they comprised the overwhelming number of inhabitants of the Swahili commercial city, living in mud, wood, and thatch huts or occasionally single-roomed stone houses surrounding the more pretentious stone structures of the patricians or spread out among the fields beyond the city walls. They were the quarrymen, stone-masons, plasterers, and carpenters. They were the shipwrights who sewed together the planks for the hull of a dhow. They wove the cotton into cloth and were sailors. Others were farmers and fishermen. Some were woodsmen, cutting the mangrove timber.

Congregational mosques were found in every stone town – without one, a town would have no legitimacy. Only a few towns possessed but one mosque; most had several, and large towns such as Mombasa more than twenty. The traditional East African mosque was rectangular in shape with the same building materials as the houses. The domed or barrel-vaulted roof was supported by either an internal wall or a column of pillars that led to the *mihrab* (pulpit), located at the northern end to enable the congregation to face Mecca while listening to the speaker. Swahili mosques have no minaret, the muezzin calling the faithful to prayer from inside the mosque. The mosque and its adjoining Quranic school (*madrasa*) were the spatial focus that linked town life with its historical past and the greater Islamic community, the *umma*. Next to the mosque and *madrasa* the cemetery was a revered place in the life of a Swahili stone town. During the flowering of Swahili civilization between the twelfth and sixteenth centuries the tombs of Swahili patricians were elaborate and unique architectural monuments. The pillar tombs of the coast were tall stone stelae rising from rectangular bases chiseled with complex geometrical carvings. Many have niches to display their beloved porcelains. Those with fewer resources had to settle for more modest burial crypts, with perhaps an arched roof and door, but the tomb of an honored holy man was often very imposing. The common Swahili man had to settle for a small pile of stones or a few flat, upright stone markers that crumbled in decay after a generation or two.

Scattered along the length of the East African coast between the stone-walled cities were the more humble Swahili towns of the countryside. They varied in size and were separated by several miles of fertile land, tilled by shifting cultivation. These country towns were invariably situated on higher ground and very old, the many generations who had lived there giving them historical stability but not the archaeological permanence of the stone towns by the shore and on the islands. Their inhabitants lived in mud-and-wattle homes clustered together, divided by streets and alleyways of sand and gardens (*shamba*) with coconut palms, mango, and citrus which produced fruit, oil, and wood. In the center of the town was the market square with a mosque, small shops, coffee-houses, and large basins for public washing. The towns were usually divided into wards that represented a kinship group that had historic and inalienable rights to the land. Surrounding the town were the fields in which sorghum, sesame, chilies, spices, and, in low-lying land, rice were cultivated, the surplus being sold in the markets of the stone towns. Although the patricians had their own estates and the artisans their fields, they were both dependent on foodstuffs from the Swahili villages in the countryside.

Slaves had been obtained from the interior of East Africa for 2,000 years; many were exported, but others remained on the coast. Every member of the patrician class had slaves, the wealthier owning them in large numbers. The Swahili, however, made a distinction between slaves for export and slaves for domestic and local use. Those shipped overseas were regarded as chattels to be used as animals, but those who were kept on the coast were divided into recognized categories of servitude. The *mtwana* were the lowest category, who labored in the fields or on the plantation estates. They were usually given a plot in which to grow their own food, but the fear of being exported across the ocean was the most effective guarantee of good behavior. The other category of slaves, *mtumwa* ("one who is sent or used"), were domestic slaves – circumcised, given a name, usually a day of the week, and having a personal relationship with the owner. These slaves provided a variety of services in the towns, where they roamed freely. Many of the *mtumwa* became trusted servants who could work on their own and receive the wages of free labor. They often possessed specialized skills as sailors, fishermen, boatmen, or artisans, and some owned slaves in their own right. Female slaves were used as domestics, field hands, and concubines for the owner. The son from such a union would be free and would bear his father's name, but he carried a lower status than his half-brothers from a free mother. Even if freed by their owners, which happened frequently, these slaves could never become full members of Swahili society, and were distinguished by their dress. Upon death the corpse had the same status as an animal carcass, and would be thrown into a pit. Slaves were seldom used in the country towns where the cultivation, processing, storage, and sale of produce did not require slave labor or specialized slave skills and consequently were carried out by the Swahili kin groups, often in conjunction with their neighbors.

The maritime Indian Ocean world of the African Swahili has obscured in the literature their relations with other Africans on the coastal plain and those in the far interior. Beyond the narrow coastal plain the land rises to a ridge that extends westward, an arid and infertile scrubland that gradually climbs into the moist and fertile highland interior. On this periphery overlooking the plain were African societies whose relationship with the rulers of the coastal city-states was symbiotic rather than subservient. They were originally known as Nyika, after the land they cultivated in the short rains in October and November or the long rains in April and May, but today are collectively called the Mijikenda. They are a Bantu-speaking people who were driven south along the coastal ridge of East Africa from Shungwaya by the Cushitic-speaking, pastoral Oromo of southern Ethiopia and Somalia. Shungwaya is the legendary place of origin in the north for both the Swahili and the Mijikenda, from which they migrated down the East African coast. By the seventeenth century the Mijikenda had established agricultural settlements, *kaya*s, in clearings on the forested ridge overlooking the coast and on the rising plateau to the west.

The Mijikenda have never been Swahili, but since they controlled the routes to the interior they acquired authority by establishing an accommodation with Swahili patricians in the stone towns, dealing with them on terms of equality. The relationship was not always harmonious, and was dependent upon slaves and food. Fugitives, children, and slaves were the resource by which local rulers in the immediate hinterland could bargain for goods and capital from the Swahili coastal towns. Food was equally important in this exchange. On the plateau above the coast the rains from the Indian Ocean were unpredictable, and when they failed, there was frequently famine among the Mijikenda; this forced them to establish an accommodation with the Swahili coastal merchants who, in times of scarcity, were self-sufficient in fish and imported foodstuffs from Asia.

The long-distance and ancient trade spanning the Indian Ocean over two millennia enabled the African societies of the East African coast to exchange the goods from the deepest interior for those from Asia. This transfer of commodities required technological and navigational skills to sail the seas and commercial acumen to barter in the marketplace. Not all were successful, but many prospered, and their wealth enabled them to pursue arts and letters, build public works, and mosques, which defined their cultural unity in the competitive commercial world of the East African city-states. The mercantile tranquility of the Sabaean Lane was suddenly and dramatically challenged by the appearance of the Europeans, when Vasco da Gama sailed into the harbor of Mombasa on April 7, 1498, where he obtained the service of Ahmad ibn Majid, a veteran pilot of the Indian Ocean, to continue north to Malindi. Here he erected a stone cross (*padrão*) that still stands. From Malindi Majid guided the Portuguese caravels on the winds and currents of the Sabaean Lane to India and the East. Vasco da Gama returned to East Africa in 1501, followed by a stream of Portuguese captains determined to carry on their crusade against Islam and to dominate and exploit the wealth of Africa, Asia, and the Indian Ocean for themselves and the kingdom of Portugal.

Further reading

East African coast and the Indian Ocean world

Jayasuniya, Shihan de Silva and Richard Pankhurst, *The African Diaspora in the Indian Ocean*, Trenton/Lawrenceville, NJ: Africa World Press, 2003
Middleton, John, *African Merchants of the Indian Ocean: Swahili of East African Coast*, Long Grove, IL: Waveland Press, 2004

Prins, A. H. J., *Sailing from Lamu: A Study of Maritime Culture in Islamic East Africa*, Assen: Van Gorcum, 1965

City-states of the African coast

Allan, J. de V., *The Swahili Origins: Swahili Culture and the Shangwaya Phenomenon*, London: James Currey and Athens, OH: Ohio University Press, 1993

Middleton, John, *The World of the Swahili: An African Mercantile Civilization*, New Haven: Yale University Press, 1992

Nurse, Derek and Thomas Spear, *The Swahili: Reconstructing the History and Language of an African Society, 800–1500*, Philadelphia: University of Pennsylvania Press, 1985

8 The Lake Plateau of East Africa

In 1860 the English explorer John Hanning Speke (1827–1864), seeking the source of the Nile, had left Bagamoyo on the Swahili coast of East Africa en route to the unexplored plateau of the interior. On his journey he was harassed by African chiefs demanding *hongo* (tolls) to pass, compromised by the Arab and Swahili slave traders, and abandoned by his porters before he arrived in 1862 at Kampala, the royal capital of the kingdom of Buganda, located in the lush vegetation of the Lake Plateau on the northeastern shore of Lake Victoria, to be enthusiastically welcomed by the *kabaka* (king), Mutesa I (1838–1884). He was astonished to discover that Buganda was a stable monarchy supported by an industrious peasantry whose markets were connected by well-maintained roads and administered by civil servants loyal to the *kabaka*, whose command of a regular army and navy held in check a subservient nobility.

Buganda was but one, albeit the most powerful, of several interlacustrine (between the lakes) states – Bunyoro, Busoga, Karagwe, and others – with complex political and social systems. Most were monarchies, and several were dominated by pastoralist aristocracies. Their economies were based on a combination of farming – particularly the cereals millet and sorghum, but also bananas – and the domestication of cattle. The peoples of these states spoke dialects of the Bantu (Congo-Niger) family of languages. Speke pondered in his journals how such large, well-organized kingdoms so, unlike the petty chieftaincies through which he had passed, had evolved in seeming isolation deep in the interior of the continent. He concluded that this remarkable state building on the Lake Plateau could only have been accomplished by the intervention of a race of "light-skinned" pastoral "Hamites" who were assumed to have come from the north to impose their political domination over the Bantu-speaking farmers.

Speke was deeply influenced by the current Victorian concepts of "race." The term "Hamite," which derived from "Ham," the name of Noah's cursed son, had been employed by Europeans to describe Africans since the Middle Ages, but in the mid-nineteenth century it had developed a new and more precise meaning. Writers influenced by the evolutionary theories of Charles Darwin now labeled those Africans whose physiognomy was more like their own or who possessed certain cultural attributes "Hamitic" to differentiate them from Africans who did not possess these superior characteristics. Moreover, this distinction appeared to confirm accepted European racial

Box 8.1 The Hamitic myth

When European explorers, missionaries, and merchants began to penetrate into the interior of Africa they were puzzled to discover that the Africans possessed complex social systems and sophisticated institutions of government. Much of this European skepticism was rooted in nineteenth-century ideas about human evolution and racial difference. This dichotomy appeared to be confirmed by the apparent technological disparity between European and African societies, which reinforced nineteenth-century ideas of the racial inferiority of blacks, forged during the centuries of the trans-Atlantic slave trade in which the Western world was increasingly reluctant to regard the African slave as an equal brother in the family of man. Victorian biologists regarded culture and race as inextricably connected. Influenced by this idea, early European travelers in East Africa put forward the theory that a group of "Caucasoid Hamites" had played an instrumental role in disseminating political institutions throughout the region. According to them, these interlopers were lighter-skinned warriors who migrated into the Lakes region from the north and imposed a monarchy on the hitherto disorganized black agricultural communities. John Hanning Speke was one of the first to argue for a "Hamitic" influence in the kingdom of Buganda. Speke's belief in the "Hamitic conquest" of East Africa was shared by the influential British administrator Sir Harry Johnston, who in his linguistic studies of Bantu languages confidently proclaimed:

> Southward, down the shores of Lake Tanganyika and thence southwest and west across the mountains and plateaus of southern Congoland to the Atlantic; eastward and southeastward across the Zambezi and Mashonaland to temperate South Africa swept the Bantu invaders, armed, it may be, with novel iron weapons and led by a Hamiticized aristocracy.
> Sir Harry H. Johnston, *A Comparative Study of the Bantu and Semi-Bantu Languages*, Oxford: Clarendon Press, 1919, p. 22

By the beginning of the twentieth century the dubious thesis of the "Caucasoid–Hamite" invasion had become accepted by most Europeans as historical fact.

During the early decades of the twentieth century, Europeans simply refused to accept the idea that black Africans were capable of creating state systems. Scholars led by E. G. Seligman, the first professor of ethnology in the University of London, proposed that the political skills of black Africans were clearly learned or borrowed from wandering bands of white Caucasians. Professor Edith R. Sanders describes the rise and fall of the Hamitic myth:

> Much of anthropology gave its support to the Hamitic myth. Seligman found a cultural substratum of supposedly great influence in Africa. In 1930 he published his famous *Races of Africa*, which went through several editions and

Box 8.1 (continued)

which was reprinted in 1966 still basically unchanged. He refined the Sergi-devised classifications of Hamitic peoples, adding the category of Nilotes or "half-Hamites." Every trace and/or sign of what is usually termed "civilized" in Africa was attributed to alien, mainly Hamitic, origin. In such a way ironworking was supposed to have been introduced to the Negroes by pastoral Hamites along with complex political institutions, irrigation, and age-grade systems. Archaeological findings of any magnitude were also ascribed to outside influences and kept the Negro African out of his own culture history. In the eyes of the world the Negro stood stripped of any intellectual or artistic genius and of any ability at all which would allow him, now, in the past, or in the future, to be master of his life and country.

The confluence of modern nationalism and the ensuing modern racism evolved from earlier nineteenth-century national romanticism and developed through theories of de Gobineau and adaptations of the Darwinian revolution. It was echoed in all western nations, culminating finally in the ideology of Nazi Germany. Because that leading exponent of racism became the enemy of most of Europe and the United States during World War II, the German-championed ideology seemed to have lost some of its popularity. The Hamitic myth ceased to be useful with African nations that have been gaining their independence one by one, and the growing African nationalism drew scholarly attention to Africa's past. Many of the scholars were unencumbered by colonial ties; some of them were themselves African. They began to discover that Africa was not a *tabula rasa*, but that it had a past, a history, which could be reconstructed; that it was a continent which knew empire builders at a time when large areas of Europe stagnated in the Dark ages; that it knew art and commerce.

Edith R. Sanders, "The Hamitic Hypothesis: Its Origin and Function in Time Perspective," *Journal of African History* 10, 4 (1969), pp. 530–531

distinctions between superior and inferior races that were later used to justify the European conquest and colonial rule of Africans, a justification seemingly supported by the technological disparity between European and African societies. Thus Speke, an ordinary, pragmatic soldier, naïvely sought to explain the complex social and political institutions he witnessed in Buganda as the work of a superior, conquering race, the Hamites, and as the first European to observe the great states of the Lake Plateau, his theory was widely accepted, refined, and became influential in forging European colonial policy in Africa. It became a pervasive and pernicious myth of racial superiority that lingers to this day in many subtle forms, and underpins the ethnic conflicts in the Lake Plateau over the past fifty years.

The Lake Plateau rises 4,000 feet above sea level and is defined, east and west, by the two great Rift Valleys, often 2,000 feet deep, that bisect the African continent. The Eastern Rift and its chain of lakes from Natron to Lake Turkana at the bottom of the trench marks the eastern boundary of the Lake Plateau, as does the Western Rift and its lakes, from Malawi and Tanganyika to Kivu, Edward, and Albert and the Ruwenzori Mountains that define the western border of the Lake Plateau and the eastern edge of the great tropical rainforest of the Congo. In the distant past the rainforest extended into the Lake Plateau, but in historical times it became a verdant region of a thousand hills in the southwest, "the green hills of Africa," while the heartland of the Lake Plateau was fertile, well-watered grass and woodlands free of the tsetse fly, whose altitude on the equator created a mild climate. At the heart of the Lake Plateau lies the imposing inland sea of Lake Victoria, lying astride the equator 2,000 feet above the two Rift Valleys and dominating the states that arose along its shores. Here there was ample room to cultivate amid rolling grasslands for the cattle of the pastoralists who came from the north down the Rift Valley and overland on the higher ground.

Unlike the states of the African coast, which had long been influenced by the Indian Ocean world, the states of the Great Lakes region were relatively isolated from the world outside Africa. The first literate visitors to the area were Arab merchants who entered Buganda in the 1840s. Speke, who arrived twenty years later, was the first European to reach the Lake Plateau and the first to write his observations of the lives of the people and their institutions; this leaves historians with very little written material to guide them in the historical reconstruction of the interlacustrine states. The many royal courts of the Lake Plateau have a rich array of oral traditions which must, however, be interpreted with caution, for they are often enshrouded in myth or hopeless hagiography, or skewed to promote contemporary political interests, all of which obscure historical reality. Archaeological surveys are limited, in part because of the political instability that has afflicted the region over the past few decades, so that historians have come to depend more on the discipline of historical linguistics to fill in the gaps in our understanding of times past on the Lake Plateau. Drawing on this body of linguistic evidence, scholars have reached a broad consensus that the region has not been as isolated as hitherto perceived and that the kingdoms of the Lake Plateau are of relatively recent vintage when compared to those in the forests, savanna, and sahel of western Africa. The accumulated traditions and linguistic evidence suggest that incomers from the north may have played some role in the development of states on the Lake Plateau, but there was most certainly no "Hamitic conquest" of their peoples.

Today, there is general agreement that the first people to inhabit the Lake Plateau were hunter-gatherers who roamed from river bank and lake shore through the forests that 4,000 years ago covered most of the region, which today have been reduced to islands of woods surrounded by rolling grasslands. They spoke languages of the Khoisan family, and their small, widely dispersed bands in all likelihood became absorbed by early farmers who occupied the land which, once under cultivation, had to be defended against the depredations of the great herds of African wildlife upon which the hunter-gatherers depended. Since there were vast stretches of uninhabited land in eastern, central, and southern Africa, the hunter-gatherers simply moved on in order to continue their lifestyle, leaving behind, however, small communities of Twa (often called "pygmies"), who continue to live on the western periphery of the Lake Plateau at the edge of the Congo rainforest.

Pollen deposits in the Lake Plateau indicate that farmers first began to clear the forests as early as 5,000 years ago. They cultivated cereal grains and raised cattle and spoke an array of languages of the Eastern Sudanic, Central Sudanic, and Southern Cushitic linguistic families. Approximately three thousand years ago, the first Bantu-speaking communities appeared in the Western Rift, at the bottom of which was fertile soil and ample water from the chain of lakes connected by rivers that traversed the valley from south to north. These newcomers had emerged from the great rainforest of the Congo River Basin to the west, where they had lived by fishing, growing root crops (particularly yams), foraging, hunting, and raising small livestock. Although initially very small in number, by the turn of the first millennium CE, they had gradually made their way, over long periods of time, to settle along the densely forested shores of lakes and the banks of rivers of the Lake Plateau where they could continue to plant their root crops from the rainforest. During the subsequent centuries the history of the Lake Plateau was dominated by this expansion of Bantu-speaking communities.

The moist lake shores and river valleys where their root crops could thrive were also, however, the home of the tsetse fly and were consequently avoided by the Southern Cushitic-speaking farmers and herders residing on higher ground between the lakes; this reduced the chance of competition for the open spaces of land between them and the Bantu speakers. These new neighbors began a long process of cultural sharing, trade, and assimilation which had profound implications for the history of the Lake Plateau. From their new neighbors the Bantu speakers may have learned how to smelt iron; they assuredly learned how to grow savanna crops such as sorghum and millet. Even more important, the Southern Cushitic-speaking pastoralists introduced the Bantu speakers to cattle-keeping, which many farmers incorporated on a small scale into their agricultural economy. Unlike the other regions of western, central, and southern Africa the Lake Plateau is relatively small. This allowed the dispersal of the Bantu languages to take place with few people actually moving from one location to another as the languages were passed from village to village during the normal social and economic interaction of neighboring peoples. The acceptance of Bantu languages and the accompanying cultural implications was obviously a gradual and cumulative process during which many people continued to live in bilingual communities for generations before Bantu became accepted as their native tongue and the interlacustrine region became a vast bloc of Bantu-speaking peoples. By 500 CE their village-based farming communities were dispersed and politically decentralized, but they shared important political and cultural traditions, including the veneration of iron-working experts, whose production of farming tools was crucial in the transformation of the land from forest to farm.

After 800 CE the spread of iron-working throughout the Lake Plateau produced increasing numbers of iron tools, which in turn stimulated an increase in agricultural productivity; this had a considerable impact on the growth of population, regional trade, and the environment. The insatiable demand for iron tools and implements was a great stimulus for inter-village trade in the commodities to exchange for them, but it also contributed to the deforestation of many areas, encouraging shifts in the population and, in some locations, an expanding emphasis on herding. The central plain of the Lake Plateau, which lay between the two great Rift Valleys, was drier, devoid of the tsetse fly, and generally better suited to raising cattle and cereal crops than its moist river valleys, lake shores, and the chain of lakes in the Rifts. The voracious consumption of charcoal for expanding iron industries, which required the wood from dozens of mature trees to produce one smelt of iron, appears to have inadvertently expanded these grasslands, enabling the pastoralists to increase the size of their herds where great forests had once stood.

The explosion of cattle-keeping among the Bantu-speaking communities appears to have been later supplemented by the arrival in the Lake Plateau of new cattle breeds, particularly the zebu. Originally from India, the zebu (*Bos indicus*) could withstand periods of drought, adapted well to tropical climates, and was resistant to heat and parasitic insects. They were readily adopted by pastoralists before they had moved south from the fertile Gezira (Arabic, "island") between the Blue and White Niles south of present-day Khartoum. These people spoke Sudanic languages of the larger Nilo-Saharan linguistic family, occupied the flat floodplains of the southern Sudan, and moved their herds annually to avoid the rising waters of the Nile flood, only to follow, in that traditional practice known as transhumance, the receding waters that left behind rich green pastures, known as *toic*, upon which their zebu cattle grew fat and prolific in milk. Some of these peoples meandered down the eastern valley from northeast Africa with their zebu cattle to settle on the pastures surrounding the lakes at the bottom of the Rift Valley, from which they spread over the upland grasslands and dry savanna to the east of the Lake Plateau. There they coexisted with the Khoisan hunters and gatherers exchanging milk and meat for their honey to distill fermented mead. The zebu cattle, however, had long preceded them by trade and ceremonial occasions to become the dominant bovine among the expanding herds of the Bantu-speaking peoples of the Lake Plateau.

At a much later date climatic change may also have encouraged economic specialization among Bantu-speaking farmers. Recent paleoenvironmental data and methods of more precise dating of climatic change indicate that a cold, dry period in the thirteenth and fourteenth centuries appears to have had an impact on the grasslands of the Lake Plateau similar to earlier deforestation. The periods of increasing desiccation during these centuries would have affected farmers, dependent on ample rainfall, more severely than the pastoralists who to combat aridity invariably sought to transform marginal land no longer suited for cultivation into pastures for their herds which, in drought, needed larger grasslands to support the same numbers of cattle, sheep, and goats. Farmers became increasingly vulnerable to pastoralists eager to augment the numbers of their clients from among increasingly desperate farmers who could no longer support themselves from cultivation. Similarly, in the fifteenth and sixteenth centuries the return of higher annual rainfalls allowed bountiful harvests of cereals and bananas, thereby giving a boost to farming communities, now at the expense of the pastoralists. Farmers adapted to these contrasting climatic episodes by raising cattle on the grasslands during the dry periods, only to return to farming during the wet ones.

The growing specialization for keeping cattle by some of the communities of the Lake Plateau also produced significant changes in traditional social relationships. Cattle, or rather an ever-increasing herd of them, brought their individual owners status and wealth far beyond that which was possible for individual cultivators to achieve in farming communities. Cattle were mobile and easily stolen, which required their owners to become proficient in arms and their communities to develop a culture of militarism to protect their animals, on which they were completely dependent. Defenders, however, were soon transformed into aggressive warriors quite prepared to raid their neighbors to augment their herds or replenish those lost in raids by others or as a result of drought and disease. Raid and counter-raid became common, punctuated by periods of peace when the elders, fearing that the spiral of violence would get out of control, established elaborate mechanisms to adjudicate disputes among rival communities. This in turn placed political power in the hands of the elders, but only so long as they could command the respect of their male warriors. In some instances the power of authority would be assumed by a religious leader or charismatic priest. The status of the priest as war leader within the society was usually determined by his success or failure. Whether led by elder or priest the creation of a warrior class among the pastoralists greatly diminished the status of their women, who were marginalized by the males responsible for the care of the cattle and their security. The principal protection for women became the institution of marriage and its obligatory dowry in cattle was negotiated by the male members of family and clan. In contrast women in agricultural societies, who were responsible for producing most of the food upon which the community depended, commanded a greater role in the decisions of the community than their pastoral sisters.

A second important development, closely tied to the spread of iron working and roughly contemporaneous with the expansion of cattle pastoralism, was the growing importance during this later moist period of the cultivation of plantains and bananas. The banana with its yellow crescent-shaped fruit (*Musa sapientum*) is a seedless perennial plant, a shoot more than a root, which provides carbohydrates similar to the yam. Unlike finger millet and sorghum, the staple cereals on the Lake Plateau, the banana requires little care, regenerates annually, and produces abundant fruit for cooking and brewing. It is indigenous to Southeast Asia, and appeared in eastern Africa early in the first centuries of the Christian era. It came from Asia by the ancient trade routes that extended from Indonesia, Malaysia, and India around the great arc of the Sabaean Lane past the Persian Gulf and across the waters of the Gulf of Arabia, to East Africa and Madagascar. From the coasts of Africa the banana may have come up the Zambezi to the interior, or perhaps directly from the East African coast, but it is more likely to have followed the fertile trench of the Rift from Ethiopia to the Lake Plateau. The first written description of the banana in Africa comes from a Greek merchant in Adulis in 525 CE, long after it had passed into the interior.

The banana became the most prolific crop on the Lake Plateau, whose cultivation was ideally suited to its climate. As a plantain it was a vegetable to bake, grind into flour, or brew into beer rather than the kind of fruit purchased in American supermarkets. Unlike the yams, beans, and sorghum brought by farmers from the equatorial forests, the cultivation of the banana requires little labor to clear the land, plant, or weed. A woman could single-handedly tend a grove large enough to feed four people that would be productive for fifty years. It produces a yield ten times greater than the savanna crops from West Africa. It is more nutritious and simple to prepare than yams. After the harvest its rotting hulks have restored the fertility of the Lake Plateau when the rains from the South Atlantic washed their fertilizer into the soils. The banana flourished in its valleys, plateaus, and hills to become a nutritious and copious harvest that replaced the yam and sorghum as the staple crop and enabled the Lakes farmers with their brittle but useful iron implements to settle permanently rather than practice shifting cultivation. With a secure and surplus supply of food the population increased from one season to the next and one generation to another.

Between 1200 and 1600 CE the village polities of the past centuries began to coalesce into kingdoms that dominated the political configuration of the Lake Plateau. These new emerging states owed their evolution to a dynamic combination of economic activities that included cattle husbandry, cereal agriculture, and the cultivation of the banana. Cattle created wealth for men who used their affluence to build and control networks of patronage and political power. Bananas gave farmers of modest means sufficient resources to secure tenure to the land and gradually enlarge their modest holdings, endowing their property with a value unprecedented in a region that still had ample uninhabited land. This economic growth produced from the pasture and the field enabled the petty traders in iron to establish more complex commercial networks to meet the demand for surplus farm commodities, iron implements, salt, hides, dried fish, bark cloth, and an array of other goods that came to be exchanged throughout the burgeoning Lake Plateau. This economic activity, in turn, gave rise to a class whose wealth enabled them to devote their energies not merely to luxurious consumption, but to insure their control of the means of production by political power.

The process by which these new leaders turned this economic dynamism into political power still remains obscure, however. Some historians regard the evolution of cohesive states and kingdoms as an ancient process rooted in traditions of the Bantu-speaking peoples of the Lakes, which emerged naturally during the economic revolution after 1200 CE. Linguistic evidence appears to support such a conclusion, for when the Bantu-speaking communities adopted new political offices and functions after 1000 CE, they did not borrow a new vocabulary from their Southern Cushitic neighbors or from subsequent incomers from the north. Had the notion of "monarchy" been imposed upon them by immigrants, it is likely that their term for "king" would have been borrowed to acknowledge new authority, but this did not happen. Linguists have amply demonstrated the continuities between the Bantu political vocabulary that existed both before and after this political transformation.

Other historians, however, emphasize the role of pastoral immigrants from the north who brought new breeds of cattle and new political institutions and traditions. Virtually all of the oral traditions of the kingdoms of the Lake Plateau attribute their founding to the arrival of itinerant heroes from faraway. The support for this tradition is to be found largely in the archaeological record, in which there are important discontinuities – particularly the sudden appearance of new pottery traditions during the period of state formation in the Lake Plateau. But this evidence is inconclusive. African dynasties throughout the continent have claimed external origins, justifiably or not, to legitimize their claims to authority. And new pottery styles do not necessarily reflect dramatic shifts in population.[1] Scholars have been somewhat reluctant to accept the necessity to have the appearance of "the great warrior" or "hunter stranger from afar" to explain state formation in Africa. Its very simplicity obscures what was probably a more complex process, and the story of wandering warrior-pastoralists stimulating political centralization is reminiscent of the discredited Hamitic myth of John Hanning Speke.

Although the process still remains unclear, by the sixteenth century several kingdoms had emerged on the Lake Plateau from the Rift Valley in the west to the western shore of Lake Victoria in the east. On the northern grasslands of the Plateau states emerged at approximately the same time. Evidence for these developments appears in the historical record in many places. First, archaeologists have excavated a handful of sites on these grasslands that were densely populated after 1000. The most famous of these are Ntusi and Bigo, which archaeologists have associated with the rise of the kingdom of Bunyoro in the northwestern corner of the Lake Plateau, above Lake Albert at the bottom of the Western Rift. After 1000 these two sites grew rapidly in size, each supported by huge herds of cattle, but Ntusi also had extensive cultivations of cereals, which played a crucial role in its economy. Of the two Bigo, however, is more famous because of its concentric earthen embanked ditches six miles in circumference and twenty-two feet high enclosing two square miles. There is no definitive explanation for these great earthworks. They may have been built to keep cattle in and predators out, or to add to the prestige of their patrons, or a combination of both, but the organization and the large number of workers required to complete such an ambitious project also required institutionalized

---

[1] The debate over "pots and people" is one of the most contentious in African archaeology. Do pottery traditions reflect specific ethnic groups? Or do language communities share and trade pottery, thus rendering them useless to archaeologists looking for "Bantu" or "Nilotic" pottery traditions?

political authority to plan and to mobilize an unprecedented number of laborers to complete the excavations.

Oral traditions also connect the origins of this kingdom with the larger empire of "Kitara," which purportedly dominated the entire Lakes region in the distant past and whose direct descendant became the kingdom of Bunyoro. The ruling dynasty of Bunyoro was from the Bito clan, traditionally one of the powerful, pastoral Luo clans that had made their way from the southern Sudan to Bunyoro-Kitara where they established themselves as a ruling minority that became assimilated by the Bantu-speaking Nyoro. The significant influence of the Luo in the history of Bunyoro is supported by linguistic and archaeological evidence. Luo names appear in the royal traditions of Bunyoro; Bunyoro pottery is markedly different from that found in the older farming communities in the region but is consistent with that of their Luo neighbors. However, the degree of Luo influence on Bunyoro history appears to have been limited to the introduction into Bunyoro of a Luo ruling class, for the changes in pottery design, settlement patterns, and economic specialization appear to have been driven more by the internal economic and social reorganization of the indigenous Bantu speakers than the smaller numbers of the Luo elite.

Southeast of Bunyoro, in the fertile highlands above Lake Kivu at the bottom of the Western Rift, the kingdoms of Rwanda and Burundi were founded in the seventeenth century, powerful monarchies supported by a dominant, aristocratic caste of pastoralists who identified themselves as "Tutsi." Like Bunyoro and many of the other states of the Lake Plateau, the oral traditions emphasized the role of northern migrants in the founding of their kingdoms. Such traditions should be viewed skeptically, however, since they reflect the living memory of rulers, not subjects, and are devoted to insuring their legitimacy. Despite the fact, however, that the Tutsi elite and the Hutu majority shared a common language and common religious traditions, they were sharply divided economically and socially. The first European observers found the Tutsi congregated on the hilltops with their large herds of cattle; the Hutu remained in the valleys below as farmers cultivating their crops. There were strict social proscriptions against intermarriage that effectively produced a single monarchy but two nations.

By 800 CE Bantu-speaking settlers in the valleys had encountered Cushitic-Bantu-speaking pastoralists in the highlands above the Western Rift Valley. During the centuries that followed, and despite the adoption of a common language, the economic and social differentiation between farmers and herdsmen became increasingly pronounced, facilitated by the terrain which differentiated hilltop cattle pastures from the fertile farms in the valleys below. Both farmers and herdsmen, however, prospered in this lush environment with its optimal zones for cattle, cereal agriculture, and banana cultivation in close proximity to one another. The fecundity of the land was matched by that of its people, whose numbers steadily increased to create, by the seventeenth century, a shortage of land. In circumstances of dearth, pastoralists with large herds of cattle could effectively introduce new relationships in which the farmers found themselves becoming the dependents of overbearing cattlemen. This process was accentuated by the growth of a strong militaristic culture in which young pastoralists, in order to obtain cattle for marriage, would place their services as warriors at the disposal of ambitious cattle barons looking to expand their influence among less well-organized and less militaristic farmers.

It was not until the seventeenth century that this collage masquerading as history received greater definition by the development of kingdoms in the highlands. In Rwanda the beginning of state building is attributed to Ruganzu Bwimba, a Tutsi who, according to tradition, established a petty principality in the sixteenth century near Kigale, the present capital of the Republic of Rwanda. The origin of the kingdom of Rwanda, however, was the work of Mwami Ruganzu Ndori (c.1600–1624) in the early seventeenth century. His leadership is more legendary than real. Like the great chieftains of the highland Scottish clans, he purportedly asserted his authority over rivals on their hills and the lowlanders in the valleys. The evolution of the state from clan to principality to kingdom was achieved by raiding, political innovation, and control of the economy. Despite the energy of Ruganzu Ndori that enterprise required another 200 years. A centralized kingdom began to take shape during the latter half of the nineteenth century during the reign of Mwami Kigeri Rwabugiri (1840–1895), but the subjugation of the Hutu in fact proved more difficult than that of rival Tutsi clans. The last independent Tutsi chiefs surrendered to Mwami Mutara Rwogera (1802–1853) in 1852, but the free Hutu communities on the Uganda frontier did not succumb to Mwami Yuli Musinga (1896–1931) until the 1920s. The ascent of the Tutsi monarchy was achieved to a great extent through intimidation, and violence. What appeared to the first European explorers to be a populous, stable, feudal kingdom was in fact an increasingly oppressive society seething with internal conflict.

Traditions attribute the founding of Rwanda's southern neighbor, the kingdom of Burundi, to the Tutsi chief Ntare Rushatsi (c. 1657–1705). Under his leadership Tutsi hegemony expanded, following much the same pattern established by Ruganzu Bwimba in Rwanda. Conquest, political organization, and the resources from the land, cattle from pastoralists, and crops from farmers made possible the centralization of the state. Like the kings in Rwanda the *mwami*s of Burundi at first pursued the course of empire by integrating important Tutsi chiefdoms. However, during the reign of Mwami Ntare Rugaamba (c. 1795–1852), the monarchy became increasingly aggressive and expansionist in its conquests. He asserted his authority not only over his thousand hills but also in the eastern savanna of modern-day Tanzania. Although the dynamics of Tutsi imperialism north and south of the Akanyaru River were similar, the kings of Burundi were more inclined to use negotiation and political accommodation with their rivals than the *mwami*s of Rwanda, who relied on the force of arms to centralize their kingdom.

In all these states, royal traditions tied their legitimacy to the role of foreign heroes who brought peace and stability to troubled communities. Many of

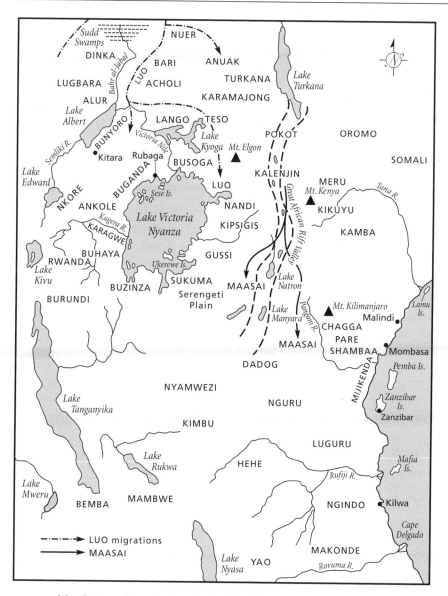

Map 8.1 *Peoples and migrations in East Africa.*

these myths of origin invoke the role of a shadowy dynasty known as the Bacwezi. Many Lakes kingdoms hold that these heroic ancestors were the first rulers in the area. What supposedly came of the Bacwezi differs from state to state – in some places they are remembered as tyrants, who were chased out by the current dynasty; in others they simply disappeared when the new rulers arrived. In Bunyoro, for example, the ruling Bito clan's legitimacy is based in part on their being the rightful successors to the Bacwezi. Today most scholars no longer consider the Bacwezi as a historical dynasty, but rather as a mythic tradition that reflects important social transformations in the region after the turn of the first millennium in which the Bacwezi appear more as revered religious figures than the builders of the earthen works at Bigo.

Although scholars have cast doubt on the role of Hamites, Bacwezi, and other foreign "king-makers" in the Lake Plateau, immigrants have undoubtedly played a significant role in its history, among them the Luo. Luo is a Nilotic language, spoken initially in the southern Sudan. Luo speakers left their homeland in southern Sudan to cross the Victoria Nile with their cattle and settle among the Bantu speakers of the northern Lake Plateau, in modern-day Uganda. These Luo-speaking migrants were not nomads, but a pastoral people seeking greener pastures, and there were ample grasslands and water on the highlands above the equatorial lakes to provide permanent pastures. They were primarily interested in grazing their herds among the farmers of the Lake Plateau whose crops were complementary and exchanged for milk, meat, and manure from Luo cattle.

The Luo speak an Eastern Sudanic language of the larger Nilo-Saharan linguistic family which in the Nile Valley is squeezed between the Afro-Asiatic languages – dynastic Egyptian, Arabic, Hebrew, and Cushitic – and the Bantu speakers in the south, whose languages belong to the Niger-Congo family. Throughout the first millennium CE the fertile Gezira was the homeland to several other Nilotic groups as well. At some time, probably after the turn of the millennium, Luo speakers gradually made their way southward from the Gezira into the southern Sudan in the vicinity of Rumbek, a contemporary administrative center in the Bahr al-Ghazal, from which they began their further migrations, reaching as far as East Africa in the sixteenth century. Their wanderings were in all likelihood related to the expansion of cattle-keeping in the Upper Nile Valley, as well as the growth of the population and the expanding militarism of their northern neighbors.

About the fifteenth century another Nilotic group, the ancestral relatives of the modern Dinka, began to follow the Luo southward. They were driven out by devastating droughts and slave raiding by nomad Arabs whose infiltration into the Nile Valley from Upper Egypt brought about the collapse of the Christian kingdom of Alwa. Their passage south was characterized by constant conflict with their predecessors or the indigenous peoples – Funj, Shilluk, Murle, Luel, and even the Luo – for land to graze and cultivate before they ultimately consolidated their presence in the Upper Nile and Bahr al-Ghazal of the southern Sudan between the sixteenth and eighteenth centuries.

Between the fourteenth and seventeenth centuries the Upper Nile Basin experienced several severe droughts, culminating in the long drought from 1587 to 1652, known among the Luo as *Nyarubanga*, the Great Famine, which coincided with their migrations – undoubtedly in their search for well-watered pastures for their cattle. The sanga and zebu humpbacked cattle that are stronger, capable of traveling longer distances, and are more disease resistant than the humpless cattle of the Luo, had yet to be introduced into the southern Sudan by the Dinka migrating from the Gezira. The peripatetic migrations of the Luo must surely have been determined by the fundamental need of their more vulnerable humpless cattle to move slowly over short distances.

Today east of the Lake Plateau in the great Eastern Rift Valley live the Maasai. Like the Luo they speak a Nilotic language of the Nilo-Saharan linguistic family and, originally from the Gezira, their ancestors migrated from southern Ethiopia down the pastures and lakes in the trench of the Rift Valley during the sixteenth century. They were a pastoral people whose society was organized by age-sets. These are associations established when adolescent boys – and often girls – of the same age are initiated together into adulthood. Each age-set had its own name, and the initiates were bound by a common name, obligations, and responsibilities, producing a powerful sense of brotherhood that remained throughout their lives, from their teens to adult warriors protecting the herds of cattle, and finally as elders. The ancestors of the Maasai had no hereditary chiefs or kings, but the power of their ritual leaders, the *laibon*, provided a religious unity. Like other pastoral peoples of East Africa their relationships with the Bantu-speaking cultivators were mostly symbiotic. There was, of course, the usual tension between the herdsman and the farmer over use of the land, but historically each needed the produce of the other. The Maasai traded milk, meat, and hides for the grain and iron implements of the Kikuyu and Kamba on the eastern highlands of the Rift. The Kikuyu in turn adopted the age-set system and initiation ceremonies of the Maasai, as did the Bantu-speaking farmers further south in the Usambara and Pare hills surrounding Mount Kilimanjaro in Tanzania.

The important trends that shaped the history of the Lake Plateau have paralells elsewhere in Africa. Traditions of heroic strangers establishing dynasties are common and reminiscent of the political revolution attributed to Luba and Lunda princes on the Central African savanna. Many of the important changes that accompanied the advent of specialized cattle pastoralism, such as a transformation of gender roles, political centralization, and growing militarism, played out in similar ways in southern and West Africa. The drama of cattle herders and agriculturalists forging new political institutions out of their ancient conflicts would be familiar to the people of the West African Sahel. The influence of an exotic crop (the banana) on culture and politics is mirrored in the similar stories of maize in southern Africa, and cassava in the Central African savanna, and the spread of iron technology with all its social, political, and unintentional environmental consequences has affected virtually all the disparate regions of the continent.

Further reading

Schoenbrun, David, *A Green Place, a Good Place: Agrarian Change, Gender, and Social Identity in the Great Lakes Region to the 15th Century,* Portsmouth: Heinemann, 1998

Vansina, Jan, *Antecedents to Modern Rwanda: The Nyiginya Kingdom,* Madison: University of Wisconsin Press, 2004

9   Societies and states of the West African forest

From the Senegambia in the west to Cameroon in the east lies a belt of dense tropical rainforest over 200 miles wide through which short but deep rivers flow to the sea. Several of these rivers make up the maze of the Niger Delta known collectively as the oil rivers. Others, such as the Bandama, Volta, Ouémé, and Benin reach the beaches that extend, with few exceptions, in an unbroken line of coast pounded by heavy surf and laced by an intricate series of lagoons beyond and parallel to the long stretches of sand. Behind the lagoons looms the West African forest that appears from the shore an impenetrable wall into the interior except for the funnel of savanna, the Dahomey Gap, a north–south corridor from the grasslands of the *bilad al-sudan* to the coast of the Bight of Benin that facilitated the flow of people and trade from the interior to the coast. This rainforest is the creation of heavy annual rainfall (50–80 inches) in two seasons, April to July and September to November, when the southwest monsoons sweep out of the South Atlantic Ocean.

In the centuries following the turn of the first millennium, some of the continent's most sophisticated states emerged from the dense undergrowth of the West African forest. Although these kingdoms never approached the size of their northern neighbors in the savanna and sahel of the Western Sudan, gold, cola nuts, and slaves from their forests were crucial commodities in the chain of commerce that stretched north to the great empires of the plains and across the Sahara to the Mediterranean. When the trade coming south from the desert could no longer compete with the new, attractive, and sought-after goods easily acquired in trade from the European sea-merchants, these forest states flourished due to their proximity to the European trading enclaves of the West African coast. Many of these states were small principalities, but there were others that rivaled in organization and power the empires of the plains; among them, however, lived numerous communities that eschewed the centralized authority that characterized their neighbors. This complex mosaic of states and stateless societies of different ethnicities and political and social complexions perhaps can best be understood by representative examples to illustrate the challenges, interactions, and responses to life in the West African rainforest by its peoples.

The first inhabitants of the forest were foragers who lived by hunting, gathering, and fishing. The expansion of agriculture into the rainforest was laborious and slow, for it required heavy work to clear the trees. Although many edible plants grew wild in the forest, there were no indigenous staples, such as the sorghum and millet of the savanna, so the evolution of farming in the rainforest was a protracted process of trial and error as crops were slowly adapted to forest conditions. African rice, which was first cultivated in the inland Niger Delta of the northern savanna, was introduced into the forest west of the Dahomey Gap.[1] The yam, a tuber that flourishes in the rainforest, had become a staple of forest agriculture during the first millennium CE.[2] Despite initial difficulties, settlements in the rainforest expanded gradually but inexorably and by 1000 villages and their surrounding earthworks had been constructed, and the fields beyond cleared from the bush with iron implements. The rivers and lagoons provided abundant fish, high-protein supplements to the carbohydrates of the yam.

Equatorial agriculture, however, required a collaborative effort that could only be accomplished by greater cohesion of community organization than in the open grasslands of the Western Sudan. The village settlements in this region were characterized by enclosed compounds surrounding a marketplace, beyond which lay the belts of farmland and then the wasteland – wild bush, inhabited by evil spirits and heroic hunters. With a slow but steady increase in population the common core of the village gradually expanded into small states that required increasingly complex political and social institutions. During the second millennium CE these clusters grew in size as they adapted to equatorial agriculture, but the forest inhibited the creation of expansive empires comparable to those found on the savanna plains.

Many forest-dwellers remained aloof from centralized states altogether, choosing to live instead in communities with no successive institutions of political authority. While this was not uncommon in Africa, it was particularly pronounced in the West African forests where one in four persons lived in what could be classified as "stateless" communities as late as the 1930s. These communities relied for governance on ritual experts or "big men," who were more mediators than rulers among the residents, whose associations were bound by kin, secret societies, age-sets, or a combination that controlled the affairs of the village without a hierarchical administration. A memorable illustration of the workings of one such society, the Igbo, is portrayed in Nobel laureate Chinua Achebe's famous novel, *Things Fall Apart*, which tells the story of Okonkwo, a successful farmer and champion wrestler who wields tremendous influence in his village by his hard work and force of will rather than from any investiture as an official of authority. Among the Igbo, Tiv, Ballanta, and

---

[1] Enslaved African rice farmers from the west of the Dahomey Gap brought their agricultural technologies to the New World, where they made possible the agricultural industry that built the British colony of South Carolina.

[2] Dating the origins of agriculture in the rainforest is difficult because of the problems of evidence. Historians, archaeologists, and historical linguists have offered wildly divergent views of the process whereby yam cultivation developed in the forests of West and Central Africa. Despite this debate, it can be said with confidence that yam cultivation had become established in areas of the forest before the first millennium CE.

other decentralized, or "stateless" West African communities, the institutions that settled disputes, organized the time to plant and the time to harvest, and dominated the rituals to propitiate the gods were invariably controlled by the elders possessing influence and wealth, not kings or emperors.

Stateless communities have long fascinated anthropologists because of their ability to manage social tensions without clearly defined, institutionalized or hierarchical forms of authority. Perhaps for this reason, they are largely forgotten in history, for they do not, as a rule, produce monumental architecture, dynastic histories, or royal artistic traditions from which the historian can reconstruct their political and cultural past. Finding it difficult to perceive change in a society with only a fragmentary oral record, social scientists, often in frustration, regard "stateless" societies as static, unchanging, and devoid of historical developments. This monolithic perspective, however, overlooks the very vibrant organizations of these societies that conduct their own affairs so successfully without an elaborate political apparatus. Indeed, "stateless" societies adapted their political and cultural traditions over time much like any other community, many of them actually evolving into states but usually without abandoning those egalitarian aspects of their past culture. For example, recent scholarship has shown that among the "stateless" Diola on the south bank of the Casamance River in southern Senegal, the role of priests and the significance of religious shrines became transformed by the arrival of new immigrants, and by the dangers and opportunities that accompanied the expansion of the Atlantic slave trade. Other "stateless" societies, such as that at Igbo-Ukwu, were involved in long-distance trade which distinguished those who prospered, who became heroic figures venerated by the common folk and acknowledged as men of authority, and were buried with all the panoply of a rich artistic tradition.

Thus, our knowledge about the early settlement of the West African forest remains fragmentary and incomplete. Relatively little archaeological work has been undertaken in the arduous conditions of the densely overgrown, hot, and humid forests. Recent fieldwork in West Africa has led to the revision of our understanding of these early rainforest settlements as new evidence produces new interpretations. For example, recent archaeological investigations in southeastern Nigeria just north of the modern coastal city of Lagos have uncovered a vast network of earthen walls known locally as Eredo. Laced with 100 miles of vertical ditches over 70 feet high in places, this honeycomb of walls is over a thousand years old, according to radiocarbon dating. Legends associate the structure with a mighty, childless queen, Bilikisu Sungbo, who patronized its construction as a legacy for her people. Who built it and why it was built remains obscure despite the fact that local traditions associate Eredo with the legend of the Queen of Sheba. Nevertheless, the authority and organization to mobilize the labor and resources to construct such a massive and intricate complex of ditches and walls for whatever purpose could hardly have been accomplished without a hierarchical, stratified society – a state – deep in the rainforest at the end of the first millennium CE.

The Yoruba

Among these early farming communities there was little to distinguish between the authority of a ritual leader, the big man in the village, or a territorial chief. As communities experienced changes in technology, agriculture, commerce, climate, demography, or some combination thereof, new and more permanent institutions emerged to coordinate more effectively the planting and harvesting of crops, the mobilization of resources, and the adjudication of disputes between increasingly diverse social groups. These political institutions often invested the elders or prominent families with hereditary authority. By the second millennium petty principalities with an acknowledged ruler began to appear among the ancestors of the modern Yoruba, Edo, Nupe, and Jukun peoples. The earliest identifiable state was Ile-Ife of the Yoruba, which developed on the fringe of forest and savanna east of the Dahomey Gap in modern Nigeria. The Yoruba language is a part of the Kwa subfamily of the Niger-Congo family. The term "Yoruba" today designates both an ethnic identity and a linguistic group that is embraced by millions of Nigerians who live in the southwestern region of the country, but in the more distant past it was adopted from a Hausa word specifically to describe the people of the empire of Oyo. Thus, the history of the Yoruba is about a people who thought of themselves as the subjects of a unified empire – quite unlike their modern descendants, who identify "Yoruba" with a people of similar ethnicity and language not attached to any Yoruba political institution.

Yoruba speakers have several traditions of their origins, but the most common is that of Oduduwa, who arrived in Ife as a heroic leader whose sons became kings and whose daughters were the mothers of rulers in collateral states: the *alafin* of Oyo whose son became the first *oba* of Benin; another son was the first *onisabe* of Sabe; a daughter bore the first *alaketu* of Ketu (in Dahomey) and another daughter gave birth to the first *olowu* of Owu. While later Yoruba historians sought legitimacy for their monarchy by claiming that the Yoruba came from Arabia, Ethiopia, or the Nile Valley, their ancestors probably migrated southward from the savanna of the Western Sudan into the bush and forest lands of West Africa about 1000 CE. Here they adapted their indigenous political ideas in a new environment to develop new institutions of governing. The legends depicting Oduduwa sending out his children to establish their own states of Yoruba origin symbolized the reality of Yoruba state building around the ruler of a great town.

The Yoruba were a forest farming people with villages, hamlets, and small market towns scattered throughout the bush, but their innovative contribution

to West African civilization was the big town, an urban center for iron smelting, terracotta figures, brass-work, cloth weaving, and the capital, the *ílú aládé*.
Ife was the first *ílú aládé* whose powerful rulers, the *oni*, were believed to be
descended from Oduduwa. These capital towns sustained large populations
with similar configurations: the palace (*afin*) at the center, from which radiated
wards that included temples, shops, and the compounds, *agbo'le*, that comprised the homes of the extended families. They were surrounded by extensive
walls; that of Old Oyo was 24 miles in circumference and 24 feet high.

By the seventeenth century, the Yoruba were joined in a confederation of
the rulers from the big towns under the spiritual and political leadership of
the senior Yoruba ruler, the *oni* of Ife. Each ruler was autonomous in his
state, but he was bound in his relations with neighboring states by elaborate
arrangements between the ruling families under the watchful eye of the *oni*
of Ife. The government of the Yoruba city-state was dominated by the king,
the *oba*, who was not, however, an autocrat, for he had to listen to the views
of his council of chiefs, the *iwarefa*, that consisted of the heads, *agba ile*, of
the extended families. The council made important political decisions, even
choosing the *oba*, but the *oba* was responsible for the carrying out of the
decisions of state by his own officials. These were his civil servants who
took their orders only from the king and were usually associated with those
special groups that were charged with the education of the age-sets in Yoruba
society. Thus the Yoruba were ruled by a monarch whose agents carried out
the important decisions of the kingdom made in a council of aristocrats. This
system functioned with remarkable results when dealing with matters of the
city-state, but it was less successful in perpetuating the revered tradition that
the Yoruba were one large family when in fact they were a family of competing
towns with intense rivalries.

These rivalries were inextricably intertwined with loyalty to the ancestors
of the founding hero, Oduduwa – and consequently the *oni* of Ife, who was the
living embodiment of those ancestors. As time passed and each Yoruba city-
state grew in power, so too did the spiritual authority of its ruler, at the expense
of the *oni* of Ife. Religion could not be divorced from government when the
powers of the ruler were sanctified by the priests and diviners and preserved
by artisans in wood, clay, brass, and ivory sculptures of power and beauty.
The ceramic clay terracotta figures celebrated life in Ife through sculptures
of its *oni* and his kinsmen. Archaeologists believe that these artistic traditions
are quite ancient, and related to clay figurines found in the Nok culture of the
Benue River region that date between 500 BCE and 300 CE. Copper and then
its alloy, brass (copper and zinc), were used by casters employing the lost-wax
technique to produce works of dramatic artistic achievement in Ife as early as
the fourteenth century, and thereafter at Benin in the fifteenth and sixteenth
centuries.

By the time that Ife had reached the height of its artistic and political influence, the Yoruba population had expanded and migrated to establish numerous

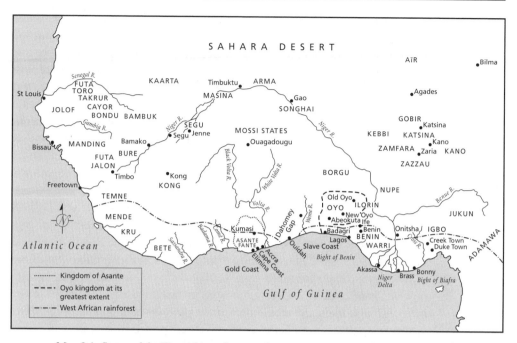

Map 9.1 *States of the West African forest and savanna.*

small city-states. Although the dispersal produced variations in spoken Yoruba, they shared a common cultural and political tradition that remained in constant tension between the central authority of Ife and the dynamic autonomy of the Yoruba towns with their own *oba*s. One of these towns was Oyo. Its inhabitants had not migrated into the rainforest but had remained in the woods and grasslands on its northern edge. Unlike the Yoruba living in walled towns whose independence was protected by the rainforest, the Yoruba of Oyo in their more open country were vulnerable to the two powerful Western Sudanic states, Borgu to the north and Nupe to the northeast, to whom they paid tribute. About 1550 Nupe conquered Oyo. Its ruler, the *alafin*, sought sanctuary in Borgu until he was allowed to return before the end of the sixteenth century to build a new capital at Igbohu.

Cavalry dominated warfare in the Western Sudan, and the horses and cavalrymen of Borgu and Nupe were famous and feared. In order to sustain its independence Oyo would also need an army of horsemen trained in cavalry warfare. Unfortunately, the woodlands of Oyo were on the fringe of the tsetse-fly zone, so that while the *alafin* was able to keep horses, unlike the Yoruba states further south, he could not breed them. The solution was to purchase horses from the savanna states to the north, but horses were the single most expensive item of trade throughout the Western Sudan. However, Oyo's marginal location, although it prevented the breeding of horses, was ideally situated at the center of the long-distance north–south trade routes for goods from the rainforest to the large markets in Hausaland to the north and those going east and west to the bustling commercial centers of the trans-Saharan trade at Gao, Timbuktu, and Jenne. Under the leadership of Alafin Orompoto (c. 1560–1580), Oyo became an enormously prosperous mercantile center trading goods from the rainforest to those of the dry savanna and manufacturing its own cloth, ironware, and pottery in return for salt and leather and – above all – horses from the Sudan. By the seventeenth century the wealth of Oyo was more than sufficient to maintain a formidable cavalry to defend its independence and expand its political power.

Benin

Southeast of the Yoruba, on the western fringe of the Niger Delta, lived Edo-speaking people, whose language, like Yoruba, is a part of the Kwa group of the Niger-Congo language family. Like the Yoruba their beginnings are obscure. They initially lived in settlements in the rainforest where they cleared bush with iron tools and supplemented their diet by hunting and fishing. The settlements grew into villages and cultivations protected by earthworks and governed by institutions of authority and social groups which were connected by trade routes through the forest to the markets of other towns, one of which was called Benin. The traditions of Benin recount that sometime in the past the Edo inhabitants became dissatisfied with their own kings and asked the legendary Yoruba ruler of Ife, Oduduwa, for one of his sons to rule them. He sent Prince Oranmiyan, who inaugurated the political development of Benin sometime before the fourteenth century.

The Edo may have borrowed Yoruba political town organization, but they retained and developed their own distinctive culture, preserved by their skilled artisans using the lost-wax technique in the famous sculptures that celebrate the authority and power of the ruler, the *oba*. The Benin Bronzes, as they are erroneously called (for they were in fact brass), were not limited to royal sculpture, as there were many brass plaques and metal pictures of warriors and acrobats to adorn the palace of the *oba*. Among the Western aficionados of African art these sculptures of kings and queens have often regrettably eclipsed the equally artistic styles of figures that were popular with the ordinary folk. This extraordinary flowering of artistic achievement could not have succeeded without the extensive trading network of the Edo- and Yoruba-speaking peoples. Brass cannot be produced without copper, and there is no copper in southern Nigeria. It had to be imported from the Western Sudan in exchange for the goods of the rainforest that provided revenue to support the state and its expansion and the surplus to support the artists.

In the mid-fifteenth century Benin accelerated its policy of expansion under the famous warrior *oba*, Ewuare (c. 1450–1480), who organized the state for imperial conquest. He exhibited his power by a sumptuous palace within

Box 9.1 The lost-wax process

The lost-wax technique was first used at Ur in Mesopotamia around 3000 BCE. It may have reached West Africa from the north or the Nile Valley, where it had long been in use, or independently developed by West Africans casting in copper. The object of the sculptor is modeled in wax, enclosed in clay and baked, the melted wax draining out through orifices. Molten metal is then poured into the mold and the openings sealed. After the metal has set, the clay covering is broken and the casting removed. The metal used was brass, an alloy of copper and zinc. When the brass contains less than 36 percent zinc it can be worked into complex shapes without frequent reheating. These extraordinary works of art are often referred to as Benin Bronze, which is technically incorrect, as bronze, as distinguished from brass, is an alloy of copper and tin, and is rarely found in Africa.

whose spacious compound, enclosed by a mighty wall and ditch, were housed the artisans, craftsmen, and courtiers. He relied for advice on a state council composed of the *uzama*, the palace chiefs who represented the heads of the powerful families, and the town chiefs who were the leaders of the craft guilds. To preserve what he had established, Ewuare introduced the principle of primogeniture to insure stability for the crown by resolving the contentious problem of succession. Having centralized and secured his authority he launched thirty years of war upon his neighbors, and had upon his death achieved a West African coastal empire extending from the Niger Delta in the east to Dahomey in the west and even incorporating Yoruba towns on his northern frontier. When the Portuguese arrived in 1486 they were duly impressed by the size, organization, and the power of the *oba* of imperial Benin.

The golden age of the empire was enjoyed by the successors of Ewuare. In 1504 his grandson, Esigie (1504–1550), succeeded to the throne. He began the erosion of the power of the *uzama* in the state council by promoting commoners as his loyal civil servants with sweeping authority. He also realized that the arrival of the Europeans would dramatically change West African societies, and made every effort to maintain good relations with the Portuguese envoys, traders, and missionaries, who responded with glowing accounts of Benin and its ruler. Esigie could speak and read Portuguese, practiced astrology (*iwe-uki*), and presided over an empire of high culture and great wealth. Primogeniture defined the succession that enabled the education of the future *oba* and the stability of the empire for another hundred years. As in Oyo the queen mother, who produced the first son and heir of the ruling *oba*, wielded enormous power, starting with Idia, the mother of Oba Esigie. She and her successors presided over a competitive court of the *oba*'s wives, female slaves, and eunuchs, and owned and managed their own village estates. The successors of Esigie all had long reigns and, despite the hagiography pervasive in royal traditions, appear to have been learned, primarily concerned with the material and spiritual well-being of their subjects, and sensitive to the Europeans without fully understanding the challenge they represented to their authority.

The Niger Delta and the Igbo

The great delta of the Niger River is a vast labyrinth of creeks and rivers, swamps and islands extending 300 miles from the Benin River in the west to the Cross River in the east. Its inhabitants in the past were fisherfolk, the Ijo, who lived in relative isolation disrupted only by those who came by canoe to visit, settle, or trade. In the sixteenth century life in the delta began to change with the arrival of the European sea-merchants who found in the maze of estuaries facing the ocean ample anchorage denied them on the surf-swept beaches to the west. Trade transformed the delta. Newcomers paddled into its rivers from the north – Igbo, Edo, Jekri, Ibibio, Efik – to position themselves in strategic settlements on the navigable estuaries as middlemen between the sea-merchants and the states of the interior. They were known as the People of the Salt Water (*ndu mili nnu*), protected by the waterways and dense vegetation of the delta from any political or commercial ambitions by their neighbors on the surrounding high ground. In this unique environment they developed in the seventeenth century institutions to govern themselves to achieve the best advantage in competitive commerce with the sea-merchants.

In order to exploit the rapidly expanding trade and now having the resources to do so, the delta peoples living in single settlements on the rivers and islands surrounded by protective intricate waterways developed systems of governance for their own city-states. City-states are well known in history, and many have in common a maritime presence. In Europe there were the famous Greek city-states, Athens and Sparta. In East Africa there were the coastal Swahili city-states of Mombasa, Malindi, and Kilwa among others. On the coast of West Africa there were the city-states of the Niger Delta whose citizens devised the means to administer law and order, justice, and to make war and peace in order to promote their commerce. Each delta city-state, like those of the Greeks, had its own distinct methods of governing. Some had kings elected by the heads of wealthy and prominent families – Bonny, New Calabar, and Warri. Others were like small republics, ruled by the members of political organizations not unlike senates – Brass and those on the Cross River in Old Calabar – Creek Town, Henshaw Town, Duke Town, and Obutong. In the city-states of Old Calabar the *ekpe* or Leopard Association of wealthy men, mostly merchants, ruled the town principally to insure the flow of peaceful trade. Anyone was free to join the *ekpe* if they could afford the exorbitant entry fee that insured that those in power represented only the interests of the wealthy merchants. They regulated the terms of trade with the Europeans and made the rules by which the community was governed by its constituent organizations, known as the "house system."

Traditional African societies were based on the clans and lineages of large families that were not always the most effective means to carry on business. Rather than the family firm, the house was a cooperative commercial trading company run not by kinship but by the ability of the head of the house, his immediate family, and a host of assistants, servants, and even slaves whose status in the company depended on their success in promoting its trade rather than kinship ties or social privilege. The house system evolved throughout the latter half of the eighteenth century as a commercial response to the dramatic increase in the slave trade and was firmly established throughout the delta by the nineteenth century. Some of the houses, the Pepples of Bonny for example, became powerful commercial firms well known in Europe and the Americas.

East of the Lower Niger River and its delta the forest continues between the ocean and the savanna grasslands, densely populated by the Igbo (Ibo) people since beyond memory. The fertility of its soil and a long tradition of iron-working enabled the Igbo to develop their own distinctive culture and way of life throughout the millennia. The tomb of what may be a ninth-century ritual leader at Igbo-Ukwu is complete with brass artifacts worked with great skill from local copper and zinc that demonstrate a remarkable continuity with contemporary Igbo motifs and an abundance of grave-goods, including cloth made of vegetable fibers and glass beads, perhaps from the Nile Valley, accompanied by the skeletons of the master's retainers.

The existence of these elite grave-goods is of particular interest, as many Igbo communities lacked powerful chiefs or hereditary rulers. While the vast Igbo-speaking region includes an array of political traditions, many lived in stateless communities at the beginning of the twentieth century. Spread over a large and fertile land, the Igbo developed differences in language, customs, and ways of living; however, these differences could not disrupt the basic commonalities of the Igbo people. All the Igbo regulate their community affairs through age-sets to which all men and women belong, and many have political associations whose leaders would take responsibility for the governance of the community. These communities, however, were composed of many individual villages, each of which had its separate local government that decided the affairs of everyday life. This was popular government, in which all the male – and occasionally the female – members of the village had a say in the local assembly where matters of common interest were decided. Many Igbo societies had women's associations to represent their interests. Among the Nnobi Igbo daughters were organized into the *umu okpu*, the oldest being the leader, to settle disputes in the lineage. All women – wives and daughters – were subject to the decisions of the women's council, the *inyom nnobi*,

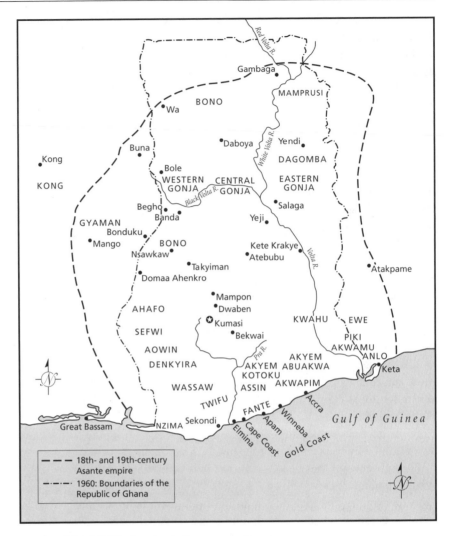

Map 9.2 *The Asante empire.*

responsible for the welfare of women with the authority to levy fines against those violating their customary rights.

The Asante

The original Asante were farmers who spoke Twi, a language that is part of the Akan cluster of the larger Kwa sub-family of Niger-Congo languages. They lived in the forest just west of the Dahomey Gap, in what is today the modern Republic of Ghana. The origins of the Asante are a matter of some debate. For a long time historians assumed that their state emerged in the northern fringes of the forest, where savanna farmers penetrated the forest in search of gold sometime during second half of the second millennium CE. However, recent archaeological and biomedical evidence indicates that the ancestors of the Asante may have been farming deep in the forest a thousand years ago or more. Regardless of when they came into the forest, by the seventeenth century Akan speakers were established in the forest to the north of Lake Bosomtwi, where they farmed and traded in gold and cola nuts. Using slaves acquired from the coast they cut clearings in the rainforest for villages and fields for the cultivation of yams. They built towns, such as Asantemanso between the Pra and the Ofin Rivers, and forged a loose alliance of Akan settlements in the rainforest – Bekwai, Kokofu Mampong, Nsuta, among others – that when threatened would band together for defense under a common leader. They paid an annual tax as well as periodic tribute in goods and slaves to the *ohene* (Twi, "King") of the neighboring state of Denkyira to the southwest, and were in constant conflict over land and trade with the neighboring Akan to the northwest.

The Akan communities underwent a dramatic transformation after the sixteenth century. Growing demand for the gold of the forests, the growth of Atlantic commerce, and the rapid spread of New World crops, such as cassava, cocoyam, and maize, ushered in an economic and demographic revolution. In this environment, new leaders would take advantage of these changes to carve out more powerful and enduring states. The most effective new leaders were the rulers of the Akan state of Asante.

At the end of the seventeenth century the Asante leader, Obiri Yeboa (*c.* 1660–1693), was killed in warfare with the Domaa and succeeded by Osei Tutu (*c.* 1695–1717), who transformed Asante society. With his friend and religious advisor, Okomfo (priest) Anokye, he forged the Asante Akan into a single strong union, symbolized by a golden stool "brought down from the sky" by Okomfo Anokye containing the soul of the Asante people, to which they swore allegiance as well as to their new *asantehene*, Osei Tutu, at his capital, Kumasi. Using the sanctity of the stool, Osei Tutu united the Asante by laws defining a common citizenship and responsibilities to serve the state, particularly in the Asante national army. Osei Tutu built his army along the lines of that in the state of Akwamu where he had grown up, but he introduced new methods of organization and fighting that transformed what had been little more than a militia into an efficient and proficient fighting force. This new ruling class derived its economic resources from its crops, largely cultivated by female slaves, and came to dominate the markets by the sale of their surplus.

In 1699 Osei Tutu launched his army against Denkyira, and by 1701 the Asante had conquered it, acquiring much booty, but – more important – the Asante "window to the sea" had been opened. They now had unrestricted contact with the sea-merchants on the coast, and particularly the Dutch at Elmina, whose trade in firearms for gold and slaves enabled the expansion of the Asante empire. Osei Tutu died in 1717, but the Akan state of Akim, an ally of Denkyira, fell in 1719, and throughout the eighteenth century, under a line of extraordinarily able *asantehene*s, the Asante kingdom became a vast empire encompassing all of modern Ghana and much of the Ivory Coast and Togo.

Opoku Ware (1720–1750) was enstooled as *asantehene* about 1720, and continued the concerted policy of territorial expansion, which occupied his long reign of thirty years. The Asante army finally crushed the revived coalition of neighboring states to the south – Denkyira, Sefwi, Akwapim, and Akim. He then turned north to defeat the states of the Black Volta – Tekyiman, Banda, Gyaaman, and Gonja – and in 1744–1745 sent his armies against the powerful state of Dagomba in the far north, whose conquest meant Asante control of the important trade routes of the Middle Niger. The expansion by military conquest resulted in the administration of the empire by men at the expense of women, who had been accustomed in a matrilineal society to a large role in the political life of Asanteland.

Opoku Ware was followed by Kusi Obodom (1750–1764), who was content to consolidate the territorial gains of his predecessor, but under his successor, Asantehene Osei Kwadwo (1764–1777), the Asante empire continued to grow as he achieved both military victories and administrative reforms, enabling the central government to rule its empire. Osei Kwadwo introduced profound changes in the appointment of the civil servants of the *asantehene* that his successors, Osei Kwame (1777–1803) and Osei Bonsu, also known as Osei Tutu Kwame (1804–1823), continued, reinforced, and expanded. *Asantehene*s inherited their position by virtue of descent through their mothers, but the men appointed to offices of political power were now chosen by patrilineal descent. Although office earned by descent, either through the mother or father within the clan or lineage, was traditional in many African societies, this system of ascription was ill-suited to govern an empire with distant provinces inhabited by non-Asante tributaries, a complex commercial network, and a military machine to defend the empire and collect the revenues on which the central government depended. The strong *asantehene*s of the latter half of the eighteenth and early nineteenth centuries relied increasingly on ability and less on birth in the selection of their officials. They wanted men personally devoted above all to the *asantehene* who had demonstrated their achievements in battle, commerce, administration, or diplomacy. They were the king's men, and their advancement and promotion in the civil service depended upon merit rather than birth.

The same principle applied to the internal security and administration of the Asante heartland, which was designed to guarantee the power of the king. The *ankobia*, a special police force, was permanently stationed in the capital, Kumasi, and major towns under an officer specially appointed by the *asantehene*. Its long-serving members were the king's bodyguard and his intelligence agency, and were equipped to prevent or crush rebellion by troublesome tributaries or hereditary Asante chiefs. The *ankobia* were complemented by the civil service, consisting of able and reliable officials within Asanteland and the outlying conquered territories. Men of humble origins rose to positions of political power as provincial governors or in the central administration at Kumasi such as Adumhene Agyei, originally a salt carrier, and Opoku Frefre (*c*. 1760–1826), who rose from a lowly position as keeper of a noble's bed-chamber to that of the wealthy advisor to the *asantehene* Osei Bonsu. This imperial administration would never have worked successfully without a swift and reliable system of communication through the rainforest and northern savanna. The empire had an extensive road network by which large quantities of trade flowed back and forth from the major commercial cities of the Middle Niger to the great European trading forts on the coast. Along these well-kept and well-used roads ran the messengers on foot to link Kumasi with the outlying administrative centers. For over a hundred years the Asante dominated government and trade in the center of the West African forest on a scale comparable to the earlier kingdoms of the Western Sudan – Mali, Songhai, Kanem-Bornu – and to the east in Benin and Oyo.

Further reading

Law, Robin, *The Oyo Empire: A West African Imperialism in the Era of the Atlantic Slave Trade*, Oxford: Clarendon Press, 1977

Ryder. A. F. C., *Benin and the Europeans, 1485–1897*, New York: Humanities Press, 1969

Smith, Robert S., *Kingdoms of the Yoruba*, 3rd ed., Madison: University of Wisconsin Press, 1988

Wilks, Ivor, *Asante in the Nineteenth Century: The Structure and Evolution of a Political Order*, London and New York: Cambridge University Press, 1975

Wilks, Ivor, *Forests of Gold: Essays on the Akan and the Kingdom of the Asante*, Athens: Ohio University Press, 1993

10 Kingdoms and trade in Central Africa

East Central Africa

South of the equatorial rainforest stretches a vast region of woodlands and savanna that includes parts of northern Angola and Zambia and the Shaba region of the Democratic Republic of Congo. The Central African savanna is bounded in the east by Lake Tanganyika, on the west by the shores of the Atlantic Ocean, and in the south by the lower tributaries of the Zambezi River. The territory is interlaced with rivers and streams that feed the southern branches of the Congo and the upper reaches of the Zambezi. This immense, often inhospitable region is home to several of the most remarkable states in the history of Africa.

The early history of the Central African savanna emerges with greater clarity after the immigration into the region by Bantu-speaking farmers from West Africa, their dispersal into small isolated communities, and the reintegration of these communities under new political institutions after 1400. Isolation was the inevitable result of the environmental challenges farmers confronted on the central savanna. The soils are generally poor in nutrients and not conducive to cereal agriculture. In the northern zone, which lies just south of the equator, the annual rainfall is dependable but steadily declines as precipitation moves southeastward, and in the far south years of drought are frequent. The valleys of the tributaries to the Congo and Zambezi are lush and heavily wooded, but the uplands between the rivers consist of lightly forested, sandy grasslands ill-suited for agriculture. Thus the early farmers descended into the valleys, lakes, and floodplains where the soils were more fertile and water more dependable. Disease also limited the size and productivity of agricultural communities in Central Africa. Malaria and sleeping sickness remain two of the most prevalent endemic diseases, the widespread presence of the tsetse fly carrying sleeping sickness (trypanosomiasis) to domestic animals, known as *nagana*, prevented the raising of cattle and horses, depriving the inhabitants of meat, milk, and transport. The environment and disease conspired to inhibit the concentration of people into larger communities, leaving the farmers to disperse into small and scattered rural settlements.

The first humans to live on the savanna were hunter-gatherers who spoke Khoisan languages. Unfortunately their history can only be reconstructed in sweeping generalizations from the scant archaeological evidence that remains.

They were gradually displaced or absorbed by the Bantu-speaking immigrants whose agriculture and technological sophistication, particularly their ability to make iron, enabled their greater numbers and military capabilities to overwhelm the hunter-gatherers. Some managed to continue their nomadic way of life among the Bantu-speaking agricultural and fishing villages, but many were driven off of their lands or integrated into settled communities. They could not compete with the economic, social, and technological accomplishments of the Bantu speakers, which were widely disseminated and shared by the peoples of the savanna.

Linguistic and archaeological evidence indicates that the way of life of these settlers – including iron-working, pottery, agriculture, and domestication of animals – spread quickly throughout Central Africa after 400 CE. The rapidity and relative ease by which hunters and gatherers appear to have been absorbed or displaced by settled agricultural communities seems to confirm an aggressive search for fertile enclaves in the great plain of inhospitable savanna by Bantu-speaking farmers whose similarities of lifestyle and language produced a cultural continuity in Central Africa throughout the centuries. Names of deities and the veneration of certain spirits developed regional variations, but the core of religious beliefs practiced by the villagers of these semi-arid plains was much the same. Most of these communities were matrilineal, but a few that became the more important in the evolution of the kingdoms of the savanna gradually evolved patrilineal systems of descent. Symbols of political authority were widely shared throughout the region, as were myths of origin featuring wandering hunters, snakes, and rainbows. When new trade and political networks emerged after the eleventh century, they linked peoples together before their relatively brief isolation had time to erode their common cultural and linguistic heritage.

These early Bantu speakers searched for islands of fertile soils adjacent to water for fish and woodlands for game. Lakes and rivers provided a livelihood for fishermen, and the rich loam of their inland deltas, such as the Upemba Depression in the north and the Kafue Flats in the south, produced bountiful harvests for the farmers. Bantu-speaking settlers also congregated at sites where they had discovered abundant mineral resources. The vast copper deposits that lay in the south were mined as early as 500 CE, and salt was an important commodity extracted from the flats lying on along the shores of northern lakes and the banks of rivers. Although the relative poverty of the environment inhibited large urban settlements, the dispersal of Bantu-speaking villages encouraged an active long-distance trade in salt, copper, foodstuffs, fabrics, and other commodities. These networks of local, regional, and long-distance trade also disseminated technologies, cultural characteristics, and political institutions among distant communities. The details of daily life in these early farming and fishing village communities remain largely unknown so that the history of the peoples of the Central African savanna is dominated by documented long-distance trade, traditions of state formation,

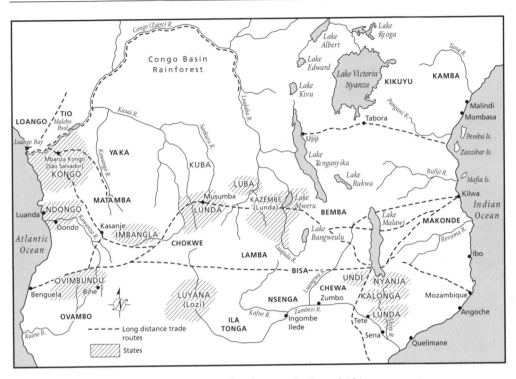

Map 10.1 *States and trade routes in Central Africa.*

and the rise of confederations and empires that demonstrate a talent for organization and political creativity.

The political history of Central Africa gradually emerges from the creation of new institutions of government among the Luba people of the Upper Kasai River Valley, the adaptation and reformulation of these Luba institutions among the neighboring Lunda, and their ensuing dissemination by the Lunda throughout the savanna. The widespread expansion of the Luba/Lunda influence has been corroborated by the many savanna states that have claimed descent from Lunda origins. The kingdom of Kazembe, which lies a few hundred miles southeast of the Lunda heartland, adopted Lunda institutions, while others, such as the more distant Bemba, insisted they had Lunda origins, most probably to bestow legitimacy on their ruling dynasties. Regardless of the historical validity of such claims, the prevalence of Lunda cultural and political characteristics throughout the savanna confirms the prestige and influence of the Luba/Lunda systems. They also indicate that after 1400 the peoples of the savanna were being drawn into closer contact with one another by exchanging goods and ideas.

Evidence for the origins of the Luba state was discovered in an archaeological site at Sanga on the shores of Lake Kisale near the Upper Kasai River, a tributary of the Congo. This region would have been particularly attractive to early Bantu-speaking settlers. It is near the fertile floodplain of the Upemba Depression, which offered opportunities for riparian agriculture. Its marshes and streams teemed with fish, and the rivers offered easy transportation for commerce. By 800 Africans in permanent settlements by the lakes, marshes, and rivers were receiving abundant protein from easily caught fish. Gradually these communities expanded their reliance on agriculture, particularly crops such as sorghum and millet, and the domestication of chickens, sheep, and goats. There were significant deposits of iron and salt, which were traded with neighbors downstream. Hunting remained an important dietary supplement, as well as a source of prestige for the hunters, who represented a special class in Luba society. This diverse economy of fishing, farming, mining, and hunting enabled the population to steadily increase by 1000. The fertility of the soils in the valleys and surrounding the lakes encouraged migrant farmers to settle and engage in trade. That an enlarged population soon produced social stratification has been confirmed by the archaeological record. Dignitaries at Sanga were buried with copper grave-goods signifying their elite status, for the copper found in its elaborate graves could only be obtained by trade with the mineral-rich regions to the south.

Why were some individuals more revered in death than others? The refinement of the Sanga grave-goods appears to confirm that a political elite had developed by 1000, and was responsible for the allocation of land and water as well as protecting and fostering commerce. Floodplain agriculture and fishing required a degree of economic specialization and political centralization that encouraged the emergence of "big men," or authorities who could organize and protect access to natural resources. Commerce could flourish only when local leaders assumed the responsibility for the protection of traders and trade routes. Political authority was usually assumed by the religious leaders, those members of society who were the intermediaries between the people and their ancestors and the spirit world, but Luba traditions clearly portray talented hunters as "big men" of authority in these early days. The first Luba king was Nkongolo, a mythical figure whose name means "rainbow" and who is remembered as a tyrannical and barbaric ruler. Luba society remained in a primitive state during his reign until the arrival of a magical hunter named Mbide Kiluwe, a foreigner who aspired to tutor the king. The two men quarreled, and Mbide Kiluwe departed, but not before he had married and impregnated two sisters of Nkongolo, each of whom bore the hunter sons, named Kalal Ilunga and Kisulu Mabele. Fearing that the son of Mbide Kiluwe would one day unseat him, Nkongolo attempted to kill the young Kalal Ilunga, who escaped to his father's village and later returned with an army to destroy the tyrannical Nkongolo.

This myth of origin appears to echo the important political transformations that took place among the Luba after 1000. The hierarchy of chiefs represented by their artifacts in the Sanga burial grounds indicates that the Luba had coalesced into a unitary state sometime before the fourteenth century. During this early era Luba kings combined existing social institutions with new political concepts to create a dynamic royal institution. Rulers over a relatively large population and wealthy in salt and iron, the Luba kings established a confederation of tributaries who recognized the authority and legitimacy of the dynasty over a wide swath of the eastern savanna. The Luba kings held that the founding myth endowed a member of the royal clan with the right to rule and that the throne could only be occupied by a descendant in the direct male line from Kalal Ilunga. Moreover, since the great ancestor was believed to have been invested with magical powers, Luba monarchs supported their authority to rule by claiming divine right. All male members of the royal family were expected to assist in the administration of the kingdom as subordinate chiefs loyal to their monarch, and his divinity defined his supreme religious role supported by the priests, secret societies, and social organizations that probably pre-dated the rise of the monarchy and were used to check the power of the political chiefs. Despite this hierarchy, cemented by pledges of allegiance to the king, the authority of the myth of origin and the appeals to divine right could not prevent weak or unpopular Luba rulers from being challenged or replaced by more able rivals.

From their homeland near the Upemba Depression, Luba culture and institutions were spread by the trade routes linking the rainforest in the north to the copper belt of the southern savanna. The court grew wealthy from tribute exacted from neighboring peoples who had accepted the authority of the Luba kings. The expansion of Luba power was made possible more by the immense prestige of its ruling dynasty than by its military force, which was never very formidable, but the extent of Luba influence was constrained by the limited size of its population and the difficulties of travel throughout the central savanna. The prestige of the monarch and his ability to exact tribute from his subjects steadily diminished with the distance from the Luba heartland. To sustain their authority and the allegiance of their tributaries, Luba kings used a system of spies, administrators, and military men, as they appear to have been reluctant to use force. They sent warriors more as a last resort than a regular means to collect tribute from recalcitrant villages, but the appearance of these punitive expeditions played an important role in disseminating the ways of the Luba.

The influence of Luba kingship was felt among the Lunda chiefdoms to the southwest. The kingdom of the Lunda first appeared in the Mbuji Mayi River Valley during the seventeenth century. Like those of the Luba, Lunda traditions of origins remember that the arrival of a foreigner inaugurated a new dynasty among a previously divided people, and that the stranger was a Luba hero named Cibunda Ilunga (*c.* 1600–1630) who married the Lunda queen Rweej. Unlike the Luba, whose homeland on the Upemba Depression enjoyed abundant natural resources, the Lunda heartland along the Kasai River possessed few minerals and its soils were relatively impoverished. The Lunda population was not large, and consequently was scattered in relatively small, dispersed chiefdoms. Thus the new Luba interlopers who followed Cibunda Ilunga brought with them not just new institutions of kingship, but the sophisticated material culture of their more prosperous homeland, which facilitated the ultimate acceptance of Luba authority.

Upon his arrival and marriage Cibunda Ilunga created a new royal office, a monarch called the *mwaant yav* ("lord of the vipers"), who like the Luba king could only be succeeded by a member of the male bloodline of the royal couple. The tradition of Cibunda Ilunga and Rweej implies that the first Lunda king was the leader of a Luba military expedition and possibly a member of the Luba ruling clan who would have possessed the immense prestige of his dynasty and the presumption of authority endowed by a member of the Luba royal house. However, no aspiring foreign rulers could simply impose their authority by decree without the assent of the entrenched chiefs who dominated Lunda society. Oral traditions indicate that the establishment of authority by these Luba intruders was a lengthy process over many years. When their rule was finally acknowledged by the Lunda, the success of the *mwaant yav* became dependent upon the support of the pre-dynastic chiefs who as tax collectors and counselors became the backbone of the royal administration. Thus the state evolved into a confederation or commonwealth of chiefdoms paying tribute to the king who redistributed a portion of his treasury to the provincial chiefs in an exchange that was as much an act of trade as royal largess.

An important innovation of the Lunda monarchy was the concept of perpetual kingship by which each new *mwaant yav* was enthroned as the living incarnation of the previous ruler. Every new monarch "became" his successor, thus severing all his existing kinship ties and adopting those of his predecessor to insure continuity from one Lunda ruler to the next and producing a durable and powerful system of administration that easily integrated new political communities. Perpetual kingship enabled the Lunda system to be grafted onto otherwise unrelated polities that facilitated the expansion of the nuclear Lunda state to the west in the valleys of the Kasai and Kwango Rivers and to the south along the upper reaches of the Zambezi. Later Lunda rulers sent military campaigns eastward to the frontiers of the Luba kingdom but never succeeded in conquering the Luba. Lunda expansion was also facilitated by the increase in long-distance trade across the savanna and the establishment of flourishing markets from which the Lunda kings extracted their share of the profits. These trade networks extended all the way to the western African coast, from which new, prolific food crops from the Americas reached the savanna plains of the interior. The most important of these New World crops was cassava or manioc (*Manihot esculenta*), introduced from the Amazon by the Portuguese in the sixteenth century and which flourished in the Lunda heartlands. It proved durable, nutritious, and relatively easy to grow in the marginal soils of the savanna. When ground, its flour could be stored for months without spoiling; it was easily transported, and a valued commodity for exchange in the marketplace that provided another catalyst for Lunda expansion and a significant increase in the population of Central Africa. The demand for and spread of cassava encouraged the creation of plantations to produce cassava for export; this required more intensive cultivation, which in turn produced a need for slave labor.

Like the Luba before them, the Lunda rulers soon learned that distance and the limits of transportation and communication on the savanna placed constraints on royal authority. Throughout a wide swath of the savanna officials of the *mwaant yav* established colonies, conquered states, and encouraged the adoption of Lunda political institutions. Many of these colonies were reluctant tributaries. They particularly resented the royal monopoly over the principal articles of trade, and as their discontent grew over time many attempted to assert their autonomy or establish their independence from the *mwaant yav*. The prosperous kingdom of Kazembe near Lake Tanganyika and far to the east of the Lunda heartland had been founded as a Lunda colony by a general of the *mwaant yav* to become an independent state, which continued to be ruled, however, by Lunda political institutions. The kingdom of Kazembe was not alone. Several other tributary states, including Yaka to the west and Pende to the north, established their autonomy but recognized the *mwaant yav* as suzerain and continued to send him nominal, symbolic tribute. Although the Lunda rulers retained relatively little influence over their satellite states beyond the traditional homeland of the kingdom, the Lunda commonwealth was still acknowledged as the most powerful and prestigious state on the savanna at the end of the eighteenth century.

Perhaps the most remarkable state within the Lunda sphere of influence was the Lozi kingdom far to the south on the flat floodplains of the Western Zambezi Valley. Like the Upemba Depression, the Zambezi floodplain enabled its settlers to fish the river and cultivate the land, but unlike the northern savanna the Zambezi Valley contained pockets of grasslands free of the tsetse fly that permitted the domestication of cattle. The ancestors of the Lozi, known as the Luyi, probably migrated into the region during the seventeenth century. Their cultural and linguistic similarities with the Lunda suggest that they had connections to the Lunda heartland. A version of the Lunda legend of Cibunda Ilunga and Rweej remembers two brothers of the queen who resented the arrival of the Luba and forthwith departed to establish their own kingdoms early in the seventeenth century. One brother, Chinyama, was reputed to have gone south to the Zambezi Valley. Unlike the Luba warriors of Cibunda Ilunga who arrived among the populous Lunda, the followers of Chinyama entered a region that was sparsely populated, and some scholars argue that the uninhabited Zambezi floodplain had recently been a great permanent lake.

Floodplain agriculture offered new challenges and opportunities to these immigrants. The annual inundation flooded virtually the entire plain, necessitating the construction of manmade mounds for villages above the waters. When the waters receded, the inhabitants would plant in the enriched soil. The leaders who built and maintained the raised villages, constructed the dams and weirs for fishing, and mobilized the labor to cultivate and tend the cattle became the rulers of the floodplain. By the end of the seventeenth century several powerful chiefs had consolidated their authority under a leader known as the *litunga* whose preeminent position was acknowledged by his title, "Keeper of the Earth." By the end of the century the Lozi "Keeper of the Earth" had expanded his authority over the chiefs and their people on the floodplain, and his raiding warriors brought tribute to the court. His slaves labored on royal plantations.

Lozi society was sharply stratified. At the apex of the social order was the king, who maintained large plantations and herds of cattle, and controlled the distribution of the important trade goods, such as iron. At the bottom of the social scale were the slaves taken as captives in local wars or given as tribute. In between were the free cultivators and fishermen from whom Lozi officials exacted tribute – foodstuffs from the farmers, fish from those by the waters, and wild game, honey, and iron from the peoples of the woodlands above the plain. Unlike the Lunda and Luba states, which employed their military superiority to expand royal authority and establish colonies, the Lozi kings remained content to confine their administration to the Zambezi floodplain, raiding their neighbors only for slaves and tribute.

Like the Luba and Lunda, Lozi political authority was characterized by new rituals and institutions that developed in response to their ecological circumstances. Lozi kings ruled through an elaborate bureaucracy, and Lozi society was dominated by an aristocratic class that was remarkable for its conspicuous consumption of luxury goods. The authority of the Lozi monarchs over the elements, the economy, and the unity of the nation was demonstrated by an elaborate ceremony that marked the advent of each rainy season. As the floodwaters rose, the king and his court embarked on a giant royal barge, signaling the annual migration to the mounds and highland villages. He returned in a similar ceremony at the onset of the dry season. The ritual was rich with symbolism, as the boat was made from materials gathered throughout the kingdom and rowed by prominent men selected from the many ethnic communities under Lozi domination.

These were the three largest and most influential savanna states before the nineteenth century. They shared a common history as well as an innovative ability to create institutions to meet diverse opportunities and new challenges. The Luba and their successors are remembered because of the scale of their accomplishments. Through trade, migration, and warfare they spread ideas, goods, and peoples throughout a wide area of the central savanna lands the size of Western Europe. Their traditions and legends tend to dominate the record of pre-colonial Central Africa, but their history is not the complete story of life on the savanna before the coming of the Europeans. Many lesser states and discreet communities established their own identities among the interstices of these great kingdoms and empires, while others lived along the margins of these centralized polities, experiencing little or no influence from their more powerful neighbors.

West Central Africa

North and west of the Lunda diaspora, in a region bordered by the equatorial rainforest to the north and the Atlantic coast on the west, several states evolved with histories similar to those found on the eastern savanna. One of these states, the kingdom of Kongo, was the best known and the most powerful kingdom in Central Africa at the time the first Portuguese mariners made landfall in the 1480s on the western African coast. South of Kongo the coastal state of Ndongo was ruled by the *ngola*, whose name is remembered by the modern state of Angola. In the northeast on the edge of the rainforest the Kuba kingdom carried on vigorous trade and accumulated considerable wealth that enabled its artists to create their renowned sculptures. These Central West African kingdoms, as well as several similar if lesser-known states, developed unique institutions and ideologies in response to the opportunities and constraints offered by their northern savanna and forest environments.

As on the eastern central savanna, West Central Africa consists of enclaves of moist fertility in a relatively dry and barren plain. This region was bounded on the north by the great Congo River whose tributaries, themselves mighty rivers, fan out to the north, east, and south and whose navigable waterways were the great highways for trade and migration, filled with fish, whose fertile valleys produced abundant crops for farmers. North of the Congo the high plateau gives way to the fringes of the equatorial rainforest. South of the river the terrain divides into three zones that run along a north–south axis. In the far west the Atlantic coast is a flat, arid plain. To the east the land rises to a wooded interior plateau. Beyond the highlands lie a higher, more arid plain and the beginning of the Central African savanna. The soils of coast and savanna are particularly poor, and for the most part unsuitable for agriculture. However, the plateau and highlands that separate coastal plain from savanna are well watered and fertile. The ecological diversity of these regions stimulated economic specialization, and the ease of travel and the transport of goods on the many rivers facilitated local and long-distance trade.

The evolution of complex, stratified societies was, as on the savanna, the result of population growth, technological innovation, and economic specialization. The crucial event in the region was the agricultural revolution introduced throughout Central Africa by Bantu-speaking farmers who arrived in the area sometime during the first millennium BCE. These early farmers cultivated root crops, such as yams, and other forest crops, such as palm kernels, without the benefit of iron metallurgy. They were soon joined in the region by immigrants from the east who were also members of the Bantu diaspora. These distant eastern cousins brought with them cereal crops, bananas, and in some places cattle obtained in eastern Africa that could thrive in the drier regions of the southern plateau.

Like the Bantu speakers on the savannas to the east, the first wave of migrants in West Central Africa settled in those fertile areas most suited to cultivation. Others established themselves on the Atlantic shore where prolific fishing in the ocean and Congo estuary compensated for the arid conditions of the coastal plain. Later these fishing communities extracted salt from seawater and briny marshes; this was much in demand, and could be profitably traded for foodstuffs cultivated by the farmers of the interior. In the south near the modern island of Luanda divers collected the valued *nzimbu* shells (cowries) that became the common currency throughout the region. In the interior the farmers, who settled on the plateau, in forests, or in fertile river valleys with dependable rainfall, were often separated from one another by large tracts of dry and inhospitable terrain where the hunters and gatherers displaced by the Bantu-speaking cultivators still lived. These early settlements of Bantu-speaking peoples were small, isolated communities growing foodstuffs, but as the immigrants adapted to their new environments by utilizing the crops and possessing the iron tools they brought with them, the population increased, the settlements grew larger, and their societies required more complex political organizations in order to take full advantage of their prosperity. The history of these Bantu speakers in West Central Africa before the arrival of the Portuguese in 1483 must be reconstructed largely through the study of oral traditions and historical linguistics. There has been little archaeological research in the region, so our knowledge of its past is more speculative than solid.

When the Portuguese first arrived at the mouth of the Congo in 1483, the population of the kingdom of the Kongo numbered more than half a million Africans, and the authority of its king, the *mani kongo*, was recognized two hundred miles into the interior from the Atlantic shore. The origins of the Kongo kingdom are situated in a small, environmentally attractive niche north of the Congo River called Vungu. Here peoples who shared a common language (Kikongo) and a similar culture raised vegetables, yams, and bananas. The Kongo heartland contained deposits of high-grade iron ore and copper, a rare metal in great demand for making jewelry. The early leaders of the Kongo communities were master smiths. As on the savanna to the east, iron-working produced a technological revolution among the farmers of West Central Africa. Those who mastered the secrets of its manufacture could exercise control over weapons, tools, and ornaments, which were the principal source of power and wealth among these farming and fishing communities. Traders exchanged the iron of Vungu throughout the region for salt, fish, cloth made from raffia palm, and other goods peculiar to the diverse regions of a growing trade network. One of the traditions of origin claims that the first rulers of the Kongo crossed the River Congo, where they came in contact with Mbundu peoples settled on the interior plateau of modern Angola. Here these Kikongo-speaking immigrants gained a position of influence among the Mbundu lineages – perhaps by intermarriage, possibly through conquest. By their mastery of iron-smelting and their control of the copper trade, the Kongo immigrants attracted merchants and supporters to their town of Mbanza Kongo and firmly established themselves as the dominant political and commercial people throughout the region.

The evolution of the Kongo monarchy began with the need for a paramount chief who could provide protection for the mining, manufacture, and trade of copper and iron goods and to keep the peace among the several powerful lineages that controlled them. The new ruler took the title of *mani kongo* ("governor of the Kongo"), and established his dynasty surrounded by an extensive royal family from whom were chosen the key officials to the royal court. The founding of the kingdom probably dates to the early fifteenth century, for when the Portuguese first arrived in 1483, the traditions of the Kongo had recognized only a few *mani kongo*s. The capital, Mbanza Kongo, was dominated by an aristocracy related and presumably loyal to the *mani kongo*, from whom were selected those nobles ordered to conquer the hinterland. In the name of the king they seized control of the fishing, salt, and seashell industries on the coast and brought the farming and fishing communities in the mountains to the north and east under his rule. They became provincial governors and exacted tribute from the subject peoples, retaining a percentage for themselves, and passing along a substantial share to the *mani kongo* and his royal court at Mbanza Kongo. In order to increase their own wealth and power these provincial leaders consequently had every incentive to expand and conquer neighboring peoples on behalf of the *mani kongo*. Since these governors raised their own armies and arranged their own tribute, they exercised a significant degree of autonomy from their ruler at Mbanza Kongo, but when the Portuguese first arrived the *mani kongo* was widely recognized as the supreme ruler over a vast territory stretching from the Atlantic Ocean several hundred miles into the interior. Although the kingdom was sharply divided between the nobility, free men, and slaves, its strength resided in the free farmers and merchants and declined when the expansion of the slave trade turned free farmers into slaves or owners of slaves.

South of the kingdom of Kongo Mbundu farmers developed their own state, which came to be called Ndongo. Here in the central Angolan highlands several clans came to be recognized as the first and therefore rightful custodians of the lands. These farmers experienced recurrent drought on the plateau, and consequently priests responsible in their shrines for the falling rain and abundant fertility shaped the evolution of political institutions. In many places the invocations of the priests were represented by carved objects called *lunga*. The symbolism of the *lunga* defined a spiritual and political identity that was connected to a fixed territory, such as a riverbed or an outcrop. The custodians of the *lunga* shrines, which were usually situated in the most fertile and well-watered lands, could employ their religious authority to acquire political power by demanding tribute, tax, and support from their religious followers. Early Mbundu political rulers were religious leaders who controlled the regimen of the agricultural season and received their resources from its harvest. The religious monopoly of authority by the priests was challenged by the ironsmiths and their masters who arrived among the Mbundu from the north. These were the same craftsmen whose secret societies enabled them to produce and share technologies that dramatically changed the waging of war and the cultivation of the soil. Their authority was represented by iron regalia called *ngola*. Unlike the *lunga*, the *ngola* were mobile, for they had no shrines, only transportable iron-smelting furnaces. Their secretive powers produced tangible results that challenged the local, sedentary religious authority of the old order. Eventually the prestige of these master smiths came to supersede that of the original *lunga*-based clans, and their chief smith took the name *ngola a kiluanje*, the conquering *ngola*, which the Portuguese transcribed as Angola.

West of Kongo on the fringe of the equatorial rainforest another centralized state emerged among the Kuba. The Kuba homeland lay between the Sankuru and Kasai Rivers, parallel tributaries of the Congo that rise south of the great river. The origins of the Kuba kingdom lie with the Mongo-speaking peoples who drifted from the rainforest southward into the borderlands of the savanna. On this fringe these immigrants encountered an ethnically diverse collection of peoples, the dominant community among them being the Bushong, a Mongo settlement along the River Sankuru. How these diverse peoples became welded into a state remains unclear. Kuba traditions remember the influence of a great leader named Shyam who led a party of adventurers into the region from the west. The arrival of Shyam is associated with the adaptation of New World crops, particularly maize and cassava, that had arrived from the coast with Portuguese traders in the early seventeenth century. Although the role of Shyam in the consolidation and expansion of the Kuba remains an enigma, his successors during the seventeenth and eighteenth centuries ruled over a growing population of farmers, traders, and warriors. The wealth of Kuba that flowed from the trade and industry of the growing agricultural population sustained one of the most creative artistic traditions in Central Africa. It supported commercial and aristocratic classes that identified themselves through the patronage and consumption of locally produced art. Kuba wooden sculpture in particular demonstrated a remarkable degree of refinement and sophistication.

All of these states of eastern and western Central Africa were roughly contemporaries of one another, and their borders and the extent of their influence inevitably overlapped and often conflicted. It is tempting to identify in

Figure 10.1 *Chokwe chair. Chokwe carvings became popular throughout the Central African savanna during the nineteenth century. The carvings on the throne reflect the power and responsibility of the ruler.*

Figure 10.2 *Chokwe carvers. Angola, 1930s.*

the simultaneous emergence of these kingdoms a significant degree of cross-fertilization of political institutions and traditions. Certainly oral traditions attest to the importance of immigrants and heroic foreigners in the origins of many of these kingdoms. However, the evolution of the states of West Central Africa is more appropriately understood as a response to the settlement, expansion, and economic specialization of the diverse communities of the region. The vast Congo and its tributaries provided a highway for the movements of peoples, goods, and ideas throughout much of the region. As migrants came to master the varied environments of the region they created more politically sophisticated communities. The complexity of the states and trade networks that existed by the end of the fifteenth century is one of the principal topics

Box 10.1 Art and history on the Central African savanna

Western views of African art have been transformed since the nineteenth century. Initially European intellectuals dismissed African arts as "primitive," and deemed them unworthy of serious study. Such attitudes began to change after the British invasion of the West African kingdom of Benin in 1897, during which the looting of the *oba*'s palace resulted in a trove of brass statuary being sent to London, where it sparked the interest of collectors. Three years later an exhibit in Paris of sculpture from Central Africa caught the attention of the artists Matisse and Picasso, who found inspiration in the "primitive" images.

In the ensuing decades African art objects collected by colonial officials, merchants, and missionaries found their way into some of the world's most prestigious museums and private collections. Today the art of the Central African savanna ranks among the most collectible "tribal" art in the world, with auction houses regularly selling masks, stools, staffs, and figurines produced by savanna peoples for tens of thousands of dollars.

But beyond its aesthetic value, the art of the savanna sheds light on important developments in the region's history. In some cases shared techniques and motifs hint at ancient and enduring connections between the Bantu-speaking peoples of the savanna. In others they reflect more recent borrowings inspired by the expanding commerce and political consolidation that accompanied the advent of ocean-borne trade from the Atlantic coast. Artistically, the era of the trans-Atlantic trade was a dynamic period on the savanna. Foreign trade expanded local trading networks, encouraged internal migrations, and in many places encouraged social stratification. New elites grew wealthy by adapting the nutritious new crops from the Americas, and from the rapid expansion of commerce. Many used their newfound wealth to patronize artists whose creations would demonstrate and memorialize their elevated status. Wood sculpture, which had traditionally been a democratic form of artistic expression, came to be increasingly produced by specialists who worked for wealthy patrons.

The link between art and elites on the savanna pre-dates the rise of the Atlantic trade. One widespread Central African motif is the decorative iron ax, which is associated with the early Luba kings. To Luba artists, and to peoples desiring to associate themselves with the prestige of Luba traditions, the iron ax harked back to the first Luba rulers, who possessed the magical secrets of iron-working. Luba political influence was widely felt throughout the region, and art that underscored Luba legitimacy was widely emulated. Though Luba artists themselves rarely worked in sculpture, artists throughout the region made the great Luba hero Cibunda Ilunga a favorite motif.

Box 10.1 (continued)

One community that adopted Luba symbolism in their art was the Chokwe of Angola, who would become among Central Africa's most accomplished artists. Their art reflects a long period of contact with Luba and Lunda rulers, and Chokwe artists helped popularize the Cibunda Ilungu motif. When Chokwe chiefs came out from under Lunda dominance in the early nineteenth century their merchants extended their trading networks toward the east, where their artistic traditions flourished. The wealth and sophistication of Chokwe traders impressed elites among the Luluwa, of the modern Democratic Republic of Congo, who began trading for, and copying art in the Chokwe style. Chokwe art was also influenced by contact with European merchants from the coast. During the nineteenth century copies of European chairs – like the one pictured on page 154 – were a popular carving produced for Chokwe chiefs. They represented a kind of furniture not widely used in Africa (carved stools are more common). Unlike its European models, the Chokwe chair was carved from a single piece of wood. Chokwe artists earned a reputation for their sculpture, which attracted patrons from Lunda elites, and became valued items of trade.

North of the Chokwe, the emergence of the Kuba state encouraged royal patronage of an array of artists and artistic forms. Sculptures of Kuba kings were commissioned to preserve their likeness for posterity, in special carved likenesses called *ndop*. Each Kuba monarch retained the royal *ndop*s of his predecessors, while commissioning the carving of his own likeness to be added to the collection. Kuba rulers also commissioned an array of other artistic objects commemorating the founding hero, King Shyam. The elevation of the Kuba rulers from chiefs to kings also entailed new rituals and ceremonies that required masks and elaborate costumes reflecting the majesty of the ruler and the wealth of his kingdom. Kuba artisans and craftsmen were also kept busy by aristocrats eager to emphasize their own elevated social status through art.

Today most major museums contain art from the savanna. Yet far from being examples of a "primitive" culture – as early Europeans would have it – most are the work of master artisans and craftsmen, who were working – as great artists have throughout history – at the behest of wealthy patrons who sought to use art for their own personal glorification.

recorded by the early Portuguese traders. Kongo and Angola attracted European merchants because they had the political authority to protect commerce, and the commercial connections that enabled the Europeans to purchase the human and material commodities of Africa from regions hundreds of miles in the interior of this vast continent.

11 The peoples and states of southern Africa

Southern Africa is a geographical region of high savanna, the *veld* (Afrikaans, "field"), mountains, and narrow coastal plain severed by short rivers lying south of the Zambezi River and comprising the modern states of Namibia, Zimbabwe, Mozambique, Botswana, Swaziland, and the Republic of South Africa, which surrounds the independent kingdom of Lesotho. Although Europeans had established stations along the coast in the sixteenth and seventeenth centuries, particularly the strategic Dutch colonial station at Cape Town near the southernmost point of the continent, they knew little of the interior of southern Africa until the latter half of the nineteenth century. However, though it is relatively new to Europeans, it is in fact geologically the oldest region of the African continent. Rocks formed more than a thousand million years ago still lie in their horizontal plane, untouched by the upheavals that have elsewhere shaped the configuration of the global landmass. Here in southern Africa protruding upward from the molten core of the earth is the massive plug of rock called the Kaapvaal Craton, which resisted the geologic turbulence that floated the other continents away to their present locations. When the African continent became stabilized about 500 million years ago, the Kaapvaal Craton, 234,000 square miles of southern Africa, remained undisturbed, along with its prodigious mineral wealth.

Geography and climate have had a profound influence over the human experience in southern Africa. The highveld is a plateau of 3,000 to 5,000 feet that rises to a chain of mountains with various names, but the entire range is called the Great Escarpment, separating the interior plateau from the coastal plain of the eastern African coast. This unbroken procession of ridges reaches its height in the peaks of the Drakensberg Mountains (9,000 to 11,000 feet). The fertile coastal belt between the Great Escarpment and the Indian Ocean sweeps around southern Africa, ranging from 30 to 150 miles – where it is commonly known as the lowveld – as the mountain ridges, now no more than 3,000 feet above sea level, merge with the interior plateau. The rolling grasslands of the highveld are broken by isolated outcrops (*kopjes*), and rocky ridges such as the Witwatersrand that are watersheds for the rivers of the plateau and the repositories of gold and precious stones. The vast grassland plateau slopes gently to the west, becoming ever more dry where it turns into the scrublands of the Great Karoo and ultimately into the sands of the Kalahari Desert. The gradual desiccation of the southern African landscape from east to west is interrupted by the microclimate of the Cape of Good Hope. Lying in the extreme southwestern corner of the continent, the Western Cape owes its unique Mediterranean climate to cold winds and rain from the Antarctic. Unlike the rest of southern Africa, the Cape receives its rain in winter (June to August), thereby permitting the cultivation of crops that cannot be grown in the summer-rainfall regions (November to April) to the north.

Rainfall and water have determined life in southern Africa since the first hominoids began to roam its savanna grasslands. The coastal plain and interior highlands get rain from the annual monsoon that blows in from the Indian Ocean each November. As the rainclouds move westward across the plain, they rise to meet the ridges of the Great Escarpment and the peaks of the Drakensberg Mountains, forming a rain-shadow that creates an increasingly arid expanse as the carrying capacity of the moisture-laden Indian Ocean cumulus steadily diminishes on their westward course over the Karoo, to die in the Kalahari. The highveld suffers from frequent droughts, and the traditional Sotho greeting "Pula" ("rain") reflects the importance of water for the peoples of the highland plateau and the rivers that flow through it, such as the majestic Zambezi and Limpopo Rivers, which flow from the interior plateau into the Indian Ocean. In the western watershed of the highveld the Vaal, the Caledon, and the Orange (Gariep) Rivers rise to fan out across the plateau and enter the Atlantic Ocean. The rivers of the coastal plain are short, unnavigable, and, like the Tugela and Great Fish Rivers, historical boundaries.

The unpredictability of the southern African climate encouraged its peoples to experiment with a wide variety of economic activities, including hunting and gathering, fishing, and, where possible, agriculture and herding. The first humans were hunter-gatherers, who left behind their stone tools, which can be found throughout southern Africa. The earliest inhabitants of the Western Cape were the ancestors of the modern San people (often still called "Bushmen"), some of whom still eke out a living as hunter-gatherers in the arid regions in and around the Kalahari Desert. These people spoke languages related to the Khoisan family of languages, which are characterized by the click sound of some of their consonants. Although the "click languages" were once spoken widely throughout the continent, there are today fewer than 130,000 Khoisan speakers, who live on the margins of southern African arid lands. These early communities were small, usually no more than fifty members, in bands spread out over large tracts of savanna and scrub. Their mobile lifestyle discouraged the development of a sophisticated material culture. They did not produce pottery. Most of their tools were made of bone and wood, and provide few clues to understand a culture whose members produced striking images painted in their many rock shelters in Botswana, South Africa, and Zimbabwe.

Sometime around 2,000 years ago groups of hunter-gatherers in the dry grasslands of modern Botswana acquired domestic cattle and sheep from people living farther to the north, which were milked and bred rather than eaten and consequently came to dominate the economic and social lives of these pastoral communities. Cattle provided a portable source of nutrition, turning otherwise infertile grasslands into sources of milk and meat that required protection and tending for their herds. Although much of their energies were spent searching for grass and water, those members of the community not immediately involved in caring for the cattle established more permanent settlements.

Livestock provided a new form of transferable wealth that could be exchanged, invested, and inherited. Men rich in cattle could enjoy an elevated social status that was unattainable in the more egalitarian hunter-gatherer bands. By sharing cattle in exchange for support and services successful herders could build a personal and loyal following. Thus cattle-keeping encouraged the creation of larger and more complex communities. Among these early pastoral groups individuals wealthy in cattle became "big men," the chiefs who assumed or were acknowledged by their contemporaries as having the authority to organize the cattle, decide disputes, and divine religious responsibilities on behalf of the community. The office of chief usually belonged to a man from a prosperous family that became even wealthier through the payments exacted from his followers in return for decisions, justice, and religious revelation. However, cattle could be a precarious source of wealth and authority, as their mobility left aspirant "big men" dependent on the consent of their followers. Discontented supporters could take their mobile assets and abandon an incompetent or unpopular leader, and ally themselves with a neighboring chief or begin a new community.

From their original home on the grassy highlands of modern Botswana, these early pastoralists in their endless search for fresh grass and a reliable source of water made their way south into the fertile river valleys of the Cape. They also pastured their cattle and sheep on the dry scrublands of the Great Karoo and the periphery of the Kalahari Desert. These herders have come to be called Khoikhoi, a name derived from the Khoisan word meaning "men of men." The original Khoikhoi communities did not produce their own iron tools and weapons, but obtained iron as well as copper in trade with Bantu-speaking neighbors in return for livestock. The manner by which the Khoikhoi came to distinguish themselves from other hunter-gatherers remains obscure, but when the first Europeans settlers arrived at the Cape during the seventeenth century they identified two distinct communities: the hunter-gatherers (the San), whom they called "Bushmen," and the Khoikhoi, whom they called "Hottentots." Today both terms are considered pejorative, and scholars – if not the general public – have replaced them with the more accurate and less demeaning linguistic terms "San" and "Khoikhoi." There are those today who prefer to distinguish between Bushmen and Hottentot by their distinctive physical differences. The Khoikhoi pastoralists tend to be taller on average than San hunter-gatherers, but these physical differences are more likely to be the result of the high-protein diet of pastoral people over many centuries. Contemporary genetic studies have conclusively demonstrated that all of the groups living in southern Africa by 1000 CE were genetically closely related despite some distinctive physical differences.

About 300 CE new communities appeared on the fertile eastern coast of southern Africa, separated from the Cape by hundreds of miles of semi-arid grasslands and deserts. These Africans, unlike the Khoisan people, made their own iron tools and weapons. They lived in settled agricultural settlements where they grew a variety of food crops, including sorghum, beans, millet, and cowpeas, but they also raised goats, sheep, and cattle. These agropastoralists also hunted, gathered, and fished in order to supplement their diet and livelihood. This successful combination of iron technology with several food-producing strategies enabled these farmer-herdsmen to expand more rapidly than the strictly pastoral Khoikhoi or the rigidly hunter-gathering San.

These agro-pastoralist immigrants appear to have been culturally related to the Bantu-speaking peoples of the Great Lakes region of East Africa, whose pottery not only distinctly resembles the ceramics of eastern Africa but the spread of its unique shape and designs can be traced along several routes from the highlands of East Africa to the cultivations and pastures of southern Africa. These early farmers spoke languages that have their roots in the Bantu languages spoken on the East African Lake Plateau and are collectively known as the Southeastern Bantu subfamily of the Benue-Congo branch of the greater Niger-Congo family. Linguists divide this subfamily into three main groups: the Nguni languages, spoken widely today from the eastern coast to the Drakensberg Mountains, which include isiZulu, isiXhosa, Siswati, and isiNdebele; the Shona languages, consisting of Chishona and Venda, both spoken north of the Limpopo River; and Sotho-Tswana, which remains the dominant language west of the Drakensberg and includes Sesotho and Setswana. Traditionally, the diffusion of this iron-age, agro-pastoral culture has been known as the "Bantu migration." There can be no doubt that there did occur a steady movement of these Bantu-speaking agro-pastoralists who introduced new and encompassing linguistic, social, economic, technological, and cultural features into southern Africa, but the subsequent domination of the Bantu speakers has often obscured the relationship and interdependence between Bantu and Khoisan, by which there was a constant exchange of customs, goods, and people from each culture.

These iron-using, Bantu-speaking farmers first trickled into the savanna lands south of the Limpopo Valley, the northern border of modern South Africa, around 200 CE, reached the eastern coast in Natal a hundred years later, and then moved onto the highveld of the Transvaal by 400. Until about 1000 they lived in sparsely settled villages, usually located in the fertile river valleys of the eastern coast, where they had access to wood for iron-smelting, fertile soil for their crops, and green pastures for their herds. Their populations on the coastal plain gradually expanded, forcing them to seek open space on the more arid grasslands west of the Great Escarpment. Although the highveld was ill-suited to intensive cultivation, it was ideal for extensive pastoralism. Indeed, the settlers coming over the escarpment from the well-watered pastures and forests of the coast and across the Limpopo from the northern savanna had stumbled upon a vast, undulating plateau whose temperate climate and sparse mobile population of hunter-gatherers was ideally suited to raise large herds of cattle and great flocks of sheep for milk, meat, and clothing, and could sustain large settlements.

The success and growing dependence of these Bantu-speaking agro-pastoralists on cattle encouraged important changes within their communities. Between 700 and 1200 their settlement sites became ever more crowded as people packed together to protect their cattle from predators. Some of these cattlemen cultivators moved away from the richest farmlands to less attractive – even stony – hilltop settlements better situated for defense and keeping watch over their herds. This explosion in cattle-keeping decisively changed almost every aspects of their social and cultural life. As caring for the cattle became the responsibility solely of men, women were expected to undertake the more arduous task of raising crops in addition to their maternal and domestic duties. Cattle became the standard of wealth, and consequently the only acceptable currency by which a man could purchase wives. Men rich in cattle were there-fore able to establish large families, social standing in the community, and political authority over those less well endowed. They were able to lend cattle from their large herds to younger, poorer men in exchange for support and services. Ownership of cattle encouraged the emergence of paternalistic, socially stratified communities in which labor and authority were severely divided between men and women and between those who were rich in cattle and those who were not.

As the agro-pastoralist way of life expanded south and west across the highveld, the farmers and herdsmen came into contact with the indigenous hunter-gatherers. Relations between these two distinct communities were com-plicated and varied over time, but generally the relationship appears to have been more symbiotic than hostile, as farmer-herders exchanged iron, pottery, crops, and cattle for wild game, fruits, berries, honey, and the lore of plant life for medicinal and spiritual purposes of which the hunter-gatherers were the acknowledged masters. Wealthy Bantu-speaking men often purchased San wives with cattle, and the presence of "click" words in some of the southern Bantu languages, such as isiXhosa, demonstrates the particularly close rela-tionships of some agro-pastoral communities with the San. By 1000 many of these communities had become involved in inter-regional and long-distance trade. Regional trade goods included ivory, foodstuffs, and livestock, and long-distance trade in copper and gold from as far away as the lands north of the Limpopo, Zambezi, and the Congo connected the highveld and coast of eastern southern Africa with the far interior.

These stratified communities were scattered all over southern Africa after 1000. By 900 a settlement located in the Toutswemogola region of Botswana

Map 11.1 *Great Zimbabwe and neighboring states.*

on the edge of the Kalahari Desert numbered over one thousand inhabitants. On a small hill overlooking the highveld, the Toutswe herders could tend their cattle and watch for thieves and predators. Although Toutswemogola was abandoned in the thirteenth century, it had exchanged goods for over a century with a similar settlement to the east at Mapungubwe Hill. Here, near the confluence of the Limpopo and Shashi Rivers, the nearby settlement of Bambandyanalo, founded sometime around 1000, was abandoned at the beginning of the thirteenth century in favor of the high, steep-sided sandstone hill of Mapungubwe. As early as the eleventh century cultivations and cattle occupied the fertile fields below the hill, and by the twelfth century the summit had been settled. Unlike the more arid climate around Toutswemogola, suitable only for grazing and marginal agriculture, the valley of the Limpopo possessed rich, well-watered alluvial soils that permitted both abundant cultivations and the raising of livestock. The craftsmen of Mapungubwe produced pottery, ivory and bone carvings, and its smiths iron tools and weapons. By 1200 its merchants were sending gold and ivory to the coastal towns in exchange for the glass beads, porcelain, and cloth of the Indian Ocean trade. Gold was melted and poured into molds to make jewelry and ornamentation for the elites, including a small golden rhinoceros dated to the thirteenth century, the earliest evidence of gold working in southern Africa.

The long-distance trade introduced the elites in settlements such as Toutswe-mogola and Mapungubwe to previously unknown luxury wares such as beads and porcelain that accentuated disparities of wealth. Those elites who owned and controlled the distribution of these new riches were able to establish their authority over their followers to an unprecedented degree. Although cattle and crops remained the fundamental resources of the community, most men could raise several cattle and grow sufficient sorghum and millet to sustain their families and even have a surplus, but the wealth in foreign trade goods was easily monopolized by the few who used their new power to wield political authority. Trade – and particularly the long-distance trade – made possible the development of a powerful, centralized polity dominated by an elite ruling class, whose authority over their more numerous followers grazing their herds and tilling the soil at the base of the hill was symbolized by the elaborate stone structures on the summit.

At the end of the thirteenth century Mapungubwe collapsed. Its decline coincided with the rise of the Zimbabwe state to the north, with its capital at Great Zimbabwe (Cishona, *dzimba dza mabwe*, "houses of stone") on the southern edge of the Zimbabwe Plateau. The rise of Zimbabwe has been attributed to its abundance of gold, which enabled Great Zimbabwe to seize control of the Indian Ocean trade and the wealth and political authority it produced. The ivory of Mapungubwe could no longer compete with the gold of Zimbabwe in the international markets on the coast, and never recovered from its loss. The original inhabitants of Great Zimbabwe practiced the mixed economy of agriculture and pastoralism that characterized most of the communities throughout southern Africa. Zimbabwe as a state emerged from its settled agro-pastoralist communities during the thirteenth century, with its center at Great Zimbabwe on a hill rising 260 feet above the plain. The southeastern region of the Zimbabwe Plateau was well watered, with fertile soil for cultivation and ample pastureland for cattle, free of the tsetse fly. Located near the Sabi River, Great Zimbabwe was situated on an important trade route linking the goldfields of the interior with the important East African coastal emporium of Kilwa. Its inhabitants became wealthy in cattle and gold and built an empire that came to dominate the Zimbabwean Plateau for two hundred years. By the twelfth century Great Zimbabwe was trading gold and ivory in exchange for a variety of exotic wares from the coast, including Chinese porcelains and beads from India. Control of these scarce goods enabled the elite to amass wealth,

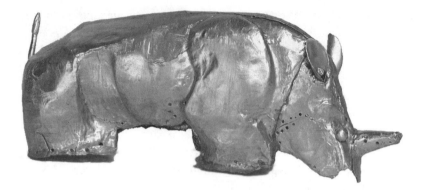

Figure 11.1 *Golden rhino discovered at Mapungubwe, on the north bank of the Limpopo River. This thirteenth-century carving was originally done in wood, and covered in gold foil.*

authority, and to develop a political system that could mobilize the human and material resources of the state to construct the magnificent stone structures that are the monuments of this civilization.

Great Zimbabwe occupies 180 acres, the core of which is a hilltop structure known as the Acropolis, a large area enclosed by massive stone walls to the south called the Great Enclosure, and a network of settlements adjacent to and outside the walls. The inhabitants on the hill only began building in stone about the middle of the twelfth century; this coincided with the expansion of trade with the coast and continued for 200 years during the height of prosperity and power of Great Zimbabwe. The complex of stone walls, for which Great Zimbabwe is famous, was erected on earthen or stone foundations, upon which were raised the walls of the Great Enclosure, 830 feet in circumference, 30 feet high, and in places over 4 feet thick, with other walls inside and a conical tower. All the walls were of similar construction. The stones themselves were so finely dressed they could be abutted firmly against one another to give structural stability without being cemented by mortar. In the valley below there are numerous stone enclosures, outside which there are the remains of many more humble dwellings that could support a population of between 11,000 and 18,000 people, making it the most densely settled town in pre-colonial southern Africa.

Since these intimidating walls clearly served no military function, their construction must reflect the desire of the ruling class to erect an edifice that symbolized their authority and prestige and the mighty, sacred power of their ruler. The walls were constructed to shelter the elite in spacious living quarters, surrounded by foreign luxury goods, and consuming prodigious amounts of beef. Even more important, however, they demonstrated the exclusive social status of those who lived within them. In the Eastern Enclosure on the hilltop was the meeting place of an exclusive cult presided over by the stunning

Box 11.1 The "lost city" of Great Zimbabwe

When the German explorer Karl Mauch stumbled on the remains of Great Zimbabwe in 1871 he was astounded to find stone ruins unlike anything he had encountered in his travels in Africa. Mauch was the first of many Europeans to assume that they had been built by foreigners. Such structures were, he believed, unknown in sub-Saharan Africa. He attributed their construction to Sabaeans from Yemen, a civilization that was linked in the Bible to the fabled Queen of Sheba.

Mauch initiated a mythology about the ruins that would survive for more than a century. Stories of an abandoned stone city fueled the fervid imagination of Victorian writers, who saw in them the basis for ancient legends about lost civilizations in the interior of Africa. The English writer H. Rider Haggard (who had lived in South Africa not long after Mauch's discovery) capitalized on the myth of the lost civilization of Zimbabwe in 1886 in his best-selling adventure story *King Solomon's Mines*, which tells the story of a group of European explorers who come across the remains of the Queen of Sheba's lost diamond mines in Central Africa.

In 1890 much of Central Africa north of the Zambezi River was claimed by Cecil Rhodes' British South Africa Company. Rhodes took a personal interest in popularizing the antiquity and exoticism of the ruins. He supported research into the history of the site and initiated its first archaeological investigation. "Rhodes recognized the considerable propaganda value that evidence of ancient foreign settlement, preferably white and successful with Biblical origins, would have. It would give a precedent and respectability to the conquest and a promise of similar prosperity to the settlers and investors in the new colony."[1]

Unfortunately for Rhodes, academic archaeologists soon began to poke holes in his "lost civilization." The first professional archaeologist to examine Great Zimbabwe was David Randall-MacIver, who had trained with the eminent Egyptologist Sir Flinders Petrie in the Nile Valley. His survey of the site, published in 1902, concluded that there was no evidence to suggest that Great Zimbabwe had been built by anyone other than the local Shona peoples. The next archaeological survey of the site was conducted in 1929 by the Englishwoman Gertrude Caton-Thompson, who had also trained with Flinders Petrie in Egypt. Caton-Thompson likewise dated the ruins to the medieval era, and pronounced them of "Bantu origin."

Such conclusions should not have been surprising to any academically trained archaeologist. The site was clearly not old enough to have any connection to events described in the Hebrew Bible, a fact that was confirmed in the 1940s with the advent of carbon dating. Nor was

[1] P. S. Garlake, "Prehistory and Ideology in Zimbabwe," *Africa* 52, 3 (1982), p. 1.

Box 11.1 (continued)

there any material evidence of extensive occupation by foreign peoples. The building materials, layout, and symbolism of the ruins all pointed to a connection with the local Shona people.

However, these conclusions were abhorrent to the white settler community in Southern Rhodesia, which shared their founder's desire to believe that an ancient "white" race had preceded them into Central Africa. To this minority community, the recognition that Rhodesia had once been the site of a sophisticated commercial kingdom threatened their claims of cultural and racial superiority. Thus, long after the academic establishment outside the country had accepted the indigenous origins of the site, the Southern Rhodesian government continued to insist, in films, books, and even in the visitors' guide sold at the park, that Great Zimbabwe was built by foreigners. It was not until majority rule came in 1980 that the indigenous roots of this civilization were officially recognized in the new nation, aptly named Zimbabwe.

Zimbabwe birds carved in soapstone. In the valley below lived the more modest members of society, huddled in densely packed settlements far removed from the elite lifestyle of their social superiors and the sacred and secular power of their rulers.

Great Zimbabwe was not an isolated city-state, but the center of an expansive economic and political network of lesser enclosures on the Zimbabwe Plateau that constituted the core of this empire that stretched east towards the coast and south across the Limpopo. The inhabitants of over 300 of these walled enclosures similar in architecture and construction owed their allegiance to Great Zimbabwe, and some of them appear to have been provincial administrative and commercial towns of the state. Although the first Europeans to stumble upon Great Zimbabwe refused to believe that these imposing stone ruins were built by Africans – attributing their origins to a variety of exotic sources, including Phoenicians, Greeks, and even extra-terrestrials – archaeologists have clearly demonstrated that the ruins were constructed by Bantu-speaking agro-pastoralists working in iron, copper, and bronze, and bear unmistakable similarities to the material culture of the Shona people who live in the region today.

This confusion was undoubtedly inspired by nineteenth-century European racism, but also by the fact that Great Zimbabwe had been long deserted when the first Europeans arrived in the region. Between 1420 and 1450 the ruling class had lost control of the coastal trade upon which they depended for their lifestyle and their monuments. When the Portuguese established trading stations in the Zambezi Valley to the north in the fifteenth century, they diverted the flow of gold and goods from Great Zimbabwe, precipitating the political

Figure 11.2 *The tower at Great Zimbabwe.*

fragmentation of the state. The demise of Great Zimbabwe, however, cannot be attributed solely to its economic and political disintegration, as there had been a steady environmental degradation by deforestation, soil erosion, and overgrazing by its citizens.

One of these provincial communities was the Mutapa state (*c.* 1450–1760) on the northern edge of the Zimbabwe Plateau in the fertile Mazoe Valley. Here on the slopes of Mount Fura (5,000 feet) the inhabitants built circular stone enclosures of rough walls with loopholes, in contrast to the more stylized stonework of Great Zimbabwe. According to tradition an emissary from Great Zimbabwe named Nyatsimbe Mutota appeared in the early fifteenth century and founded a new kingdom. His successors took the title *munhumutapa* (Cishona, "ravager of the lands"), who lived with his extended family, advisers, and religious and military functionaries and ruled over his provincial chiefs, whom the Portuguese called governors. The *munhumutapa* received his revenue from the coastal trade, agriculture, pastoralism, and mining, which were the economic foundations of this powerful state, as well as tribute from his subject peoples. Although the Portuguese first arrived in the sixteenth century, they were content to establish only markets (*feira*), but by the seventeenth century they had gained control over the gold and ivory trade, and reduced the *munhumutapa* to a Portuguese puppet. Although the *munhumutapa* appears to have reasserted his control over his kingdom sometime after 1663 when the Portuguese withdrew from the Upper Zambezi, he was unable to recapture the peripheral tributaries or to suppress the internal insurrections that forced the state into steady decline.

Another satellite of Great Zimbabwe was situated on the Khami River near the modern city of Bulawayo. Khami was the second-largest town on the Zimbabwe Plateau, with some 7,000 inhabitants, and the capital of the state of Torwa (Cishona, "stranger," "foreigner"), which dominated the southwestern Zimbabwe Plateau from about 1450 to 1700. Like Great Zimbabwe, an elite ruling class lived in Khami, supported by the profits from long-distance trade, the resources from cultivation and cattle, and enjoying a life of privilege surrounded by their subjects. The stone-built structures of Torwa continued the building traditions of Great Zimbabwe but adapted them to local conditions. Construction was characterized by terraced-stone platforms and elaborately decorated stone retaining walls much smaller than those of Great Zimbabwe. Sometime around 1680 the rulers of Torwa were conquered by the Changamire-Rozvi dynasty, about which little is known except that its rulers came to rule most of the Zimbabwe Plateau until the early nineteenth century.

For centuries these states of the Zimbabwe Plateau were in constant contact with the East African trading emporiums and the commerce of the Indian Ocean. Largely dependent upon the Asian trade to supply the wealth for luxurious living in elaborate and permanent stone buildings, the ruling class was quite content to remain in a sedentary community, for they had no reason to wander in search of greener pastures. Between 900 and 1200, however, there were lesser-known communities whose ancestors had entered the eastern and southern regions of the modern Republic of South Africa in the early centuries of the Christian era and who had remained outside the orbit of the Indian Ocean commercial world. They were Bantu-speaking farmers and herdsmen who with their iron tools and weapons enjoyed a greater degree of mobility and economic egalitarianism, and little of the pronounced social stratification that characterized the societies in the northern states. The presence of vast tracts of sparsely inhabited savanna and agricultural land that enabled the southern Bantu speakers to wander widely did not, however, inhibit these peoples after 900 from undergoing social and political transformations. In the familiar pattern of southern Africa, those men rich in cattle were able to raise large families and gather clients, thereby establishing themselves as chiefs and converting their families into royal lineages. These leaders faced the same limitations to their authority that confronted all pastoral communities in the region, and the history of these communities is characterized by unrecorded separation and consolidation throughout the centuries.

The early Bantu-speaking communities on the well-watered lands of the coastal plain stretched from Delagoa Bay in the north to the Kei River in the south. The rich alluvial soil produced lush grass for pasture and fertile loam for cultivation that could sustain a greater population density than the more arid highveld across the Drakensberg to the west. Although little is known about the political history of the early southern Bantu speakers before the eighteenth century, they appear to have entered the region by gradually moving down the fertile eastern coast. The southernmost of these communities, the Xhosa, adopted a large percentage of Khoisan words into their language, having clearly absorbed many San peoples during their migrations. Although little is known of the Xhosa before this date, it appears that by the eighteenth century they had a long history of living in relatively densely settled chiefdoms and were the first Bantu-speaking Africans to encounter white settlers moving eastward from the Cape.

On the great central savanna plateau of southern Africa lived the Sotho-Tswana, another group of southern Bantu-speaking peoples. This cluster of related languages can be roughly divided into Setswana, dialects of which are spoken among Bantu-speaking communities further west of the highveld, and Sesotho. Like the Xhosa, the first Sesotho speakers during their migrations southward appear to have developed close relations with the local Khoisan peoples. As their herds grew and their numbers increased Sotho chiefdoms were formed and by 1000 the ancestors of the modern Sotho were living in communities of over a thousand inhabitants. The first Setswana speakers appear to have first settled in the region of the Vaal River sometime around the eleventh century. Like the Sotho, the prolific increase in cattle in a propitious environment produced an increase in the human population that in turn provided the impetus for the development of chiefdoms and royal lineages. Although the various dialects of the southern Bantu languages are mutually intelligible, there are cultural and economic variations among these communities that make them distinctive.

During the last thousand years the common cultural tradition of the southern Bantu speakers became inexorably differentiated by geography, particularly the barrier of the Drakensberg, which divided the Bantu speakers of the coast from those of the highveld, and each had to adapt to their diverse environments; this produced regional differences in dialect, material culture, and social organization. Despite these variations the southern Bantu speakers culturally and historically have far more uniting them than dividing them. By the early sixteenth century improvements in the use of iron tools in agriculture and the dramatic growth of their herds of cattle spread the lifestyle of the Bantu-speaking farmers south and west into the sparsely populated grasslands of the subcontinent. During this expansion of the Bantu speakers many of the indigenous Khoisan peoples were pushed to the periphery or absorbed into Bantu-speaking communities. In the dry lands of the west, however, the Khoikhoi pastoralists continued to water their herds in the valleys and streams near the Cape with little interference, and the San, sprinkled throughout the region, kept on hunting and gathering unmolested in the traditional manner. When the first Portuguese explorers arrived in southern Africa in the late fifteenth century they were oblivious to this ancient and profound Khoisan association with the land. To them and the Dutch colonists who later arrived in the mid-seventeenth century, southern Africa was underpopulated, underutilized, and available to anyone willing to claim it.

PART II

Africa in world history

12   The arrival of Europeans in sub-Saharan Africa

Although Africa north of the Sahara and the coasts of the Red Sea and East Africa were well known to the ancient Mediterranean world, Africa south of the desert was not. By the fifteenth century European perceptions of the land and people of sub-Saharan Africa were shrouded in myth, distorted by legends of ferocious peoples with bizarre physical features. Africans were collectively called *Ethiopians*, a pejorative term having nothing to do with the Ethiopians of northeast Africa. From the middle of the fifteenth century the dramatic discovery of Africa by Europe was made possible by the Portuguese voyages of exploration around the African coast. These voyages were carefully planned, but their execution down the African coast was painfully slow. The long, inhospitable western African coast had few natural harbors and dangerous shores, shoals, and ocean currents that required methodical exploration to understand and chart accurate nautical maps; this could only be achieved by substantial innovations in shipbuilding, seamanship, and navigation, which required over six decades to devise before the Portuguese captains could round the Cape of Good Hope.

The Portuguese had ample reasons to launch this remarkable program of organized exploration of western Africa and the South Atlantic Ocean. Its monarchy had captured the last Muslim stronghold in Portugal in 1249 and in 1385 had initiated a stable political system under the new dynasty, the house of Avis, isolated on the western coast of Europe with a powerful and suspicious Spain as its neighbor to the east. The gold of Africa would provide the resources to defend the kingdom and finance Portuguese expeditions around Africa to the Indian Ocean and Asia in order to reap the wealth from the spice trade. Moreover, beyond the Sahara Desert lived the non-Muslim peoples of West Africa who perhaps could be converted to Christianity and enlisted in the crusade against the Muslims which Portugal had been waging for over a century. And then there was the compelling legend of Prester John, which ignited the desire of medieval European monarchs to succor this beleaguered Christian king surrounded by Muslim enemies somewhere in the East. By the fifteenth century the legend of Prester John had come to be associated with Abyssinia (Ethiopia) in northeast Africa; his Christian subjects were said to be defending the faith against the *jihad* (holy war) of Islam. No Portuguese king, noble, or peasant could neglect their Christian responsibility to come to the aid of Prester John and his people.

The ocean of the Portuguese was the illimitable Atlantic, which surged against their shores, rather than the tranquil waters of the Mediterranean Sea. Portuguese captains, strongly supported by the Crown, knew that to traverse the Atlantic required new ships, the application of Islamic and Hebraic astronomy and mathematics to celestial navigation, new instruments to fix accurately one's location on the high seas, and more skillful seamanship than that required for the more placid currents and steady winds of the Mediterranean. The new ship was the caravel, at most sixty feet long and twenty feet wide with two or three masts with lateen – and later square – sails to tack into the wind, whose shallow draft could easily maneuver around the shoals of the West African coast. Navigation was more difficult. Unlike the Mediterranean, the high seas of the Atlantic required knowledge of the ship's position east and west (longitude) and, particularly in the South Atlantic, north and south (latitude). Although the Portuguese were able to calculate approximate longitudes, it was not until the eighteenth century that an accurate chronometer, fixed on Greenwich, England, could give correct locations around the globe.

More important, they invented a simple but accurate means for any pilot to determine the latitude on any ocean or landmass by applying medieval Islamic astronomy and mathematics. Although the Muslims had been driven out of Portugal in the mid-thirteenth century, they had left behind a deep heritage of celestial calculations originally developed to fix the position of Mecca with precision by advanced trigonometric solutions that could also be applied to navigation. After the expulsion of the Muslims, Jewish astronomers and mathematicians interpreted the Arabic scientific texts and continued the Islamic scientific legacy in Portugal until the beginning of the sixteenth century. Many of these Jewish scientists arrived in more tolerant Portugal as part of the massive migration of Jews fleeing from Christian pogroms in the Iberian Peninsula in 1391 and 1412. They were given refuge and safety by Prince Henry and the Crown in return for their resolution of the practical problems of navigation. The Jewish cartographer Jacob ben Abraham Cresques produced an accurate method to determine tides, so important to Portuguese captains leaving or approaching a landing on the western African coast.

No exploration of the South Atlantic could be successful, however, without accurate charts. At first the Portuguese began to measure the polestar above the horizon in order to fix latitude, but south of the equator they could no longer see it, and so adapted the mariner's astrolabe, an instrument that had been invented by the Greeks sometime in the second or third century and improved by Arab astronomers, into a sophisticated device to track constellations at night. The vital Portuguese contribution to the adaptation of the astrolabe was in measuring latitude from the sun rather than the stars. This precipitated an intense compilation of nautical measurements throughout the remainder of the fifteenth century. By 1484 Abraham Zacuto's *Rules for the Astrolabe* (*Regimento do astrolabo*) had become the standard manual for Portuguese navigation in the South Atlantic, and later in the Red Sea and Indian Ocean.

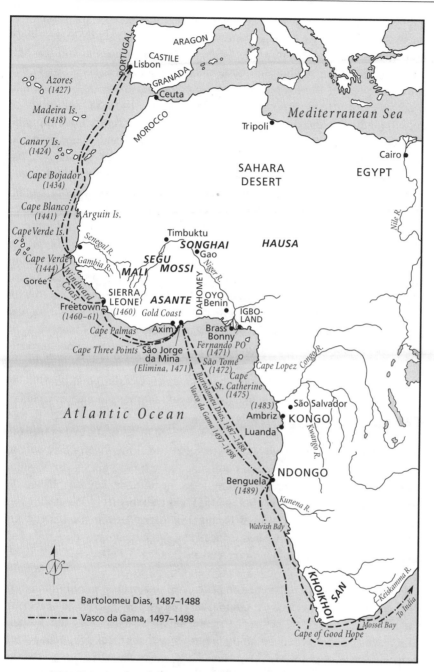

Map 12.1 *Portuguese explorations of the West African coast.*

Armed with the astrolabe, the new caravels first reached the uninhabited Atlantic Ocean islands of Madeira and the Azores. Sugar plantations established by the mid-fifteenth century helped to finance other expeditions down the mainland coast of Africa. In 1434 Prince Henry the Navigator sent Gil Eannes, the best sailor in Portugal, to seek gold beyond the feared Cape Bojador in the western Sahara. He returned with only a sprig of rosemary. Prince Henry ordered him to retrace his route the following year, a voyage that brought him a further 150 miles, south to find footprints of men and camels at Angra dos Ruivos ("creek of the red-haired men," now Garnet Bay). In 1436 another agent of Prince Henry, Afonso Baldaia, reached the Rio do Ouro ("river of gold"). Finding no gold, he continued to sail further south to a promontory he called Cabo Branco (Cape Blanco) because of its white sands. They found no gold and no slaves, but in 1441 Prince Henry sent two new captains, Antão Gonçalves and Nuno Tristão, to Cape Blanco. They bartered for gold dust and seized a dozen slaves, and a second expedition in 1442 to the Bay of Arguin returned with gold, salt, and ten slaves. The success of the mission persuaded Prince Henry and his successors of the profits to be made on the western coast of Africa.

The pace of exploration accelerated rapidly, driven by commerce, missionary fervor, and the technological innovations in navigation and ships. Between 1450 and 1458 a dozen ships left Portugal for West Africa, and returned with a profit of 50 to 800 percent in gold, slaves, and spices. A Portuguese trading post was started during Henry's lifetime and completed in 1461 at Arguin (an island off the coast of modern Mauritania), a barren place more noted for its rich fishing grounds than gold or slaves. The Portuguese traders brought cloth, silver, hardware, maize (corn), and horses, which were in great demand, in return for hides, beeswax, fish, and ostrich eggs, additions to the principals of trade – gold and slaves. The reputed piety of Prince Henry and recognition of the expense of African exploration were rewarded by several papal bulls from Pope Eugenius IV (1431–1447). The king of Portugal was given a commercial monopoly in all African territories colonized by the Portuguese and jurisdiction over all Christian churches and religious institutions they established. In the 1450s Popes Nicholas V (1447–1455) and Calixtus III (1455–1458) had confirmed the exclusive rights of Portugal in Africa, advocated the conversion of Africans, and encouraged Prince Henry to circumnavigate Africa and reach the Indies. Their bulls were read in Latin and Portuguese in Lisbon Cathedral.

Prince Henry died in 1460 before he learned that his last expedition led by Pedro de Sintra had reached the Grain Coast (today Sierra Leone and Liberia), named for its malaguetta pepper (*Aframomum melegueta*), or "grains of paradise," which competed successfully in Europe with the black pepper imported from the East through the Mediterranean. Here, where the African coast swings to the east, new opportunities for Portuguese enterprise were undertaken by a wealthy Lisbon merchant, Fernão Gomes. Although he was more interested in the domestic affairs of Portugal and crusading in North Africa, King Afonso V (1438–1481) could not ignore his nephew Prince Henry's enterprise in sub-Saharan western Africa. His solution in 1469 was to grant Gomes exclusive rights to explore and trade in Africa for five years. In return Gomes would advance from the Grain Coast 300 hundred miles a year along the West African coast, and contribute to the royal treasury an annual payment of 200,000 reis, a very substantial sum.

Fernão Gomes represented a new generation of entrepreneurs who were to capitalize on the vision of Prince Henry, the improvements in maritime technology, and the insatiable European demand for the human and material wealth of Africa. His coat of arms was composed of three African heads with gold rings on a silver background. Gomes, the monarchy, and Portugal profited from this commercial arrangement, which was extended to 1475. His well-organized expeditions swept along the coast. His captains reached Cape Palmas, Cape Three Points (the Ivory Coast), and in January 1472 anchored at the mouth of the River Pra, close to where the Portuguese in 1482 constructed their great trading fort of São Jorge da Mina at Elmina, "the Mine," in modern Ghana. A fleet of nine caravels and two huge provision ships carried the stone, brick, timber, tools, nails, and 100 stonemasons and carpenters, who erected the fortress walls and town in twenty days. The gold of the Akan forest and West Africa was now brought here to the Gold Coast. Forty years after Prince Henry had set out to divert the trans-Saharan golden trade of the Muslims, his agents had succeeded. The gold trade was extremely profitable to Gomes and the Crown. The royal treasury in Lisbon recorded that the annual average amount of gold deposited between 1487 and 1489 was 8,000 ounces. By the fifteenth century the monarchy's profits had increased to 24,000 and 30,000 ounces. These royal figures may be inflated, and did not take into account smuggling and loss at sea, but the fact remains that the Portuguese seaborne trade was annually exporting half a ton of bullion to Europe; this financed their further explorations around the coasts of Africa to the Indian Ocean and Asia.

How to pay for the gold? The usual European trade goods – cloth, hardware – so profitable on the Senegal and Gambia were of little value in the equatorial climate of the Gold Coast. Although horses were in great demand by chiefs in the savanna lands of the Western Sudan, where they would exchange fourteen slaves for a stallion, domestic animals could not survive in the coastal rainforests because of the trypanosomiasis carried by the tsetse fly. Firearms were in great demand, but were banned by the Papal bulls. The most available commodity were Africans taken in trade and war by the Ijo and Itsekiri in the estuaries of the Niger Delta and later by the coastal Africans living along the Slave Coast (between Cape Saint Paul and Lagos – Togo, Benin, and Nigeria). They were willing to sell slaves to the Portuguese, who in turn exchanged them for gold at Elmina. In 1471 and 1472 Gomes's captains discovered the islands of Fernando Po, Príncipe, and São Tomé in the Gulf of Guinea, crossed the equator, and in 1475 when his contract expired Rui de Sequeira had reached Cabo Santa Catarina (Cape Saint Catherine) south of the equator and the Gabon River. These were extraordinary accomplishments, for the currents that carried them down the African coast frustrated their return. There was no polestar to guide them south of the equator. The mists, sandbars, and shoals of the West African coast were treacherous.

While Portuguese artisans were transferring stone for the walls of Elmina through the surf, humidity, and heat of the Gold Coast, two ships under the command of Diogo Cão (d. 1486), an old associate of Prince Henry, set sail to pass beyond the southernmost known headland at Cape Saint Catherine. He carried with him, as did all subsequent voyages of exploration, stone pillars, each seven feet high and topped with a cross, a *padrão*, inscribed in Latin and Portuguese with the year and the names of the king and explorer. These *padrão*s not only symbolized the nautical achievements of the Portuguese, but were a visible manifestation of their claim to the lands they had discovered – lands on the African continent hitherto unknown to the Europeans. Always placed on a hill or headland visible from the ocean, they became navigational landmarks for future mariners. Cão erected his first *padrão* at Mpindi on the southern shore of the estuary of a colossal river he called the Rio do Padrão. The local people called it Nzadi ("the great river"). Luis Vaz de Camões in his great epic poem, *The Lusiad*, called it Zaire. Today it is known as the Congo. Cão sailed up the river to Yelala Falls (near the present point of Matadi), where he made contact with officials of the kingdom of Kongo. Proceeding down the long coast of western Africa to a headland, Cape Santa Maria south of Benguela in Angola, he left another *padrão*. In 1485 Diogo Cão returned to complete the circumnavigation of Africa he had failed to accomplish in his previous expedition. He sailed south from Cape Santa Maria along the barren sands of what later became known as the Skeleton Coast of Namibia, where he erected a fourth *padrão* at Cape Cross north of Walfish Bay in 1486 and where he died, his ships returning to Portugal.

During this expedition Diogo Cão established relations with the *mani kongo*, Nzinga Nkuwu, ruler of the kingdom of Kongo, whose capital was at Mbanza Kongo thirty miles south of the river. The kingdom had been established in the fourteenth century, and was the most organized state that the Portuguese had yet found in Africa. The king ruled from a palace, accompanied by elaborate ceremony, through a network of officials and nobles who administered the provinces of the state to collect tribute in copper, iron, and slaves. Trade was conducted in the state currency, *nzimbu* (cowrie shells). The arrival of Diogo Cão in the kingdom of Kongo was the beginning of a long and complicated relationship between Europe and the kings of Kongo and Angola. His last voyage, however, had convinced King João II (1481–1495), against the advice from his royal counselors, that Portuguese commerce relied upon the expansion of the sea routes to India. In 1487 he ordered Bartolomeu Dias (1450–1500) to complete the circumnavigation of the African continent in search of Prester John and the Indies that had eluded Diogo Cão.

Sailing far out into the South Atlantic, Dias made his landfall on the western African coast at the promontory of Lüderitz Bay in Namibia, where he raised his *padrão*, only to be blown by the powerful winds and seas of southern Africa far from land and around Cape Agulhas, the southern tip of the African continent. Working his way north he made a landfall for fresh water at Angra de São Brás (Cape Saint Blaise, now known as Mossel Bay) on February 3, 1488. Here there was a confrontation between the Portuguese and Khoikhoi herdsmen, one of whom Dias killed with his crossbow. They continued eastward along the coast for several more days and erected another *padrão* at a promontory now called Kwaaihoek before turning back for Portugal and the great headland Dias named Cabo da Boa Esperança (the Cape of Good Hope), where another *padrão* was placed. He had confirmed the medieval belief that Africa could be circumnavigated. The way to Prester John and the Indies was now open.

The king's failing health meant that it was another ten years before a major expedition could be launched to complete the contact with the Indies that Dias had failed to accomplish. King João II had sent two emissaries, Afonso de Paiva and Pero da Covilhã, overland to seek Prester John. They never returned. Then in 1497 a fleet of four caravels, two of which were specially built under Dias's supervision without regard to expense, departed from Lisbon under the command of Vasco da Gama (1460–1524). Dias had recorded the latitude of the Cape of Good Hope, enabling da Gama to sail on the prevailing winds in a wide arc through the South Atlantic to make his landfall in Saint Helena Bay on November 8, 1497. In stormy seas he rounded the Cape of Good Hope 125 miles to the south, and on November 25 put into Angra de São Brás. His remaining three ships then sailed up the East African coast on currents and fair winds, passing the green, wooded promontories of Natal and Mozambique, where they encountered the Arab dhows of the Indian Ocean trade whose pilots' instruments for navigation were as good as if not superior to those of the Portuguese. As they sailed up the East African coast they received the hospitality of the Swahilis, whose wealth in cloth, gold, porcelains, and produce surpassed any of the gifts da Gama could offer. The Portuguese superiority was in cannons and muskets. With crusading zeal they bombarded and plundered Mozambique, repelled a Swahili attack at Mombasa, and negotiated with its rival Malindi for a Gujarati pilot and sufficient provisions to reach the port of Calicut in India in the summer of 1498. In January 1499, they returned to Malindi, where da Gama erected a stone *padrão* that still stands. The crews had been decimated by disease and scurvy, and only enough sailors remained alive to man two caravels, which rounded the Cape of Good Hope on March 20, 1499; one of them entered the Tagus Estuary at Lisbon in July and the other in August. It had been an epic journey, and honors were heaped upon Vasco da Gama, who had revealed the wealth of East Africa, Asia, and India. Europe, Asia, and particularly Africa would never be the same.

Exploration, Christian zeal, and commercial exploitation characterized the arrival of the Portuguese and their intervention in Africa. Although they had engaged in the colonization of Portuguese settlers on the islands – the Madeiras, Azores, Cape Verde, São Tomé, and Fernando Po, where they established sugar

Figure 12.1 *Quelimane, in modern Mozambique, was founded by the Portuguese in the sixteenth century.*

plantations and vineyards – the Portuguese made no sustained effort to venture into the interior of Africa from their coastal commercial enclaves. Their few initial attempts to march inland were thwarted by disease, mostly malaria, and the military strength of the Africans. The technological superiority of the Portuguese, with their cannons and muskets, enabled them to dominate coastal towns, but these weapons were useless in the heavily forested hinterland, where African weapons and organized opposition were able to repel the firearms of the Portuguese. Throughout the sixteenth century the Portuguese repeatedly tried to control the interior of Angola for slaves, only to be repulsed. In Mozambique they sought to move up the Zambezi River Valley, but in 1571 a Portuguese expedition was driven back to the East African coast. The population of Portugal was insufficient to sustain expensive expeditions and imperial ambitions in Africa, India, and the Far East. They consequently concentrated their energies on building heavily fortified coastal trading forts to protect themselves from the Africans, and later from their more powerful European rivals for the wealth of Africa and Asia.

On his first voyage in 1483 Diogo Cão had returned to Portugal with hostages and an emissary from the *mani kongo*, Caçuta, who was baptized João da Silva and learned Portuguese. He returned to Mbanza Kongo in 1491 with a Portuguese ambassador, Gonçalo de Sousa, who came to encourage commerce and Christian civilization. Thereafter, artisans, masons, and women arrived to teach carpentry, stonework, and housekeeping. In 1492 two printers from

Figure 12.2 *A Portuguese legation visiting the king of Kongo.*

Nuremberg traveled to São Tomé, presumably to spread literacy by the press. Priests were ever present and successful. On May 3, 1491 the *mani kongo*, Nzinga Nkuwu (d. 1505) had been baptized King João I; others followed suit, numerous chiefs taking the titles of Portuguese noblemen. This attempt to create a black Christian Portugal in the Kongo proved illusory. During the next 200 years Christianity came to combine indigenous beliefs with Catholicism into a system in which the veneration of ancestors and local deities was integrated with that of the saints of the European Church. The Portuguese masons rebuilt Mbanza Kongo into a capital of stone buildings renamed São Salvador, but despite the introduction of new crops and technology commerce was soon dominated by the single most important commodity the kingdom of the Kongo had to offer – slaves. The increasing demand for slaves by Portuguese traders inexorably destroyed the civilizing mission envisioned by the Portuguese monarchy at the end of the fifteenth century.

When the Portuguese mission had arrived in 1491 Nzinga Mbemba was a provincial governor of northeast Kongo, son of the principal wife of King João, and a devout convert to Christianity. When he seized the throne in 1506 from rivals on the death of the *mani kongo*, he was beholden to the African Christians and the Portuguese. His long rule as Afonso I (1506–1543) witnessed profound changes in the kingdom of Kongo. As a convert to Christianity he sought to consolidate his claim to the throne by making Catholicism the state religion, and with the support of the Catholic Church he was able to increase the central power of the Crown. He never abandoned the traditional African acceptance of polygyny, however, and rejected the European concept of primogeniture, thereby permitting his many sons to plunge the kingdom into a series of succession struggles upon his death. Although slavery was an integral part of Kongo society, the slave trade was not. By 1514 the Portuguese demand for slaves turned a domestic institution into an international trade. Afonso understood the dangers to his authority by rapacious Portuguese slave traders and their African agents, the *pombeiros*. He sought to restrict the trade by making it a royal monopoly. In frustration, he abolished it by decree in 1526. Both policies failed. At his death in 1543 7,000 slaves were passing annually from the Kongo and Angola through São Tomé.

The slave trade brought the monarchy of Kongo substantial revenues, which were largely dissipated in the consumption of cloth, wine, guns, and hardware. Moreover, the slave trade and Christianity created a widening gulf between the aristocracy and the commoners. The nobility was Christian, literate (the first transcription of a Bantu language was the Kikongo catechism published in 1555), and traded in slaves. The free farmers continued to worship their traditional spirits, remained illiterate, and were exploited for their crops. When socially or economically impoverished, they were taken as slaves.

In 1568 the kingdom of the Kongo was confronted by an African threat more formidable than the Portuguese. The Jaga (Yaka) stormed out of the Kwango River Valley in the interior to defeat the armies of the *mani kongo*, Dom Alvaro I (1542–1587), sacked São Salvador, and forced the king to seek sanctuary on Hippopotamus Island in the estuary of the Congo River. The origins of the Jaga remain a mystery. They were depicted by the Portuguese as marauding cannibals from a single ethnic group, but they were more likely to have been a composite of different ethnic groups and dissidents in Kongo, forged together into disciplined raiders who pillaged the towns and countryside of the kingdom. Alvaro appealed to the king of Portugal for assistance, and King Sebastian promptly ordered 400 Portuguese musketeers from São Tomé to come to his aid. They drove the Jaga south to Angola and restored Alvaro in his capital, São Salvador, with a fort to resist any future Jaga attacks.

Portuguese support for Alvaro demonstrably increased their presence in the kingdom while Alvaro and his successors sought to invoke the power of the Vatican at Rome to counter their influence in order to strengthen the central authority of the *mani kongo*. Profits from the slave trade enabled the kings of Kongo to purchase muskets and the hired guns of the Portuguese to restore and protect the monarchy. The Crown also began to receive revenue from the new crops introduced from the New World by the Portuguese – maize (corn), cassava (manioc), and citrus – that were to become the future staples and nutritious crops of Africa. Literacy was essential in the policies of centralization by the kings of Kongo in the latter half of the sixteenth

Box 12.1 Who were the Jaga?

Andrew Battell (1565–1614) was an English sailor who was seized from a British privateer operating in the South Atlantic and imprisoned in Luanda by the Portuguese authorities. After numerous adventures, Battell lived with the Jaga for twenty-one months, and consequently his account of these mysterious and warlike people became the most authoritative. He claimed that the Jaga suddenly appeared in 1568, overran the kingdom of Kongo, and destroyed the capital, São Salvador. Their military superiority was irresistible, and they roamed widely, spreading terror from the Congo to the Cunene River, during which they assimilated conquered peoples. In one of the more interesting debates among Africanists, Joseph Miller argued in 1973 that the Jaga never existed.[1] In 1979 John K. Thornton refuted Miller's interpretation, declaring that not only had the Jaga existed, but that they were just as Battell had described them.[2] Miller's rejoinder, "Thanatopsis," upheld his earlier arguments,[3] but later Anne Hilton in "The Jaga Reconsidered" supported Thornton's "resurrection" of the Jaga.[4] If indeed the Jaga were present in the Kongo during this period, as Thornton and Hilton argue, they probably had cultural connections with the Luba–Lunda peoples of the interior of Central Africa.

[1] Joseph Miller, "Requiem for the Jaga," *Cahiers d'Etudes africaines* 49, 13-1 (1973), pp. 121–149.
[2] John K. Thornton, "A Resurrection for the Jaga," *Cahiers d'Etudes africaines* 69–70, 18-1-2 (1979), pp. 223–227.
[3] Joseph Miller, "Thanatopsis," *Cahiers d'Etudes Africaines* 69–70, 18-1-2 (1979), pp. 229–231.
[4] Anne Hilton, "The Jaga Reconsidered," *Journal of African History* 11, 2 (1981), pp. 191–202.

century and the first half of the seventeenth. The alliance between Crown and Church resulted in the establishment of mission schools that produced a class of Africans literate in Portuguese who came to wield the enormous power of the pen. The provincial governors had clerks who corresponded with the *mani kongo* and in turn could now communicate with merchants in Lisbon and with the Vatican in Rome.

These centralizing policies of the *mani kongo* could not be sustained. New trade routes for slaves were established to the south through Angola and those for copper shifted north of the Congo River, depriving the royal treasury of critical revenue. In the past the king had controlled the appointment of the non-hereditary nobility to be his provincial governors, *mani mpembe*, whose loyalty to the throne had been eroded by the power of the *pombeiros*, who supplied the guns in return for slaves. One governor in the northeast could mobilize a private army of 5,000 archers and 100 musketeers. European rivalries between

Box 12.2 Kongo letter

The conversion of the first *mani kongo* to Christianity opened the door to Iberian and Vatican influence in West Africa. But it also brought the rulers of Kongo powerful allies against their enemies. The following letters from the newly crowned Alvaro III to Pope Paul V reflects the many challenges the Catholic kings faced in Kongo. Alvaro III seeks assistance against the growing demands of Portuguese merchants, African raiders (known as "Jaga") and rival claimants to his throne.

Alvaro III to Pope Paul V

San Salvador,

25 October 1617

Very Holy Father, Myself, Dom Alvaro the Third, by divine grace, augmenter of the faith of Jesus Christ and defender of the faith in these lands of Ethiopia, king of the very ancient kingdom of Congo, Angola, Matamba, Ocanga, and of the Ambandu, here and beyond the marvelous river Zaire [Congo], and of many other kingdoms and neighboring sovereignties . . .

As the very humble and very obedient son of Your Holiness, I kiss his very holy feet in my name and of my royal person as well as in the name of all my kingdoms and states, I give him the allegiance due him as the universal pastor of the flock of Christ. I beg Your Holiness with all possible ardor to accept the above-said allegiance, which I have given and offered by the intermediary of my procurer, Dom Jean-Baptiste Vivis of Valencia. The prothonotary and referendary [arbitrator] of Your Holiness will remit it, according to the mode and manner which the other Catholic Kings are accustomed to in dealing with the apostolic Holy See. I give him all necessary faculties to pledge allegiance as well as to treat affairs in my name to Your Holiness and to all the Roman pontiffs, his successors. If for any reason he cannot do so, we would like Your Holiness and his successor to have the power to name other procurers in my name and in the name of my kingdoms. In this way the designs of King Dom Alvaro II, my lord and father whom God has, in His glory, taken up again. This is what he had in mind when he sent Dom Antonio Manuel, who died in Rome, to the apostolic Holy See. He entrusted letters to him, affairs to be discussed and commissioned him with an embassy. It is necessary that these projects be developed for the greater service of God and for the greater good of Christianity . . .

I reconfirm the instructions he gave and the business he negotiated, and I humbly beg Your Holiness to give orders so that old requests and those which more recently have been addressed to the above-named procurer, to be submitted by him to Your Holiness, may be examined. All

Box 12.2 (continued)

these affairs are contained in instructions that I have sent, signed by my hand, which manifest that my goal is to promote the divine cult for the greater glory of God, the exaltation of His Church, the confusion of barbarians and pagans, and the consolidation of Catholics.

By other routes I have written to Your Holiness, to the Seignior Cardinal, protector of these kingdoms, and to the above-named procurer, my ordinary ambassador resident at that Roman court, Dom Jean-Baptiste Vivis.

In those letters I announced the death of King Alvaro III, my lord and father. I related that after his death, given my young age, the kingdom was put in the possession of Dom Bernard, my uncle, bastard half-brother of the above-named king, with the help of a few important people. But after less than a year, the kingdom, seeing the injustices done to me, scandalized by some disorders indicative of little Christian religion, took up arms against him without my knowing. This was under the command of Dom Antonio da Silva, Grand Duke of Mbamba, a province of the kingdom, and general of the kingdom, to whom the above-named king, my lord and father, before dying, had given over my person, as executor of his will. Dom Bernard was deprived of the kingdom and his life, and I was reestablished in power to the great joy of all, and was recognized by all the states as their king and their universal lord.

I beg Your Holiness to deign to send many favors and spiritual graces to me and to all my subjects, to deign to let us rejoice in his letters, which will bring us many benefits and much honor, and the courage to resist the barbarous pride of paganism by which, from all sides of our kingdom, we are besieged.

We also beg Your Holiness to deign to receive us forever under the protection and defense of the apostolic Holy See and to make his Catholic Majesty, King Dom Philippe [of Spain], whom we greatly esteem and honor as our well-loved brother, favorable to us, recognizing the great benefits that I and all these kingdoms and this Christianity owe to his magnificence. These benefits have cost His Majesty great expenditures, which he has not ceased to make in favor of this Christianity whose culture he assures. Even so, we are under the weight of injustice on the part of his captains-general and governors who reside in Angola. They enter the lands belonging to our crown and make themselves masters there, as if it were enemy territory, without receiving any such orders from His Majesty. On the contrary, the king orders them in his instructions, which he gives them, to aid and serve us in all instances. They do not do this, having only their own interests in mind. They commit numerous unjust acts, making alliance with a nation of extremely

Box 12.2 (continued)

barbarous men called Gindas and Ingas [Jagas], who live on human flesh.

May Your Holiness deign to find a remedy for this. I beg him to accord me his immediate protection.

May the Lord care for the very holy person of Your Holiness in the measure that his very humble and very obedient son desires . . .

Primary Source: "Relations between the kingdom of the Kongo and the papacy, Alvaro III to Pope Paul V," in Robert O. Collins (ed.), *Documents from the African Past*, Princeton: Markus Wiener, 2001, pp. 84–87.

the Dutch and Portuguese at Luanda in Angola would later seal the collapse of the kingdom of Kongo. In 1575 Paulo Dias de Novais (d. 1589) returned to Luanda Bay with a charter from the king of Portugal to establish a fortified trading post that became the center for the Brazilian slave trade. After his death in 1589 the Portuguese Crown took over the post as the capital of its colony of Angola. During the mercantile wars of the seventeenth century the Dutch seized Luanda in 1641, only to lose it in 1648 to the Portuguese from Brazil led by Salvador Correia de Sá (1602–1681) who restored the Angolan–Brazilian slave trade. Triumphant at Luanda, Salvador de Sá was determined to establish Portuguese control over the interior, including Angola and the kingdom of Kongo. The *mani kongo*, Antonio I (1661–1665) mobilized his nobles of dubious loyalty against the advancing Afro-Portuguese force. On October 30, 1665, at the great battle of Mbwila, Antonio and most of his noble title-holders, court officials, and 5,000 Kongolese troops were killed. Mbwila was the ultimate contest between the kingdom of Kongo and the Portuguese which had begun 200 years before. The kingdom of Kongo dissolved into petty chiefdoms and never recovered.

Portuguese policy in East Africa at the beginning of the sixteenth century was far different from that in the west. There was no centralized state with a powerful animist king who could become a Christian ally with Portuguese spiritual and technical assistance. On the East African coast there was an archipelago of wealthy independent Swahili trading cities, extending 1,500 miles from Sofala in the south to Mogadishu in the north. Unlike West Africa and its powerful kingdoms the rival, individual mercantile ports of East Africa that in the past had had no reason to defend themselves against attack from the sea were no match for the cannons and muskets of the Portuguese on their way to the riches of India and the Orient. The city-states were ports of call for the Portuguese, who put in for fresh water and supplies and then plundered the Muslim inhabitants in the name of Christ. On his second voyage to India in 1502 Vasco da Gama encountered a dhow with several hundred pilgrims returning from their *hajj* (pilgrimage to Mecca). He loaded gunpowder in the hold, set fire, and blew up the ship and its passengers. Subsequently, flotillas of armed Portuguese ships seized control of the Swahili towns on their way to establish Portuguese colonial enclaves in Asia.

In 1503 Ruy Lourenço Ravasco seized dhows and their crews in East African waters for ransom, and with his cannons forced the sultan of Zanzibar to pay an annual tribute. These piratical raids were followed by an official task force under the command of Francisco de Almeida (1450–1510), who sacked Kilwa and Mombasa in 1505 and broke the power of the Swahili traders before sailing to Goa on the west coast of India to be governor of the Portuguese eastern empire. The Portuguese reaped immediate profits from their pillage of gold from Sofala, where a fort was built to protect the golden trade from the interior. In fact, the gold mines of Zimbabwe were near exhaustion and the recorded amount of bullion to reach Lisbon was modest. More important was control of the lucrative trade of the Sabaean Lane between Asia and Africa, which had made possible the wealth and public buildings of the Swahili coast – the harbors, coral houses, mosques, palaces, public baths, and burial monuments. Portuguese commercial policy was that of the eighteenth century – mercantile – whereby it was argued that since global resources were finite, the prosperity of the state could only survive if it monopolized a substantial portion of the world's wealth at the expense of other nations. Thus the Portuguese sought to impose a commercial monopoly by introducing regulations that would require all Indian Ocean commerce to be carried in Portuguese ships. To enforce these decrees and sustain Portuguese control of the Sabaean Lane, trading forts were constructed at Sofala, Mozambique Island, Kilwa, and the commanding fortress of Fort Jesus at Mombasa. These efforts to restrict trade to Portuguese vessels failed, as rebellious Swahili merchants and mariners easily evaded Portuguese prohibitions, officials, and their ships ordered to enforce them. Nevertheless, the damage caused by these restrictive policies eroded the prosperity of previous centuries and plunged the East African coast into economic depression during the seventeenth and eighteenth centuries.

Despite their fortified enclaves overlooking the Indian Ocean the Portuguese simply did not have the human and material resources to dominate the trade and people of the Swahili coast. They could exert their authority in the vicinity of the forts to make an alliance for mutual benefit with local leaders, as they did at Malindi, but there were never a sufficient number of Portuguese administrators, soldiers, or priests to consolidate the authority of Portugal in East Africa as they did in India and the Orient. Challenged by the growing imperial mercantile power of Britain and France in the Indian Ocean, Portuguese East Africa became a backwater. Although Portugal remained in Mozambique until 1975, the Portuguese period in East Africa had come to an end when Fort Jesus fell to the Swahili people of Mombasa in 1792. The harsh judgment of Justus Strandes has withstood the test of time: "Portuguese rule in East Africa was the rule of alien conquerors based on force and destined to greater strength when it appeared. It had no lasting influence whatsoever on the country and East Africa today would appear the same even if there had been no Portuguese period in her past."[1]

At the beginning of the nineteenth century the sultan of Oman, Sayyid Sa 'id, arrived on the East African coast to take up permanent residence at Zanzibar. He was determined to forge the Swahili city-states of the East African coast, which had recovered their traditional independence, into an Omani empire to replace the imperial pretensions of Portugal.

Further reading

Diffie, Bailey W. and George D. Winius, *Foundations of the Portuguese Empire, 1415–580*, Minneapolis: University of Minnesota Press, 1977

Russell, Peter, *Prince Henry "the Navigator": A Life*, New Haven: Yale University Press, 2000

Seed, Patricia, *Ceremonies of Possession in Europe's Conquest of the New World, 1492–1640*, Cambridge: Cambridge University Press, 1995, esp. chapter 4

Thomas, Hugh, *The Slave Trade: The Story of the Atlantic Slave Trade, 1440–1870*, New York: Simon & Schuster, 1997

Thornton, John K., *Africa and the Africans in the Making of the Atlantic World, 1400–1800*, New York: Cambridge University Press, 1998

---

[1] Justus Strandes, *The Portuguese Period in East Africa*, Nairobi: East African Literature Bureau, 1961, p. 320.

13 Diseases and crops: old and new

Diseases

When modern humans began to move out of Africa to Asia and beyond 100,000 years ago, the number of *Homo sapiens sapiens* was probably no more than a million, most of whom lived in Africa. They were hunters and gatherers in small family groups who foraged for food in a radius not more than one day's walk from water. There was ample room to roam, 6 million square miles through grass and woodlands, which bipedal modern humans did with increasing vigor. The family clans and groups were consequently widely distributed and few in number compared to the continental landmass. Today Africa has a higher birthrate than any other continent, but this is a phenomenon of the last century. In the past the rate of population growth in Africa has been consistently lower than that in more temperate climates. While many explanations have been put forward, the most likely is the inability of the environment to sustain an increase in the population of Africa. When the capacity of the land was limited, the number of Africans remained relatively constant. When the climate, land, and inhabitants produced food in abundance, their numbers rapidly expanded, and as mobility of those with tools and fire increased, they migrated into the more productive regions of the continent. One would expect the increased birthrate, made possible by the increase in food production, to result in a concomitant increase in the total population of Africa, but this did not happen. To be sure, the numbers of Africans steadily but gradually expanded, but those who survived were far fewer than those who roamed and then settled in Asia, Europe, and ultimately in North and South America. They had all come from the same evolutionary beginnings, but the enormous disparity in terms of population growth between those who had moved out of Africa and those who remained can best be explained by the tropical diseases that debilitated the Africans.

From their evolutionary beginnings humans in Africa have been afflicted by a proliferation of parasites and organisms. During the many centuries before the European conquest and colonization of Africa the spread of disease was gradual but steady, characterized by contact between neighboring communities and along established routes for trade or war. Although the years of European colonial rule encompassed little more than a half-century, they produced a dramatic transformation to create an environment in which the diseases of

Africa could flourish. The introduction of river steamers, railroads, and later the automobile resulted in large numbers of rural Africans migrating to the new urban areas and the mining enclaves that transformed the environment and enabled Africa's endemic disease to afflict ever more Africans. Although European scientists and doctors had discovered the complex morphology of many African diseases, which resulted in the birth of the discipline of tropical medicine, and the authoritarian colonial administration possessed the power to contain epidemics, Africans were increasingly exposed to contagion in their congested cities.

Disease in Africa was usually carried by resilient members of its rich insect population, which multiplied profusely in a tropical environment unchecked by the climatic change of seasons that occurs in the temperate continents. The tropics have been the home of the greatest diversity of living organisms – animal or vegetable – as well as the parasites they carry from one host to another. Until the twentieth century the means of infection remained obscure and treatment more spiritual than medicinal. The diseases were many. One source lists 296 infectious diseases, but there were three that accounted for the steady decline in the African population and consequently their inability to populate the vast landmass of their continent: sleeping sickness; bilharzia; and the endemic killer, malaria.

Sleeping sickness (trypanosomiasis) infects humans and domestic animals, in which it is called *nagana*. The parasites that infect humans are the *Trypanosome brucei rhodesiense*, a parasite of game animals, and the *T. brucei gamiense*, transmitted by humans. They are carried by the testse flies, *Glossina mortisans* and *G. palpalis* respectively, which are about the size of the common house fly. *G. mortisans* occupies the low-lying savanna lands that spread across Africa from west to east and south. The more aggressive *G. palpalis* prefers the thick bush by streams, rivers, and lakes from western to eastern Africa. The female tsetse develops a single larva containing the vector from the fertilized egg in her abdomen, which she deposits in the moist soils by streams and rivers. In her lifetime she will produce only a few larvae. The adult fly emerges within five weeks carrying the trypanosome and passes it into the bloodstreams of those humans and animals that come to drink. Once injected, the parasite works ruthlessly on the immune system of its victim; it possesses the ability to change its antigens and thereby frustrate attempts by the host to combat it. Trypanosomes and the tsetse fly that distributes them have been in Africa since long before the evolution of the hominids or *H. sapiens sapiens*. Together they have contained the expansion of the African human population and their domestic livestock. Numerous species of antelope have developed a resistance to the parasite of the tsetse fly, but neither humans nor the domestic animals upon which they depend can survive in the fly zone or acquire immunity.

Sir David Bruce (1855–1931) was the first to discover in 1894 that trypanosomiasis in South Africa was transmitted by the tsetse flies; this work led to the administrative and medical controls to contain the devastating sleeping sickness epidemics then ravaging the Africans living around Lake Victoria and in the Congo and Sudan. The success of these programs was instrumental in the establishment of schools of tropical medicine in Europe and the organization of hospitals and rural public health services in colonial sub-Saharan Africa. Geographically, the tsetse flies and their trypanosomes have throughout the millennia infested two-thirds of Africa's most productive land. Historically, trypanosomiasis has been a major deterrent in the development of Africa, preventing the utilization of vast areas of savanna by humans and their domestic animals. Those Africans living on the marginal lands paid the price of debilitation, death, and depopulation. Today, trypanosomiasis infects some 500,000 Africans, 80 percent of whom will perish, and 3 million head of their livestock. Ironically, the inability of humans to expand into much of Africa's savanna contributed significantly to the preservation of the great herds of game animals that were immune, as they were able to roam unaffected across the grasslands of eastern and southern Africa.

Bilharzia (schistosomiasis) is more insidious than sleeping sickness, for it is a debilitating disease rather than a killer. It is named after Dr. Theodor Bilharz (1825–1862) who discovered the parasites *Schistosoma mansoni* and *S. haematobium* and their snail hosts in 1851. Bilharzia originated in the waters of the Lake Plateau of East Africa and traveled down the Nile to infect the dynastic Egyptians and their pharaohs. Eggs of the schistosoma fluke have been found in Egyptian mummies from as early as 1200 BCE. There are numerous species of schistosomes in animals; *S. mansoni*, for instance, is readily carried by baboons. Just as the trypanosomes of sleeping sickness require the tsetse flies as a host, the schistosoma parasites need small aquatic snails that proliferate in the quiet waters of African lakes, rivers, and canals, in which the parasite produces the schistosoma larvae. Those who come to bathe, wash, drink, or work in contaminated water are infected through the skin with the snail's fluke, whose arrow-sharp schistosomes multiply in the human bloodstream and throughout the organs. There are three schistosomes widespread throughout sub-Saharan Africa that infect humans: *S. mansoni*, which develops in the liver; *S. haematobium*, which attacks the bladder and kidneys; and *S. intercalatum*, which is less severe and found in the Congo and West Africa. Bilharzia is not a killer until adulthood, but children who live in the waters of Africa soon became debilitated, lethargic, and unproductive. Historically, it has been the second-greatest deterrent to population growth in Africa after malaria, and today more than 200 million Africans are infected.

Malaria (Italian *mal' aria*, "bad air") was attributed by the Romans to swampy vapors; this was widely accepted until the end of the nineteenth century when (in 1897) the anopheles mosquito was found to be the vector for the disease. Malaria was indigenous to Africa, and is endemic in all but the cool and dry regions of the earth. It has been the greatest tropical killer disease throughout history, and today causes two-and-a-half million deaths annually.

In Africa one child dies from malaria every thirty seconds. Until two French chemists, Joseph-Bienaimé Caventou and Pierre-Joseph Pelletier, extracted the alkaloid of quinine from the bark of the cinchona tree of the Andes in the 1880s as a prophylactic, malaria was the principal reason why Europeans were confined to their African coastal enclaves and unable to penetrate into the interior. It is the oldest and most persistent known disease, whose four single-cell species infect humans. Its origins were in the African anthropoid apes, from which the species found its way into the bloodstream of the anopheles mosquito some 35 million years ago. There are some 3,000 species of mosquito, but it is the female *Anopheles gambiae* that seeks out human blood, and prefers to breed in the pools or watered grasslands and forest clearings where Africans farm and graze their herds. Here she transfers the plasmodium parasite from one human to another through her proboscis while searching for blood to lay her eggs. The most virulent form of the plasmodium parasite is *Plasmodium falciparum*, which circulates in the bloodstream to the brain causing cerebral (malignant tertiary) malaria and death. Falciparum malaria has been endemic in Africa and the tropical regions of the globe wherever the female *A. gambiae* flourished, leaving other mosquito species to be satisfied with animal blood.

The spread of malaria throughout sub-Saharan Africa accompanied the expansion of agricultural settlements. When forests were cleared for cultivation, there was a significant increase in the number of stagnant pools, in which the anopheles mosquito rapidly multiplied to infect villagers, particularly the sedentary old, infants, and women – who experienced intrauterine death of the embryo, premature birth, and spontaneous abortion. The increased incidence of infant mortality appears to have lowered the birthrate; this led inevitably to a decrease in the total population until the farmers could, in time, adjust to a new symbiotic relationship to their environment. To ingest the malarial parasite the anopheles mosquito must first bite an infected person or animal and then transfer it to another mammal to begin the life cycle of the parasite, which can only be sustained if the host is reinfected within ten days. Since the initial infection is followed by fever and chills, the incapacitated host becomes a vulnerable target for the second crucial bite. Consequently, among hunter-gatherers, who were constantly on the move, the incidence of malaria was very low, but when Africans began to settle to tend their crops, they became the ideal incapacitated hosts for the malarial parasite.

The human immune system has long been a losing battle against falciparum. Historically, some Africans have developed by genetic selection the ability to limit the growth of the parasite in red blood cells in order to survive the lethal effect of *P. falciparum*. Some, particularly those in western Africa, evolved by genetic mutations a red blood cell shaped like a sickle that destroyed the malaria parasite, but by denying it penetration produced a variety of side-effects, from anemia to heart failure.

Sleeping sickness, bilharzia, and malaria were the major parasitic diseases that depended and flourished on a vector – fly, snail, and mosquito. There were others. The site of the simulium blackflies that breed along the great rivers of Africa transmits to humans the larval microfilariae that migrate to the eye to blind and the skin to blotch with black spots. Sand flies carry the parasite leishmania, which spreads kala-azar, which killed 100,000 Sudanese in 2001, and *Leishmania aethiopica* in East Africa. Several species of worms originating in monkeys create severe intestinal disease, usually from contaminated drinking water.

There were many other lethal diseases indigenous to Africa, transmitted through viruses rather than parasites, that inhibited the growth of its population. The yellow fever pathogen had its origins in tree-dwelling monkeys and was transferred to humans by the mosquito *Aedes simpsoni*, from which it was easily transmitted to the numerous species of domestic mosquitoes such as *A. aegypti*. Yellow fever was first identified in the seventeenth century among African slaves brought to the Caribbean, but it had long been prevalent, often in epidemics, from West Africa to Ethiopia. The mutilating disease of leprosy was endemic in rural Ethiopia by the fourth century, and was found throughout all the humid tropical areas of the continent when the Europeans penetrated the interior in the nineteenth century. Most of these African diseases were exported during the slave trade to the other tropical regions of the New World and Asia, where they flourished in the heat and humidity.

The early hunters and gatherers of Africa were probably infected by those parasites carried by the higher apes and animal herds whose carcasses they scavenged. These nomadic foraging families, however, were few, and their wanderings over many square miles prevented infection growing into the epidemics: the disease would die with the individual in some remote location. Agriculture and the concentration of farmers in villages beside the fields destroyed the prophylactic of space and exposed the closely packed residents to the intensity of a confined disease. After 1600 the spread of endemic diseases accelerated with the expansion of long-distance trade, which nourished the fledgling towns. The village, town, and city have historically been hothouses of epidemics. Africa was no different except that it had many more virulent diseases, placing greater constraints on the growth of its population. In order to survive, the Africans had to adapt to the very harsh ecology of disease that limited their ability to proliferate at the same rate as those who had migrated to more temperate climates.

Crops

The African continent is the most ancient, and its soils the most impoverished. The hunters and gatherers learned to exploit the variegated indigenous plants they domesticated on marginal land to begin African agriculture. Throughout the great swath of sahel and savanna from the Atlantic to the Indian

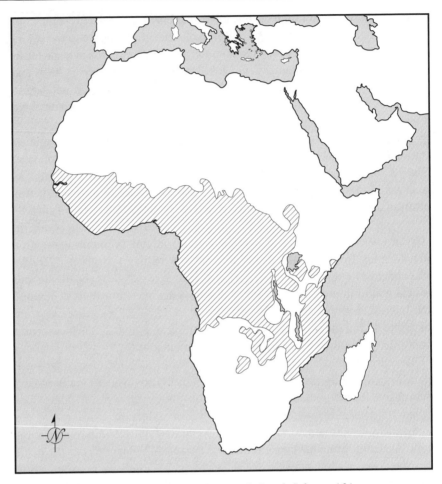

Map 13.1 *The distribution of the tsetse fly in sub-Saharan Africa.*

Ocean an African agricultural complex emerged, which enabled the building of villages, towns, cities, and states. Here the Africans developed and cultivated indigenous savanna plants – cereals, tubers, vegetables, and stimulants. In a large continent with different ecologies, climate, and terrain, the agricultural diversity of African crops developed individual varieties and different techniques to grow them. Indigenous African agriculture can be arbitrarily divided into crops grown from seeds, roots, or plantains. Cereals and grains require seeds saved from the previous harvest sown in savanna lands with medium rainfall. The collected grains are ground into flour to produce a wide variety of porridges, bread, and beer. Root crops are derived from tubers or shoots that are planted individually in whole or in part into the moist soil of the forest regions of Africa. They are high in carbohydrates, but can be stored for long periods in the heat and humidity of the rainforest to provide a tasty staple prepared in many ways. Plantains are more like a seedless vegetable that sprouts to bear an edible fruit high in carbohydrates such as the banana.

The most important food in the history of Africa is the perennial crop that produces small grains, sorghum (*Sorghum bicolor*), known colloquially as *durra*. Sorghum has been a staple food for 7,000 years since its grains were first gathered from wild grasses in the savanna west of the Nile. During the subsequent millennia the seeds were domesticated and spread throughout the savanna lands of western, eastern, and southern Africa, where new strains were developed to accommodate the variety of soils, rainfall, and human preference. By the beginning of the Christian era sorghum was the staple food of Africans of the savanna and sahel. The intensification of sorghum cultivation was made possible by the rapid development of iron tools, which could clear the fields, weed, and harvest. Hoes and axes forged by local smiths enabled the expansion of sorghum cultivation as well as of other indigenous cereals.

Sorghum became the staple food, but millet was the crop that survived when sorghum failed in times of drought. Millet, like sorghum, is indigenous to Africa. A perennial, it grows in arid and marginal lands, looks like a weed, and has a variety of species. The pearl or bullrush millet (*Pennisetum glaucum*) originated in the western Sahel in the Tichit region of Mauritania as early as the second century BCE, from where it spread to be widely exploited. Another species, the finger millet (*Eleusine coracana*), is native to Ethiopia and the East African highlands.

Rice is the African grain that grows best in wet lowlands watered either by rain or rivers. There are two species common in Africa, one indigenous, the other imported. The distinct *Oryza glaberrima*, Guinea rice, originated in regions of ample rainfall in the hinterland of the Guinea coast and in the wetlands of the delta basin of the Middle Niger River. By the beginning of the Christian era farmers had domesticated Guinea rice, which became a staple for their diet and a commodity to trade. The rice commonly used throughout the world today is *Oryza sativa*; its origin is in India and Southeast Asia, where it was domesticated as early as the third millennium BCE. It was carried to the East African coast by traders plying the Sabaean Lane from India more than a thousand years ago, where it was regarded by the Swahili as a cosmopolitan food, superior to the finger millet, which was seen as fit only for farmers.

Sorghum, millet, and rice provided nourishment for Africans in the savanna and along the rivers, but only root crops could be grown in the African forest, the most abundant being the yam (*Discorea cayensis*). The domestication of the yam was less complicated, and consequently very ancient. Yams are tasty and high in carbohydrates, but low in any other nutritional value, and consequently require supplements of vegetables, fish, palm oil, goats, and chickens, which can survive in the tsetse-fly zone. The planting and harvesting of yams have been celebrated by African societies in the forest for centuries. Nigeria today produces half the world's supply of yams, and it is from West Africa that the African yam became a staple in the Caribbean, Southeast Asia, and Oceania. The yam was the principal food that made possible the expansion of the Bantu-speaking people, through the rainforest of equatorial Africa.

The other crop that shaped the history of Africa is the plantain, the best known form being the banana (*Musa sapientium*), which originated in Southeast Asia. Numerous varieties were carried to East Africa by mariners and traders of the Sabaean Lane during the first millennium of the Christian era. The banana flourished in the ample rainfall of the Lake Plateau of East Africa, where it became the staple food crop for the inhabitants of the states scattered around the equatorial lakes and the equatorial rainforest to the west. Africa has its own banana (*Ensete edulis*, known as the false banana), indigenous to Ethiopia, which does not bear edible fruit, but for the Africans of southwest Ethiopia its tubers pounded and cooked are the dietary staple, its stems make ropes, and its seeds are used for ornamental and medicinal purposes. These crops enabled the Bantu speakers to expand throughout the continent, but they were heavy in carbohydrates and deficient in nutrients. Childbearing women were vulnerable to disease and early death due to an unbalanced diet, particularly when the scarcity of food combined with their demanding domestic chores limited their reproductive capacity. Infant mortality before the age of five has been estimated at over 30 percent. Children were socially, economically, and culturally essential to African society. The need for children and their short lives made polygynous marriage a practical solution, but even multiple wives could not increase the population more than two or three per thousand when it was decimated by disease and a diet that did not have the basic nutrients for healthy reproduction.

Ironically, it was the arrival of the Europeans in the sixteenth century, who were to transport millions out of Africa to the New World as slaves, that enabled the Africans to increase their population. This was not due to the containment of disease – in fact, the Europeans introduced new and very deadly diseases; rather, the growth in the number of Africans after the sixteenth century has been attributed to the introduction of new crops from the New World, especially by the Portuguese. Today the major foodstuffs in Africa are both seed and root, as in the past, but they are not indigenous to Africa. Maize (corn) has replaced sorghum as the preferred grain and cassava (manioc), rather than the yam, soon became the dominant African tuber food.

Maize (*Zea mays*) originated in the coastal regions of Peru and was cultivated for over two millennia in Mexico, from which it reached Spain and was brought to Delagoa Bay in Mozambique by the Portuguese in the sixteenth century. Maize grows well in humid and sunny weather, and by the nineteenth century had spread erratically but steadily from southern and Central Africa to the northern grasslands of the continent. Its high yields – twice as many calories as millet and 50 percent more than sorghum – and pleasant taste made it the staple, prestigious grain food in Africa. Unlike flowering sorghum the compact corn cob is sheathed (its defense against voracious birds), and it is easily stored in large corn cribs, while sorghum seeds were kept in fragile baskets. The cobs became the standard food for the itinerant trader over long distances.

The cassava plant is only a few feet high, but it produces fat roots of varying length. Cassava (manioc, *Manihot esculenta*) was carried by the Portuguese from the Amazon in Brazil to Africa, also in the sixteenth century. Transplanted to West Africa and the Congo rainforest, it flourished in the heat, humidity, and poor soils to become the staple tuber crop. Cassava produces 150 percent more calories than maize, and like maize had spread throughout most of sub-Saharan Africa by the nineteenth century. Its tubers are prolific and low in protein, but, like the banana, they require little land and labor compared to sorghum and maize. Cassava was an efficient food in regions of dense population, as it could survive drought and be easily stored as insurance against famine.

These new staples, which began to change the demography of Africa, should not diminish the importance of other New World crops – most of them brought by the Portuguese – that have contributed to the increase in the population of the African continent during the last 400 years. There were beans in all varieties – kidney, lima, navy – that grow well where there is water. Like maize, beans were first domesticated by the Indians of the Americas. Ancient Peruvian pottery inscriptions portray Indians holding beans in one hand and maize in the other to acknowledge their dependence upon them. The Spanish carried beans to the Philippines and Asia. The Portuguese transplanted them to Africa, but several important varieties arrived with the Atlantic slave trade, such as the lima bean, which came from Brazil. Sweet potatoes were popular and widely grown throughout Africa. Another crop of the Indians in the valleys of the Andes, the potato, found its way to Africa in the eighteenth century via Florida, Spain, and England in the eighteenth century. Peanuts, first domesticated from the wild in Brazil and Paraguay, spread northward through Central America and Mexico. The Spanish brought them to Iberia, and in the sixteenth century the Portuguese introduced them to West Africa, where they flourished and spread throughout the continent. The tomato also arrived in Africa from South and Central America along the same route. Peas, sesame, and sugar cane came from Asia, carried by Asian and European merchants in the globalization of international trade that followed the Portuguese pioneering voyages of discovery.

The introduction of New World and Asian crops transformed many African agricultural societies, enabling them to expand into the vast unpopulated lands of the continent. The Europeans did indeed transport the agricultural innovations of the Indians of South America, but they also carried with them the diseases of the Old World that were to infect the peoples of Africa and add to their multiplicity of tropical endemic diseases. Like the indigenous peoples of the New World the Africans had no immunity to new and deadly Old World parasites. Smallpox (originally, *small pockes*, *pocke* meaning sac) had been the major killer disease in the temperate climates. It first appeared around 10,000 BCE in northeast Africa, from where it spread to Persia, India, and China. Its scars have been found on the mummies of ancient Egyptians and among the peoples of the Ethiopian highlands during the early centuries of the Christian era, and those of a mild indigenous strain in West and East Africa. The virulent variety of smallpox, against which Africans had no natural immunity, however, came with the Europeans. As early as 1589 a smallpox epidemic was reported in Mozambique by João dos Santos, and during subsequent centuries epidemics erupted during periods of severe drought. Epidemics of European smallpox ravaged West Africa from the sixteenth to the nineteenth centuries, particularly in the equatorial regions of Kongo in 1560 and Angola between 1625 and 1628. In 1864, 1867, and 1873 the Igbo and others in West Africa were decimated by smallpox epidemics; one-quarter of the population of Luanda perished in the epidemic of 1864. Smallpox arrived in Cape Town from Asia with the Dutch, in 1713 killing one-quarter of the settlement's population and devastating the Khoisan people. Only one in ten is recorded to have survived. The epidemic swept north across the Orange (Gariep) River, and there were extensive outbreaks in 1755 and 1767 that proved fatal to unrecorded numbers. Epidemics were frequent and episodic, but it was not until the twentieth century and the introduction of vaccination that the spread of smallpox was limited (but never completely eliminated) in Africa.

There were other diseases carried out of Europe to which the Africans had no natural immunity. Like smallpox, syphilis seems to be indigenous to Africa in a mild form, but after the introduction of venereal syphilis from the New World by Europeans in the sixteenth century it became widespread. Typhus and tuberculosis appeared in Africa during the seventeenth century. The desert prevented the plague, the Black Death, from advancing into sub-Saharan Africa, but in the seventeenth century it arrived in Kongo and Angola via the Atlantic slave trade and appeared in Senegal and Guinea in the eighteenth century.

Africa was an agricultural continent with many indigenous endemic tropical diseases to which were added those carried by the Europeans. Disease was the principal factor that prevented the African population from growing at the same rate as in more temperate climates. The arrival of the Europeans contributed new parasites against which Africans had no natural immunities. At the same time, the Europeans brought from the New World crops of great productivity that enabled the Africans to begin a steady increase in population to fill a relatively empty continent.

Further reading

Clark, J. D. and S. A. Brandt (eds.), *From Hunters to Farmers: The Causes and Consequences of Food Production in Africa*, Berkeley: University of California Press, 1984

Connah, Graham, *African Civilizations: An Archaeological Perspective*, Cambridge: Cambridge University Press, 2001

Harlan, J. R., J. M. J. de Wet, and A. B. L. Stemler (eds.), *Origins of African Plant Domestication*, The Hague: Mouton, 1976

Hartwig, G. W. and K. D. Patterson, *Disease in African History*, Chapel Hill: Duke University Press, 1978

Ransford, Oliver, *"Bid the Sickness Cease": Disease in the History of Black Africa*, London: John Murray, 1983

Vansina, Jan, *Paths in the Rainforest: Toward a History of Political Traditions in Equatorial Africa*, Madison: University of Wisconsin Press, 1990

14   Slavery in Africa

Slavery is an institution with ancient roots. It is one of many unequal social relationships that humans have created over time, and has existed in many forms. Some societies have treated slaves as family members, allowing them to marry, inherit property, and even earn their freedom. Others have dehumanized them, terrorizing them psychologically, exploiting them sexually, and treating them as beasts of burden, often to be worked to death. While all human societies have social inequalities, slavery is common in those in which human labor is scarce and in demand. Ancient Rome, Eastern Europe in the Medieval era, and Africa for much of its history have been societies in which there was more work to be done than people to do it.

Slavery has deep roots in Western civilization. It was firmly established in the Mediterranean world by the Greek and Roman Empires, which acquired millions of slaves in wars and raids against the peoples living in the geographical arc that spanned Europe from the Caucasus in southern Russia to Spain. To the ancients, slavery was an institution that required no justification; even those guardians of ethical behavior such as the Greek philosopher Aristotle regarded it as an indispensable, normal, and acceptable feature of society. In the Roman Empire many slaves were Slavs – from which the word slave is derived – as well as other Europeans, such as Germans, Saxons, Normans, Celts, and Gauls. The Romans enslaved some black Africans as well, though they did not appear to have associated slavery with skin color and there were numerous free Africans in their societies. Slaves were distinguished by custom and law, in which the slave was an object (*res*), property with few rights.

In Africa, slavery was practiced at least 5,000 years ago. In the ancient world slavery was an important component of Africa's trade to other continents, down the Nile, across the Sahara Desert, over the Indian Ocean, and later, across the Atlantic Ocean to the New World. The oldest evidence of the enslavement of Africans appears in the carvings and inscriptions at the Second Cataract of the Nile representing Pharaoh Djer of the first Egyptian dynasty of the Old Kingdom taking slaves in a boat from Nubia to Egypt in about 2900 BCE. During the next millennia the number of slaves taken out of Africa was relatively small compared to the substantial numbers that followed after the eighth century CE. The dynastic Egyptians regularly raided for captives in the Nile Valley south of Aswan, most of whom remained enslaved in Egypt. In the first millennium

CE. there was also a diminutive flow across the Sahara to Europe and from Ethiopia and the East African coast to Asia.

The advent of the Islamic age coincided with a sharp increase in the African slave trade. After the death of the Prophet Muhammad in 632 the expansion of the Arabs and the spread of Islam became the dominant force in world history for the next 500 years. Within a short period of time most of the peoples of North Africa had embraced Islam, and Islamic communities were established in West and East Africa, where the inhabitants became Muslims, though most did not speak Arabic. This new Islamic world – which stretched from Baghdad to Morocco – had a steady demand for slaves which could not be satisfied through trade with Christian Europe. As the expanding Islamic world demanded more slave labor, the feudal economies of Europe that had replaced the Roman Empire were witnessing rapid population growth. In Europe the demand for slave labor significantly diminished as European slavery gradually transformed into serfdom.

The expansion of the trans-Saharan slave trade (which we associate with the Sahelian empire of Ghana) was the commercial response to the demand in the markets of the Mahgrib. The moral justification for the enslavement of Africans south of the Sahara by Muslims was accepted by the fact they were "unbelievers" (*kafirin*) practicing their traditional religions with many gods, not the one God of Islam. The need for slaves, whether acquired by violence or by commercial exchange, revived the ancient but somnolent trans-Saharan trade, which became a major supplier of slaves for North Africa and Islamic Spain. The earliest Muslim account of slaves crossing the Sahara from the Fezzan in southern Libya to Tripoli on the Mediterranean coast was written in the seventh century, but from the ninth century to the nineteenth there are a multitude of accounts of the pillage by military states of the Sahel, known to North African Muslims as *bilad al-sudan*, ("land of the blacks"), of pagan Africans who were sold to Muslim merchants and marched across the desert as a most profitable commodity in their elaborate commercial networks. By the tenth century there was a steady stream of slaves taken from the kingdoms of the Western Sudan and the Chad Basin crossing the Sahara. Many died on the way, but the survivors fetched a great profit in the vibrant markets of Sijilmasa, Tripoli, and Cairo.

As in the Western Sudan, Islam stimulated the ancient trade in slaves in East Africa, as Muslim merchants looked to expand their Indian Ocean commerce along the maritime arc across East Africa, the Persian Gulf, and India known as the Sabaean Lane. The slaves from East Africa and its Horn were called *zanj* (Arabic, "black"), and became laborers, soldiers, and concubines in the Muslim world of the eastern Mediterranean, Mesopotamia, the Persian Gulf, the Indian subcontinent, and Central Asia. A few became powerful officials, *wazirs*; most worked the fields or in households, and thousands were concentrated in the salt mines of southern Iraq at the head of the Persian Gulf. In 869 Ali ibn

Muhammad ibn Abd al-Rahim (d. 883), an outspoken critic of the Abbasid caliphate in Baghdad, led the *zanj* in rebellion against their harsh treatment, and under his able leadership sustained a revolt that shook the Islamic community of the Middle East. The *zanj* revolt was finally suppressed in 883, but the spectacle of a successful rebellion by African slaves did not diminish the demand for slaves in Arabia and the Persian Gulf or the supply from East Africa.

For those enslaved peoples who remained within Africa, there were myriad variations in their status and in their treatment. Scholars Suzanne Miers and Igor Kopytoff describe African slavery as "simply one part of a continuum of relations, which at one end are part of the realm of kinship and at the other involve using people as chattels. Slavery is a combination of elements, which if differently combined – an ingredient added here or subtracted there – might become adoption, marriage, parentage, obligations to kinsmen, clientship, and so forth."[1] The variables that shaped the nature of slavery were many. Slaves in village-based societies often lived and worked with their masters' families, and were more likely to enjoy some protection and status within the community. Slaves who worked in large groups – in the salt mines of the Sahara and on the agricultural plantations that emerged in West Africa after 1500 – were more likely to be treated as chattels. Slaves in communities in which they outnumbered their masters, such as the Dutch Cape Colony in the late eighteenth century, could expect draconian punishments from their fearful owners for even trivial transgressions. Slaves in Muslim societies enjoyed some rights and protection under Islamic jurisprudence, but these were more often observed in theory rather than practice.

Any discussion of African slavery inevitably leads to a comparison with the forms of slavery practiced in the New World. It is true that New World slavery – characterized by large gangs of slaves toiling in mines and on plantations, justified by the most naked forms of racism – was at the most extreme end of that "continuum of relations" described by Miers and Kopytoff. In such comparisons African slavery has often been characterized as relatively benign because slaves could be assimilated into communities, earn freedom for themselves or their descendants, and even, in a few remarkable instances, attain eminent social and political status. The numbers of African slaves integrated into any community, however, were relatively few compared to those who were abused like the slaves in the Americas. While African slavery was in many cases qualitatively different from that found in the colonies of the Atlantic world, it was still slavery.

Although the treatment of slaves in Africa varied from the benign to the brutal, the severity of punishments usually diminished from one slave generation to another as the community became more accustomed to the slaves, who no longer possessed a memory of a past in which they were free. Assimilated by

---

[1] Suzanne Miers and Igor Kopytoff, introduction to Suzanne Miers and Igor Kopytoff (eds.), *Slavery in Africa: Historical and Anthropological Perspectives*, Madison: University of Wisconsin Press, 1977, p. 66.

language and culture into that of the masters the offspring of slaves became less like outsiders and consequently more acceptable to the community. The constraints of nature and disease that limited population growth throughout Africa discouraged the sale of slaves either temporarily or permanently, for the needs, social status, and importance of the master could best be satisfied by large numbers of slaves. As early as the eleventh century there were merchants in the trans-Saharan trade who owned more than a thousand slaves. In southern Nigeria at the end of the nineteenth century there were numerous wealthy merchants who possessed hundreds. In northern Nigeria by the 1850s half of the inhabitants of the sultanate of Sokoto were slaves, a pattern that continued into the twentieth century. In the French territories of the Western Sudan, French officials estimated that 30 to 50 percent of the African population, some 5 million people, were slaves.[2] Further east in the great basin of Lake Chad in the states of Kanem-Bornu, Bagirmi, and Wadai the ratio of slave to free person was much the same.

The Africans were not the only ones to practice slavery in Africa. Among the resident Europeans on the coast, slavery was regarded as a legitimate and acceptable necessity. Merchants, missionaries, officials, plantation owners, and Afro-Europeans who were their agents or independent traders themselves became a class with many names – *pombeiros*, *prazeros*, Creole – many of whom owned slaves that were not for export. The slaves resident on the coast served in many capacities from those trained to operate the commercial stations to the most menial tasks – loading ships, porterage, common labor, concubinage, and guarding other slaves for the overseas trade. By the end of the eighteenth century there were some 60,000 to 100,000 slaves owned by Europeans and Afro-Europeans in Africa. They were scattered in the European enclaves along the coast from West to East Africa, but the greatest concentration was on the western African coast in Angola around the two large enclaves of Luanda and Benguela. Here the majority of slaves were women, the men being exported while the women remained in Africa to perform the agricultural labor on the European and Afro-European plantations as they had in many traditional societies.

Slavery in Cape Town and its immediate interior developed a different pattern from that in the other European coastal cantons. In 1652 the Dutch East India Company established a permanent settlement at Cape Town to provide supplies for its ships making the long passage from the Netherlands to India and Indonesia. Since the Dutch West India Company, which held a monopoly of the Dutch Atlantic slave trade from western Africa, prohibited the Dutch East India Company from poaching on their west coast slave preserves, and the indigenous Khoikhoi at the Cape were disinclined to become menial laborers, the company imported slaves from other parts of Africa, from the island of

---

[2] Paul E. Lovejoy, *Transformations in Slavery: A History of Slavery in Africa*, 2nd ed., Cambridge: Cambridge University Press, 2000, pp. 183–184, 202.

Madagascar, from India, and from Indonesia to the Cape. During the seventeenth century tensions between the Dutch employees and the company led to the flight of many Dutch farmers, *boers*, into the interior, resulting in the decision by the directors in 1717 to restrict immigration of free or indentured Dutch labor from the Netherlands in favor of importing additional slaves from Asia. At the end of the eighteenth century the slave population had increased to 25,000, outnumbering the colony's 20,000 free colonists. Many of these Cape slaves learned skills the company needed in transit between Europe and Asia.

On the eastern African coast in the valley of the Zambezi the Portuguese settlers, who as early as the sixteenth century had established themselves as warlords on their *prazo*s (Portuguese, *prazo*, "estate"), were granted vast tracts of land by the Portuguese Crown to enlarge their plantations worked largely by female slaves. To defend and expand the *prazo*s the Portuguese *prazero*s, many of them Afro-Portuguese, filled their private armies with slave soldiers (*achikunda*), who lived off the produce and tribute exacted from the African cultivators by them and the *prazero*s. Armed and organized into regiments, to which they were fiercely loyal, the *achikunda* could not be treated as chattels, for the *prazero*s were dependent upon them to protect and enlarge their holdings; this gave them status and treatment superior to that of the free farmers. Five hundred *achikunda* on a *prazo* was not uncommon; some armies numbered a thousand, but most *prazero*s had a hundred or less of these African mercenary slaves.

How did Africans become enslaved? Most slaves were taken in wars or slave raids (*razzia*) or kidnapped, and consequently were outsiders who were particularly vulnerable to the demands and exploitation by those of different ethnicity, language, and culture who had acquired them. There were many reasons to declare war, but prisoners were a ready sale that helped defray the cost of maintaining mercenary armies. Kings made wars in the name of the state, but many of these hostilities were an ill-disguised excuse to raid for slaves. In the fifteenth century the larger kingdom of Jolof in the Senegal Valley on the frontier of Islam disintegrated before the assaults of Wolof warlords and their armies of mounted slaves (*ceddo*, *tyeddo*). These warlords threatened the rule of kings, and many became mythical heroes struggling against real or imagined royal tyranny in the legends recited by the *griot*s, the West African praise-singers. African kings in time of war had the right to demand military service from the aristocratic heads of clans. They were, like the nobility in Europe, notoriously unreliable when called to honor their allegiance and fight for the king, who consequently came to rely increasingly on slave soldiers loyal only to him and not to clan, lineage, or ethnicity. These slave troops have formed the core of the royal armies in dynastic Egypt, the kingdom of Kush, the empires of the Western Sudan, and the kingdoms of Asante, Benin, Dahomey, Kongo, Bagirmi, and the Luba Lunda of Central Africa. The king provided arms and horses, and the armed slaves were fed at his expense or were billeted in the villages ready to march immediately at the king's order. The kingdom of Kayor in the Senegal was typical, for here the "*ceddo* were the only section of the population [on] which the king [the *damel*] could absolutely depend."[3] Among the Mossi, Nupe, and Hausa the kings also employed slaves as police upon whose loyalty they could count to keep order in the towns and cities.

Bandits were more straightforward if more vicious than kings, for the *razzia* was their principal occupation. Brigands are as old as history, as common in Africa as they have been throughout the world. These gangs were usually led by a chief in rebellion against a central authority for personal gain, who would willingly provide refuge for escaped slaves. Banditry is violent theft, and the Africans made the distinction between highway robbery and kidnapping, which was a much more common means to acquire slaves. The widespread use of kidnapping is often overshadowed by the more dramatic enslavement by war and banditry, but it was common, and was a measure of domestic insecurity within many African states. The *Hudud al-alam*, a tenth-century Persian account, describes the land and its people between the Atlantic and the Nile where "the [Egyptian] merchants steal their children and bring them [with them]. Then they castrate them, import them into Egypt and sell them. Among themselves there are people who steal each other's children and sell them to the [Egyptian] merchants when the latter arrive."[4] Olaudah Equiano (1745–1797) was an Igbo child who was presumably kidnapped and sold into slavery. He was later given his freedom and educated in England, where in 1789 he published the story of his abduction, the authenticity of which has recently been challenged:

> Generally when the grown people in the neighbourhood were gone far in [the] fields to labour, the children assembled together in some of the neighbourhood premises to play; and commonly some of us used to get up a tree to look out for any assailant or kidnapper, that might come upon us . . . One day when all of our people were gone out to their works as usual, and only I and my dear sister were left to mind the house, two men and a woman got over the walls, and in a moment seized us both, and without giving us time to cry out, or make resistance, they stopped our mouths, and ran off with us.[5]

A slave who shared the same language, culture, and religion of the owner would usually be accepted as part of the family, but not a member of the clan or lineage. There were those, however, who belonged to the same ethnic

---

[3] V. Monteil, "The Wolof Kingdom of Kayor," in D. Forde and P. M. Kaberry (eds.), *West African Kingdoms in the 19th Century*, London: International African Institute, 1951, p. 269.

[4] *Hūdud al-'ālam (The Regions of the World)*, trans. V. Minorsky, 2nd ed., C. E. Bosworth, London: Luzac & Company, 1970, p. 165.

[5] Olaudah Equiano, *The Life of Olaudah Equiano, or Gustavus Vassa the African*, ed. Paul Edwards, London: Longman, 1989, pp. 15–16.

group but became outsiders when they were regarded by the community as undesirable – criminals for murder, theft, adultery, sorcery; those afflicted with a deforming disease, particularly the hated leprosy; or people accused of other anti-social activities who were sold into slavery rather than imprisoned or put to death. African slavery also purged the unwanted from society – the old, widows, feeble-minded, destitute, debtors, and the homeless in search of food in times of famine. The threat of starvation, which was frequent in times of drought, often resulted in voluntary enslavement. Those upon whom society imposed its sanctions were at times victims of ritual sacrifice, as in Benin, but most undesirables were more easily eliminated by a profitable sale to foreign traders, particularly after the introduction of the trans-Oceanic slave trade to the New World or Asia.

Coercion by the master was usually administered in one of two ways – the brutal and the more subtle. To insure obedience, discipline, and service slaves were intimidated by flogging, dismemberment, castration, sacrifice to the gods, or put to death as spectacle for the crowd. The use of force was common in all slave societies and not peculiar to Africa. There was, however, an equally powerful psychological means of coercion, which tended to result in the meek acceptance of servitude. The insubordinate or hostile slave ran the risk of sale into situations, such as ritual sacrifice, that were far worse than his existing servitude. This imminent threat was, for many slaves, more feared than harsh punishment because it was always present and its results uncertain.

Though slaves were vulnerable to abuse by their masters, they were also a valuable asset, which their owners were wise to protect. They filled a number of roles beyond the obvious tasks of concubinage and manual labour. Simply being the slave of another gave that person social stature. Slaves were also trusted with many important functions, and served as warriors, traders, and as agents of chiefs and kings, Such responsibilities could offer a talented and ambitious slave the opportunity to win status and wealth; but the greatest aspiration of any slave was to gain freedom. Manumission was not uncommon, particularly among Muslims, and Islamic law held that children of concubines were free. Some slaves earned enough to purchase their freedom, while in other cases a master might free his slaves upon his death. Mostly, however, slaves were passed on to the heirs of a deceased owner, along with whatever land or livestock he possessed.

Slavery in Africa took many forms, depending on the needs and occupations of the slave owners, and often the work of slaves was hardly distinguishable from that of free Africans in the society – those who were serfs, those who labored for wages, or those working on traditional communal lands or pastures. Yet all of these workers had, theoretically, the freedom to walk away, a choice that the slave did not possess except to flee, aware of the retribution that would follow recapture. Slave owners controlled the sexual and reproductive capacities as well as the physical and mental lives of their slaves. Demand, largely regulated by the marketplace, determined the price of slaves. Women and young girls commanded higher prices than men and boys of similar age. The master's right to sexual access drove up the price of female slaves to twice that of males of comparable age. Moreover, a female slave had to have the consent of her master to have a relationship with another, and her children became his property. Bonds of affection could develop between owners and their slaves, but in the end the master controlled the reward system. In Africa as in the Americas and Asia the short life-span of a slave, largely from overwork, and the very low birthrate among slave women, who did not wish to bear children that were not to be their own, constituted the driving-force to seek new sources of slaves by warfare, *razzia*, or trade to replace losses and to increase the slave population.

Of all African slaves the eunuch was the most highly prized and the most expensive. The demand for eunuchs always exceeded the supply, and consequently their price in the African slave markets could often be ten times that of a female slave. The making of a eunuch by castration has historically been extremely hazardous, with an estimated mortality of 70 to 90 percent, depending who was doing the operation. In the literature and mythology of the West the eunuch was the guardian of the ruler's harem, but in fact the primary role of the eunuch was not protecting the concubines, but as political advisor to the ruler, whether in the African kingdoms of Asante, Oyo, Dahomey, Bagirmi, the Arab, Turkish, and Persian empires of the Middle East, or the Tang and Ming dynasties of China. The eunuch was the quintessential slave. He could not pass on life, goods, titles, or functions. He was beholden to no clan, chief, or noble. He remained aloof from the intrigues of imperial courtesans and was not dependent upon the supplications of the king's own family and kin.

After eunuchs, women were the most valued slaves, for they could perform more functions than any male. They could cook at the hearth, cultivate and carry, act as concubines and bear children, conduct business, and themselves often dealt in slaves. The average estimated demand for women to men slaves over time and place in Africa was usually two to one, and that was reflected in numbers and price. Female slaves were often purchased for their ability to reproduce, but it could be a bad investment, as female slaves had few children. In eighteenth-century Cape Town slave women had only one or at most two children, while free women had three or more. In the nineteenth-century Congo and West Africa slave women had on average less than one child. These examples reflect the sad fact that motherhood was not desirable to female slaves, as they knew that their children would be born into a life of slavery.

It was not through procreation, but in their agricultural labor, that female slaves made their most important contribution to African economies. Women in Africa traditionally perform 60 to 70 percent of the agricultural labor and virtually all the housekeeping, but none of the pastoral work. Women have not just been the laborers in the fields, but also the artisans in intensive crafts such as weaving. The men did the heavy work of clearing and planting, but it was women's work to cultivate the crop, weed, and prepare for the harvest. Since women did the agricultural fieldwork in free African societies, they were expected to do the same as slaves, and consequently were worth twice the price in the marketplace. Young girls were frequently used in the form of slavery known as "pawning" whereby a slave was pawned by a parent or seller to a creditor in return for cash, to be recovered on repayment; this was widely practiced throughout Africa. Young girls were also given to reward soldiers or as booty, payment of fines, and bride-wealth. In some African societies women were also warriors. There are romantic descriptions of the corps of 3,000 Amazons in Dahomey during the eighteenth and nineteenth centuries, who were celibate female slaves and the loyal bodyguards of the king.

The export trade in slaves was Africa's most dependable commodity, but within the markets of the continent the slave was the most convertible of all currencies – more so than gold or cowries, and became the essential medium in the transactions of the internal trade. The buying and selling of slaves was not a male monopoly: female owners and traders in slaves were not uncommon. They were free women who kept their property separate from that of their men, according to local custom and traditions. The female head of the house dominated and controlled the household slaves. She did hesitate to exploit female African slaves in the pursuit of commercial profit in the marketplace. In many African societies, particularly in West Africa, there was a long and respected tradition of female mercantile enterprise.

Many of these women were the offspring of transient European male traders and African women from the social elite given the name "Eurafricans" by the historian George E. Brooks. They were cultivated, multilingual, and frequently entrepreneurial. They were slave owners who played a crucial role in the commercial and social relations between the Africans and European merchants, and who often practiced Catholicism without abandoning their traditional religious rituals. In the seventeenth century the Luso-African Senhora Catarine (Seignora Catti) was the commercial agent for the *damel* (king) of Cayor and interpreter for the Compagnie du Sénégal, who traded the *damel*'s slaves on his behalf and for her own profit. Bibiana Vaz was the wife of one of the most successful Portuguese traders, Ambrosio Gomes, and, upon his death in 1679, used his two-master schooner to consolidate an extensive commercial network in the Senegambia. A Luso-African contemporary of Bibiana Vaz, La Belinguere, of royal blood, became one of the most influential persons in the Gambia and amassed a fortune in cattle, gold, and slaves. In the eighteenth century Senhora Doll from the Ya Kumba family dominated trade in the Sherbro Estuary with her English husband; their descendants established a mercantile dynasty including control of the Plaintain and Banana Islands. A Bullom woman, Seniore Maria, made a fortune in the salt trade near Cape Sierra Leone and became an interpreter for the Royal African Company, and another Eurafrican, Betsy Heard, was one of numerous Eurafrican children sent to England to learn reading, writing, and arithmetic. She returned to the West African coast to manage a profitable slave factory on the Bereira River.

These African and Eurafrican female slave owners could prosper by marrying a male slave and exploiting his labor. There is an Igbo saying that "Those who have people are wealthier than those with money." Woman marriage was widespread, in which a female slave owner assumed the role of legal genitor whereby all the children of the younger women slaves belonged to her female husband. A prosperous female slave owner in Sierra Leone was Madam Yoko, a Mende. She was "the possessor of many slaves, who live in small towns owned by her, near and around Sennehoo. These work her farms, and she is supported solely by their labor and industry. About her person is a train of female attendants – about twenty in number – who are her ladies-in-waiting, and minister to her wants and wishes."[6]

Ironically, the abolition of the Atlantic slave trade in the nineteenth century produced a dramatic increase in slavery within Africa. When slaves could no longer be exported, the trade expanded into the interior regions of the continent where slaving and slavery had hitherto been of little importance. The Mossi on the Upper Volta River and the Luba and the Ovambo in the interior of Angola were now enslaved by African slave traders. No longer exportable, the number of slaves in Africa increased, and their masters now feared that the concentration of slaves in their territory, most of whom were men, would overwhelm them in times of trouble. There were slave rebellions in the Futa Jalon, the Niger Delta, and among the Yoruba, the suppression of which was accompanied by an increase in ritual killings and human sacrifice – often perfunctory, but usually attached to a festival, funeral, or a religious rite. The *asantehene* Kwaku Dua I (1833–1867) justified the practice to a missionary: "If I were to abolish human sacrifices, I should deprive myself of one of the most effectual means of keeping the people in subjection."[7]

Slavery in Africa was a historic and accepted institution whose numbers throughout the millennia undoubtedly surpassed the estimated sixteen-and-a-half million slaves who were forcefully exported out of Africa between the seventeenth and twentieth centuries to the Americas and Asia.

> A history of Africa claims that between 30 and 60 percent of the entire population were slaves during historical times. If this is correct, the number of people enslaved in Africa far exceeded the number taken from the continent by the slave trade. In fact, given the volume of the demand for slaves within

[6] Reverend Thomas H. Carthew, letter in the *United Methodist Free Churches' Magazine*, January 1885, p. 68. See Christopher Fyfe, *Sierra Leone Inheritance*, London: Oxford University Press, 1964, p. 238.

[7] T. B. Freeman, *Journal of Various Visits to the Kingdoms of Ashanti, Aku, and Dahomi*, 2nd ed., London: J. Mason, 1844, p. 164.

the continent, the shipping of slaves across the Atlantic should perhaps be seen as an extension of the internal market.[8]

Even today there are accounts by journalists, academics, and investigators from numerous agencies such as Human Rights Watch describing pockets of slavery that are still scattered throughout the continent.

What the sterile statistics do not record and the factual descriptions of slavery often fail to emphasize is the indescribable amount of suffering – physical, psychological, emotional – of the slaves who were the victims of this system, which until the nineteenth century was universally accepted. A few slaves survived to enjoy positions of power and pleasure. However, most who did not perish when captured or during transport to the slave markets lost everything, including their individual identities. They were transformed into dehumanized beings to serve their masters. No words can convey the enormous and tragic loss to mankind wrought by this "peculiar institution."

Further reading

Lovejoy, Paul E., *Transformations in Slavery: A History of Slavery in Africa*, 2nd ed., Cambridge: Cambridge University Press, 2000

Lovejoy, Paul E. (ed.), *Slavery on the Frontiers of Islam*, Princeton: Markus Wiener, 2004

Lovejoy, Paul E. and Toyin Falola (eds.), *Pawnship, Slavery, and Colonialism in Africa*, Trenton, NJ: Africa World Press, 2003

Miers, Suzanne and Igor Kopytoff (eds.), *Slavery in Africa: Historical and Anthropological Perspectives*, Madison: University of Wisconsin Press, 1977

Robertson, Claire C. and Martin Klein (eds.), *Women and Slavery in Africa*, Portsmouth, NH: Heinemann, 1997

[8] John Reader, *Africa: A Biography of the Continent*, New York: Alfred A. Knopf, 1998, p. 291; see also Claude Meillassoux (ed.), *The Development of Indigenous Trade and Markets in West Africa: Studies Presented and Discussed at the Tenth International African Seminar at Fourah Bay College, Freetown, December 1969*, London: Oxford University Press, 1971, pp. 20–22.

15 The Atlantic slave trade

Although slavery had been an established institution in Africa for over a millennium and the trans-Saharan, Red Sea, and East African slave trade had been pervasive for many centuries, the Atlantic slave trade differed from them by its numbers, intensity, and the changes it produced within the societies of the African continent. More than 11 million Africans were exported to the Americas from the coast of western Africa. It was mostly conducted in just 300 years and concentrated in specific regions during different centuries, creating an uneven disruption of African societies along the coast. Over half the trade took place in the eighteenth century; the Bights of Benin and Biafra contributed significantly to the total, but the greatest number came from Loango and Angola further down the African coast. Africans developed new forms of political and social organizations in response to the Atlantic slave trade, but the skills and equipment that made the trans-Atlantic trade possible accelerated the growing technological gap between Africa and Europe. The demand for slaves increased the incidence of slavery in Africa, contributed to the disruption of traditional cultures, and encouraged a callous disregard for human life as persons became property. The brutality that accompanied the capture, sale, service, and ultimately transport across the Atlantic of Africans produced a great misery that cannot be ignored by the fact that the human resiliency of the Africans and their institutions survived the suffering.

In 1441 Antão Gonçalves arrived at Cape Blanco on the northern coast of present-day Mauritania. This was the forerunner of later expeditions sent down the coast of West Africa by Prince Henry the Navigator, and after his death the kings of Portugal, to divert the trans-Saharan gold trade for Portugal, convert African pagans to Christianity in the crusade against Islam, and discover a route around Africa to Asia and along the way find that legendary Christian king, Prester John. At Cape Blanco Gonçalves traded with Muslim merchants – and, to impress Prince Henry – seized twelve black Africans, including one woman. The prince was indeed interested. He knighted Gonçalves and sent him back the following year to round Cape Blanco into the Bay of Arguin, where he seized another ten Africans. The Atlantic slave trade had begun, and to encourage the conversion of African slaves and inhabitants to Christianity Pope Nicholas V issued his bull *Romanus Pontifex* on January 8, 1454, granting to the Portuguese a monopoly of trade with Africa, including slaves. Thereafter, Portuguese captains slowly made their way down the West African coast until

Table 15.1 *Slave exports from Africa across the Atlantic, 1450–1900*

Years	Number	Percent of total Atlantic trade
1450–1600	409,000	3.6%
1601–1700	1,348,000	11.9%
1701–1800	6,090,000	53.8%
1801–1900	3,466,000	30.6%
Total	11,313,000	100.0%

Source: Lovejoy, *Transformations in Slavery*, table 1.1.

Bartolomeu Dias reached the southern tip of Africa in 1488. During the half-century (1441–1488) between the encounter at Cape Blanco and their landing at the Cape of Good Hope gold had been the primary Portuguese export from West Africa – and remained so for another century – but during those years the Portuguese captains and merchants became increasingly involved in the trade in slaves as a secondary but profitable commodity. Since the Americas had yet to be discovered and it was to be another century after 1492 before slaves were in great demand in the Caribbean, the total volume of slaves to reach the islands in the Atlantic – Madeira, the Canaries, and Cape Verde – and Portugal for resale in southern Europe was no more than 80,000 from 1441 to 1500, an average of less than 1,400 per year. On the Gold Coast, however, the Portuguese were hard-pressed to find goods acceptable to the Africans in return for gold. Cloth and metals had a good but limited market. Since the Akan coastal merchants wanted slaves as porters, agricultural laborers, and for resale in the interior, the most prized commodity were slaves taken further east in the Bight of Benin, which became known as the Slave Coast, to exchange for gold. By the early sixteenth century Europeans had become directly involved in the internal African slave trade, transporting some 500 slaves a year from the Niger Delta to Elmina on the Gold Coast – not for export, but in exchange for gold in the local markets.

In 1482 the Portuguese arrived at the mouth of the great River Zaire, the Congo, and soon thereafter reached the flourishing inland kingdom of the *mani kongo* (king) with his capital at Mbanza Kongo (see chapter 10). The nobility and free commoners of the kingdom of Kongo owned slaves, as did the king, whose authority was dependent upon his slave army. Portuguese influence soon became dominant at the court after King Nzinga converted to Christianity and was baptized King João I in 1491, and slaves became the kingdom's principal export to the islands of São Tomé and Principe in the Bight of Biafra to labor on the new Portuguese sugar plantations or to await trans-shipment to the established plantations on Madeira and Cape Verde or to Elmina for gold. During the first two decades of the sixteenth century the kingdom of Kongo annually exported some 2,000 to 3,000 slaves; this increased to over 5,000 per year by the middle of the sixteenth century. When Nzinga Mbemba, a son of King João I, usurped the throne in 1506 to reign as Afonso I, he bitterly complained to the king of Portugal:

> Many of our subjects eagerly covet Portuguese merchandize, which your people bring into our kingdoms. To satisfy this disordered appetite, they seize numbers of our free or freed black subjects, and even nobles, sons of nobles, even the members of our own family. They sell them to the white people . . . This corruption and depravity is so widespread that our land is entirely depopulated by it . . . It is in fact our wish that this kingdom should be a place neither of trade nor of transit for slaves.[1]

King Afonso I (1506–1545) was not satisfied with the king of Portugal's contemptuous response that the Kongo had nothing to sell but slaves, and the subsequent history of the kingdom became one of conflict between the Kongolese monarchy's efforts to regulate the trade as a royal monopoly and the private traders, Portuguese and Afro-Portuguese (*pombeiros*), who were determined to subvert it. Neither was entirely successful. The traders failed to meet the increasing demand from the Spanish Caribbean, while the kingdom of Kongo was overwhelmed in 1568 by the invasion of the savage Jaga from the interior. The Jaga occupation of the kingdom until 1572 effectively ended attempts by the *mani kongo* to restrict the trade or to manipulate it to his advantage. Equally frustrated by the Jaga, the Portuguese turned south to Luanda, the gateway to Angola, for a new and plentiful supply of slaves who no longer had to be trans-shipped through São Tomé but were sent directly to the Americas.

In 1492 Christopher Columbus had discovered the Caribbean islands for Spain; in 1500 Pedro Álvares Cabral discovered Brazil for Portugal. Both regions were admirably suited to the cultivation of sugar on large plantations. Europe had an insatiable taste for sugar, and the plantations an insatiable demand for the labor to produce it. The first cargo of African slaves to arrive in the Americas came from Spain on a Spanish ship in 1501, followed by a second shipment of seventeen slaves in 1505, but it was not until 1518 that the first cargo of slaves reached the Caribbean directly from Africa. At first the nascent plantations were worked by Amerindians, but by the middle of the sixteenth century their population had been decimated by European and African diseases, and had to be replaced by Africans to meet the increasing demand for labor from plantation owners. African slaves were cheaper than European white indentured servants, and better able to withstand the tropical climate and disease of the Caribbean and Brazil. By the end of the sixteenth century 80 percent of the African slave trade went directly to the Americas, mostly to

---

[1] Afonso I to João III, October 18, 1526 and July 6, 1526, in Louis Jadin and Mireille Dicorate (eds.), *Correspondence de Dom Afonso, roi du Congo 1506–1543*, Brussels: Academie royale des sciences d'outre-mer, 1974, pp. 167, 156. See also John Illife, *Africans: The History of a Continent*, Cambridge: Cambridge University Press, 1995, p. 130.

Brazil. The remaining 20 percent was absorbed by the internal African markets and those on the Atlantic islands off the African coast, but in the sixteenth century the total volume of the Atlantic trade amounted to only a third of the combined trade in slaves across the Sahara, Red Sea, and the Indian Ocean to Asia. Between 1450 and 1600 the number of Africans exported from the continent into the Atlantic basin was about 410,000 or some 2,700 per year, a relatively small percentage (3.6 percent) of the total volume of slaves exported out of Africa during the 350 years of the Atlantic trade.

If the volume of the Atlantic slave trade remained relatively modest during the sixteenth century, the need for labor on the sugar plantations of the Americas increased, to remain steady at 10,000 slaves exported annually until the mid-seventeenth century, by which time the Protestant Dutch had destroyed the 200-year Catholic Portuguese monopoly granted by Pope Nicholas V in 1454. The Portuguese had neither the manpower nor the resources to sustain a far-flung fragile empire extending from Lisbon to the island of Macao in the South China Sea or to defeat the new European maritime power, the Dutch. The Dutch conquered northern Brazil, captured Elmina in 1637, and seized Luanda in 1641 until the return of the Portuguese in 1648. They established the famous trading fort for slaves at Gorée on the island of Bir on the coast of Senegal opposite modern Dakar during the 1630s and controlled the trade to Brazil and the Caribbean. The Dutch supplied slaves at prices the owners of new plantations in the Americas could afford, which greatly stimulated the expansion of the trade. The dramatic increase and subsequent profits in the Dutch trade in the latter half of the seventeenth century naturally attracted their fierce mercantile rivals, the British and the French. These interlopers had been active in the trade in the past, but between 1650 and 1700 they gradually overwhelmed the Dutch – at first by organizing companies such as the Royal African Company chartered in 1672; but later, particularly in the eighteenth century, the trade became dominated by private, individual British and French merchants working out of Liverpool, Nantes, and other Atlantic coast ports who now supplied the increasing number of Africans needed to work the new large sugar islands in the Caribbean, Jamaica, and Saint-Domingue (Hispaniola, later Haiti). During the seventeenth century the trade's trajectory peaked at an estimated average of 18,680 annually, and by the end of the century it is now calculated that 1,348,000 slaves had landed in the Americas between 1601 and 1700, but this number was only a trickle, and was to become a mighty river in the eighteenth century.[2]

The eighteenth century marked the zenith of the slave trade, as the annual estimated trajectory continued to a figure of 61,330 slaves per year. By the eighteenth century the focus of Atlantic trade had moved steadily along the coast from the Senegambia, where it began, to Upper Guinea and the Windward

---

[2] Paul E. Lovejoy, *Transformations in Slavery: A History of Slavery in Africa*, 2nd ed., Cambridge: Cambridge University Press, 2000, pp. 46–49.

Table 15.2 *The trans-Atlantic trade, 1601–1700*

Years	Number	Annual average
1601–1650	616,000	12,300
1651–1675	217,000	8,700
1676–1700	515,000	20,600

Source: Lovejoy, *Transformations in Slavery*, table 3.2.

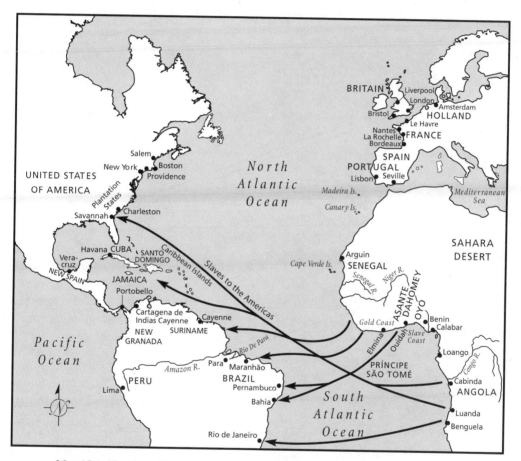

Map 15.1 *The trans-Atlantic slave trade.*

Coast, and then to the Gold Coast, the Bights of Benin and Biafra, and West–Central Africa, particularly Angola. Over 6 million slaves or 54 percent of the assumed total during 1450–1900 were exported from these four regions in just one century. The Gold Coast exported 881,200 (15 percent). Another 1,223,100 (20 percent) came from the Bight of Benin, while further east 900,100 (15 percent) were exported from the Bight of Biafra, most coming from the

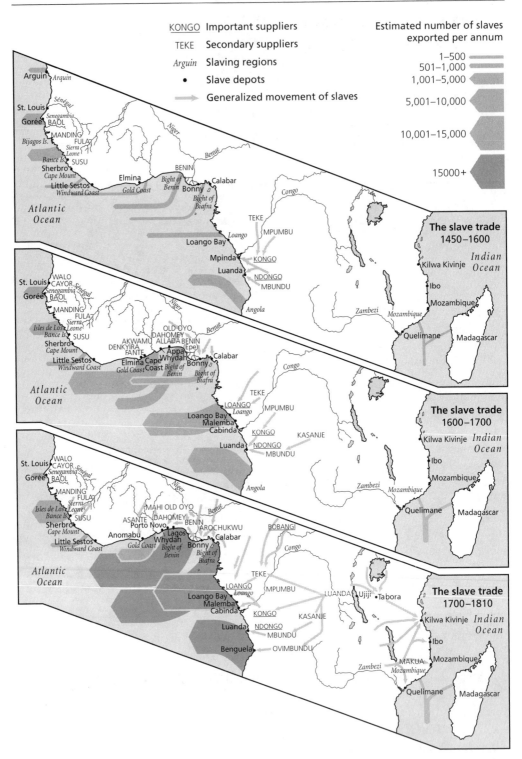

Map 15.2 *The slave trade.* Source: *Historical Atlas of Africa,* ed. J. F. Ade Ajayi and Michael Crowder, Cambridge: Cambridge University Press, 1985.

Table 15.3 *Regional origin, number, and percent of slaves in the eighteenth-century Atlantic trade*

Origin	Number	Percent
Senegambia	314,900	5%
Upper Guinea	230,900	4%
Windward Coast	143,200	2%
Gold Coast	881,200	14.5%
Bight of Benin	1,223,200	20%
Bight of Biafra	901,100	14.7%
West–Central coast	2,331,800	38.2%

Source: Lovejoy, *Transformations in Slavery*, table 3.4.

Niger Delta. By far the greatest number, however, 2,331,800 (38 percent), were taken from the West–Central African coast, particularly Angola.[3]

Unlike the internal slave trade within African societies or across the Sahara, where the demand for female slaves outnumbered the males two to one, the Atlantic trade was almost exactly the opposite. Women were deemed unsuited for the very heavy, intensive labor required to plant and harvest the cane on the sugar plantations of the Americas. European agents on the coast were given precise instructions to purchase young men in their prime: "Always observe that the Negroes be well-liking and healthy from the age of 15 years not exceeding 40; and at least two 3rds. men slaves."[4] European merchants were reluctant to take children under fifteen years of age, but more children could be packed into the ships than adults, and at less cost. Moreover, children soon reach maturity, which would ultimately justify the cheaper investment for their purchase at a time when there was an unequivocal growing demand for adult male slaves.

In the last quarter of the eighteenth century the estimated annual supply of slaves increased to 78,000 from the 30,900 exported during a comparable period in the seventeenth century, and their price rose four or five times, which leads one to conclude that the economic motive of supply and demand determined the price. The extent to which African suppliers responded to market forces has puzzled historians attempting to explain the dramatic increase of slaves exported during the eighteenth century. "Was the increase in volume related to the conscious decisions of slavers who were responding to higher prices, or was the increase in supply a relatively incidental feature of the extension of enslavement that resulted from the spread of warfare and other politically-motivated actions?"[5] There appears little doubt that the demand of the marketplace encouraged a rise in price, but that steady demand also contributed to the acceptance of the slave trade as an institution of investment.

[3] Ibid., pp. 46–50.   [4] Iliffe, *Africans*, p. 132.
[5] Lovejoy, *Transformations in Slavery*, p. 53.

Slaves were purchased with a wide variety of currencies and goods, many of high value. There is a commonly held view that they were acquired with worthless items of conspicuous consumption – liquor, beads, cheap trinkets. This is a myth. To purchase slaves on the western African coast for the Atlantic trade cash was essential – cowries, silver coins, and gold bullion – and quality goods – textiles, iron, copper, brass bars and wire, firearms, fine glass beads, and porcelain. Throughout the centuries of the trade the cargo most carried by the slave traders was cloth – woolen and later cotton – mostly made in Europe and India. The Africans, of course, had been weaving and dyeing cloth long before the arrival of the Europeans, but there was an insufficient supply for the insatiable demand, and the choices in color and design offered by the Europeans were very attractive.

The cowrie shell (Hindi, *kauri*; Kikongo, *nzimbu*; Latin, *Cypraea moneta*) was the most widespread and commonly accepted currency in the markets of Africa. It is found principally on the reefs of the Maldive Islands in the Indian Ocean, some 200 miles southwest of the Indian subcontinent. Here they were gathered in abundance from coral and marine plants, washed, and polished to sparkle like money from a mint. Long used as currency in India, cowries were brought to Africa by the early Portuguese expeditions, and became the standard currency on the African coasts and in the slave markets of the interior. There was a flourishing trade in cowries in Amsterdam and London for slavers going out to Africa. The number of cowries in circulation expanded during the eighteenth century proportionately with the increasing number of slaves. Two billion were imported by slave traders who were paying as much as 176,000 cowries for a single slave, an amount that required eight porters to carry.[6] During the eighteenth century cowries represented one-third the value of all trade goods, or £4 million – a staggering sum with a per capita money supply for West Africa equal to that of the early twentieth century.[7] Indian and later European cloth cut into narrow strips was used to supplement currency, or used where cowries were not accepted in commercial transactions. Iron, copper, and brass bars and wire were popular in the Bight of Biafra, and although the Asante produced gold, they were eager to accept gold from European traders in return for slaves. The import of currencies whether cowries or metals, did little for the economies of Africa. They certainly facilitated the trade in slaves, but this loss of manpower effected a decline in the productive capacity of the society, and since cowries were not acceptable as international currency, the European goods Africans could purchase with them for productive purposes were very limited.

6 Jan Hogdorn and Marion Johnson, *The Shell Money of the Slave Trade*, Cambridge: Cambridge University Press, 1986, pp. 58, 111; John Reader, *Africa: A Biography of the Continent*, New York: Alfred A. Knopf, 1998, p. 398.
7 Lovejoy, *Transformations in Slavery*, p. 107; Patrick Manning, *Slavery, Colonialism, and Economic Growth in Dahomey*, Cambridge: Cambridge University Press, 1982, pp. 156–161.

In the eighteenth century military hardware – firearms, ammunition, knives, swords – became staple commodities nearly equal in value to cowries. In the fifteenth century the Portuguese had sought to use firearms in trade until prohibited by the papacy, and it was not until the early eighteenth century that a flood of muskets and flintlocks became the principal article of trade preferred by British merchants. In 1730 over 180,000 guns were imported; from 1750 to 1800 the annual average fluctuated between 283,000 and 394,000. By the end of the eighteenth century an estimated 20 million guns had been sold to Africans, along with another 22,000 tons of gunpowder.[8] Such staples as currency and guns cannot discount the demand for luxury goods for the wealthy, particularly expensive cloth, mirrors, alcohol, and tobacco. The simplistic theory of the "gun–slave cycle," whereby guns and luxury goods were sold to encourage enslavement, fails to take into account the complexities of the slave trade, in which powerful African rulers, chiefs, and wealthy merchants set the terms of trade for what they perceived as their own best interests. Their desire for wealth and status, not their vulnerability to external pressure, kept the trade flowing.

Profits from the trade depended upon the prompt sale of a valuable but perishable human commodity before it died or escaped. Until the arrival of a European buyer, the slaves were incarcerated in barracks known as "traders' houses" or barracoons where they were fed, and oiled in anticipation of a quick sale. If slave ships did not arrive promptly, however, the slaves might attempt to escape or sometimes rebel, which usually ended in brutal suppression. Many more slaves, however, died of disease or neglect when forced to languish for months before shipment. The European merchants' associations operated from permanent coastal trading forts, known as "factories," and there were also private traders cruising along the coast purchasing slaves until they filled their ships. Most of the elaborate negotiations with European merchants were conducted by coastal middlemen whose main concern, besides profit, was to keep the Europeans from the interior and the African rulers and their merchants from the coast. These middlemen were mostly Africans, but some were Afro-European, particularly of Portuguese descent, called *lançados* or *pombeiros*, who represented many generations of the Portuguese presence on the western African coast. The subsequent negotiations for the terms of sale were controlled by the middlemen and their African patrons, and accompanied by lengthy haggling, expansive hospitality, bribery, abundant quantities of alcohol, and frequently trust and good faith between individuals who had conducted business in the past and expected to continue in the future.

Having been sold, a slave was branded, as in Roman times, with the mark of his owner and marched or taken in canoes in chains to the hold of the slave ship. By 1701 British merchants and their ships had come to dominate the trade and the trans-Atlantic crossing, the infamous Middle Passage. Throughout the

---

[8] Lovejoy, *Transformations in Slavery*, p. 109.

eighteenth century they carried an estimated 2,468,000 slaves (40.5 percent) compared to the Portuguese, 1,888,000 (31.0 percent), the French 1,104,000 (18.1 percent), and other Europeans with modest numbers.[9] In the fifteenth century the Portuguese began the Atlantic trade in small, single-decked caravels of a hundred tons with square or lateen sails that could carry 150 slaves. During the sixteenth and seventeenth centuries the technology of shipbuilding became increasingly complex, a work of art in design and skill in joinery. By the eighteenth century the typical slave ship was not specifically built for the trade but was a converted wooden cargo ship with square sails, three masts, and armed with muskets and cannons. More than half the British ships of that century had been obtained by capture during the European mercantile wars. The remainder were built in British and French shipyards specifically designed for the trade. "At the end of the eighteenth century, the best-known shipbuilder of Nantes, Vial de Chabois, would declare that the ideal *négrier* was between three and four hundred (old) tons, with ten feet of hold, and four feet, four inches between decks."[10] Slave ships were short-lived: no owner expected his ship to be seaworthy for more than ten years, and few European ships made more than six trans-Atlantic voyages. The number of officers and crew varied throughout the century, averaging about thirty officers and sailors in their twenties, often recruited while drunk in the local taverns of the European ports that catered to the trade. There was harsh discipline in the violent world of a slave ship, where 20 percent of the crew died on an average voyage, but the survivors were well paid, with bonuses related to the number of slaves delivered alive. Freed African slaves were often sailors, and sometimes slaves were rented out by their owners as crew.

The slaves were terrified of the vast, mysterious sea, and many – especially those from the interior – believed that the crew were cannibals whose red wine was African blood and gunpowder crushed African bones. Once underway and with a steady flow from the southeast trade winds and high pressure in the mid-Atlantic, the average time in the eighteenth century to cross the Middle Passage was thirty days. In 1754 the *Saint-Philippe* of Nantes carrying 460 Africans from Whydah established a record of twenty-five days. In 1727 the *Sainte-Anne*, also from Nantes, established a less enviable record of nine months from Whydah to Saint-Domingue, during which fifty-five slaves perished.[11] Below decks each slave was tightly packed into a space normally five feet high and four feet wide, with the sexes separated. The quantity was limited, for the space given to supplies of food and water reduced that available for slaves. The eatables varied with the nationality of the ship. On Portuguese slavers manioc (cassava) was the staple food. British ships carried maize (Indian corn) and the French oats. The daily ration averaged about three pounds, accompanied

[9] Ibid., p. 48.
[10] Hugh Thomas, *The Slave Trade: The Story of the Atlantic Slave Trade: 1440–1870*, New York: Simon & Schuster, 1997, p. 304.
[11] Ibid., p. 411.

by a few ounces of flour, beans, and salted beef. A greater problem was space for drinking water. Water is heavy, cumbersome, and requires a lot of room, yet water more than food determined the success of a slave voyage – success being measured by the number of slaves who survived. Slave voyages were hot and crowded, and many slaves suffered from dysentery, the "flux," and its dehydration, which claimed a third of the dead from disease on any voyage. Smallpox, scurvy, and a variety of other tropical diseases accounted for the remainder. Losses from sickness were usually recorded in the ship's ledgers of expenditure, and diminished during the centuries of the trade because of better food, water, and innovations such as limes to combat scurvy. In the sixteenth century the loss of slaves during the passage was as high as 20 percent; in the nineteenth, 10 percent. During the eighteenth century deaths steadily declined from a high (32 percent) in 1732 to a low (5.6 percent) in 1800. A century average (12.5 percent) was considered normal.

Many deaths were the result of violence, particularly rebellions. These insurrections were common on slave ships of every nationality, estimated at one in every eight or ten voyages. They almost always occurred during embarkation, before sailing, or when the ship was still in sight of the coast.[12] Most mutinies were promptly suppressed, for the crews were always alert and well armed at the dangerous times – when loading slaves or taking their meals on deck. All hands not involved in distributing the food stood to arms with cannon loaded and aimed at the crowded, hungry, and hostile slaves. The eighteenth century was a violent age, and it is not surprising that the leaders of unsuccessful revolts were frequently tortured, mutilated, and decapitated if not already dead.

At the end of the eighteenth century the Atlantic slave trade represented the largest involuntary migration in human history. Although the trade temporarily declined from 1790 to 1815 during the Napoleonic wars, the volume crossing the Atlantic revived to previous levels by 1820. The organization of this forced transfer of millions of Africans across the Atlantic became extremely complex. The internal African systems of slavery, the rituals of trade on the coast, and the transport across the Atlantic Ocean were inextricably woven together so that to operate successfully required the mobilization of the human and material resources of both Africa and Europe. Slavery in Africa became more common, and the increase in numbers of slaves encouraged an increasingly systematic process of enslavement – not only for export, but also for greater exploitation of slave labor within African societies. The vast system of slave labor in Africa that had grown in tandem with the rise of the Atlantic trade would continue long after the ocean-borne trade had ended.

In the eighteenth century European intellectuals and clergy began working to end the trade in slaves. The Abolitionist Movement had its origins in the eighteenth-century Enlightenment, the Age of Reason, which eroded the foundations of those institutions that had dominated European societies for

---

[12] Ibid., p. 424.

centuries. During the first half of that century English poets began to condemn the slave trade in their widely read verse, and in the American colonies the Quakers denounced the immorality of the trade in their meetings and polemical tracts amidst the rising fear of many colonists that to continue to increase the number of slaves would lead to the "great danger" – slave rebellions. In France the great intellectuals – Voltaire, Montesquieu, contributors to Diderot's *Encyclopédie*, and especially Jean-Jacques Rousseau – denounced slavery, under the illusion that the government would act on their beliefs and end it. By mid-century the cause of abolition in England had shifted from the poets to the lawyers. In 1755 Francis Hutcheson, an Irish Protestant and professor of philosophy in Glasgow, published *A System of Moral Philosophy*, in which he argued that no one can change a rational human being into "a piece of goods" with no rights. Other Scottish intellectuals expanded on this theme, but it was the English jurist Sir William Blackstone who laid the foundations for the legal case against slavery in his *Commentaries on the Laws of England*. In a case involving a slave named Somerset, however, the Lord Chief Justice of England, Lord Mansfield, decided there was no legal definition as to whether one could or could not be a slave in England, but since slavery was "odious," he reluctantly set Somerset free in 1772; this was widely, if wrongly, interpreted by many blacks as meaning that one could not be a slave in England. John Wesley and his Methodists went further than the lord chief justice and declared in pamphlet and pulpit that Englishmen must repent for the crime of the slave trade, a crime in which England, as its most enthusiastic participant, reaped the greatest profit.

Hesitant legal opinions and religious appeals would never have made the Abolitionist Movement the powerful force it became without the ability, energy, and conviction of three remarkable Englishmen – Granville Sharp (1735–1813), Thomas Clarkson (1760–1846), and William Wilberforce (1759–1833). Granville Sharp was a junior government clerk who befriended a slave in the streets of London and, moved by his plight, learned of the ambiguities in English law concerning slavery; this led him to argue the case on behalf of the slave Somerset before the Lord Chief Justice in the "Mansfield judgment" of 1772. Thereafter, as a persistent philanthropist he rallied the support of the influential Anglican bishops of England, which galvanized non-sectarian polemicists and theologians. In 1785 he met a young Cambridge graduate, Thomas Clarkson, who thereafter devoted all his energy and research skills to the rapidly growing Abolitionist Movement. He founded the Committee for the Effective Abolition of the Slave Trade in 1787, the same year he met the Member of Parliament for Hull, William Wilberforce, who was also a Cambridge graduate, and convinced him to become the political leader of the movement for the abolition of the slave trade. Sharp constructed the legal case against the slave trade, Clarkson supplied the detailed factual information about its operations, and Wilberforce, who was a close friend of Prime Minister William Pitt, led the charge in Parliament for its abolition.

The turning-point in the campaign came in 1788 when the Committee for the Abolition of the Privy Council was established; this was followed by a blizzard of pamphlets to arouse the moral indignation of the nation. The immediate result was the founding of a colony for freed slaves in Sierra Leone. The following year, Wilberforce launched, with the support of Pitt, Edmund Burke, and Charles James Fox, the debate on the voluminous Report of the Committee for Abolition, which was followed by bills in the House of Commons to abolish the trade. This galvanized the formidable vested interests in the slave trade to defeat them. The opposition was an amalgam of powerful economic and political interests who were joined by those who held sincere but often bizarre perceptions of the trade. Much of the opposition came from the cities of Bristol and Liverpool, whose inhabitants were, directly or indirectly, dependent on the slave trade. Then there were those who were convinced that the African slave in the New World was more content than his free brethren in Africa. Others ludicrously dismissed the horrors of the Middle Passage as sheer fabrication, while many regarded the continuance of the slave trade as essential to state revenue and the aggregate wealth of the nation. The bankers of London were opposed to its abolition, as was the textile industry, which prospered from cheap cotton cultivated and picked by African slaves transported to the American South. The pro-slavery lobby in Parliament successfully opposed the bills proposed by Wilberforce for nearly twenty years until Prime Minister Lord George Grenville, now supported by new men convinced that the trade was morally wrong and those who had been converted from the opposition, quietly introduced yet another bill in January 1807, which passed overwhelmingly, to make the trade in slaves illegal. But their crusade had not yet come to an end, as slavery was only abolished throughout the British empire in 1833, after another twenty-seven years of ceaseless campaigning and heated debate in Parliament. The Abolitionist Movement could not have succeeded without the contribution of Africans to their own liberation. Freed slaves were the most compelling critics of the horrors of the trade. And any discussion of the Abolitionist Movement must recognize the role that slave rebellions – particularly the Haitian revolution of 1791 – played in persuading Europeans in slave-owning societies to accede to the end of the trade.

Although three-and a-half million slaves were shipped across the Atlantic to the New World during the nineteenth century, the volume was 42 percent less than in the eighteenth, and mostly in the first half of the century. The efforts of the abolitionists, their governments, and the navies of Britain, France, and the United States enforced this steady decline from 1801 to 1851, when the trade was virtually terminated – except by the Portuguese in the west–central region of the Atlantic coast, and even there much reduced. The success of the abolitionists did not prevent those who sought by euphemisms and legal chicanery to circumvent the international prohibitions against the trade in the legal conventions signed by the relevant nation-states. The French and the Portuguese, in particular, used the status of contract labor under various names,

Table 15.4 *Regional origin, number, and percent of slaves in the Atlantic trade, 1801–1867*

Origin	Number	Percent
Senegambia	113,900	3.6%
Upper Guinea	176,200	5.3%
Windward Coast	39,200	1.1%
Gold Coast	68,600	2.0%
Bight of Benin	546,200	16.4%
Bight of Biafra	453,700	13.7%
West–Central Coast	1,613,200	48.7%
Southeast Africa	407,537	12.3%
Total	3,313,600	100.0%

Source: Lovejoy, *Transformations in Slavery*, table 7.4.

whereby the indentured slave would work his contractual engagement for a certain number of years and then be free of all obligations. These contracts, however, could be renegotiated, sold, and lengthened, and since life in slavery was usually short, such a slave was unlikely to live to his end of his contract. In the latter half of the nineteenth century more than 150,000 servile laborers were exported from Africa on contract at a time when the abolitionists had virtually ended the former trade in slaves.[13]

During the 450 years of the Atlantic slave trade an estimated 11,313,000 Africans were exported to the Americas. Although the exports from Africa have been calculated from an extraordinary amount of evidence from many sources, which has bestowed upon them their credibility, the estimates of losses during the march from the interior to the coast and at the port of embarkation are based on more fragmentary and scattered documentation, from which only broad generalizations may be established. There were unknown Africans who perished in the slave raids and wars, but were not slaves. There were significant numbers who died at the moment of enslavement, for which there is no information and therefore no statistics. The number who died on the march to the coast can only be an educated guess on the reasonable assumption that the number who died increased with the distance. Joseph Miller has demonstrated that many slave deaths occurred during the early days of the ocean voyage, indicating that they came aboard with diseases already contracted on land, which may have been a greater cause of death than conditions onboard ship. Since these rates varied from 9 to 15 percent of shipboard deaths, it would seem reasonable to accept Miller's estimate of a loss of 10 percent on the march to the coast.[14]

[13] Lovejoy, *Transformations in Slavery*, pp. 142, 151–152.
[14] Joseph C. Miller, "Mortality in the Atlantic Slave Trade: Statistical Evidence on Causality," *Journal of Interdisciplinary History* 11 (1981), pp. 385–423.

Most of the evidence of losses at the point of embarkation came from the established trading forts, such as the Dutch at Cape Castle, which kept more scrupulous records than other European trading posts. The data from the Gold Coast suggests that 6 to 7 percent of those brought to the coast died or escaped before embarkation. Losses on the west–central coast, Kongo and Angola, were as high as 11 to 12 percent on the march from the interior. Since the European merchants carefully inspected slaves for sale, they rejected all but the healthiest or those over thirty; the rest were sold cheap in the local markets and are thus lost as a statistic. Since healthy young men were the substance of the Atlantic trade, a disproportionate number of women, children, and elderly slaves were retained in Africa. Paul Lovejoy, relying on data compiled by Patrick Manning, has estimated that if "equal numbers of males and females were enslaved and that the percentage of children (aged 13 and under), young adults (aged 14–30), and older people (over 30) in the enslaved population was 30 percent, 50 percent, and 20 percent respectively," then the export of slaves would account for only 44.6 percent of the total enslaved population, leaving 55.4 percent in Africa.[15] There are, of course, innumerable variations of the numbers of children, women, and the elderly in various times and places that would distort this model from one decade and century to the next. Nevertheless, this estimate, no matter how rough, clearly demonstrates that a significant number of slaves destined for the Middle Passage and the Americas remained in Africa.

Further reading

Hawthorne, Walter, *Planting Rice and Harvesting Slaves: Transformations along the Guinea-Bissau Coast, 1400–1900*, Portsmouth, NH: Heinemann, 2003

Hogendorn, Jan and Marion Johnson, *The Shell Money of the Slave Trade*, Cambridge: Cambridge University Press, 1986

Millar, Joseph, *Way of Death: Merchant Capitalism and the Angolan Slave Trade, 1730–1830*, London and Madison: James Currey and University of Wisconsin Press, 1988

Rodney, Walter, *A History of the Upper Guinea Coast, 1545–1897*, New York: Oxford University Press, 1970

Rodney, Walter, *How Europe Underdeveloped Africa*, Washington, DC: Howard University Press, 1974

Thomas, Hugh, *The Slave Trade: The Story of the Atlantic Slave Trade, 1440–1870*, New York: Simon & Schuster, 1997

Thornton, John K., *Africa and the Africans in the Making of the Atlantic World, 1400–1800*, New York: Cambridge University Press, 1998

[15] Lovejoy, *Transformations in Slavery*, p. 65.

16   The Asian slave trade

Unlike the Atlantic slave trade, the transportation of slaves from Africa to Asia and the Mediterranean was of great antiquity. The first evidence is a carving in stone from 2900 BCE at the Second Cataract depicting a boat on the Nile packed with Nubian captives for enslavement in Egypt. Over the next 5,000 years African slaves captured in war and raids or purchased in the market were marched down the Nile, across the Sahara Desert to the Mediterranean, or transported over the Red Sea and from the East African coast to Asia. The dynastic Egyptians also took slaves from the Red Sea region and the Horn of Africa, known to them as Punt. Phoenician settlers along the North African littoral enslaved Africans from the immediate hinterland. The Greek and the Roman rulers of Egypt continued the practice of raids into Nubia, and sent military expeditions from their cities along the southern Mediterranean shore, which returned with slaves from the Fezzan and the highlands of the Sahara. African slaves, like those from Europe, were used in the households, fields, mines, and armies of Mediterranean and Asian empires, but Africans were only a modest portion of the Roman slave community since the abundant supply of Caucasians from Asia Minor and Europe was more than adequate for the economic and military needs of the empire. Not surprisingly, African slaves were more numerous in the Roman cities of the Mediterranean littoral.

There can be no reasonable estimate of the number of slaves exported from Africa to the Mediterranean basin, the Middle East, and the Indian Ocean before the arrival of the Arabs in Africa during the seventh century. Between 800 and 1600 the quantity of evidence for the estimated volume of slaves improves slightly. Until the seventeenth century the evidence is derived mostly from accounts of travelers and descriptions of slave markets in the commercial towns of North Africa, from which only maximum and minimum numbers at best can be extrapolated, given the paucity of direct data. There is, however, a considerable amount of indirect evidence from accounts of the trade, and evidence of strong demand for slaves for military service, from which general but not unreasonable estimates of the Asian slave trade can be proposed.

When European states directly entered the world of Indian Ocean trade in the seventeenth century, the estimates of the number of slaves become increasingly reliable. There is a striking similarity between the total estimated number of slaves exported across the Atlantic and those sent to Asia. The Atlantic trade carried an estimated 11,313,000 slaves from 1450 to 1900. The Asian trade numbered an estimated total of 12,580,000 slaves from 800 to 1900. The important difference between the Atlantic and Asian slave trades, however, is the time span in which the export of the slaves took place. The 11 million slaves of the Atlantic trade were exported to the Americas in only 400 years, an intensity that had a much more traumatic impact on the African societies engaged in the trade than did the 12.5 million slaves exported to Asia over eleven centuries. During the period 1600–1900, for which there is more credible evidence, the volume of the Asian trade is estimated at 5,510,000 slaves – half that of the Atlantic.

Moreover, the use of slaves in the Islamic world was somewhat different from that in the Americas. Slaves were very much in demand as household slaves, cultivators and herdsmen, oarsmen, concubines, and soldiers; but with the exception of the salt mines of the Sahara and the salt marshes of the Lower Tigris and Euphrates Rivers, gangs of slaves organized for intensive labor with the kind of high mortality rates experienced in the New World were rare until the establishment of clove and sugar plantations on the islands scattered along the East African periphery of the Indian Ocean. At the end of the Napoleonic wars during the first half of the nineteenth century an extensive plantation economy was developed on the East African coast and the islands of Zanzibar, Pemba, and the Mascarenes in the Indian Ocean, which demanded greater numbers of slaves from the interior. In a brief spasm of fifty years until the impact of the European abolitionists after 1860 dramatically restrained and then ended the trade to Asia, the eastern African slave trade was more reminiscent of the West African experience than in any of the preceding centuries.

Until the arrival of the Portuguese on the coasts of sub-Saharan Africa in the fifteenth century, only Islam had introduced a systematic regulation of slavery. By the tenth century the Arabs, who had conquered North Africa, the Middle East, and Persia, had absorbed the ancient institution of slavery, but as Muslims they shaped it to conform to Islamic laws and jurisprudence. Their legal definition and treatment of slaves, however, was more a modification in the status and function of a slave than any fundamental change in the practice of involuntary servitude. The slave remained property to be used as the master wished – as an agricultural laborer, soldier, domestic, concubine, or even a high official, a *wazir*. Thousands of slaves were taken in the holy wars (*jihad*) during the expansion of the Islamic world, for their enslavement was legally and morally justified because they were not Muslims but unbelievers (*kafirin*), expected to abandon their traditional religions and embrace in slavery the true faith.

As the Islamic empire expanded, slaves came increasingly from conquests of non-Muslim Africans on the frontiers of Islam to the slave markets in the Arab Middle East. Young women became domestics or concubines; young men were trained for military or administrative service. Apart from the constant demand of the Moroccan sultans in the seventeenth and

Table 16.1 *Slave exports acoss the Sahara, Red Sea, and East Africa and the Indian Ocean, 800–1900 and 1600–1900*

Trans-Saharan:		
800–1600	4,670,000	
1601–1800	1,400,000	
1801–1900	1,200,000	
800–1900	Total	7,270,000

Source: Lovejoy, *Transformations in Slavery*, tables 2.1, 3.7, 7.1.

Red Sea:		
800–1600	1,600,000	
1601–1800	300,000	
1801–1900	492,000	
800–1900	Total	2,392,000

Source: Lovejoy, *Transformations in Slavery*, tables 2.2, 3.7, 7.1.

East Africa and Indian Ocean:		
800–1600	800,000	
1601–1800	500,000	
1801–1900	1,618,000	
800–1900	Total	2,918,000

Slave exports from the Sahara, Red Sea, and East Africa and Indian Ocean, 800–1900

Total   12,580,000

Slave exports from the Sahara, Red Sea, and East Africa and Indian Ocean, 1600–1900

Total   5,510,000

Source: Lovejoy, *Transformations in Slavery*, tables 2.2, 3.7, 7.7.

eighteenth centuries for young men as slave soldiers, mature males and women were preferred to perform the menial tasks of field and household under harsh conditions; it was a short life, and consequently they had to be regularly replaced by newly acquired slaves, preferably females.

Since the young were absorbed into Muslim society and the old perished, the need for constant replenishment of slaves was not impeded by race or color. The only requirement for the Muslim was that the slave be pagan, and since African traditional religions were not recognized as legitimate religions, sub-Saharan Africa became the most important source of slaves for the Muslim merchants, who established elaborate commercial networks to transport them out of Africa across the Sahara, the Red Sea, and the Indian Ocean. Europeans had frequently justified slavery by arguing that exposure to Christianity, the religion of the slave owners, would lead to conversion, bringing civilization and salvation to slaves otherwise condemned to eternal damnation. Islam, however, imposed upon the Muslim master an obligation to convert non-Muslim slaves in order for them to become members of the greater Islamic society, in which the beneficence of the afterlife was assumed. Unlike Christianity and African religions the act of emancipation was explicitly defined in Islamic jurisprudence, granting the slave immediate freedom rather than the lengthy African generational process of acceptance by social assimilation. Conversion also enabled slaves to perform different functions unknown in the slavery of the New World. The Arab conquests had produced a far-flung empire whose bureaucracy utilized slave officials and slave soldiers loyal to the state. These slave officials were frequently empowered to have authority over free members of the state. Often Muslim slaves became highly specialized in commerce and industry through the acquisition of skills in the more advanced technology of the Islamic world.

Female slaves also occupied a different status in Islam from that in African or Atlantic slavery. Islamic law limited the number of legal wives to four, but it recognized concubinage, and gave rights to the children of such unions. Slave women were given as concubines to other slaves, to freed slaves, or to the master's sons. The relationship between the male master and the female slave, however, was clearly defined in theory by the legal Islamic sanctions that applied to emancipation. A concubine became legally free upon the death of her owner. If she bore him children, she could not be sold and her children were free, but in practice they had a lower status than children of free wives.

Trans-Saharan slave trade

Humans have always crossed the Sahara, even after it became a desert some 5,000 years ago. Why? The way was long, 1,500 miles more or less. The dangers from predators, both animal and human, were real. The terrain of gravel, rock, and sand was treacherous. There was a dearth of water, and food was found only in isolated oases. The need and desire of Berbers, Arabs, and other Africans for goods foreign traders could provide made it worth their while to confront the dangers of the trans-Saharan crossing. Human portage was the first means to carry salt both north and south from the mines of the Saharan oases in return for food as early as 1000 BCE. The prosperity of the Phoenician colony of Carthage in 600 BCE stimulated the trans-Saharan trade, which became a more reliable network when the Berber pastoralists established settlements in the desert oases and thereafter contact with the Africans living on the southern shore of the Sahara, the Sahel. Oxen acclimatized to desert travel could carry heavy loads without water for several days from one oasis to the next; the horse and the mule were swifter but carried less. During these centuries the trade was modest, being carried along routes defined by the string

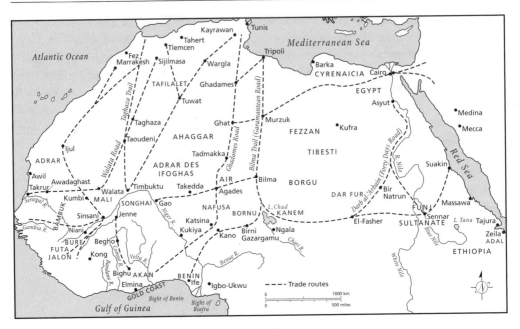

Map 16.1 *Trans-Saharan trade routes.*

of oases and limited by the capacity and resistance to thirst of the pack animals. Moreover, it was local, rather than long distance, being passed from one oasis to another until the arrival of the camel from Asia in the fourth century of the Christian era.

The camel revolutionized trans-Saharan travel and trade. The single-humped camel, the dromedary, could travel at two-and-a-half miles an hour, the same as humans, or 30 miles a day. Depending on terrain and its condition the camel could even cover twice that distance. A well-fed camel could carry the same load as an ox, 350 pounds, but the dramatic difference was its freedom of movement. With fat stored in its hump and a water tank in its belly the camel could move methodically for ten days without a drink, three times as long as the ox or horse. It could withstand the extreme desert heat of the day and the extreme desert cold of the night. Its splayed feet were cushions on sand and gravel.

The Persians had introduced the camel into Egypt as early as the sixth century BCE, but it did not flourish in the humid canals and cultivated fields of the Nile Delta. It was not until the first century CE that it moved westward along the sands of the Mediterranean littoral, and by the fourth century the Berbers had made the camel the principal beast of burden throughout the Mahgrib. By the fifth century they had trained the camel to be the primary vehicle for desert travel. It gave the nomadic Sanhaja Berbers of the west and the Tuareg of the central Sahara astonishing mobility and transport. They could now reach remote pastures in the great upland massifs of the Sahara – the Fezzan, Tibesti, and Ahaggar – whose valleys contained wadis with sufficient water and oases to sustain Saharan nomadic life. The new mobility also enabled the Berber to conduct raids from their desert sanctuaries to plunder the agricultural settlements of the Sahel and savanna to the south and the villages and towns of the Maghrib to the north.

The camel also enabled the Berbers to organize the long-distance trans-Saharan trade. Until then the passage through the Sahara had been in stages and periodic. With the camel the trans-Saharan trade evolved through the centuries into organized and regular caravans, crossing the whole of the Sahara with Sanhaja and Tuareg cameleers and led by Toubou guides. Documentary evidence suggests that by the twelfth century caravans of 12,000 camels were crossing the Sahara. The caravans traversed the most favorable terrain along an archipelago of well-watered oases, but with heavy losses in camels and men and the payment of tolls to Sanhaja, Tuareg, and Toubou who controlled these oases. Sometimes a caravan would be totally annihilated by one of the great sandstorms that swept the desert. Many did not survive the crossing, but the prospect of huge profits always brought men back to the desert.

Until the exploitation of the New World in the sixteenth century the gold for European kings, Arab sultans, and their merchants came from West Africa. Until the twentieth century gold was the economic symbol of the state, for no ruler can command authority if he cannot control the accepted coinage of commercial transactions. The legitimacy of every ruler is symbolized by the minting of currency that confirms his authority, whether in Cairo, London, or Rome. Rulers and merchants along the Mediterranean littoral have known from antiquity that the gold came from mines in West Africa, but they did not know precisely where. The African producers kept the location of their mines a closely guarded secret that has led to much fantasy, myth, and legend. In fact, there were four gold-producing regions: Bambuk, between the Senegal and Falme Rivers, whose gold went up the Walata Road; the gold of Bure, between the Upper Niger and Tinkisso Rivers, was sent down the Niger to Jenne, Timbuktu, and then north up the Taghaza Trail; the bullion of the Lobi mines on the Upper Black Volta River was sent north on the Taghaza Trail but also to Tripoli on the Garamantean Road; the mines of the Akan forests of northern Ghana, opened in the thirteenth and fourteenth centuries, also used the Garamantean Road to Tripoli.

The gold was mined from thousands of holes, shafts no more than 40 feet deep, and extracted from gold-bearing alluvium by women, who separated the gold from the gravel in the same manner as California miners panning gold dust in 1849. The mining required the organization of labor around a chief who collected the gold dust and nuggets, and negotiated the sale. The gold, which was mostly dust and the occasional gold nugget, became a royal monopoly of the rulers of the Western Sudanic kingdoms; they derived great wealth from it, but never minted their gold into coins.

Box 16.1 Gold of the Sahara

It is quite impossible to calculate the amount of gold brought out of West Africa to the Mediterranean world and Europe, but there is an account of thirty camels carrying gold that reached Sijilmasa in 1600. The standard load for a camel in good condition, then and now, is 300 pounds, or in this instance for the caravan 9,000 pounds. It is difficult to imagine that a camel would carry less for the trans-Saharan crossing in which carrying the maximum amount without endangering the camel would have the highest priority. At current prices of gold today one pound would be worth $6,000 and 9,000 pounds $54 million for this caravan. There is insufficient evidence to translate the value of 9,000 pounds of gold in 1600 into the monetary purchasing power of that amount of gold. Since the purchasing power of gold, however, is equal to the price of gold divided by the price of commodities, Roy W. Jastram has demonstrated[1] that in 1600 the price of gold was 70 percent and the commodity prices 55 percent of gold and goods respectively in 1930. Thus, the purchasing price of gold in 1600 would be 127 percent greater than in 1930. These comparisons are still difficult to translate into current dollars for gold is not money, but they do demonstrate that those camels in Sijilmasa in 1600 were carrying a great deal of purchasing power.

[1] Roy W. Jastram, *The Golden Constant*, New York: John Wiley & Sons, 1977, tables 2 and 3.

The West Africans were not about to part from their gold without an equally valuable commodity in exchange – salt. Man can live without gold, but he cannot live without salt. Salt (sodium chloride) is essential to most bodily functions, animal and human, and can become addictive. The individual African of the Western Sudan in the past and present has consumed about ten pounds of salt per year. It was also used as a preservative and for medicinal purposes. The demand for salt in sub-Saharan Africa was insatiable, for there are few sources of it in Africa south of the Sahara, and the desert remains its greatest repository. When the desiccation of the Sahara ended 5,000 years ago, its waters had evaporated, leaving behind great salt beds from its briny lakes containing millions of tons of salt. Salt deposits are scattered everywhere throughout the Sahara, and over the centuries it has been mined by slaves and cut into pure white blocks weighing 66 pounds to fit either side of a camel's hump. The volume of the trade throughout two millennia was enormous. The salt deposits at Bilma sent 6,000 tons annually to the salt-parched regions of the sahel and savanna of Niger, Chad, Nigeria, and the forest regions of sub-Saharan Africa. In the west thousands of tons of salt on many thousands of camels came to the Niger and Senegal regions from the mines at Taghaza and Taoudeni, to be passed on in stages by donkey to the edge of the tsetse-fly belt from where it was then carried by human porters into the rainforest. From Timbuktu on the Niger it was transported up and down the river by canoe, and its price often increased a hundredfold from its source to its ultimate destination.

The labor required by the salt industry – for mining, porterage, and the protection of commerce – fueled the demand for slaves to be used within the continent. Beyond Africa's borders the Islamic world's appetite for slave labor was equally voracious. Until the fifteenth century the export of slaves across the Sahara, the Red Sea, and the Indian Ocean was believed to be relatively constant, an estimated 5,000–10,000 per year throughout these many centuries, whose modest numbers mitigated the impact of loss among African societies. The estimate of the number of slaves, 4,670,000, exported across the Sahara between 800 and 1600 can only be a reasonable guess based on diffuse evidence, and acceptable simply for lack of a better figure. Undoubtedly, there was a demonstrable demand for slaves from sub-Saharan Africa that resulted in continuous contact between the Muslim merchants, who organized the trans-Saharan slave trade, and the rulers of the Sudanic states, who supplied them. The presence of Muslim traders had a profound influence at the courts of African kings. They not only conducted commerce, but also introduced literacy and Islamic law as it pertained to their transactions – principally slaves. Although the *bilad al-sudan* stretched from the Atlantic Ocean to the Red Sea, there were only six established north–south routes across the Sahara that resulted in well-defined markets at their terminals in the Sudan and North Africa. There was the Walata Road from ancient Ghana to Sijilmasa in Morocco; the Taghaza Trail from Timbuktu at the great bend of the Niger north to Taghaza and Sijilmasa or to Tuwat and Tunis; the Ghadames Road from Gao on the Lower Niger to Agades, Ghat, Ghadames, and Tripoli; the Bilma Trail or the Garamantean Road that left the Hausa states at Kano and Lake Chad north to Bilma, Murzuk in the Fezzan, and on to Tripoli; the Forty Days' Road or *darb al-'arbain* from El-Fasher in Darfur north to the Nile at Asyut; and the route furthest east that began at Suakin on the Red Sea, swung southwest to Sennar on the Blue Nile, and thence followed the Nile to Egypt. There was also a vigorous and often ignored east–west trade, which connected the great market towns of the Sahel overland and on the Niger River, along which slaves were moved for sale locally by Dyula traders or to the larger markets in one of the Sudanic terminals of the trans-Saharan trade.

As in the Atlantic trade, the largest number of slaves did not come from the same region throughout the millennium of the trans-Saharan trade, and although it was a very important source of revenue, the savanna states of the Western and Central Sudan were not dependent upon the slave trade for their rise, expansion, and decline. They were important suppliers of slaves, but not at the expense of their political and cultural independence. Slaves had long been taken from the headwaters of the Senegal and Niger Rivers up the Walata Road to Sijilmasa in Morocco. During the three centuries (1235–1492) of the Keita dynasty and the expansion of the empire of Mali slaves were captured south of the Niger and from its headwaters and taken to Gao, after which they were exported from Timbuktu up the Taghaza Trail or, less frequently, from Gao up the Ghadames Road. The Songhai empire (1492–1599) succeeded that of Mali when Sunni Ali of the Songhai established his authority over the whole of the Middle Niger River Valley. His wars and those of his successors produced a substantial increase in the number of slaves exported across the Sahara in the sixteenth century, partially to offset the loss of revenue from the declining gold trade. When the Moroccan army crossed the Sahara to conquer Songhai in 1591, the large number of Songhai captured produced an ample supply of slaves in the markets of North Africa before returning to the traditional pattern of the past. Further east in the central Sudan west of Lake Chad during the same century the kingdom of Bornu acquired an excessive number of slaves during its wars of expansion under Idris Alawma (*c.* 1571–1610); they were exported up the Bilma Trail to Tripoli. The *mai* (kings) of Bornu utilized this ancient route, which had been established many centuries before by the Saifawa dynasty in Kanem. In the nineteenth century the largest number of slaves to cross the Sahara had shifted from the western and central Sudan to the two routes for the Nilotic slave trade, the Forty Days' Road (*darb al-'arbain*) from Darfur and the route from Sennar to Nubia and Egypt. The estimated 1,200,000 slaves exported across the Sahara in the nineteenth century, compared to 700,000 in the eighteenth, can only be explained by the increase taken from the Upper Nile Basin, as the numbers exported from the states of the western and central Sudan had steadily declined.[1]

During the seventeenth and eighteenth centuries the trans-Saharan trade steadily increased to some 700,000 in each century, or 67 percent of the total exported across the Sahara in the preceding 800 years. This estimated average of 7,000 per year for these two centuries, based on limited evidence, may be greater than the real numbers, but indirect evidence indicates that there was a considerable supply of slaves from the savanna and sahel because of drought and warfare. When the rains did not come, the fields were barren and the free cultivators vulnerable to slavers when wandering the countryside in search of food. During the increasing aridity of the seventeenth and eighteenth centuries the northern environmental frontier between desert, sahel, and savanna retreated some 150 miles southward before the irresistible march of desertification. In order to survive Africans often voluntarily enslaved themselves to those with something to eat.

Between 1639 and 1643 a serious drought spread from the Senegambia to the great bend of the Niger. After a period of adequate rainfall the severe dry years returned during the last quarter of the seventeenth century. Desiccation in the *bilad al-sudan* proved worse in the next century. A major drought brought

---

[1] Paul E. Lovejoy, *Transformations in Slavery: A History of Slavery in Africa*, 2nd ed., Cambridge: Cambridge University Press, 2000, pp. 24–29.

famine to the Middle Niger Valley from 1711 to 1716 and again during the early 1720s, but the great drought of the eighteenth century on the Niger and in Senegambia lasted from 1738 to 1756. Bornu in the central Sudan suffered correspondingly in the 1740s and 1750s. Thereafter sporadic and localized years of little or no rainfall were recorded in 1770–1771 at Timbuktu, 1786 in the Gambia, and during the 1790s in the central Sudan.

These two centuries also experienced the dissolution of the old Sudanic empires into petty states whose warlords carried on interminable warfare with local rivals, producing an abundance of captives who became slaves and were exchanged in ever-increasing numbers for the North African horse. From the fourteenth to the late nineteenth centuries the insatiable demand for horses by the rulers of Sudanic states, large and small, from the Atlantic to the Nile, transformed the horse into an important commodity in the trans-Saharan slave trade. The mounted warriors, the cavalry, constituted the most effective force to assure victory in large battles, pursue the vanquished, and raid the sedentary farming communities. The North African, Barbary, or Saharan horse was the showpiece of the cavalry, for it was taller and heavier, which endowed it with greater speed and carrying capacity over long distances, and a more intimidating appearance than the smaller indigenous breeds of the savanna. Unfortunately, the imported North African horse was particularly vulnerable to savanna diseases, particularly trypanosomiasis. Although cross-breeding resulted in a hardy West African pony more resistant to disease, the Barbary and Saharan breeds could not long survive in the environment of the savanna with annual losses of 30 or even 50 percent that insured a steady flow of slaves to use as currency to replace them. Similarly, the high rate of mortality among slaves during the Sahara crossing required, in turn, a regular supply of slaves captured as prisoners of war or by the institutionalized *razzia*. This solidified a continuous and dynamic spiral of violence of slaves for horses.

The demand for and importance of the imported horse can perhaps be best understood by the size of the state cavalries. In the sixteenth century the Jolof empire in the Sengambia could mobilize 10,000 mounted warriors, while far to the east the *mai* of the Empire of Bornu, Idris Alawma, boasted that his cavalry numbered 40,000. In the smaller satellite states the number of cavalry horses would range from a few hundred to a few thousand. The horse, however, did not become the formidable animal of war and the *razzia* until the cavalry of sahel and savanna adopted the Arab saddle, which was more stable than the indigenous saddles of the Western Sudan, and the Arab stirrup, which enabled the rider to use his lance and swords with greater maneuverability and force to break and scatter infantry, and against which the communities of cultivators were defenseless. The Arab saddle and stirrup, however, required the large North African horse to be most effective, and as it was more expensive than the local savanna pony, this led to an overall increase in price. Although the cost in slaves varied with supply and demand and the quality of the horse, the price generally was one slave for the small savanna horse, while a good desert horse could command ten to fifteen slaves and sometimes as many as twenty-five. In some instances an infatuated buyer would pay a hundred slaves for a spectacular Barbary. Although the evidence is speculative, the number of slaves in the Senegambia purchased for the trans-Saharan trade by the eighteenth century exceeded those sold for the Atlantic. The rulers of the Senegambia appear to have been able to satisfy their need for European guns and powder with an ever smaller expenditure of slaves, leaving a larger number of slaves to be exchanged for the North African horses, upon which their style of warfare depended.

The wars in the Western Sudan, which followed the fragmentation of the old empires, were conflicts between Muslims and non-Muslims, or Muslims and those who claimed to be Muslims but did not practice orthodox Islam, such as Islamic mystics (Sufis), whom many considered religious renegades. Muslims regarded these wars as *jihad*s led by holy men, and as an important goal for Muslims was to convert unbelievers to Islam, their enslavement for conversion was both legally and morally correct. These reasons, however, were often an excuse for the warlord to replace his lost imported horses and to offset the high rate of attrition of slaves crossing the desert by exploiting new sources whose sale would provide revenue to maintain the cavalry and therefore the state. The organized *razzia* became commonplace with a variety of official names – *ghazwa* or *salatiya* in Darfur and Sennar, for instance – and were carried out more often than not by slave soldiers. Some of the enslaved were retained – women as concubines, men as soldiers or agricultural laborers – but a far greater number were sold, and for most warlords slaves, after direct taxes, were the greatest source of revenue. During the innumerable petty wars among the Hausa city-states Muslim prisoners were illegally sold for the trans-Saharan trade along with non-Muslims, to the dismay and condemnation of Islamic jurists. Further west on the Middle and Upper Niger and the plateau of the Senegambia the distinction between Muslim and non-Muslim was more well defined, but this did not inhibit the Muslim reformers from leading their followers (*talibes*) in holy wars against apostate Muslims, who were enslaved when they refused to accept Islam as practiced by dogmatic Muslim clerics or the political authorities of the theocratic Islamist states they founded.

Those who supplied slaves for the trans-Saharan trade were not always Muslims. The powerful Bambara pagan state of Segu established on the Niger southwest of Timbuktu was a major supplier in the seventeenth and eighteenth centuries. The hunting associations of young Bambara men were easily transformed into mercenaries to loot for petty warlords or organized bands to raid for status and profit. Slave soldiers were the largest contingent in the armies of the Bambara and in the states of the Senegambia where they collected taxes, held administrative offices, and were often the powerbrokers at the royal court. Similarly, the kingdom of Bagirmi southwest of Lake Chad provided a steady

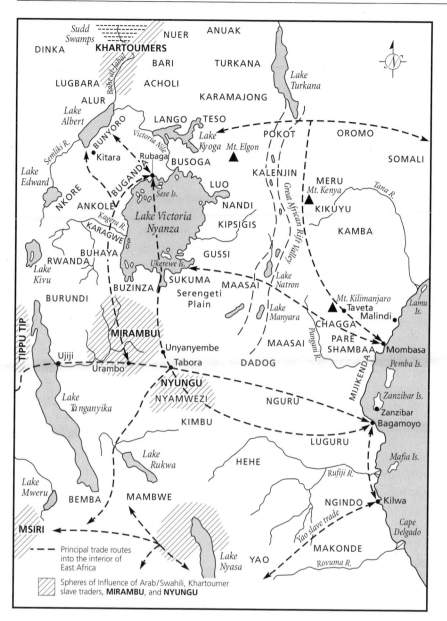

Map 16.2 *East Africa in the nineteenth century.*

flow of slaves to the trans-Saharan trade after the sixteenth century, which remained the principal source of revenue for its "Sun King."

The reduction in the number of slaves crossing the desert that accompanied the steady decline of the established trans-Saharan trade in the nineteenth century was offset by the astonishing growth of the Nilotic slave trade. In 1820 the army of the able and dynamic ruler of Egypt, Muhammad Ali, invaded the

Table 16.2 *Estimated slave exports across the Sahara, 1600–1900, with percent of the total Asian trade, 1600–1900*

	1600–1700	%	1701–1800	%	1801–1900	%	Total & Percent
Trans-Saharan:	700,000	12.7%	700,000	12.7%	1,200,000	21.7%	2,600,000 47.1%

Source: Lovejoy, *Transformations in Slavery*, tables 3.1, 7.1.

Sudan. Although nominally the viceroy of the Ottoman sultan, Muhammad Ali was in fact an independent ruler whose armies had conquered the Hijaz and its holy cities, Mecca and Medina, and advanced through Palestine to the frontiers of Syria at great expense to both his army and treasury. He therefore invaded the Sudan to exploit its gold and to enslave the pagan Sudanese to rebuild his army, and succinctly summed up his purpose to his commander in the Sudan: "You are aware that the end of all our effort and expense is to procure Negroes. Please show zeal in carrying out our wishes in this capital matter."[2]

Hitherto the Funj kingdom of Sennar had exported some 1,500 slaves per year to Egypt. Muhammad Ali wanted 20,000. A military training camp was constructed at Isna, and a special depot to receive slaves from the Sudan at Aswan. From the administrative capital at Khartoum the Egyptian governor-general organized military expeditions up the Blue and White Niles to enslave the Nilotes. Despite heavy losses from disease on the march down the Nile and across the Nubian Desert, by 1838 10,000–12,000 slaves reached Egypt every year. Under pressure from the British government the Ottoman sultan and the khedive of Egypt officially declared the slave trade illegal in the Commercial Convention of 1838, but on the Nile the trade shifted from the Egyptian government to an elaborate private commercial network constructed by Muslim merchants to continue and expand the trade throughout the Upper Nile Basin. By the 1870s tens of thousands of slaves were exported to Egypt and Arabia from ports on the Red Sea, and although the numbers dramatically declined during the years of the Mahdist state in the Sudan (1881–1898), the Red Sea trade only came to an end after the Anglo-Egyptian conquest of the Sudan in 1898.

The Red Sea slave trade

The Red Sea slave trade was, ironically, older than the trans-Saharan. The dynastic Egyptians regularly sent expeditions to the land of Punt, which

---

[2] Muhammad Ali to *sar-i 'askar* (commander-in chief) of the Sudan and Kordofan (Muhammad Bey Khusraw, *Daftardar*), September 23, 1823, quoted in Richard Hill, *Egypt in the Sudan, 1820–1881*, London: Oxford University Press, 1959, p. 13.

Figure 16.1 *Slaves, Indian Ocean.*

was their name for the coasts of the Red Sea and northern Somalia, to return with ivory, perfumes, and slaves. Slaves were undoubtedly among the commodities exported from Africa to Arabia across the Red Sea and the Gulf of Arabia during the centuries of Greek and Roman rule in Egypt. Direct evidence for the period between 800 and 1600 remains scanty, but the numbers of slaves transported to Arabia were not large, and the trade was localized rather than organized. One estimate holds that 1,600,000 slaves were exported during this period, or an annual average of 2,000. The sources of slaves for the Red Sea trade were limited to Nubia, the Nile north of its confluence at the modern capital of Khartoum, and Ethiopia, but the total Red Sea trade amounted to only 34 percent of the trans-Saharan trade during these 800 years. The ports were few – Aidhab in Egypt until destroyed by the Ottoman Turks in 1416, Suakin in the Sudan, and Adulis on the Red Sea coast of Ethiopia.

During the seventeenth century the Red Sea export trade appears to have been a steady but modest figure of 1,000 slaves per year. The estimated number of slaves increased in the eighteenth century to some 2,000 slaves annually from Ethiopia and the Nile Valley, but that was only a symbolically small portion of the increasing world-wide export of African slaves, which continued into the nineteenth century. Throughout the eighteenth and early nineteenth centuries Darfur in the Nile Basin sent several thousand slaves per year to Egypt, and also to the Red Sea through Sennar on the Blue Nile and thence east along the established trade route to Suakin. The Funj kingdom of Sennar itself exported some 1,500 slaves per year until conquered by the forces of Muhammad Ali

Figure 16.2 *Ivory for export. Dar es-Salaam, Tanganyika, late nineteenth century.*

in 1821. Thereafter, Egyptian government *razzia*s and, later in the century, powerful merchant-adventurers organized the Nilotic trade for Egypt, but they also sent a substantial number of Sudanese slaves to Arabia through the Red Sea ports, which the Egyptian government controlled. Slaves in the Upper Nile Basin were captured by the private armies (*bazinqir*) of these merchants, who

Table 16.3 *Estimated slave exports from the Red Sea, 1600–1900, with percent of the total Asian trade, 1600–1900*

	1600–1700	%	1701–1800	%	1801–1900	%	Total	Percent
Red Sea	100,000	1.8%	200,000	3.6%	492,000	8.9%	792,000	14.4%

Source: Lovejoy, *Transformations in Slavery*, tables 3.1, 7.1.

raided as far as Dar Fertit in the west and southwest into the kingdoms of the Azande and Bagirmi deep in equatorial Africa.

These centuries also experienced an increase in the slave trade from the Ethiopian highlands. Slavery in Ethiopia had been an accepted institution in the long history of that Christian kingdom, and slaves had regularly been sent to the Yemen and Arabia from the ancient port of Adulis (later Massawa). Although there had been frequent conflicts throughout the centuries between Christian Ethiopians in the fertile highlands and the Muslim Somalis on the arid plains below, it was not until the sixteenth century that the famous imam of Harar Ibrahim al-Ghazi, known as Grañ (the left-handed), and his Somali warriors ravaged Ethiopia, destroying churches, monasteries, and enslaving large numbers of Ethiopian Christians until he was killed in 1543 by Portuguese musketeers who had arrived to defend the emperor and his Christian kingdom. Thereafter Muslim control of the Red Sea continued to insure a dependable supply of Ethiopian slaves through Massawa during the seventeenth and eighteenth centuries when the centralized authority of imperial Ethiopia collapsed. Ethiopia dissolved into a state of anarchy known as the *Masafant* ("the period of judges") for 200 years, during which the rival warlords of the nobility obtained many slaves in their petty wars and *razzia*s. They retained some slaves for agriculture and domestic chores, selling the surplus captives to Muslim merchants. In the nineteenth century strong emperors returned internal stability to Ethiopia, but they waged continuous warfare on their frontiers against the Egyptian government, whose armies raided the border hill country, while the Muslim Galla (Oromo) pillaged southwestern Ethiopia for thousands of slaves who were exported across the Gulf of Arabia from the Somali ports of Berbera and Zeila. Children, girls, and young women were particularly prized in the Ethiopian trade, outnumbering males two to one and commanding three times their price in the marketplace. During the first half of the nineteenth century the Ethiopian Red Sea trade peaked at 6,000 to 7,000 slaves each year, amounting to an estimated 175,000 exported in the second quarter of that century.

East Africa and the Indian Ocean slave trade

During the centuries of the early Christian era Greek traders had been making their way down the coast of East Africa, where they conducted a

Table 16.4 *Estimated slave exports from East Africa, 1600–1900, with the percent of the total Asian trade, 1600–1900*

	1600–1700	%	1701–1800	%	1801–1900	%	Total	Percent
East Africa	100,000	1.8%	400,000	7.3%	1,618,000	29.4%	2,118,000	38.4%

Source: Lovejoy, *Transformations in African Slavery*, tables 3.7, 7.3.

profitable trade that included slaves. The Greek mercantile presence in the Indian Ocean did not survive the dominance of Rome in the Mediterranean, but trade on the East African coast was continued, as in the past, by merchants from Arabia, Persia, India, and China, who plied the waters of the Indian Ocean on the monsoon winds of the Sabaean Lane. The Arabs brought goods from Asia – cloth, porcelains, glassware, and hardware – and, after the seventh century, Islam. They returned to Asia with ivory, gold, rhino horn, spices, and always slaves, for fields, mines, armies, and households. The Arabs were followed by the Persians and the Chinese, who traded on the East African coast during the Southern Sung (1127–1279) and Ming (1368–1644) dynasties for ivory, rhino horn, and tortoise shells, which were highly valued in Asia, and a few slaves – mostly as concubines.

Although there are Arabic, Persian, and Chinese documents which describe East Africa and its trade, there is little direct evidence as to the number of slaves exported to Asia until the nineteenth century. By extrapolation with the slave trade in the Red Sea, an estimate of 1,000 per year throughout the centuries until the eighteenth does not appear unreasonable. At the end of the eighteenth century there are records of the number of slaves (2,500 per year) from the mainland that passed through Kilwa to the French sugar and coffee plantations on the Mascarene Islands and slaves exported from Mozambique to Cape Town and Brazil to add another 4,000 to 5,000 per year from the historical ports of the East African coast.[3] This was a dramatic increase during the last three decades of the eighteenth century; it was, however, only the harbinger of the massive numbers exported during the first half of the nineteenth century.

In the first decade of the nineteenth century 80,000 slaves are estimated to have been brought from the interior of East Africa. Over a third (30,000) were retained on the coast; the other 50,000 were shipped to the Asian mainland (Arabia, Persia, and India), the Mascarene Islands, and the Americas. During the next four decades the decline in the Mascarene trade was offset by a regular increase in the number of slaves sent to the Americas, mainly Brazil, that reached a high of 100,000 per decade during the 1830s and 1840s thereafter to decrease to only a trickle by mid-century. During this first half-century the

[3] Lovejoy, *Transformations in Slavery*, pp. 61–62.

export trade from the East African coast to the Asian mainland experienced a modest but firm increase to a high of 65,000 per decade in the 1850s and 1860s until 1873, when the sultan of Zanzibar was forced by the British government and its navy to ban all trade in slaves by sea. Despite the British intervention at Zanzibar the retention of slaves to work the growing number of plantations on the East African mainland coast rose an average 20 percent per decade, from 35,000 slaves in the first decade of the century to a high of 188,000 for the 1870s, at a time when the Indian Ocean trade was first restricted and then suppressed. When confronted by the power of British abolitionists, the slave traders brought fewer slaves to the coast – 28,000 in the decade of the 1880s – but the dynamics of the slave system enabled them to continue successfully smuggling as many as 16,000 from 1890 to 1896.[4]

This spectacular increase in the nineteenth-century East African slave trade was caused by the development of plantations requiring large numbers of unskilled laborers on the islands of Zanzibar and Pemba, where Arab immigrants from the Hadhramaut and Oman and Swahili entrepreneurs from the mainland had established extensive plantations of cloves, coconuts, and grain. The Swahili traffic in slaves from the mainland to the offshore islands dates from the late sixteenth century when patrician Swahili families, the Nabhany of Pate and the Mazrui from Mombasa, acquired estates on Pemba and Zanzibar. The fertile soils and timely rainfall of Pemba, in particular, produced sufficient rice and cereals to become the granary for the whole of the Swahili coast throughout the seventeenth and eighteenth centuries. Under the leadership of Sultan Sayyid Said, who arrived in Zanzibar from Oman in the 1820s, cloves were being exported by 1827, and thereafter the island became the principal supplier to the international market. The clove, like cotton, is a labor-intensive crop, and required an ever-increasing supply of slaves, so it is no coincidence that the demand for slaves was greatest during the peak of clove production in the 1860s and 1870s. Ironically, the needs of the nineteenth-century plantation economy of East Africa for slaves were similar to those in the Americas that produced the expansion of the trans-Atlantic slave trade in the eighteenth century.

During the seventeenth and eighteenth centuries slaves for the East African coast and Asia came mainly from the hinterland of the Zambezi Valley, controlled by the Portuguese. By the nineteenth century the sources of supply had shifted north where African traders, the Nyamwezi and the Yao, brought slaves to the coast from the interior of Lakes Tanganyika and Nyasa (Malawi). Kilwa, which had been reduced by the Portuguese to a commercial backwater, now became the principal slave entrepôt for the Zanzibar clove plantations, supplying nearly 95 percent by 1866. After the prohibition against exporting slaves across the Indian Ocean in 1873, Kilwa

---

[4] *Ibid.*, p. 155–156.

Table 16.5 *Estimated slave exports from East Africa, 1800–1900, with percent of the total Asian trade, 1800–1900*

Region	Volume	Percent East African Trade	Percent Asian Trade
Arabia, Persia, India	347,000	21.4%	10.5%
Southeast Africa	407,000	25.1%	12.3%
Mascarene Islands	95,000	5.9%	2.9%
East African coast	769,000	47.5%	24.6%
Total	1,618,000		

Source: Lovejoy, *Transformations in Slavery*, table 7.7.

continued to supply slaves for the mainland plantations by marching them up the coast.[5]

During the early decades of the nineteenth century Arab and Swahili traders from the East African coast developed a second route for slaves and ivory, using the old road into the interior that led them to the Africans living in the vicinity of the great equatorial lakes of Tanganyika and Victoria. Their success brought them into competition with the Nyamwezi and Yao traders, and precipitated hostilities with the Africans of the lakes, who at first supplied slaves only to be taken as slaves themselves by the heavily armed agents of the coastal merchants. The interior of eastern Africa erupted in raiding and petty wars, from which the African victims became slaves in these local struggles between rival warlords, traders, and warrior bands known as the *ruga-ruga*. The *ruga-ruga* had fled north in the 1840s and 1850s from the intense warfare that plagued southern Africa in the 1830s, which itself was probably related to the demand for slaves from new French sugar plantations in the Indian Ocean.

Summing up

The history of slavery in Africa and the slave trade cannot be measured only in terms of numbers or statistics, which obscure the complexities of the system and the enormity of the misery that accompanied the institution. Yet numbers do serve a purpose, for they quantify to give a means, no matter how sterile, to understand this otherwise incomprehensible human tragedy. There are pitfalls to avoid in reading the numbers. There was, of course, no trade with the Americas until they were discovered at the end of the fifteenth century, yet slaves had been taken out of Africa across the Sahara, the Red Sea,

[5] Frederick Cooper, *Plantation Slavery on the East Coast of Africa*, New Haven: Yale University Press, 1977, pp. 115–130.

and East Africa for many centuries before Columbus. Their numbers can only be estimated, precariously, from indirect evidence and extrapolation after the coming of the Arabs from 800 to the great surge in the Atlantic slave trade in the seventeenth century, at some 7 million, or less than 9,000 per year. This figure is not very helpful, for the number of slaves taken to the Mediterranean and Asia varied dramatically in time and place. Not until the seventeenth century does evidence, direct and indirect, permit greater certainty as to the estimated numbers of slaves taken out of Africa. From 1600 to 1900 the Atlantic and the Asian slave trades together systematically exported an estimated 16,414,000 slaves from Africa – 10,904,000 to the Americas and 5,510,000 to the Indian Ocean islands and Asia. This represents an average of 54,713 slaves per year, or over 36,347 exported cross the Atlantic and another 18,367 to Asia.

In Africa there are no statistics, but many accounts and oral traditions confirm that the slave trade and slavery were very much a part of African life until the 1930s. Thereafter numerous incidents of slavery have been reported up to the present day, and involuntary servitude still exists under new names, but after 5,000 years the institution of slavery as a system has come to an end, leaving behind both myths and truths. The historical obsession with the Atlantic slave trade and slavery in the Americas has often obscured the extent of the trade to Asia.

Further reading

Alpers, Edward A., *Ivory and Slaves in East Central Africa – Changing Patterns of International Trade to the Late Nineteenth Century*, Berkeley: University of California Press, 1975

Beachey, R. W., *The Slave Trade of Eastern Africa*, London: Rex Collings, 1976

Bovill, Edward W., *The Golden Trade of the Moors*, new introduction by Robert O. Collins, Princeton: Markus Wiener, 1995

Chaudhuri, K. N., *Trade and Civilization in the Indian Ocean: An Economic History from the Rise of Islam to 1750*, Cambridge: Cambridge University Press, 1985

Cooper, Frederick, *Plantation Slavery on the East Coast of Africa*, New Haven: Yale University Press, 1977

Cordell, Dennis, *Dar Kuti and the Last Years of the Trans-Saharan Slave Trade*, Madison: University of Wisconsin Press, 1985

Lovejoy, Paul E., *Salt of the Desert Sun: A History of Salt Production and Trade in the Central Sahara*, Cambridge: Cambridge University Press, 1986

Webb, James L. A., *Desert Frontier: Ecological and Economic Change along the Western Sahel, 1600–1850*, Madison: University of Wisconsin Press, 1995

PART III

Imperial Africa

17 Prelude to the European conquest of Africa

In 1787 a party of settlers disembarked from a British ship moored at the mouth of the Sherbro River in West Africa. Many of the new arrivals were freed slaves from England and her North American colonies, some of whom had found themselves destitute on the streets of London. Their passage had been paid by a group of affluent British abolitionists, who symbolically called their new settlement Freetown. These idealistic humanitarians envisaged that this new colony would become a model for the regeneration of freed African slaves by a combination of Protestant Christianity and European capitalism that would then spread their civilizing mission throughout the continent. Although many African settlers died from disease and violent confrontations with the indigenous Temne peoples, the Freetown colony eventually flourished to become a safe haven for tens for thousands of freed slaves, an important West African base for the Royal Navy of the anti-slave trade patrol, and a hub of commercial activity. The descendants of the original colonists developed their own distinctive culture, which was thoroughly Western in outlook, and the subsequent diaspora of this Krio population, as they called themselves, proved instrumental in disseminating Christianity and commerce throughout West Africa.

At the time when Freetown was founded, before it became the colony of Sierra Leone, no one perceived that this philanthropic enterprise was a harbinger of the changing relationship between Africa and Europe. During the first 400 years of their contact with sub-Saharan Africa, Europeans were confined to a handful of scattered trading stations along the coast. There was a vigorous trade in gold and slaves, profitable to Europeans and Africans alike, but African rulers and merchants were determined to prevent any Europeans from venturing beyond their coastal enclaves for trade or exploration. Moreover, European traders had little incentive to seek out the interior regions when the Africans themselves could supply slaves and other commodities for the European sea-merchants. On the West African coast strong kingdoms – Asante, Dahomey, and the Niger Delta states – controlled the passage to the interior. On the East African coast the independent Swahili city-states – Mombasa, Malindi, and Kilwa – blocked the way to the interior despite the theoretical suzerainty of Portugal. Among the Europeans, only two groups – the Dutch on the Cape Colony frontier and the Portuguese in the Zambezi

River Valley – made successful, though sporadic, efforts to venture into the interior.

The founding of Freetown was a symbol that this arrangement was changing, and that Europeans would exert increasingly greater influence over African communities in the coming century. New forces emerging from Europe, many of them present in the Freetown experiment, were slowly transforming the Atlantic world. One was the spirit of Evangelical Christianity, which swept through the industrial cities of Great Britain early in the eighteenth century. The eighteenth century had witnessed a revival of popular piety and the aggressive evangelism of the Anglican clergyman John Wesley (1703–1791), the founder of the Methodists, who attracted a massive following among the growing working classes of northern England. Inspired by the zeal of Wesley, Evangelical Protestant missionaries spread throughout the globe to establish missions in order to convert the heathens. Animated by this missionary zeal, the British businessmen who had helped to establish Freetown firmly believed that the alliance between Evangelical Christianity and commercial capitalism would bring civilization to West Africa.

One of the central beliefs of the eighteenth-century European Enlightenment was in natural law, which forcefully affirmed the universal equality of all men of whatever race or color, the corollary of which was that involuntary servitude was anathema to natural law and therefore could not be condoned. Thus economists of the Enlightenment opposed slavery; the Scottish moral philosopher Adam Smith (1723–1790) argued that slavery was an economically inefficient form of labor. Armed with ethical and pragmatic arguments, British abolitionists demanded that their government outlaw the slave trade by international treaty and use the ships of the Royal Navy to suppress it. The campaign to abolish the slave trade would force the European traders in Africa to diversify into purchasing commodities that came to be referred to as legitimate commerce. The changing European economy, brought about by industrialization and urbanization, particularly in England, relentlessly transformed the terms of trade on the eastern and western African coasts throughout the nineteenth century. Tropical products – including animal hides, gum arabic, palm oil, and cloves – steadily assumed a much greater proportion of the African trade, which had previously been dominated by ivory, gold, and slaves.

The Enlightenment also fostered a growing curiosity about the peoples and geography of Africa. As one group of philanthropists was planning the establishment of Freetown in the name of universal human equality, others were organizing expeditions to map the uncharted interior of the continent. This new age of exploration was quite different from the earlier Portuguese expeditions of Prince Henry the Navigator. These had mapped the outline of the continent for very specific national goals – to circumnavigate it in order to acquire the gold of Africa and the rich spice trade of Asia for the king's treasury and to undertake the conversion of Africans to Christianity. The new explorers of the

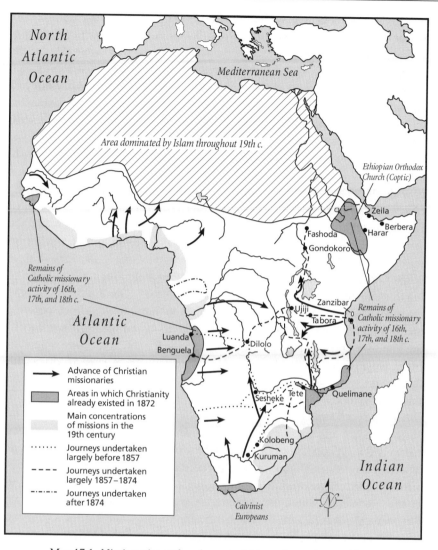

North
Atlantic
Ocean

Mediterranean Sea

Area dominated by Islam throughout 19th c.

*Ethiopian Orthodox
Church (Coptic)*

Zeila

Berbera

Fashoda   Harar

Gondokoro

*Remains of
Catholic missionary
activity of 16th,
17th, and 18th c.*

*Atlantic
Ocean*

Zanzibar

Ujiji   *Remains of
Catholic missionary
activity of 16th,
17th, and 18th c.*

Tabora

Luanda

Benguela

Dilolo

	Advance of Christian missionaries
	Areas in which Christianity already existed in 1872
	Main concentrations of missions in the 19th century
......	Journeys undertaken largely before 1857
- - - -	Journeys undertaken largely 1857–1874
-..-..-	Journeys undertaken after 1874

Sesheke   Tete   Quelimane

Kolobeng

Kuruman

*Indian
Ocean*

*Calvinist
Europeans*

N

Map 17.1 *Missionaries and explorers in Africa prior to the partition.*

nineteenth century claimed to be motivated by the simple desire to discover the
unknown, not realizing that their footsteps through forest and savanna would
be followed by those of conquering armies. In the century following 1787
abolitionists, missionaries, merchants, and explorers descended on the continent in unprecedented numbers, and with unprecedented vigor. In this era new
ethnic groups, such as the Krio of Freetown, were created, new commodities
were traded, old ideas were widely shared, and vast areas of the continent were
made intelligible to European cartographers.

If the eighteenth-century Enlightenment provided the vision to seek newfound lands, the nineteenth was the heroic age of exploration and their discovery. Neither the elites who sponsored these great expeditions nor the men

who undertook them perceived of themselves as the vanguard of empire. Those businessmen, politicians, and scientists who sponsored the discovery of Timbuktu or the search for the Nile were motivated by their passionate belief in the importance of enlarging the fund of human knowledge, a quest upon which no European government in the nineteenth century was officially willing to embark. If knowledge about the African interior proved to be of some commercial value, all the better for the participants and the nation, but the rhetoric of exploration was that of objective scientific inquiry.

The explorers recruited to map the interior of Africa were mostly British, French, and German, with very complex personalities; but they shared some characteristics. Most of them were wanderers who had traveled extensively before venturing into Africa. They possessed a curiosity of the unknown which was made legitimate by appeals to science despite the fact that few had the rigor of a scientific education. Some of them, like the missionary David Livingstone, were driven by the humanitarian mission to abolish the African slave trade. Others were motivated by the thrill of adventure or the challenge of hunting elusive and often dangerous African game. There were those who came to Africa to amuse themselves; others to subsume their own personal and emotional inadequacies. Many were soldiers bored with garrison duty in the Victorian era, when there were few wars to be fought. Some were supported by the Royal Geographical Society of Great Britain; others came to Africa with their own wealth. They were a host of romantic, beguiling, attractive, and often cruel characters.

The impact of their adventures in Africa on their fellow Europeans who stayed at home was not so much their discoveries but the crucial way by which their vivid and popular accounts skewed Europe's perceptions of the Africans and their land. Virtually all the explorers returned from Africa to write irresistible descriptions of dramatic landscapes, bizarre fauna, exotic flora, and strange people, by which they hoped to reap the rewards of discovery – fame for many, the redemption of a hitherto aimless personal life for some, and fortune for a few. Their discoveries were not to serve the Africans – except perhaps those vulnerable to the slave trade, which the explorers relished exposing – for most of their accounts disparaged the Africans. Their body of writings collectively presented them as primitive, barbaric, and exotic, and since there were no previous accounts of the continent's interior to contradict often fantastic descriptions, hasty judgments, ignorant assumptions, and tendentious commentary came to be accepted as fact.

One of the first was James Bruce (1730–1794), a Scottish laird, who traveled through Ethiopia to reach the source of the Blue Nile in 1770. Although his graphic account of his travels was disbelieved and ridiculed by the wits of eighteenth-century London, his adventures inspired others to follow him into Africa. There was Captain Sir Richard Francis Burton (1821–1890), who was the first European to visit Lake Tanganyika but failed to find the source of the Nile. Burton was a romantic figure who detested the stultifying society of the

Victorians – who were captivated, however, by his journey to the forbidden cities of Mecca and Medina. His contempt for Victorian sexual mores was only matched by his disdain for the Africans. Then there were the Bakers, Sir Samuel White Baker (1821–1893) and his beautiful blonde Hungarian wife, Florence (1845–1916). Possessing great wealth, Sir Samuel did not need the Royal Geographical Society to sponsor him, and the two lovers wandered in the Upper Nile for five years of adventure and hunting, all of which "Sam" vigorously recounted in wonderful best-selling books. John Hanning Speke (1827–1864), who discovered a source of the Nile at Lake Victoria, sought fame but left behind as his only memorial an obscure obelisk in Kensington Gardens. Others came for their own satisfaction – René Caillié (1799–1838), Gerhard Rolfs (1831–1896), Gustav Nachtigal (1834–1885), Georg Schweinfurth (1836–1925), and Joseph Thomson (1858–1895). Their tales of adventure and exploration, which emphasized the economic value of Africa's interior and the desperate needs of its peoples, were powerful instruments in the education of the reading public, and profoundly shaped its later approval and support for imperialism, resulting in the European conquest of and colonial rule in Africa.

Towering above all the other explorers in popularity was Dr. David Livingstone (1813–1873), a Scottish missionary and physician who established for himself a unique and revered position in British society as an explorer. He made four great African journeys. The first was in southern Africa in 1841, which was but a prelude to his momentous trans-African journey from Luanda (Angola) on the Atlantic to Quelimane (Mozambique) on the Indian Ocean, made between 1853 and 1856. There was a third expedition to the Zambezi, sponsored by the British government from 1858 to 1863, and his last journeys from 1866 to 1873, which were more wanderings than exploration. He was a man of great humility who could be cantankerous, but his explorations and passionate writings against the slave trade made him something of a Victorian saint. Though a missionary, Livingstone made very few converts to Christianity, for he was never in one place long enough, nor did he possess the patience to persevere in the time-consuming task of conversion. He saw himself as the forerunner of the main missionary movement that he anticipated would follow him. He went on foot, with a dozen porters. His personal relationships with his wife, children, and other Europeans were dysfunctional. His only positive personal relationships were with Africans, who saw him as an old man possessed by *baraka* (Arabic, "spirituality") who posed no threat, carried no guns, and treated Africans with civility, which they returned.

If Livingstone failed at conversion, he succeeded as an explorer. He demonstrated that the interior of southern Africa was not the desert many thought, but in fact a vast verdant, fertile, well-populated savanna. His greatest contributions, however, were his writings – not only descriptions of the interior of Africa, but of the slave trade. Through his letters and books he did more than any other single individual to focus the determination of Great Britain to end the trade in East Africa. The conquest of Africa began a decade after his death in 1873. He would have welcomed the intervention to end the slave trade, but would have been appalled to learn that he had done more than any other explorer to encourage the bloody conquest of those very Africans he sought to uplift by their peaceful conversion to Christianity.

African exploration took a dramatic turn after the 1860s, when the wandering romantics and eccentrics were replaced by explorers superbly equipped, more rigorous in their observations, and more precise in their measurements, all of which required large expeditions that often appeared like armies on the march. This change was to some extent related to the growing celebrity of famous explorers. Today, the media is a massive industry that dominates contemporary life. In the nineteenth century it was just beginning to do so, with the advent of a popular press in which the public could read the accounts of African explorers. Cheap newspapers, often branded with the sobriquet *Yellow*, tantamount to today's tabloids, had increasing influence among urban workers, who devoured their stories with enthusiasm. The most famous of these new explorers was the journalist Henry Morton Stanley (1841–1904). Unlike the gentleman explorers who had preceded him, Stanley was of humble origins, an orphan and an abused child in a workhouse in Wales. After many misadventures, which included fighting for both sides in the American Civil War, he became an ace reporter for the *New York Herald*, which sent him to find Dr. David Livingstone somewhere in the heart of Africa.

He stumbled upon Livingstone at Ujiji on Lake Tanganyika on November 10, 1871, and chronicled his journey in a bestseller, *How I Found Livingstone*. Florence Nightingale, the famous founder of the nursing profession, described it as "without exception, the very worst book about the very best subject," but this did not prevent her from "devouring the book to the end."[1] Finding Livingstone brought Stanley fame, fortune, and the jealousy and enmity of the British establishment, but he also revolutionized African exploration. Stanley was neither a self-indulgent individual nor a wanderer. He defined the objective, mobilized a huge expedition in which money was no object, then went ahead, dispensing generosity to compliant Africans, but shooting down fractious opposition, intent on achieving his goal and writing a lucrative account of his adventures. Not surprisingly, in Africa he was known as *Bula Matari* ("the breaker of rocks"). His trans-African journey of 1874–1877, which established the sources of both the Nile and Congo Rivers, was written up in another bestseller, *In Darkest Africa*. His subsequent expedition of 1887–1889 opened the way for the acquisition of the vast basin of the Congo by King Leopold of the Belgians and resulted in the widely popular *Through the Dark Continent*. With Stanley the golden age of African exploration came to an end, and the age of European conquest began in earnest.

[1] Florence Nightingale to Julius Mohl, November 24, 1872, in Sir Edward Cook, *The Life of Florence Nightingale*, New York: The Macmillan Company, 1942, vol. II, p. 315.

Livingstone inspired a generation of missionaries who were more interested in saving souls than in exploration. Since the sixteenth century Catholic
missionaries had accompanied the Portuguese expeditions around the African
coast, but it was the teachings and preaching by Protestant Evangelicals in the
eighteenth century that inaugurated a new era in the conversion of Africans
to Christianity. Evangelical Protestantism was practical and private, devoid
of the elaborate ritual and panoply of Rome or the solemn ceremonies of the
English state church in Canterbury. Its message of spiritual surcease from the
tawdry travail that accompanied life in the industrial cities had great appeal to
those who had come off the land where the Anglican Church was the stuffy
preserve of the landed gentry. If, indeed, Christ had come to save mankind,
not just the elite, then it logically followed that the evangelical message of
Christian salvation should apply equally to those in Africa, who never had the
opportunity to hear it.

Each of the Evangelical churches organized its own missionary society
during the early nineteenth century, all financially supported by their large
constituencies in Europe, particularly Great Britain; these could not be politically ignored or have their motivations questioned. They all had close ties
with the influential British and other European abolitionists whose secular
principles were indivisible from their religious ideology. The British scientific
community, most of whom were affiliated with the Evangelicals, welcomed the
prospect of new knowledge in the pursuit of new Christians. The British commercial community lent their financial support to the missionary societies who
by their very presence in Africa would open new markets for the manufactured
goods of their industries.

This enthusiasm to carry Christianity from the industrial workers to the
African farmers and herdsmen was tempered by the recognition that mission
work in the tropics was hazardous. Europeans were susceptible to numerous
tropical diseases, of which malaria was the most fatal. They knew little of
African societies or their traditional religions with which Christianity would
have to compete. It was not surprising, therefore, that the European missionaries in the first half of the nineteenth century perceived that the success of their
mission depended on the conversion and training of an African clergy who,
in turn, would be the vanguard in the spread of Christianity throughout the
continent. This attitude was commensurate with the humility of Evangelical
Christianity and acknowledged that Africans would be intuitively suspicious of
those who challenged their traditional beliefs, particularly if they were related
by color and culture with those who had carried them into slavery. The new missionary societies were not without African recruits for Christ. The slaves freed
by the West African Squadron of the Royal Navy and deposited in Freetown in
Sierra Leone were taught English, practical skills, and Protestant Christianity
by British missionaries, who then sent them throughout West Africa to serve as
models of liberated Christian men. Many of these freed slaves were the Krio

from Sierra Leone, who returned to spread the Christian faith among their fellow Yoruba, who called them Saro.

As outsiders, the first missionaries had to make concessions that accommodated their vulnerability among the communities that tolerated them. The early clergymen, African and European alike, attempted to present the Christian message in a local idiom. Since many African belief systems recognized one supreme deity, Christian evangelists worked to persuade their flock that they worshiped the same God, if by different names. They were also wise to ignore those aspects of African cultural and social life that challenged Christian teachings. Veneration of ancestors and polygamy, in particular, were widespread practices which the clergy frequently overlooked when cultivating new converts. However, challenging the status quo could work to the advantage of missionaries as well. The defense of the rights of freed slaves by British clergy in Cape Colony earned them the enmity of rural Afrikaners, but won the appreciation of many former slaves. In general, early missions had their greatest success among the marginalized members of African communities – the slaves, the poor, the needy, criminals, persons afflicted by disease or accused of witchcraft, and particularly women and orphans. In some African kingdoms the support of the rulers – Mutesa (1838–1884) in Buganda, Moshoeshoe (1786–1870) among the Sotho – aided missionaries in the conversion of large numbers of their subjects.

Christianity not only questioned African religious practices, it challenged established society and the accepted laws and traditions to which the people were accustomed, and for the most part faithfully observed. Yet the missionaries had more to offer than just faith. Africans may have been indifferent to the Christian message, but they could not and did not want to ignore the skills of the European missionaries or their African disciples who had acquired them. Africans wanted the knowledge and material goods of the European missionaries, the price for which was often the acceptance of the Christian faith. The role of the missionary in numerous African societies frequently evolved from disruptive agent to neutral mediator in the internal disputes of the traditional community – a role the missionaries were eager to play, as it gave them increasing knowledge and insight into the local culture that was invaluable in their primary goal of conversion. Most African languages had never been transcribed, and the task of translating the Gospels into an indigenous language often fell to African ministers, for the very foundation of conversion was literacy, which could only be taught from translations in which only the African catechists and clergy knew the idiomatic intricacies of local languages.

Although African catechists and clergy were instrumental in the spread of Christianity in West Africa during the first decades of the nineteenth century, they occupied an uncomfortable position between the white ministers who trained them and the black Africans among whom they preached. On the one hand, they sought to be true to their new faith, but on the other, they could not completely disassociate themselves from their traditional culture. This dilemma was most visible in the career of Samuel Ajayi Crowther (*c.* 1807–1891), a freed slave who rose through the hierarchy of the Church of England to become the Anglican bishop of West Africa. He was born in the Yoruba-speaking region of modern Nigeria during the first decade of the nineteenth century, perhaps in the same year that the British Parliament voted to abolish the slave trade. In 1821 Crowther was captured by slavers and sold to Portuguese merchants, who packed him into a slave ship bound for Brazil which was intercepted by the Royal Navy. He was promptly freed and deposited in Sierra Leone, where he was baptized in 1821 by missionaries of the British Church Missionary Society (CMS). He eventually made his way to Bathurst in the Gambia, and from there where he went on to study at Fourah Bay College, the first European university in Africa founded by British missionaries to train African catechists and clergy.

A brilliant student, Crowther became a very successful Anglican missionary and minister, and did more than any other single individual to promote the spread of Christianity in West Africa. He accompanied several expeditions to explore the Niger and open the river to Christian missions and British commerce. In 1864 he was appointed the first bishop of Western Equatorial Africa, as West Africa was known in the Anglican Church. Despite his dedication to the Church and Christianity, however, he never was fully accepted by the white hierarchy in the Anglican Church. Unlike British missionaries in the early nineteenth century who were imbued with that fundamental concept of the Enlightenment, the universality of the human race, the later Victorians were deeply influenced by the belief that white people were superior to those with darker skins. Protected from malaria by the discovery of an effective prophylactic, quinine, white missionaries could now carry the faith directly to the Africans rather than leave the task to black clergy. Consequently, his elevation to the bishopric was criticized on unabashedly racist grounds by his white fellow clergymen, making his position within the Church untenable, and he was forced to resign in 1890. Upon his death in 1891, his followers, led by one of his sons, left the Anglican Church to found their own African church, with African clergy administering to Africans, thus beginning the movement by African Christians frustrated by white domination to form their own churches throughout Africa which continued during the next century.

If the missionaries were the new harbingers of change by faith in nineteenth century Africa, European traders had been transforming African coastal societies by the trade in slaves since the end of the sixteenth century. Throughout 300 years of West African trade the commercial and mercantile interests of both the European merchants and the African traders remained much the same. The terms of the trade, the commodities to be exchanged, and its organization were unusually consistent for such a long period of commercial intercourse. Both the Africans and the Europeans were free traders, and their commercial transactions were invariably accompanied by much socializing and copious quantities of alcohol. Some agreements were reached quickly, to the satisfaction of each party. Other transactions were concluded only after days or weeks of hard bargaining and occasional threats of violence. Nevertheless, during the centuries of their mutual trading arrangements each side realized that there was little to be gained and much to lose by the domination on the coast of any single European government. The African traders realized that they would gain more by competition with individual European merchants or their loose associations in a free market rather than a monopoly controlled by a single European government. In the East African trade in particular, the disastrous attempts by the Portuguese to dominate the trade in the sixteenth century had led to a suffocation of commerce that benefited no one.

This fundamental issue of the manner by which African trade should be conducted vacillated throughout the centuries, depending largely on domestic politics in the capitals of Europe. Although the Dutch East and West India companies constructed trading forts at the Cape and in West Africa respectively, the others were mostly built from the resources of European state treasuries. These formidable structures, however, were scattered along the West African coast, and between them lay vast reaches of unrestricted beaches, lagoons, and estuaries that provided ready access to coastal markets for individual European sea-merchants. Moreover, the great expense of building and maintaining these trading posts required, from the African point of view, the imposition of disadvantageous terms of trade compared with those offered by individual traders who created their own associations. The loose association of the Merchants Adventurers to Africa, for instance, did not have to maintain expensive permanent trading forts and, consequently, were able to negotiate greater profits for themselves and their African suppliers.

The longstanding commercial rivalries for the African trade came to an end when Parliament made the slave trade in the British empire illegal in 1807, as did the other nations of Europe by 1815, and in 1833, despite the efforts of the powerful pro-slavery interests, William Wilberforce (1759–1833), who had introduced a bill abolishing slavery every year for the past eighteen years, succeeded in maneuvering such a bill through Parliament a month before his death. British merchants, now forced to abandon the slave trade, looked for new opportunities in what came to be known as "legitimate" commerce. Their search for new markets and tropical raw materials drew their agents into the interior, which was being opened up by European explorers and Christian missionaries. They were encouraged by the free-trade principles of the British government and, by the mid-nineteenth century, had abandoned the mercantile policies of the past, leaving the commercial exploitation of the African interior to individual entrepreneurs. When Richard Lander discovered that the Oil Rivers of the Niger Delta were in fact the many mouths of the Niger flowing 2,600 miles out of Africa, individual traders immediately sought to penetrate the branches of its delta to reach the open river and the dynamic populous markets

Box 17.1 The campaign to abolish the trans-Atlantic slave trade

The beginning of the end for the trans-Atlantic slave trade came in 1807 when the British Parliament outlawed the trade, and subsequently threw the nation's formidable diplomatic and naval weight behind abolition worldwide. Why did British politicians vote to end a trade that had profited the nation handsomely for more than a century? In the nearly 200 years since abolition historians have debated this question. Until the Second World War most scholars viewed the decision as an act of remarkable selflessness. In this view, it was the British public, roused by the campaign of a handful of passionate Evangelical Christians and Enlightenment *philosophes*, who found the conscience to end the nation's association with a profitable but inhumane commerce.

Then in 1944 the Caribbean historian and future politician Eric Williams published his ground-breaking work *Capitalism and Slavery*, in which he argued that abolition was not an act of selflessness, but was instead motivated by national self-interest. The campaign to end the trade, which began in the British Parliament in 1787, only gathered momentum as the British Caribbean sugar industry declined. Slave owners in Jamaica and other British sugar colonies in the New World suffered from diminishing soil productivity and indebtedness, which undercut both their demand for slaves and their political influence in London. Williams argued further that slavery was a mode of labor which had become obsolete to a nation that was in the process of embarking on the world's first industrial revolution. The growing enthusiasm for free trade principles, enshrined in Adam Smith's *The Wealth of Nations* (1776), encouraged many people to see the "free labor" that characterized the growing industrial workplace as preferable to the less efficient slave mode of labor. Abolitionists were therefore kicking at an open door when they called for an end to the trade.

Williams' argument proved influential, and became orthodoxy in some academic quarters. However, recent scholarship has cast doubt on many of his assertions. For example, it is now evident that though the Caribbean sugar industry was experiencing economic problems in the early nineteenth century, the slave plantations remained profitable. Indeed, one work critical of Williams' thesis, titled *Econocide*,[1] argues that the abolition of the trade, and its ensuing implications for the Caribbean plantation colonies, proved to be an act of "economic suicide." But if abolition was not a cynical attempt to justify the transition from slave to wage labor, neither was it simply an act of altruism. Once Great Britain

[1] Seymour Drescher, *Econocide: British Slavery in the Era of Abolition*, Pittsburgh: University of Pittsburg Press, 1977.

outlawed the slave trade in its own parliament, its vigorous campaign to stop slave ships from leaving Africa – and to force other Great Powers to join their campaign – was motivated in part from the fear of competition from slave plantations in foreign empires. Nor did the Act of 1807 make the institution of slavery itself illegal. Slaves in South Africa, Jamaica, and elsewhere in the British empire would have to wait another three decades for their emancipation.

Scholars have also begun to move beyond the domestic issues involved in the abolition movement to explore the role African slaves played in the ending of the trade. Many historians have shifted their focus to the influence of freed slaves and former slave traders who played an important role in making the abolition campaign into a mass movement. Others have considered the importance of the threat of future slave rebellions in the calculus of British politicians, who were debating abolition as the largest and most successful slave rebellion in modern history unfolded in Haiti after 1791.

on its banks. The disastrous Niger expeditions of Macgregor Laird in 1832 and Richard Lander in 1841 discouraged further attempts to open the river to commerce until the use of quinine made possible survival in the forests and woodland savanna of tropical Africa. In 1854 W. B. Baikie (1825–1864) led another official British expedition up the Niger to seek Heinrich Barth or word of his explorations, particularly seeking information as to the commercial prospects in the Western Sudan for British merchants. The search was unsuccessful, but Baikie and his men reached the confluence of the Niger and the Benue Rivers without losing a single man, thanks to the systematic application of quinine. The commercial exploitation of the interior by European entrepreneurs could now follow the explorers and missionaries to advance national interests without the state having to occupy unwanted territory or create troublesome military and administrative responsibilities at great expense.

In the nineteenth century the European mercantile community in the coastal settlements of West Africa coexisted with a new class of African entrepreneurs consisting of freed slaves. Educated in mission schools, they learned the fundamentals of commercial transactions from European merchants, who also supplied credit for them to become successful traders on their own initiative. These African traders were convinced that education was essential to their financial success, and became a powerful elite in Freetown, known as *aristos*, although many continued to participate in African religious rituals and festivities and ignored missionary denunciation of polygyny. Although they carried out their commercial transactions on the coast, they also had extensive contacts in the interior, which opened the way for the advance of European interests, authority, and, ultimately, conquest. Ironically, by the 1880s many of these independent prosperous African merchants, who had helped the Europeans open the interior, were reduced to agents of European companies no longer interested in free trade and determined to establish a monopoly of commerce by their superior supply of capital and technology.

After the mid-nineteenth century the terms of trade began to shift between Europe and Africa, particularly on the west coast, where commercial contacts were the most ancient. There tropical products began to supplement the dominant trade in slaves, and eventually eclipsed the trade almost entirely, as international efforts at abolition gradually choked off the main sites of export. The new emphasis on legitimate commerce offered fresh opportunities for some individuals and regions, and posed challenges to others. The vigorous competition to master the new terms of trade came to be perceived as threatening to European merchants, who increasingly used claims of instability to call for a greater imperial presence on the western African coast.

After nearly 200 years during which Portuguese mercantile policies on the East African coast had effectively stifled the once-flourishing commerce, Portuguese authority collapsed at the beginning of the nineteenth century, thereby allowing a revival of the long-distance trade of the Indian Ocean world. The commercial vacuum left by the Portuguese was soon filled by the sultan of Oman, Sayyid Sa'id (1790–1856), who had established the Busaidi dynasty on the island of Zanzibar and on the East African coast. By 1827 he dominated the historical commerce of eastern Africa by his commercial acumen and his introduction of valuable spices, mainly cloves, and slaves to cultivate the labor-intensive work on his large plantations. After a contentious struggle with the independent city-states on the mainland, he gained control of the strategic port of Mombasa from the Mazrui dynasty in 1837. He and his successors thereafter managed the profitable slave trade with Arabia, the Persian Gulf, and the new French sugar plantations on the Indian Ocean islands of Mauritius and Réunion; this ultimately precipitated British intervention by the Royal Navy, which forced the sultan, Barghash ibn Said (1833–1888), to end the East African slave trade and accept the imperial paramountcy of Great Britain at Zanzibar and on the east coast of Africa as in West Africa.

The changing terms of trade offered numerous challenges and great risks. But they also offered opportunities to those Africans with the talents to take advantage of the new situation. This new generation of entrepreneurial Africans is best personified in the career of Jaja (1821–1891) of the city-state of Opobo in the Niger Delta. Like Bishop Crowther, Jaja was enslaved in Nigeria as an Igbo child, and eventually purchased by a merchant in the Niger Delta trading state of Bonny. His rise from slave to ruler was not unknown in West Africa – Sakura (1285–1300) the emperor of Mali, was a freed slave, and Jaja's principal rival in the Niger Delta had also been born into slavery. But it was nevertheless a remarkable achievement, which reflects his own talents, as well as the opportunities offered by the quickening pace of commerce, which permitted Africans to circumvent established social hierarchies in order to acquire wealth and power. In Jaja's case, it transformed him from a petty trader to king of Opobo and the principal middleman between the European merchants on the coast and the sources of palm oil in the interior.

Initially Jaja appeared to be a successful participant in the shift from the trade in slaves to the legitimate commerce sought by British abolitionists when he began to export tropical products, particularly the valuable palm oil – which, ironically, was tapped and processed by slaves. Jaja was an astute and dependable trading partner with European merchants and a reliable ally to British authorities, whom he supported during their invasion of neighboring Asante in 1873 and for which he received honors from Queen Victoria in 1875. Jaja effectively monopolized the palm-oil trade, selling 8,000 tons a year, mostly to British merchants from Liverpool in defiance of a rival monopoly being imposed by the Royal Niger Company. Although Jaja was not squeamish about using force to defend his monopoly, the British government – presumably in the name of free trade, despite the fact that the Royal Niger Company sought its own monopoly – declared Opobo a protectorate in 1885, which Jaja ignored. He was deported to the West Indies in 1887, but his loyal followers, who included the influential Liverpool merchants and the Irish members of the House of Commons as well as his compatriots, secured his release in 1891 only for him to die on the return journey.

By 1873 few Europeans or Africans recognized that they were experiencing the prelude to the conquest of the continent, but astute observers perceived that European influence had been steadily increasing throughout the nineteenth century. European trade goods and religious traditions percolated into the interior far beyond those regions opened up by explorers or missionaries. European influence on the coastal enclaves, such as Freetown and Zanzibar, was soon to become dominant. No one in Europe at that time contemplated the conquest of Africa, but the foundations for the partition, scramble, and conquest were now in place.

Further reading

Ajay, J. F. A., *Christian Missions in Nigeria, 1841–1891: The Making of an Educated Elite*, London: Longman, 1965

Blackburn, Robin, *The Overthrow of Colonial Slavery, 1776–1848*, New York: Verso, 1988

Hargreaves, John D., *Prelude to the Partition of West Africa*, London: Macmillan, 1963

Hochschild, Adam, *Bury the Chains: Prophets and Rebels in the Fight to Free an Empire's Slaves*, Boston: Houghton Mifflin, 2005

Hopkins, A. G., *An Economic History of West Africa*, London: Longman, 1973

Sanneh, Lamin, *Abolitionists Abroad: American Blacks and the Making of Modern West Africa*, Cambridge, MA: Harvard University Press, 1999

Williams, Eric, *Capitalism and Slavery*, London: A. Deutsch, 1987

18 The European conquest of Africa

After 400 years during which Europe had displayed little or no interest in Africa beyond its coastline, suddenly – in the twenty years between 1878 and 1898 – the European states partitioned and conquered virtually the entire continent. To observers in the last quarter of the nineteenth century this sudden conquest was a frantic, often unseemly, and largely unexpected scramble for territory in a continent about which the Europeans knew little and for which most cared nothing. Their sentiments were encapsulated in the famous remark by the English imperial historian John H. Seeley, that his generation had conquered half of the world "in a fit of absence of mind." Today, however, with the advantage of hindsight historians have perceived several fundamental causes and events which combined to upset 400 years of equilibrium between Africa and Europe and precipitate the European conquest and colonial rule of virtually the entire continent. The Industrial Revolution in several European nations resulted in a need for raw material from Africa, while at the same time the Africans represented a large, new market for European manufactured goods. Moreover, the new technologies produced by the Industrial Revolution provided the instruments that upset the longstanding balance of power between Africa and Europe. Popular nationalism was transformed into imperial rivalry, as imperial strategy and the defense of empire became of great concern to European statesmen. Changing terms of trade required European merchants to seek political stability in Africa, where for centuries they had profited from the instability that had fostered the slave trade. Christianity was also changing in the nineteenth century, as the new and powerful Evangelical movement inspired aggressive missionary activity, which in the past had been fragmentary and largely confined to the African coast, throughout the continent.

This "scramble for Africa," however, should be perceived as but another chapter in the larger story of nineteenth-century global imperialism by the West. While Western statesmen were asserting claims to large portions of African territory, they were also staking out spheres of influence in China, prying open Japanese trade with gunboats, and dispatching armies to conquer much of Southeast Asia. The progress of the European conquest in Africa was in many ways determined by the actions of the inhabitants, and differed according to region, state, or even village. Some communities fought ferociously against European encroachment; there were those who successfully forestalled or mitigated European influence, while others profited little from

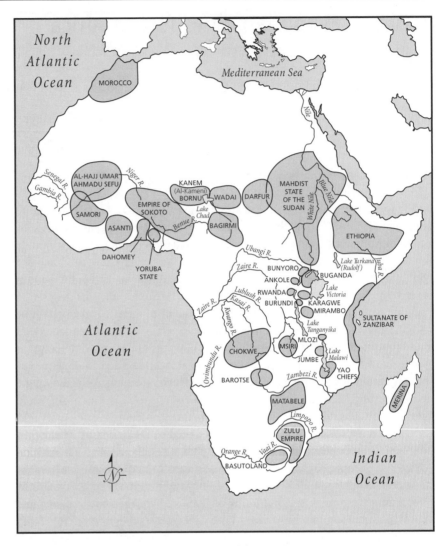

Map 18.1 *African states on the eve of the partition.*

their defiance. Numerous Africans welcomed the European imperial powers as potential allies against their enemies. Some in the more remote and isolated regions of the continent remained oblivious for years to the fact that they had become a part of one or the other European empire.

The conquest of Africa was a manifestation of the European Industrial Revolution, and the principal instrument for its accomplishment was the steam engine. Steam was the driving force of those industries that produced railroads and steamships to conquer land and sea. This revolution in transportation had particular significance in Africa, for unlike the other continents it possessed no great navigable rivers that could provide a passage from the oceans into the heart of the continent – no Amazon, Mississippi, Rhine, Ganges, or Yangtze.

Figure 18.1 *Steamboat on the Zambezi River, Portuguese East Africa. Steam-powered gunboats allowed European armies to project their power along Africa's great river systems.*

Except for the Gambia all the great rivers of Africa were obstructed by cataracts and falls at the lip of the African Plateau, whose waters tumble down onto the short coastal plain and over the shoals of their estuaries. Once above the falls, however, the African rivers – the Congo, Niger, Nile, Zambezi – were navigable for hundreds of miles. On these broad and placid reaches European steamers and gunboats dominated the vigorous and profitable flow of commerce on the rivers and could intimidate African authorities to obtain favorable terms of trade in their markets.

The nineteenth century was also the great age of the steam locomotive and its railways that spanned continents. It was the railway that enabled the imperialists to avoid the rapids and gain supremacy of the navigable rivers. These rail lines were built primarily to carry and support sufficient military forces to conquer Africa, but after the subjugation of the Africans was complete, the railways become the means to spread colonial administration and the transport of colonial commerce. Railway building was a long, expensive, and arduous process. In 1879 the French government appropriated funds for the Senegal Railway to link the Senegal River with the Niger, the construction of which was not completed until 1905. In the 1890s Henry Morton Stanley cut a passage around thirty-two cataracts for a railway from the port of Matadi on the Congo Estuary to Stanley (Malebo) Pool on the navigable Congo that enabled King Leopold of the Belgians to conquer the vast interior beyond the banks of the river and its tributaries. Between 1896 and 1898 the British constructed a railway across the Nubian Desert to bypass five cataracts to the navigable Nile in order to conquer the Sudan; this was later extended, for administrative and commercial needs, to the capital, Khartoum. In Uganda the British constructed a railway from Mombasa to Lake Victoria to forestall French encroachment at Fashoda on the Upper Nile, but it was not completed until 1902, and the cost of its construction could only be justified by the British commercial exploitation of East Africa.

In southern Africa the railway was instrumental in the growth of the mining industry, whose riches fueled imperial expansion. After the discovery of diamonds at Kimberley in 1867, railways from the southern ports of Cape Town, Port Elizabeth, East London, and Durban were constructed to supply the miners, bring out the diamonds, and insure that the mines became part of the British empire. When gold was discovered on the Witwatersrand in the Transvaal in 1885, it was the extension of the rail line to Johannesburg in the independent Republic of the Transvaal that symbolized the advance of British power into southern Africa, contributing to the outbreak of the South African (Anglo-Boer) War in 1899. North of the Transvaal the conquest of the Ndebele kingdom of Lobengula, which became part of Southern Rhodesia, was accomplished by a mercenary army, mostly of British subjects, which entered Mashonaland in 1890. It was no coincidence, however, that the first train to arrive at Bulawayo seven years later carried sufficient arms and ammunition to suppress the Ndebele–Shona revolt of 1896–1897 against the British occupation of their country, in which 10 percent of the settler population had been killed.

African railways were built for the most part by forced labor (called by the French the *corvée*), and conditions of railway construction were dangerous, with a high rate of mortality. Although apologists for colonialism later argued that railways were a beneficent legacy of imperial rule, they were built by African labor, mostly for the benefit of the Europeans. Railway construction was very hard, debilitating work, of little or no interest to African farmers and pastoralists. In some areas, such as British East Africa, it proved impossible to coerce them into construction work, so the Ugandan railway was built in large part by South Asian laborers, indentured servants, from British India, who after its completion remained to form the nucleus of the Asian community in British East Africa.

Each of these European innovations presented different challenges for the Africans, but the most devastating technological disparity to emerge in the nineteenth century was the revolution in firearms. For over 300 years the musket had been an inefficient weapon, and its short range and inaccuracy against individual moving targets was not much superior to the spear, arrow, knife, and second-hand muskets used by Africans, particularly in the coastal rainforests, where it frequently misfired from moisture-saturated powder. In the 1860s the muzzle-loading musket of the Napoleonic era was replaced by the single breech-loader, and, by the 1880s, the magazine repeating rifle. The change from musket to rifle dramatically upset the balance of African warfare. The repeating rifle with its bullets, rather than powder and ball, was easy to load for rapid fire, and was reliable. It was very accurate at long range against massed or mobile targets, with speed improved by the smooth ejection of the used cartridge. In 1885 Hiram S. Maxim (1840–1916) took the logic of the repeating rifle one step further by binding several rifle barrels into a revolving column, the Maxim gun, the prototype of the modern machine gun. Although the trade in firearms remained as vigorous as ever on the African coast, African leaders found it increasingly difficult to equip their armies with these new weapons. The European imperial nations, determined to maintain their superiority in firearms, were increasingly reluctant to export modern weapons to African leaders who resorted to purchasing rifles from unreliable and often untrustworthy arms merchants. Moreover, unlike the eighteenth-century muskets, these new rifles were mass-produced by machine tools and could not be repaired by African blacksmiths using their traditional technology.

Artillery was used infrequently in Africa. In Europe, particularly during the Napoleonic wars, it had often been the decisive factor in battle. In Africa artillery only became significant in the late nineteenth century when light mobile field guns were introduced to breach the walled cities of the Western Sudan. Moreover, combat on the savanna and sahel was dominated by cavalry and light infantry whose maneuverability limited the value of heavy artillery, which would have to be carried long distances across difficult terrain. However, artillery had not been unknown in Africa before the nineteenth century. The fortifications of the slave-trading forts of the West African coast all had cannons – pointing seaward to defend them against European rivals – and one of the most sumptuous gifts for a West African chief in the elaborate negotiations accompanying the slave trade was a cannon for him to fire on ceremonial occasions.

All of these instruments of empire building would have remained useless so long as disease threatened to strike down European invaders. There were numerous diseases – yellow fever, sleeping sickness, yaws, leprosy – but the greatest killer for Europeans in the nineteenth century, as well as Africans then and now, was malaria, which is endemic throughout Africa, except in the cooler and less humid uplands. Until the mid-nineteenth century the average annual death rate of British garrisons on the coast and the Royal Naval Squadron at sea was 77 percent, overwhelmingly from malaria. Another 21 percent became invalids, and only 2 percent remained fit for further service. Explorers, missionaries, and merchants suffered similarly, and empires could not be established or expanded at such human cost. European missionaries in West Africa rarely ventured from their coastal stations, leaving Christian evangelism in the interior to freed slaves converted to the faith at the British colony of Sierra Leone. Malaria as well as the other endemic diseases also kept European traders and explorers from venturing far into the interior, leaving large blank spaces on European maps. In 1854 the Scottish doctor W. B. Baikie successfully demonstrated that by taking the prophylactic quinine, an extract taken from the bark of a tree native to Brazil, the men of his ship were able to reach the pestilential confluence of the Niger and Benue Rivers without loss. By the 1860s and 1870s quinine was in regular use by European missionaries, merchants, and soldiers and even more than steam, telegraphy, and firearms made possible the new imperialism.

The imperialism of the nineteenth century was also accompanied by a new self-confidence, which cannot be measured like ships, guns, or quinine. The unprecedented productivity of European industrialization gave the Victorians a sense of superiority and invincibility that drove them to use their new technologies to control continents, command millions, and harness knowledge for prosperity, progress, and prestige. Was it not their duty, the Victorians insisted – indeed, moral obligation – to promote the advancement of European civilization in Africa? Were they not ordained to bring light to those living in darkness and to march with the civilized vanguard of humanity motivated by a supreme calling, what the Anglo-Indian writer Rudyard Kipling called the "White Man's Burden"? The Victorians invoked this humanitarian crusade to justify the imposition upon the Africans of a new – and presumably better – way of living by the extension of empire, even if it required the slaughter of those who refused to accept an alien culture and its civilization. The conquest of Africa could not have been accomplished without this sincere faith in their mission. Although in retrospect the fervor of their convictions today appears naïve, if not hypocritical, many of the Victorians firmly believed in the ultimate beneficence of their actions.

The scramble for Africa was also spurred by the rise of popular nationalism in late nineteenth-century Europe. Before the rise of the new nations of Germany and Italy, the older imperial powers expressed little interest in African expansion. While the local agents of France, Britain, and Portugal in Africa had from time to time encouraged an expansion of their small African holdings, their governments had consistently refused to support them. African colonies were rightly perceived as expensive, and tolerated more to stop the trade in slaves than to make a profit. Unlike the eighteenth century, when European governments sought to control commerce, the old and the new nations of the nineteenth century were committed to the principles of "free trade" whereby commerce along the African coast was regulated by the current market price, safeguarded by the occasional display of gunboat diplomacy.

The creation of the new nations of Italy in 1866 and Germany in 1870 threatened the European balance of power, which had governed international relations since the age of Napoleon. European nationalists came to see African colonization as a prerequisite for great power status, and they envied the extensive and established empires of Great Britain and France. Their jealousy, however, was to some extent an illusion, for the colonies of France brought her considerable expense and little profit, and the British thought so little of their insignificant holdings in West Africa that in 1868 Parliament seriously considered abandoning all of them. Perceptions, however, were more appealing and

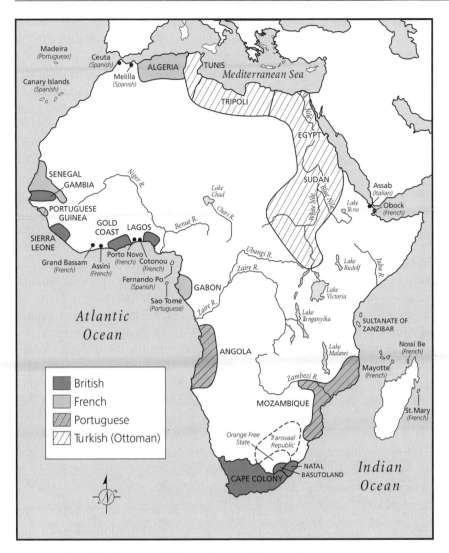

Map 18.2 *Europe in Africa on the eve of the partition.*

powerful than the costs and realities of empire, and the voters in Germany and Italy supported the imperial ambitions of their leaders to challenge the older empires of Britain and France.

The first European to take the initiative to acquire an African empire was, surprisingly, King Leopold of tiny Belgium. He created the façade of a supposedly scientific Committee for the Study of the Upper Congo, but his agents were instructed to obtain large tracts of territory rather than pursue any scientific investigations. They coerced African chiefs to sign treaties by which they unwittingly granted to Leopold more than a million square miles of the vast Congo Basin as his own personal colony. The king's astonishing success immediately motivated France to secure the territory north of the Congo River, and even the German chancellor, Otto von Bismarck (1815–1898), who at first resisted any colonial ambitions in Africa, sought to placate the increasingly vocal groups of merchants, missionaries, and nationalists who insisted that the German empire in Europe must now expand into Africa. Eventually, a reluctant Bismarck perceived that he could use an African empire as diplomatic leverage with his European rivals – particularly France and Great Britain, who were suddenly and to their surprise confronted with German colonies in Togo, Kamerun, South West Africa, and German East Africa (Tanganyika).

Like the Germans, the Italians, seeking to convince themselves they were a great power, used the growing power of Italian nationalism to justify their colonial ambitions. Although Italian imperial designs in Tunisia were checked by the French occupation in 1881, the Italians eventually conquered the vast, arid territory of Libya in order to claim both shores of the Mediterranean as their *mare nostra*, but in fact their principal designs were in Ethiopia, although these were crushed by the victory of Emperor Menelik II (1844–1913) over the Italian army at the battle of Adua in 1896. The Italians fared better in the Horn of Africa, where they established a colony in the sands of Somaliland.

Faced with these developments the older imperial powers could no longer remain idle. Portugal, a nation whose fortunes had declined precipitously since the days of Henry the Navigator, rallied to consolidate its African empire in the belief that this would secure its future status in Europe. Portuguese expeditions sought to expand the colonies of Mozambique and Angola from the coasts deep into the interior. French governments, which had long tried to restrain the enthusiasm for expansion by their men in Senegal, the infamous *officiers soudannais*, now became ardent advocates of a forward policy in what would become the French Soudan. British politicians, who in the past had been stalwart "Little Englanders," now found themselves reluctant imperialists, acquiescing to new conquests or supporting the expansion of allies in order to preserve free trade for British merchants and to placate the vociferous demands of the missionaries for the government to protect and support their missions.

European imperialism was not simply a nationalistic urge, as many Europeans had concluded that the tropical commodities of Africa were essential to the industrial growth of Britain, France, Belgium, Germany, and Italy, all with rapidly growing urban populations. When merchants sought to protect their profits on the West African coast or missionaries insisted on the expansion of their endeavors in southern Africa, the politicians and statesmen began to listen to their arguments and to believe that imperial conquest would open African markets for European manufactured goods, thereby protecting the jobs of workers at home, while enabling missionaries to bring their civilizing mission to the African peoples. These were powerful and persuasive interests who converted their nationalist leaders into global imperialists in which the promise of new colonies in Africa would contribute to the prosperity of the nation and thwart the ambitions of rival states, all in the name of civilization, commerce, and Christianity. In the end these promises were to prove illusory, a testament to the profound European ignorance of Africa and the Africans.

While Africa was not to be a new India for European economies, it did nevertheless produce a variety of tropical products that were in demand by manufacturers in the new industrial cities. Indeed, the abrupt partition of the continent exposed Africa's growing vulnerability to dramatic changes in global commerce ushered in by the Industrial Revolution. The demand for East African ivory in Europe and America for piano keys and billiard balls was only exceeded by the insatiable demand from Asia for the highly prized ivory ornamentation and carvings. The need for soap to cleanse the body from the industrial dirt of machines and mines strengthened the demands by European merchants for the British government to insure political stability for the palm-oil markets of the Niger Delta. The invention of the pneumatic tire and the subsequent mania for cycling among the middle classes of Europe and America in the 1880s suddenly made the wild rubber trees of the Central African rainforest an essential commodity. In an increasingly competitive marketplace, European merchants frequently sought to lower their costs by cutting out traditional African middlemen – who, not surprisingly, resisted, which in turn provoked European military punitive expeditions. Merchants also hoped that imperial rule would guarantee supplies of tropical products that could not be acquired elsewhere, and upon which industrial manufacturing depended. Rivalries among commercial firms in London, North Germany, and Paris led to demands for imperial conquest in East Africa and the Niger Delta.

A justification for empire equal in importance to commerce or Christianity was the strategic and diplomatic consideration of consolidating and defending existing empires. Indeed, some historians have viewed the advent of the "scramble" as the defensive reflex of European politicians anxious to protect their imperial possessions. Many of these statesmen were from the European aristocracy, who frequently regarded merchants and manufacturers with disdain and evangelists with contempt. Bismarck was surrounded by his circle of Prussian nobility, Lord Salisbury by Tory ministers and conservative civil servants. They were deeply imbued with the responsibility of defending the empire by diplomacy and military might, and were not sympathetic to the activities of European adventurers, traders, or missionaries in Africa if they did not coincide with their own views and needs for imperial defense and expansion. These were the men who constituted the official mind of the Victorians, and who were directly responsible for the imperial decisions and diplomacy of empire.

Most of Africa was partitioned in Europe's corridors of power by men totally ignorant of Africa drawing lines on maps of territory about which they knew little or nothing. It was empire on the cheap, for it was easily acquired by the stroke of a pen. All that was required by the European statesmen was a map of Africa and a fistful of treaties – usually obtained by false promises or veiled threats. To actually occupy and assert European authority over these new possessions, however, was quite another matter, which frequently required the military subjugation of formidable African opposition. The African armies that confronted the European imperialists were either those that had sought to adopt European weaponry and military tactics – the Asante of modern Ghana, the armies of the Tukulor in modern Mali, and the Dyula leader Samori Turé (1830–1900), whose sprawling empire encompassed much of modern Guinea and Côte d'Ivoire, and the Ethiopians – or those who relied upon their traditional weapons and ways of waging war – the Sokoto caliphate of northern Nigeria and the Zulu kingdom of South Africa. Each in their own way proved to be impressive opponents to the African armies led and equipped by Europeans. The Asante army numbered some 40,000 infantry equipped with obsolete but serviceable muskets and led by an effective command structure centered on the *asantehene*. The Tukulor army and that of Samori Turé were composed of *sofa*s, infantry armed with muskets and later repeating rifles purchased from the English, cavalry with traditional weapons, and artillery captured from the French. The Ethiopians had first experienced the power of modern breech-loading rifles during a brief punitive campaign in 1867 when a British column assaulted the royal residence at Magdala to free the British ambassador from captivity. After Menelik II succeeded the emperor Yohannes IV to the Ethiopian throne in 1889, he assiduously acquired modern European weapons that enabled him to mobilize an army of 70,000 repeating rifles and quick-firing artillery against the Italians in 1896. The army of Sokoto, however, remained dominated by the ideal of the Hausa warrior and relied on its aristocratic cavalry equipped with lance, sword, and bows with arrows. The more disciplined Zulu army with its age-set regiments (*impi*s), warriors in superb physical condition who could perform complex tactical maneuvers, and led by officers, the *induna*s, would advance against the enemy behind their walls of great shields to destroy them at close quarters with their short stabbing assegai, an eighteen-inch broad-bladed spear (*iklwa*). The Zulu armies had long familiarity with European firearms, and some warriors carried rifles into battle, but they never integrated firearms into their *impi*s, relying on their traditional tactics which had served them well for a generation and inflicted a devastating defeat on a British army at the battle of Isandlwana in 1879.

Not every colonial acquisition was preceded by violence. Many African leaders willingly, if unwittingly, signed treaties that effectively placed their territory under the protection of a European patron. Some believed that a voluntary submission to European colonial rule was an opportunity to acquire a powerful ally – and perhaps firearms – that would consolidate their personal power and insure the continuation of the indigenous political system, with themselves as the local ruling authority. Others, like the king of the Tio, whose agreement with the French explorer Savorgnan de Brazza (1852–1905) placed much of the modern Congo Republic under French rule, had little concept of what their treaties entailed. Others, such as the Ndebele king Lobengula (*c.* 1836–1894), bartered away the autonomy of their neighbors in order to retain the integrity of their own kingdoms. Most African rulers were painfully aware during these negotiations of the possibility that the Europeans would use their superior weaponry, if their demands were not met.

The swift defeat of African armies by European forces has produced among the public and historians alike the false impression that those who did resist gained little, but upon closer examination this does not prove to be the case. Shona and Ndebele resistance to the British South Africa Company forced Cecil Rhodes to grant important concessions in a negotiated peace. Although the bloody uprising against German rule in Tanganyika, known as Maji-Maji, claimed over 100,000 African lives, fear of another uprising ultimately forced the German government to temper some of the demands it made on the survivors as well as agreeing to a host of administrative reforms. In Asante and Zululand those rulers who resisted were initially exiled after their defeat, but eventually their dynasties were restored. Despite their ultimate defeat, armed resistance by Africans against European-led armies later was to become the focus of important and symbolic remembrance, providing a rallying point for independence movements after the Second World War. In the Sudan the family of the Muhammad Ahmad al-Mahdi, the religious founder of the Mahdist state (1885–1898), became an important political force in nationalist politics. In Zimbabwe the struggle against white rule which emerged during the 1970s, came to be called the Second Chimurenga, a name that harkened back to the Chimurenga or war of liberation fought against the agents of Cecil Rhodes in 1896. In Guinea during the 1950s the nationalist Sekou Turé drew legitimacy from his claim to be the grandson of the great warrior Samori Turé (*c.* 1830–1900).

Although the conquest of Africa took place during the last twenty years of the nineteenth century, the coastal roots of European expansion had been inexorably spreading into the interior of Africa since the 1850s. The foundations for a French empire, later known as the French Soudan, had been established as early as 1860 in the valley of the Upper Niger River where in the remote garrison of the forgotten French colony of Senegal ambitious French officers initiated an aggressive military policy – to further their own careers as much as to extend the French empire. Their ambition placed them in the path of the expanding power of the Tukulor empire of al-Haj Umar (*c.* 1794–1864). Al-Haj Umar was always wary of the French and reluctant to make war against them, as his *jihad* (holy war) was not with the Christian French, with whom he carried on a vigorous trade in arms, but the non-Muslim Africans, the *kafirin* (infidels) of the savanna. From April to July 1857 his army of 15,000 had besieged the advanced French fort at Médine, the end of navigation on the Senegal. After losing 2,000 of his *talibe*s (Arabic, "student"; the name applied to his disciples) Umar withdrew eastward into the vast hinterland of the Western Sudan. His Tukulor *talibe*s, inspired by his appeals to *jihad*, did not lack courage – only the artillery to breach the walls of French forts and sink their gunboats on the Niger. Having lost Médine, al-Haj Umar negotiated a strategic armistice with the exhausted French in 1860 that checked their conquest of the Western Sudan for another ten years.

After 1870 the advance of the French into the hinterland of the Western Sudan was revived, but its pace was painfully slow. Under a succession of French commanders, the *officiers soudanais* – who frequently ignored orders from Paris to seize large tracts of territory for France and win medals and promotion for themselves – the struggling columns of their African troops, the *tirailleurs sénégalais*, equipped with repeating rifles and artillery, marched eastward into the heartland of the Sudanic kingdoms. Segu did not fall until 1889, but its capture opened the navigable Niger to French gunboats, which bombarded and secured the surrender of Timbuktu in December 1893. The *seku* Ahmadu Tal (1836–1902), son and successor to al-Hajj Umar, implacably opposed the French advance until he was forced to flee for safety to the caliphate of Sokoto, where he died in 1902. He left his empire in the hands of a few French officers, who did not know what to do with the vast territory they had finally occupied.

The French had even more difficulty establishing control over the empire of Samori Turé. Samori was a Dyula trader who became one of the most famous soldiers in pre-colonial Africa due to a combination of political acumen and military genius. He forged a multi-ethnic empire from his capital at Bissandugu, which was divided into administrative districts and controlled by a 5,000-man army of *sofa*s loyal only to him and equipped with muskets and, by 1890, rifles. He learned early to avoid the French in set-piece battles, preferring to have his highly mobile columns of *sofa*s harass the French lines of communication and attack their isolated units. He employed scorched-earth tactics, but after the British refused to supply him with rifles from Sierra Leone, he could no longer sustain his forces in the field and in 1898 surrendered to the French, who sent him into exile in Gabon. Despite the collapse of his empire, he remains for many one of the first African modernizers in trade, politics, and war.

The French-led African armies had won for France a vast empire across the Western Sudan which consisted for the most part, however, of sandy "light soil," as the British prime minister Lord Salisbury commented undiplomatically, but the enormous geographical sweep of their new African empire restored French national pride, which had been badly tarnished by the French defeat at Sedan at the hands of Prussia in 1870.

In Central Africa, Leopold, king of the Belgians, sought to exploit the natural wealth of the Congo Basin by raising a private army of mercenaries, who collected wild rubber and ivory using intimidation, torture, and mutilation to build a vast private estate for the monarch. During the first decade of the twentieth century the scandal of his gross exploitation of the Africans was fully exposed by the reformer E. D. Morel (1873–1924), Christian missionaries, and the British consul, Roger Casement (1864–1916). This compelled the Belgian parliament in 1908 to demand that the king relinquish his personal control to a reluctant Belgian government to become the Belgian Congo – but not before he had spent many of his ill-gotten gains on the beautification of Brussels at an estimated cost of some 3 to 10 million African lives, before he died the following year. Events far to the North on the Nile Valley also drew Europeans more deeply into the affairs of African states. In 1869 the khedive of Egypt, Ismail Pasha (1830–1895), opened the Suez Canal with panache and splendor. There were four days of massive festivities, and armies of servants and cooks to entertain the guests from every royal house in Europe. Giuseppe Verdi was commissioned to compose the opera *Aida*. Religious patriarchs from Islam, Christianity of every persuasion, and even a Hindu priest blessed the waters. This grand event in one stroke dramatically changed the global defensive strategy of the British empire. Suddenly, the Suez Canal – and with it all of Egypt and the Nile Valley stretching all the way to the Great Lakes in the interior – became the linchpin of Great Britain's vast South Asian empire.

Although the British had long been fascinated with Egypt, their interests were largely concerned with its long history, dynastic monuments, and its strategic location in the eastern Mediterranean. Since 1801 the country had been ruled by a dynasty founded by an astute and ruthless Rumelian Turk, Muhammad Ali (1796–1849), who had come to Egypt in command of a Macedonian detachment of the Ottoman army to fight the French and had seized power in 1805. He and his successors sought to modernize the agricultural economy of Egypt, a policy that culminated in the 1860s when Egypt became the principal source of long-staple cotton for the textile mills of Lancashire during and after the American Civil War. The enormous profits from the Egyptian cotton crop enabled Ismail Pasha to embark upon the modernization of Egypt. He built palaces, an opera house, railways, and irrigation canals, but his greatest achievement was the Suez Canal. When Egyptian revenues could no longer service the interest on its debt, Britain and France imposed a European commission, the Caisse de la Dette Publique, in 1879 that effectively took over control of the Egyptian government by ruthlessly reducing expenditure, particularly in the army. When Ismail objected, he was forced to abdicate by Britain and France in place of his son, Muhammad Tawfiq Pasha (1852–1892), who was disdainfully dismissed by the Egyptian nationalists as a European puppet.

The political situation in Egypt rapidly deteriorated as the various classes of the Egyptian establishment – the liberal Western-oriented professionals, the conservative Muslim clerics, and the powerful landlords – rallied around the leader of Egyptian nationalism, Colonel Ahmad Arabi Pasha (1839–1896). Neither the British nor the French had any desire to occupy Egypt in order to continue their financial reform program, but when British and French citizens were killed in anti-European riots and Arabi threatened to seize the Suez Canal, a British expeditionary force landed at Ismailia and on September 13, 1882 destroyed the Egyptian army at Tel el-Kebir to occupy Egypt. Prime Minister

William Ewart Gladstone (1809–1898) announced that the British troops would be withdrawn from Egypt as soon as law and order were established. They were to remain for another seventy-five years.

The British occupation of Egypt insured control of the Suez Canal, but its security depended on a constant flow of water from the Nile. Without the Nile Egypt would be nothing but sand and rock and wind. The desire to protect the Nile water obliged the British to go thousands of miles up the river to secure it from any encroachment by potential rivals. By 1889, twenty years after the opening of the Suez Canal, the British were completely committed to employ all their considerable military, diplomatic, and economic power to exclude any European or African state from the Nile waters in order to secure Egypt and Suez. Although the Germans and Italians were restrained from any Nilotic adventures by British diplomacy, the French sought to challenge British control in Egypt by seizing the Upper White Nile at Fashoda, which precipitated the Anglo-Egyptian invasion of the Sudan, the conquest of the Mahdist state, and the humiliation of France when it was compelled to recall its filibustering expedition under Captain Jean-Baptiste Marchand (1863–1934) from Fashoda in 1898; this marked the end of the European scramble for Africa.

Often overlooked in the conquest of this vast continent was the crucial role played by Africans in the process. Despite the technological sophistication of the imperial armies, black African soldiers recruited by Europeans did most of the fighting. They were less susceptible to tropical diseases than their European allies, and much cheaper. The French employed the largest number of African troops, the famous Senegalese light infantry, the *tirailleurs sénégalais*, who subsequently conquered all of French West Africa. In 1900, at the end of their conquest of West, East, and Central Africa, British African troops numbered 11,500 African soldiers, commanded by no more than 300 British officers and NCOs. In the west there was the British West African Frontier Force, composed of men of numerous African ethnicities, but in which the language of command was Hausa. In the east Nilotes and Luo dominated the battalions of the King's African Rifles and the Sudanese battalions of the Anglo-Egyptian army. The German East African *Schutztruppe* relied heavily on its African askaris, led by a handful of white German officers. The Italians also had askaris, who won victories over the Sudanese Mahdists at Agordat in 1893 and the Ethiopians at Coatit in 1895; and even during their disastrous defeat by the Ethiopian host of Emperor Menelik II at Adua in 1896 the Italian troops were supported by over 10,000 askaris and Tigrayan irregulars. Portugal, the oldest European colonial power in Africa, had used African troops for centuries. In one of their last colonial campaigns, in 1902, against the kingdom of Barue in the Zambezi Valley of Mozambique, only 477 of its 15,000 men were Portuguese. Although not officially a colony even the Congo Free State recruited its *force publique* to conquer the vast expanse of the Congo for King Leopold. An ethnic conglomeration of 6,000 African mercenaries infamous for their brutality, they ultimately defeated the Arabs in the Upper Congo, the Zande kingdoms in the north, the Yaka of the western Congo, and the Luba at the headwaters of the Lualaba River.

The composition and motivations of these African troopers were strikingly similar. They were often marginalized members of their societies, or bound by personal and ethnic friendship to accept the pay, prestige, and security of the battalion in return for their submission to European discipline, demands, and their lives in combat against other Africans. Many learned skills for later civilian employment after demobilization. Others established family traditions for sons to follow fathers in the colonial and, after independence, the national armed forces.

The European conquest of Africa was shrouded in misconceptions by all of its participants. European statesmen knew little about African geography or the natural resources of its interior. What information they did receive came from explorers, merchants, and missionaries, who invariably embellished the truth to further their own ends. Lamenting the dearth of reliable information at his disposal, Lord Salisbury once remarked that he knew more about the moon than the interior of Africa, because at least he could see the moon. Ignorance bred mystery, and mystery led Europeans to harbor unrealistic expectations of the wealth that African imperialism might offer. African ignorance of European culture played an equally important role in the scramble. European notions of international law and freehold property were nonsensical to many of the Africans – accustomed to their communal control of land – who were signatories of the treaties that gave a patina of legitimacy to the European seizure of their land. It was only after the conquest that the reality of European imperialism in Africa became increasingly apparent. The European powers found that their new colonies were likely to require greater expense in men and money than they were worth, and the African communities discovered that the treaties signed by their hapless leaders legalized European rule. By the beginning of the twentieth century the popular enthusiasm for empire began to fade, symbolically, with the death of Queen Victoria in 1901. The European public soon lost interest in Africa. It would pay little attention to the affairs of the continent for the next fifty years.

Further reading

Headrick, Daniel R., *The Tools of Empire: Technology and European Imperialism in the Nineteenth Century*, New York: Oxford University Press, 1981

Pakenham, Thomas, *The Scramble for Africa, 1876–1912*, New York: Random House, 1991

Robinson, Ronald and John Gallagher with Alice Denny, *Africa and the Victorians: The Official Mind of Imperialism*, London: Macmillan, 1961

Vandervost, Bruce, *Wars of Imperial Conquest in Africa, 1830–1914*, Bloomington: Indiana University Press, 1998

19 Africans, Dutch, and the British in South Africa 1486–1910

At the end of the fifteenth century southern Africa was populated by peoples who spoke languages of either the Khoisan or Bantu families. Some of the Khoisan were hunter-gatherers, while others lived in small communities, raising livestock. The Bantu speakers clustered roughly into two groups: the Sotho-Tswana, who occupied the highveld, and the Nguni, who had settled on the coast. The Khoisan-speaking herders lived along the fertile valleys of the Cape Peninsula. Although the enormous landmass of this southern subcontinent of Africa seemed very large for the Khoisan and Bantu-speaking peoples, they had successfully exploited its diverse environment – the arid Karoo of the San (often pejoratively called Bushmen), the grasslands of the Khoi (often pejoratively called Hottentots), and the moist grasslands of the coast and drier savanna of the highlands of the Bantu speakers. This was the world into which the first Portuguese mariners made landfall in southern Africa in 1486, to be followed in 1488 by Bartolomeu Dias, who rounded the Cape of Good Hope as far as Algoa Bay, and on his return voyage discovered the safe and strategic anchorage of Table Bay, modern Cape Town.

The arrival of the Portuguese was made possible by their skill in organizing expeditions and the development of new naval technologies – ships, instruments, maps – that enabled them to navigate the treacherous winds, tides, and shoals of the western African coast and the violent seas off the Cape. These Portuguese captains and their crews were the vanguard of a new age of maritime global commerce that would bind Europe to Africa and Asia. By the end of the sixteenth century Dutch, English, French, and Scandinavian mariners would follow the Portuguese to the Cape to take on fresh water and barter iron tools and weapons for Khoi cattle and sheep. The trade of these early years was at times marred by violence precipitated by disputes over the terms of trade, drunken sailors, mutually unintelligible languages, and cultural ignorance. From the African perspective these European visitors were a curious, if insignificant, spectacle – hungry and thirsty sailors looking for provisions and fresh water or victims of shipwrecks in desperate straits. During the next 150 years the influence of these passing sea-merchants in the region was negligible, but the needs of the ships for fresh water and food and the desire of the Khoi for manufactured goods assured the continuation of these sporadic contacts. In 1649 a stranded Dutchman who had wintered at Table Bay proposed to the Dutch East India Company (Dutch Vereenigde Oost-Indisch Compagnie,

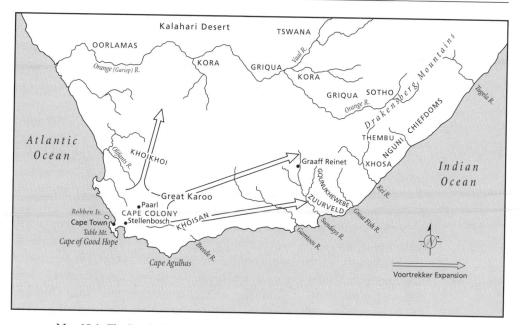

Map 19.1 *The Dutch Cape Colony and its settlements.*

VOC) that it establish a settlement to supply its ships making the long voyage to and from Asia. Three years later Jan van Riebeeck (1619–1677) arrived in command of eighty company employees to build a fort and supply their ships.

The company had no intention of remaining in Africa permanently, yet when van Riebeeck left in 1662 this Dutch outpost at the tip of the continent had been inadvertently transformed into a colony with a complex racial and social structure. In 1657 the company had begun to release its employees from their contracts and give them land as free burghers to be *boer*s (Dutch, "farmers"). Throughout the seventeenth and eighteenth centuries the number of settlers gradually increased by the additional discharge of company servants, immigrants from the Netherlands, including French Protestant refugees, the Huguenots, fleeing from Catholic persecution. Despite their diverse origins the new settlers were soon assimilated into Dutch culture, language, and the religion of the Dutch Reformed Church. By the beginning of the nineteenth century over 15,000 free burghers were resident at the Cape. Many of these settlers failed as farmers, for there was only a limited amount of arable land surrounding the Cape, and became artisans and merchants who catered to the visiting ships. The more successful burghers acquired ever larger holdings that they converted into heavily capitalized farms growing wheat and grapes worked by slaves.

When the company decided to establish a station at the Cape, it had not contemplated the use of slaves, but the Dutch were averse to the arduous physical labor required to make a farm productive, and the Khoi were unwilling to become their slaves. Since the company already used slave labor on their Asian settlements, van Riebeeck quite naturally requested permission to import slaves, and in 1658 the first shipment arrived from Dahomey in West Africa. Within a decade the company and the free burghers were dependent upon slave labor, and by the eighteenth century the distinctive characteristics of slavery at the Cape had become solidified. Cape slavery was characterized by a greater linguistic, cultural, and religious diversity than was to be found among slave populations in the New World. Only a few of the Cape slaves came from the African mainland, usually Mozambique; most arrived from Indonesia, India, Ceylon (Sri Lanka), and Madagascar. A minority were Muslims. Since slave societies historically do not reproduce themselves and at the Cape the ratio of male to female was four to one, it was only possible to meet the demand, particularly after the high mortality rate caused by intermittent epidemics of smallpox, by the continuous and steady importation of slaves. By 1711 and thereafter slaves outnumbered the free burghers, but the scale of slave enterprises at the Cape differed dramatically from the plantation system in the Americas. Only a few officials and farmers owned more than a hundred slaves, several burghers possessed less than fifty, and half of them no more than six.

When van Riebeeck and his company servants arrived in 1652, the indigenous Khoi pastoralists were accustomed to the occasional visit by European seamen, with whom they readily traded for iron, cooper, and brass. Relations between the Dutch settlers and the Khoi pastoralists were at first cordial, but they soon deteriorated after the completion of the company fort. Quarrels erupted – mostly over cattle – and when the Khoi refused the terms or quantity demanded by the company, the Dutch simply stole them. When the free burghers were given land in 1657, the Khoi burned five settler farms and recaptured stolen cattle, beginning a spiral of violence that ultimately ended with the destruction of Khoi society. During the next fifty years the settlers branded, flogged, and imprisoned any Khoi suspected of theft, and after 1673 declared total war against them. By 1713 the white settlers controlled all the territory in a circumference extending 50 miles below the mountain escarpment. Ravaged by European diseases, their cattle confiscated, their chiefs reduced to clients of the company, and their peoples technically free but treated as slaves, Khoi society disintegrated.

For fifty years the Dutch settlement at the Cape was hemmed in by the Khoi and the arid Karoo, the vast scrubland that stretched to the north and east, but gradually throughout the eighteenth century younger sons of farmers and landless settlers began to make their way through the Khoi territories and across the Karoo to the more attractive grasslands that lay beyond. They drifted into the interior, living by herding and hunting and becoming increasingly removed from life at the Cape. These white pastoralists were called *trekboers* (Dutch, "migrant farmers"), and wandered over the vast grasslands for hundreds of miles carving out their vast farms as far north as the Orange (Gariep) River and the eastern frontier town of Graaff-Reinet. They sold their cattle and sheep to itinerant Cape tradesmen in return for coffee, tea, tobacco, and in particular gunpowder and lead. Some would make an annual pilgrimage to the Cape from frontier towns such as Graaff-Reinet and return by ox-cart over rutted tracks, a journey that could take three months.

The *trekboers* lived the independent, spartan, and often violent life of the frontier which frequently brought them into conflict with Khoi pastoralists and San hunter-gatherers, who in turn would often rustle their cattle and sheep and even attack their homes. The *trekboers* retaliated by organizing their own military operations called commandos. Originally founded by the company for defense at the Cape, the mobile horse commando was ideally suited to combat on the plains. Consisting of *trekboers* and often their African servants and slaves equipped with firearms, they could swiftly descend on the Khoi and San, whom they regarded as little more than vermin to be eliminated, with devastating destruction. In one infamous raid in 1774 a large commando claimed to have murdered over 500 Khoisan in one day; in 1795, 2,430 were reported killed. By the end of the eighteenth century the indigenous people of southwestern Africa could no longer resist. Many became virtual slaves of their Dutch masters; others, seeking safety, fled deeper into the interior of southwestern Africa.

Living beyond the periphery of Dutch society, these refugees, many of mixed European, Asian, and African ancestry, were joined by runaway slaves and European renegades. These mixed communities spoke Dutch, practiced Christianity, and dressed in Western clothing. They also had access to horses and firearms, and used them with great skill to form their own commandos. They hunted wild game on horseback and traded the skins and ivory to merchants from the Cape in return for coffee, tea, tobacco, and above all powder and lead. These communities came to be called by a variety of names, including Bastaards, Griqua, and Kora. During the same period a similar community of mixed parentage, descendants of those of who had remained behind in the Cape Colony, emerged as a distinctive society known as the Cape Coloured.

Far to the east of the Cape on the high plateau of southern Africa lived Bantu-speaking communities divided by language, material culture, and political organization; but this diversity was relatively superficial and frequently concealed the fundamental continuities that bound them together. All spoke languages of the Bantu branch (Benue-Congo) of the greater Niger-Congo language family, and many were mutually intelligible. Most of the Bantu speakers practiced agriculture with the keeping of livestock, especially cattle, and the first of them to encounter the advancing white Dutch *trekboers* were the Xhosa, the southernmost of the Nguni communities. Long before the appearance of the Europeans the Xhosa had had close relationships with the Khoi pastoralists, and even integrated the distinctive "click" sounds of Khoisan into their language. The Xhosa lived on relatively fertile grasslands that permitted them to practice a mixed economy combining agriculture, animal husbandry, hunting, and gathering. They also lived in semi-permanent villages where they produced durable homes as well as ceramics and iron tools and weapons that gave them greater population densities than the Khoi or San, and would make them a formidable obstacle to European expansion.

As the Khoi buffer between Dutch and Xhosa collapsed in the latter half of the eighteenth century the *trekboers* began to insert themselves among the westernmost Xhosa settlements. During the ensuing competition for grass, water, and cattle conflict was all but inevitable along the frontier. The first violence between Europeans and the Xhosa arose from competition for water and pasture, as well as stock theft around the area of the Great Fish River, which erupted into open warfare in 1779. These frontier wars continued intermittently for the rest of the eighteenth century, during which the competition for grass, water, and cattle ironically often found Xhosa and *trekboer* in alliances against their African and European rivals. It was not until the nineteenth century that these incessant wars, characterized by a good deal of intercourse between *trekboers* and Xhosa, changed into a racially defined struggle of European against African for control of the frontier.

By 1800 the *trekboers* remained hemmed in by the Xhosa in the east, and at the Cape memories of the glorious Dutch past had faded. Cape Town had settled into a sleepy existence as just another port of call in a declining empire. The French Revolution and the subsequent Napoleonic wars suddenly revealed the enormous strategic importance of the Cape Peninsula to Great Britain, now the world's dominant sea power. Determined to protect its far-flung maritime empire and secure her trade routes to Asia, the British occupation of the Cape in 1806 was a decisive event in the history of South Africa. Although the presence of a major British naval base stimulated local commerce and the introduction of merino sheep made South Africa a major wool producer, its exports amounted only to a fraction of British foreign trade, and there was no substantial investment or immigration from Britain. Nevertheless, Great Britain could not ignore the administration of its new colony, which soon and somewhat to their surprise confronted British rulers with complex problems of governance.

The arrival of the British proved to be a mixed blessing for the Dutch living at the Cape. On the one hand, the British presence stimulated a sluggish local economy. On the other, English replaced Dutch as the official language of government, English law began to take precedence over the codified Roman Dutch law, and the languid, inefficient Dutch administration was replaced by a modern bureaucracy. To be sure, Britain introduced a modern army fashioned during the Napoleonic wars that soon tipped the balance in favor of the Dutch during their interminable wars with the Xhosa; but, determined to avoid unnecessary loss of life and reluctant to take on new administrative responsibilities on the eastern frontier, the British proved unwilling to press the Xhosa for concessions as hard as the Dutch had expected. Finally and to the total exasperation of the Cape Dutch, the British occupation permitted the presence of radical Evangelical missionaries whose spiritual message demanding the liberation of all oppressed peoples was anathema to the stolid Calvinism of the Dutch Reformed Church. In 1828 the promulgation of the fiftieth Ordinance giving the Khoi and "free people of colour" equality with whites before the law, to be followed in 1833 by the emancipation of slaves throughout the British empire, produced outrage and hostility among the Dutch at these egregious attacks on their way of life. The abolition of slavery appeared to threaten the prosperity of Dutch farms and ranches. It challenged the passionate conviction that Africans were inferior to Europeans and fit only to serve them. Discontent ran deep, and a handful of Dutch farming families determined to protect their way of life by moving from the Cape beyond the control of misguided and oppressive authority, in the tradition of the eighteenth-century *trekboers*.

Northeast of the Cape Colony, along the fertile coastal shelf of Natal, the early nineteenth century witnessed a remarkable period of conflict among rival Nguni groups that would reverberate throughout southern Africa. Warfare, banditry, and forced migration created a ripple effect that left the social geography of the region transformed. Entire communities were displaced, and new states absorbed the streams of refugees created by the crisis. This period of southern African history is often referred to as the Mfecane, an Nguni term that means "the crushing," and which came into use long after the events it was coined to describe. In the highveld the same process is known by the analogous Sesotho term Difaqane.

What caused the Mfecane is one of the most hotly disputed issues in southern African history. During the ninetenth century many observers – European and African alike – connected the origins of the Mfecane to the rise of Shaka (*c.* 1787–1828), the warrior-king who created the Zulu empire. More recently scholars have suggested that the introduction of food crops from the New World into the Nguni regions – particularly maize (corn) – may have put pressure on populations, thereby encouraging social and political innovations and conflict. There is little evidence, however, that demographic growth was outstripping the capacity of the land at the end of the eighteenth century. Other scholars have argued that at the beginning of the nineteenth century the amount of arable land available to the northern Nguni became more limited, precipitating increased competition for water, grass, and fertile soil at a time of severe droughts, which afflicted the area periodically during the first decades of the nineteenth century. The failure of the rains may have accentuated the competition over cattle, water, and pasture that was endemic to cattle-keeping societies. Still other scholars have emphasized the pressure on the Nguni by *trekboer* and Kora bands, who used horses and firearms to expand their settlements. For some combination of the above reasons the states of the northern Nguni were becoming larger in size, more rigorously organized, and were led by rulers who were able to demand an unprecedented degree of loyalty from their followers.

One feature of this transformation among the Nguni was the militarization of their age-sets. In Nguni society boys of similar age from different lineages were traditionally initiated together into adulthood to assume the responsibilities of the community, but also to bind them for life as a corporate fraternal body known as an age-set. Sometime before the advent of the nineteenth century these age-sets appear to have undergone a subtle but decisive reconstruction from an institution originally set up to preserve social stability and continuity into cohesive fighting units that enabled several Nguni confederations to fight more aggressively and to integrate more effectively the diverse peoples living on the fertile grasslands of the southeast African coast. Sometime around 1810 two rival confederations, the Ndwandwe led by Zwide (*c.* 1770s–1825) and the Mthethwa of Dingiswayo (*c.* 1770s–1816), fought for supremacy on the coastal plain with a ferocity that was remarkable among the Nguni.

Out of this conflict emerged a new and powerful Zulu state. Oral traditions attribute its foundation to Shaka (*c.* 1790–1828), a lieutenant of Dingiswayo, the leader of one of the most powerful of the Nguni confederations. With the help of Dingiswayo, Shaka had become chief of his small Zulu chieftaincy in 1816 and reorganized the Zulu army. When Dingiswayo was soon captured and killed by the Ndwandwe, Shaka assumed the leadership of the Mthethwa and with his Zulu army in the vanguard defeated the Ndwandwe in 1818 at the battle of the Mhlatuse River. This decisive victory confirmed that Shaka was the dominant power among the northern Nguni, and by 1820 he and his armies controlled the coastal plain from the Pongola River in the north to beyond the Tugela River in the south.

Shaka's role in instigating the Mfecane is subject to much debate. Historians actually have very little first-hand evidence about Nguni society before him, or about Shaka himself. An array of interested parties shaped the Shaka legend over time, including Zulu nationalists, British officials, and *trekboer*s. These groups found advantage in laying the credit, or blame, for the Mfecane at the feet of one man. Thus Shaka's actual role in creating the disorders may never be fully known. Many scholars choose instead to see the rise of Shaka and his Zulu state as a result, rather than a cause, of a phenomenon that was more likely to have been instigated by demography, military technology, regional trade, and other factors with deep roots in the region's history.

Though Shaka's role in fomenting the Mfecane is disputed, the significance of his Zulu state is not. This was a state organized for war, with a permanent standing army of some 40,000 warriors dedicated to expansion. It was constantly mobilized for raids against its neighbors. The success of Shaka soon resulted in the organization of other similar militarized societies that became states in order to defend themselves during the Mfecane, and refugees fleeing the conflict often organized into their own militant bands and employed Nguni military and administrative techniques to carry out their own plunder and conquest. Some crossed the Drakensberg to the highveld in the west, establishing themselves by force of arms among the Sotho-Tswana communities. Others

Figure 19.1 *European engraving of a Zulu village, early nineteenth century.*

headed south among the Xhosa, ultimately destabilizing their frontier with the
Cape Colony. One group, led by the Zulu leader Mzilikazi (*c.* 1790–1868),
embarked in 1821 on a long odyssey throughout the highveld, eventually settling in the western region of modern Zimbabwe where he founded the Ndebele
kingdom. The Sotho leader, Moshoeshoe (1786–1870), gathered together the
refugees in the Caledon River Valley on a mesa called Thaba Bosiu to drive off
the Ndebele of Mzilikazi and establish the present-day kingdom of Lesotho.
In the mountains northwest of Zululand Sobhuza (1780–1839) laid the foundations for the kingdom of Swaziland. Still other parties of warriors carved
out the Gaza kingdom in Mozambique, while yet more continued north to raid
as far as modern Tanzania. Shaka did not live to see the end of this traumatic
restructuring of African society throughout much of southern Africa. He was
assassinated by his half-brother, Dingane (*c.* 1795–1840), on September 24,
1828.

Confused accounts of events in Zululand were reported in the Cape Colony
by English merchants from Natal. Descriptions of the fertile lands of the coastal
plain depopulated by Zulu raiders attracted the attention of the Cape Afrikaners, who detested British rule and in the traditional fashion of the *trekboers*
were seeking new lands beyond the reach of the British authorities. By 1836
reconnaissance parties claimed to have discovered abundant grasslands depopulated by the Mfecane in the highveld beyond the Orange River and on the

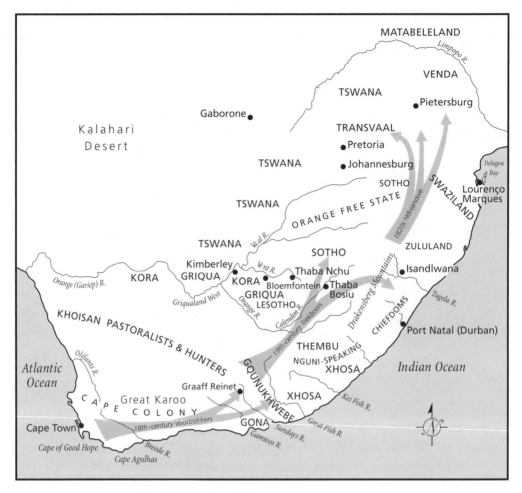

Map 19.2 *Southern Africa.*

coastal plain south of the Tugela. Parties of Afrikaners, called Voortrekkers, were soon on the move in what came to be known as the Great Trek, and by 1840 some 6,000 Afrikaners, 10 percent of the white population, had left the Cape. Some crossed the Vaal River, ultimately settling on the edge of the highveld at Soupantsberg. Others moved north across the Orange River, where they clashed with the Ndebele warriors of Mzilikazi, and yet another party led by Piet Retief (1780–1838) came over the Drakensberg Mountains seeking from Dingane a grant of land on the Zulu coastal plain inland from the British trading station of Port Natal.

Alarmed by the Voortrekker victory over the Ndebele and threatened by those now descending from the highveld into Natal, Dingane, during the final negotiations with Retief, sought to end the white invasion by clubbing him and his party to death on February 6, 1838 and launching his Zulu regiments against the Voortrekkers, killing many and capturing huge herds of cattle and sheep. When news of the massacre reached Natal, a Voortrekker commando led by Andries Pretorius (1798–1853) was mobilized to exact revenge. On December 16, 1838 Pretorius and 500 men encircled their wagons at the Ncome River (later renamed Blood River by the Voortrekkers) where some 10,000 Zulu attacked with incomparable courage, only to retreat, leaving behind some 3,000 dead. The Afrikaners suffered not a single casualty. This was a dramatic example of the power of the new European technology that was to be relentlessly repeated against African military forces until the end of the European conquest. In the aftermath of Blood River the Zulu kingdom declined into disarray as the Voortrekkers established their supremacy south of the Tugela River in Natal.

British officials at the Cape watched the expansion of the Voortrekkers with considerable trepidation, fearing that conflict in the far interior between Voortrekkers and Africans would require British intervention. The British thought that they had resolved this dilemma in 1854 when the Cape government officially recognized the autonomy of the two largest Voortrekker settlements, the Orange Free State north of the Orange River and the South African Republic beyond the Vaal. Though the territorial expanse of these "republics" looked impressive on a map, they were in fact poorly organized congeries of settlers grouped around influential family heads. None had an efficient system of taxation, administration, or defense, and all lived in a perpetual state of anxiety caused by the presence of the Bantu-speaking communities among whom they had insinuated themselves. British administrators at the Cape would have preferred to keep the Voortrekkers in the imperial fold, if only to constrain them from hostilities against African states, but the human and material price of imposing very unpopular British rule upon those who had fled from it was not worth the cost.

By the middle of the nineteenth century the Voortrekker descendants of the original Dutch colonists were beginning to forge a new sense of identity. As early as 1709 white farmers, the Boers, had referred to themselves as "Afrikanders" to distinguish themselves from the wealthier, urban Cape Dutch. During the next 150 years events in the Cape – and particularly on the frontier – had convinced them that indeed *trekboer*s were different from the Africans in southern Africa and the British settlers in the Cape Colony and Natal. The Great Trek and the victory over the Zulu at Blood River became the historical traditions that linked the Voortrekkers into what they perceived as their national struggle. By the end of the nineteenth century the Dutch and Boers had become Afrikaners.

As the Boers carved out their independent states in the north, British and Dutch settlers at the Cape were expanding east at the expense of the Xhosa. The 5,000 British settlers who in 1820 had been placed along the western border of the Cape Colony around the city of Grahamstown as a buffer to keep the Dutch and Xhosa apart had turned to farming and commerce rather than cattle ranching. Thirty years later, between 1849 and 1851, a second wave of 5,000 British men, women, and children settled further east on the fertile coastal plains of Natal. Most of them failed as farmers and departed to join the Voortrekkers on the highveld or returned to Port Natal as clerks and shopkeepers, renting their land to African tenant farmers they called *kaffirs*, a pejorative term derived from an Arabic word that means "infidel." Others were more successful, establishing sugar plantations, which, however, required an intensive and disciplined labor force that had no appeal to Africans accustomed to growing grain and raising cattle and sheep. When the colonial government forbade the "recruitment" of workers from the established African reserves, the plantation owners in 1860 began to import workers from British India. Twenty-five Indian women were permitted to accompany every hundred men, and by the end of the nineteenth century a permanent Indian community had emerged in Natal, outnumbering the whites and contributing yet another minority in the increasingly complicated racial mosaic of South African life.

By 1862 two centuries of European settlement in southern Africa had destroyed some indigenous societies and transformed others, but beyond the Cape Colony settler control over African communities was tenuous. Powerful African states on the highveld, in Natal and Zululand had contained the insatiable territorial ambitions of the Afrikaners in an uneasy equilibrium that was soon upset by the South African mineral revolution, which proved a greater threat to African societies than European farmers and pastoralists, and ultimately determined the triumph of white domination throughout southern Africa.

In 1867 on the northern border of the Cape Colony alluvial diamonds were discovered on a Boer farm, and by 1872 20,000 Europeans and 30,000 Africans were engaged digging diamonds on the site they called Kimberley. Since the diamonds lay in a shallow clay bed, they could initially be mined by simple tools that enabled Africans to extract the diamonds. They soon outnumbered European miners, who formed "digger committees" that used threats and violence to prevent Africans from owning their diggings, forcing them to labor in European-owned sites. Having summarily annexed Kimberley the British left labor relations, for which the Cape government was responsible, to these committees, whose industrial rules defined and hardened the racism of the Dutch agrarian settlers. Kimberley quickly became a rough-and-ready frontier town with a plethora of competing, often petty, mining claims that within a decade had been consolidated into the mining monopoly of De Beers Consolidated Mines led by Cecil Rhodes (1853–1902), Alfred Beit (1853–1906), and Barney Barnato (1852–1897). Those diamonds scraped from the surface soil were, in fact, only outcrops of deep diamondiferous plugs, which could only be successfully excavated by advanced technology that was available only to highly capitalized companies. Rhodes provided the organization, his associates the capital, and steam replaced man and animal power. The itinerant African diggers-turned-wage-laborers were replaced by a permanent, disciplined workforce of African miners living in all-male compounds.

The discovery of diamonds had produced a massive influx of immigrants and wealth into southern Africa. The newcomers were miners whose interests, outlook, and industrial pursuits were drastically different from the agrarian, pastoral Afrikaners. These new developments awoke the somnolent Cape politicians and their complacent businessmen to the possibility of even greater wealth in the interior of southern Africa, which could best be exploited by a closer political association of its territories. A confederation of southern Africa would provide the governing structure that would guarantee African labor for mining, agriculture, and the administration of the Cape Colony and Natal, a reduction in the cost of policing African communities, and the peace and security necessary to develop infrastructure and attract foreign investment. In theory confederation had considerable appeal; in practice its formation would require the approval of very different, independent, and powerful states – the Xhosa chiefdoms, the Zulu kingdom, the Afrikaner republics of the Orange Free State and the South African Republic – commonly known as the Transvaal – and the British-dominated Cape and Natal.

The first of these states to be incorporated into the British sphere of influence were the Xhosa. Since the middle of the eighteenth century they had been caught in a spiral of intermittent frontier wars with the European settlers of the eastern Cape. The final destruction of Xhosa autonomy was precipitated by an extraordinary event in 1857. In 1855 a deadly cattle disease (bovine pleuropneumonia) introduce from Europe began to destroy Xhosa herds in a seemingly inexplicable calamity. A young prophetess called Nongqawuse announced that she had been visited by her ancestors, who had informed her that the calamity befalling her people could only be reversed by a profound act of expiation – the destruction of the wealth of the Xhosa people. Her uncle Mhlakaza, who had lived for some time in the household of an Anglican bishop, was a spiritual advisor to the Xhosa chief Sarhili, and assured the ruler that if the Xhosa slaughtered their remaining cattle and destroyed their grain, the ancestors would expel the whites from their lands. Through Mhlakaza's influence a frenzy of cattle-killing and grain-burning broke out, which reached its climax in February 1857. Over 400,000 cattle and many grain stores were destroyed. More than 40,000 Xhosa died of starvation and another 33,000 were reduced to working as laborers on white-owned farms. The remnants of the Xhosa chieftaincies were eventually incorporated into the Cape Colony in 1866. The Xhosa cattle-killing is a remarkable incident in southern African history, whose roots lie in both African and European cultures. It drew on Xhosa and Christian theology in formulating its vision of a massive act of atonement, and the promise of a resurrection of the faithful. In many ways it paralleled nearly simultaneous millenarian movements taking place among the Plains Indians of North America and the Tai Ping rebels in China.

The next people to be drawn into the British plans for confederation were the Zulu. In 1872 the successor to Dingane, Mpande (b. c. 1800) died, and Cetshwayo (c. 1832–1884) became king of the Zulus. Cetshwayo was determined to restore his authority and that of his central government and to revive the glorious days of Shaka. The powerful secretary of native affairs and British agent in Natal, Theophilus Shepstone (1817–1893), had annexed the Transvaal republic to the British Crown in 1877, and then to secure the support of the Afrikaners for his policy of humbling Cetshwayo and containing the Zulu, he encouraged their insatiable demands for Zulu territory. The following year Shepstone and his officials in Natal had become convinced that only by the destruction of Zulu independence would confederation, enhanced by the annexation of the Transvaal, be further promoted and the mighty Zulu warriors be reduced to wage laborers. Shepstone demanded that Cetshwayo disband the Zulu army; the king refused and mobilized 30,000 Zulu warriors. In January 1879 a column of 15,000 British regulars, Natal African levies, and colonial volunteers launched the invasion of Zululand. On January 22 1,600 British troops were surrounded and massacred at the highland pass of Isandlwana. It was the greatest British military defeat since the Crimean war; British reinforcements were rushed to Natal and after heavy fighting captured the Zulu capital, Ulundi, in July. The Zulu kingdom never recovered, and it was annexed, and partitioned between the British and the Transvaal in 1887.

Once the Zulu threat had been broken, the Afrikaners in the Transvaal, chafing under British governance, once again proclaimed their independence in 1881 and after their victory over a British force at Majuba Hill, the British government conceded self-government to the Transvaal but retained control of the republic's foreign policy and native affairs. The British might have possibly remained satisfied with this somewhat ambiguous relationship if not for the discovery of the world's largest deposits of gold in 1886 at the Witwatersrand in the heart of the Transvaal, 40 miles south of the capital, Pretoria. The goldfields ran for miles in "reefs," but their seemingly unlimited quantities were not nuggets but flecks, requiring the most advanced mining technology to extract a few ounces of gold from a ton of rock. There would not, as at Kimberley, be a flood of impecunious miners hoping to strike it rich; only massive investment, heavy machinery, and a large, disciplined labor force could extract the gold.

The phenomenal wealth of the Witwatersrand, however, threatened to upset the balance of power in southern Africa. Efforts by British officials to draw the Transvaal into closer union with the Cape proved fruitless, as the president of the republic, Paul Kruger (1825–1904), sought to use his newfound wealth to increase the Transvaal's independence by channeling foreign trade through the Portuguese port at Delagoa Bay rather than to Cape Town. A filibustering raid in 1896 led by Dr. Leander Starr Jameson (1853–1917) on behalf of Rhodes and his British South Africa Company utterly failed to overthrow the Transvaal government. Jameson surrendered to Afrikaner commandos, but the raid made war between Great Britain and the Afrikaner republics all but inevitable. Three years later the governments of the Orange Free State and the Transvaal had become convinced that the British government was determined to destroy the independence of the Transvaal. On October 11, 1899 the war began, called the Boer War by the British, the Second War of Freedom by the Afrikaners, and by historians today the South African War.

The British government had made two serious miscalculations. They exaggerated the Afrikaner threat to British interests in southern Africa, and they underestimated the Afrikaner confidence in their military prowess, particularly after the British defeat at Majuba Hill in 1881 and their determination to remain independent. For two-and-a-half years a small Afrikaner force was able to harass and hold in check 450,000 British troops and their imperial allies from Canada, Australia, and New Zealand. The final defeat of the Afrikaners was only achieved after Lord Kitchener introduced scorched-earth policies, which destroyed over 30,000 Afrikaner farms, and established concentration camps where the civilian population was incarcerated, in which nearly 28,000 Afrikaner women and children died of disease. The republics were laced with 3,700 miles of barbed wire laid down between 8,000 blockhouses. Overwhelmed by death, disease, desertions, and fears of widespread rebellion among their African subjects, the Afrikaner armies surrendered and their commando officers signed the Peace of Vereeniging on 31 May 1902.

The war had profound effects on black Africans as well as white Afrikaners. Tens of thousands of Africans served with the belligerent armies. Most (approximately 100,000) threw in their lot with the British, who, it was hoped, would offer some political concessions to Africans if they won. Their hopes would be dashed, however, as the British bargained away their political rights in the ensuing peace negotiations. Approximately 10,000 Africans served with the Afrikaner armies, and an additional 28,000 were herded into the infamous concentration camps run by the British army. Over 14,000 of these prisoners died, a mortality rate that exceeded that of the Afrikaner civilians in the camps.

The defeat of the Afrikaner republics did not, however, resolve the future political configuration of South Africa nor fulfill the illusory goal of a British confederation. In defeat the Afrikaners were more united and more committed to Afrikaner nationalism than ever before. They were determined to insist on the clause in the Peace of Vereeniging that granted the Afrikaners of the Transvaal and Orange Free State the right to decide whether their black African subjects would be permitted to vote, which most recognized would never happen. Afrikaner solidarity was accompanied by postwar disenchantment with South Africa in England, which convinced the British government to appease the Afrikaners in order to protect its financial, mining, and business interests. The Transvaal and the Orange River Colony were granted self-government in 1907, which insured the vote for whites only – including white British South Africans, most of whom now supported the Afrikaners in denying the franchise to Africans. When the South African Party came to power in the Cape with the support of the Afrikaner Bond, it became increasingly clear to most

Figure 19.2 *African, European, and Chinese miners, South Africa. Mining labor became so scarce after the war of 1899–1902 that 60,000 Chinese men were imported to the goldfields of the Witwatersrand.*

whites that as a minority their position could only be protected by some sort of political union. The nineteenth-century vision of an imperial confederation and schemes by Cecil Rhodes for a British southern Africa from the Cape to the Zambezi had never died, and in October 1908 the all-white national constitutional convention for a united South Africa was convened in Durban. The constitution they drafted was overwhelmingly approved by the individual colonial governments, and on May 31, 1910, eight years to the day after the Afrikaner military forces had surrendered, the four colonies of the Transvaal, Orange River, Natal, and the Cape became the Union of South Africa.

The war's ultimate victors were the white supremacist settlers, purveyors of an emerging Afrikaner ideology, who ascended to power in the wake of the 1910 settlement. Before the war there had been a sharp cultural divide separating the more cosmopolitan Cape Dutch from their distant cousins living in the primitive Voortrekker republics. While Dutch speakers in Cape Town recognized an affinity to the Trekker communities, most were unenthusiastic about the prospect of these independent republics severing their ties to the Cape. Likewise the Voortrekker republics had a long history of conflict among themselves, and many of the influential burghers in the republics viewed the Cape Dutch as foreigners. However, the war proved a fillip for the emergence of a common "Afrikaner" identity. The perfidious aggression of the

British government and the atrocities committed in the concentration camps became part of a national myth of persecution. In the postwar era Afrikaner intellectuals and politicians in the Cape Colony constructed an agenda that placed the economic and cultural supremacy of the Afrikaner people above all considerations.

Further reading

de Villiers, Mark, *White Tribe Dreaming*, New York: Penguin USA, 1989

Etherington, Norman, *The Great Treks: The Transformation of Southern Africa, 1815–1854*, New York: Longman, 2001

Makinnon, Aran, *The Making of South Africa: Culture and Politics*, Upper Saddle River, NJ: Prentice Hall, 2003

Mostert, Noël, *Frontiers: The Epic of South Africa's Creation and the Tragedy of the Xhosa People*, New York: Knopf, 1992

Rotberg, Robert I., *The Founder: Cecil Rhodes and the Pursuit of Power*, New York: Oxford University Press, 1988

20 European colonial rule in Africa

The era of European colonial rule in Africa was relatively brief. Most of the colonies conquered or annexed after 1885 were independent less than eighty years later. Yet this brisk episode produced a massive disruption of African societies and left a legacy of strong, centralized, authoritarian governments. European colonial states differed dramatically from the traditional political systems Africans had developed during their long pre-colonial history, and not surprisingly most Africans regarded them as the imposition of an unfamiliar, unwanted, and unnecessary means of governance. Within a generation of colonization their discontent began to be organized into movements that soon demanded political equality and ultimately independence, but by then the European ideas of strong, protective governments had become so deeply entrenched that, ironically, on independence leaders of the new post-colonial states perpetuated colonial-style government, the very system they had vowed to dismantle. Even today the administrative structure in most African states has changed little from that bequeathed to them by their European conquerors. Although that European inheritance differed according to the traditions of law and government introduced by French, British, Portuguese, Belgian, German, and Italian officials into their African colonies, the diverse methods of administration employed by these imperial rulers shared some fundamental features in the governance of their colonies.

Like the nation-states of nineteenth-century Europe, the African colonies were demarcated – at least on maps, if not always on the ground – by territorial boundaries. Although political authority in pre-colonial Africa was sometimes defined by specific geographical space whose borders were natural features of the landscape – rivers, mountains, deserts – political authority was more closely associated with communities of people than territory, and the bonds of the state were social networks of lineage and kinship rather than arbitrary borders drawn on the ground. Some Africans now found themselves thrown together with others with whom they had little or no previous contact, and other homogeneous ethnic groups discovered themselves divided between two alien rulers by a boundary that for them made no sense, and caused a great deal of inconvenience, if not hardship. In defining their colonial territories the Europeans sometimes could not help but utilize natural landmarks or the obvious presence of pre-colonial ethnicities, but most frontiers were arbitrarily defined by treaty in the corridors of power in Europe, based on the often erroneous

Figure 20.1 *Asante troops enlisted to fight for Great Britain during the Second World War.*

observations of European explorers. Some of the largest colonies, such as British Nigeria and French West Africa, were the creation of an incremental process of conquest and annexation often the result of competition between rival European states. These boundaries had little to do with pre-colonial communities or natural landmarks, and encompassed a remarkably diverse array of geographical environments, economic practices, and ethnic identities under a single administration. This insured that few colonies would have a linguistically homogeneous population and guaranteed that most would contain an array of ethnically diverse peoples. Upon independence African leaders, fearing that the redrafting of boundaries would lead to endless and even bloody boundary disputes, retained this European legacy that is the jigsaw-puzzle political geography of modern Africa.

Another common feature of European rule was the ability of the colonial power to extend its authority throughout the colony largely by the sophisticated toolbox of industrial technology – telegraphs, railways, steamboats, repeating rifles – enabling the Europeans to impose an unprecedented degree of communication, coercion, and centralization. Pre-colonial African rulers often claimed they governed vast geographical regions, but the authority of most pre-colonial states in reality diminished in direct proportion to the distance from its center. A Lunda king might claim to rule over the entire Central African savanna, but his ability to collect tribute or impose his will on his peripheral communities was erratic. The sultan of Zanzibar might grandly assert that his authority spread deep into the interior of East Africa, but in fact he exerted little influence beyond the coast. Although there were remote pockets of unknown Africans that the colonial administration never reached and isolated communities that never fully submitted to the new European order, European technologies and the colonial armies equipped with them imposed and enforced an unprecedented degree of political consolidation within their African colonies.

Astonishingly, the European conquest of Africa was carried out without any preparation, planning, or even an ideology by which to establish the governance of colonies once pacified. European states with no previous imperial traditions or empirical experience seized African territory with little or no thought as to the manner and methods of administration for their new colonies. Once Britain and France had pacified their African colonies, they imported those imperial administrative devices that had served them well in their old empires. In India the British had ruled indirectly through the traditional maharajahs since the eighteenth century, while the French sought to impose on their African colonies the more centralized authority direct from Paris they had employed in Indochina. The result in virtually every colony was a jerrybuilt administrative structure that was the product of ad hoc decisions resulting from the many unexpected challenges of ruling vast regions of the African continent. This failure to prepare for colonial rule in Africa was in some ways inevitable. The European conquest of Africa was completed very rapidly – less than twenty years – giving officials in London, Paris, Brussels, Berlin, and Rome little opportunity to prepare for the administration of their colonies. This was left largely to the European officials on the ground – usually white soldiers leading African armies. This explains the diverse administrative systems that took root in the colonies, and the absence of clear administrative objectives and standardized institutions that characterized the early colonial era.

Although the colonial rulers came to Africa with different European national cultures, the colonial officers – British, French, Belgian, Portuguese, German, and Italian – were guided by a shared set of assumptions. They all would agree that their colonies would not be governed like European nation-states. Although most of the imperial powers accepted some form of democratic government at home, none of them ever considered applying the principles of popular representation in their new territories. After all, it was argued, the failure of pre-colonial African communities to rule themselves effectively had justified colonial conquest, and they could hardly be permitted to participate in the political process of colonial government. Another assumption shared by all the imperialists was that colonies should be financially self-sufficient – and most certainly not a burden on the domestic taxpayer, many of whom were ambivalent about the imperial missions of their governments. On the one hand, this principle required that colonial governments practice a frugality that precluded the recruitment of a sufficient number of European officials to administer vast territories inhabited by different Africans with differing needs. On the other, the thin khaki line of colonial administrators that arrived in Africa was expected to extract as much desperately needed revenue as possible with very little concern for the most egregious and visible human abuse.

Consequently, colonial governments were staffed by an astonishingly small number of European officials, who held all the principal political administrative positions and constituted most of the officer corps of the colonial armies. Although in West Africa in the nineteenth century there was an educated African elite that had participated in the early decades of British colonial administration, they were shunted aside in the 1890s by young, arrogant white Victorians who arrived in Africa quite convinced of their racial superiority. Therefore, the colonial bureaucracies soon came to be dependent upon Africans with only a rudimentary Western education to act as interpreters, policemen, clerks, typists, and to do a variety of other menial jobs in the colonial service. These positions were poorly paid and offered few opportunities for advancement, but Africans were eager to accept them, as government service was secure and the only alternative to life in the traditional economy. In return for low pay, long hours, and few psychological rewards these recruits, who often had some training in a mission school, learned linguistic, clerical, and technical skills that set them apart from their brothers on the farm and in the cattle byre. Within less than a generation this colonial system had created a class of Western-educated men – for virtually all of them were men – who were often scornfully referred to by their white superiors as "half-educated" but who had achieved an understanding of the workings of the colonial state. However, they could never aspire to exert real influence over the colonial political or economic system, and their frustration, combined with their knowledge, would play an important role in the subsequent movements for independence.

This cadre of minor civil servants was necessary to make the colonial administration function, but they could not be and were never considered as political leaders. With limited resources and few European political and administrative officials, all the colonial governments were therefore forced to rely on the traditional or accepted African leaders to carry out colonial policy and practice. During and after the conquest the administration sought the cooperation of the existing African political leaders by the use of flattery, bribery, rewards, or threats. When the collaboration of a traditional leader was not forthcoming, a pliant nonentity was often given a position of authority and expected to execute the wishes of his colonial overseer. The British in Africa enthusiastically embraced this concept of ruling through native authorities; it became known as indirect rule, and evolved from preexisting British domestic and imperial institutions. As subjects of the queen, British administrators acknowledged that monarchy was a natural and legitimate form of government, and the British empire in India provided the model for ruling subject peoples through traditional institutions. The intellectual architect of indirect rule in British Africa was Lord Lugard (1858–1945), an officer in the Indian army who had served in Nyasaland and Buganda and later as governor and governor-general of Nigeria, whose book *The Dual Mandate in British Tropical Africa* extolling the virtues of indirect rule became "first, a useful administrative device, then that of a political doctrine, and finally that of a religious dogma" and the manual for virtually every British African administrator.[1]

The two principles of indirect rule were decentralization and continuity. The foundation for law and order and material and moral progress could only be achieved by delegating authority to British officials in their territories with strict instructions to maintain a balance between indigenous traditions and imperial rule. This would achieve law and order and introduce change without disruption. These objectives could not be accomplished, however, without a continuity of personnel committed to these policies. In Lugard's view, the progressive development of "primitive peoples" would be retarded by a revolving-door of administrative officials without the language and understanding of the customs of the people.

The indirect rule of 129 million subjects of British colonial Africa required the cooperation of the traditional authorities or their pliable surrogates, who would employ traditional laws and customs that encouraged subject peoples to associate closely with those of their own ethnic identity, often in competition with neighboring ethnic communities. They would be advised by a British official who knew the language – and, hopefully, the laws and customs – of the people under his tutelage. In theory indirect rule would cause the least possible disruption in the lives of Africans during a time of gradual change by allowing their traditional leaders to administer justice, collect taxes, and implement the policies of the colonial government. In practice, however, indirect rule contained numerous inherent contradictions that unintentionally transformed African custom, law, and politics.

First, the system confirmed traditional rulers in their positions of leadership, but the British advisors demanded that the chiefs undertake a host of new and unpopular responsibilities, including raising soldiers for colonial service, collecting new taxes, and providing laborers for public works projects or for white-owned farms. Chiefs charged with imposing these new demands on their subjects often became lightning-rods for public dissent. Second, indirect rule aspired to govern Africans through their own laws in native courts, but that "customary law" was inevitably transformed by the demands and presence of the colonial administration. British district officers reserved the right to

---

[1] Address given at Chatham House by Lord Hailey on December 8, 1938, in *International Affairs* 18, 2 (1939), p. 202.

prohibit practices that they considered barbarous – slavery, witchcraft, trial by ordeal, human sacrifice, and blood feuds. To Europeans, the prohibition of these activities was a beneficent aspect of their civilizing mission, but by criminalizing these practices, indirect rule invariably changed the legal and administrative functions of the traditional leaders. They could no longer use these "barbaric customs" to eliminate rivals and malcontents or to over-awe and intimidate their followers, which had been essential instruments for the maintenance of political and social order. For example, under colonial rule the traditional right of aggrieved individuals to retaliate against their enemies was made illegal. However, colonial jurists failed to recognize that the threat of violence was itself an important mechanism for maintaining social stability, as it encouraged lineage leaders to put pressure on feuding parties to settle their disputes amicably. When the punishment for theft, adultery, or assault became the payment of compensation rather than the infliction of bodily harm, such offences became viewed as less serious – and some of them, as a result, more common.

Indirect rule also changed African jurisprudence by the simple act of cod-ifying and standardizing "customary law." Many Islamic African states had relied on written law codes for centuries, but in the non-Muslim kingdoms custom and law were part of an oral tradition that was constantly subject to interpretation to meet new circumstances and could vary widely within a single linguistic or ethnic community. The very act of writing down customary laws, however, made them uniform, static, and unable to respond to changing con-ditions, which entrenched the privileges and interests of those whose version happened to be the one that was codified. The status of women, in particular, was acutely affected. In virtually every African society the elders were held in the highest respect as the living embodiment of the laws, mores, and spirit of the community. Consequently, when European administrators sought out the traditional leaders to advise and cooperate in establishing colonial gover-nance, they were invariably senior men, the guardians of the customary laws that were now reduced to legal paper. Not surprisingly, patriarchal authority was reinforced and fixed in place, solidifying the second-class status of women in African societies. When the British introduced and installed warrant chiefs (non-traditional appointed chiefs, sometimes of a different ethnicity) with judi-cial powers in Igboland in eastern Nigeria in the 1920s, the women feared they would abuse their authority, particularly in the adjudication of matters involv-ing taxation of families, bride-wealth, and marriage. Their anger turned into a mass protest in which British troops killed fifty women and injured fifty more, forcing the colonial authorities to reconsider their imposition of indirect rule in the region.

The introduction of indirect rule in British Africa did indeed confirm the authority, legitimacy, and prestige of some traditional rulers, but it also invested other chiefs, who in fact had only a very precarious control over the commu-nities they presumed to rule, with an unprecedented degree of power. Many of these leaders had only recently come to power, and could hardly claim to be the heirs of a long dynasty. Indeed, the late eighteenth and early nineteenth centuries saw unprecedented state expansion in sub-Saharan Africa, and many new leaders were willing if not eager to reach an accord with the Europeans to consolidate their recently acquired authority. In return for cooperation and collaboration these rulers found themselves supported by the powerful bureaucracy and military forces of their colonial patrons, giving them a hitherto unprecedented control over their subjects. There were other African societies that were more difficult to fit into the pattern of indirect rule, for their communities had no clearly recognizable political offices or hierarchies – stateless societies, in the language of colonial anthropologists. Their presence created a good deal of consternation among the colonial authorities, who had difficulty grasping the idea that a society could manage its affairs, settle disputes, and contain malcontents without an identifiable leader, chief, or king. The British resolved this dilemma by simply inventing traditions and institutions, and appointing leaders where none had previously existed. The lack of authority and respect accorded to these chiefs meant that their tenure in office was often brief, with one British puppet following another in rapid succession.

Although every colonial power at one time or another contemplated, imposed, or abandoned some version of indirect rule, the French at first experimented with a policy of assimilation, which has left a deep and influential legacy throughout Francophone Africa. Like indirect rule in British colonies, it was the product of French history, its revolutionary and imperial institutions and the political traditions of France. The French Revolution had translated the philosophical beliefs of the eighteenth-century Enlightenment about the universality of man into practical ideas of action in the Declaration of the Rights of Man and of the Citizen of 1789, which triumphantly proclaimed that all men – not just Frenchmen – are born and live free and equal in rights. These egalitarian principles obviously had to apply to the inhabitants of the French colonies, and throughout the nineteenth century France aspired to assimilate its colonial subjects, making them French by means of French language and culture. French enthusiasm for creating an empire of 100 million Frenchmen was rooted not only in the egalitarian traditions of the French Revolution, but also the imperial heritage of Napoleon, who had sought by conquest in Europe – and his military successors by conquest in Africa – to spread the ideas of the revolution founded on the superiority of French culture. When the French conquered Algeria in the 1830s, and much of West Africa in the 1880s and 1890s, many French politicians, officials, and the French people themselves expected that the inhabitants of these new territories would become black Frenchmen.

On the surface indirect rule and assimilation appeared dramatically different. Indirect rule assumed that Europeans and Africans had separate capabilities and destinies. Assimilation anticipated that French culture could be accepted and absorbed by all peoples regardless of ethnicity; this appeared to render it less overtly racist than indirect rule. However, it also presumed that French culture was superior and therefore preferable to the diverse African cultures to be found in the colonies. In practice the early influence of assimilation required the presence of a far larger number of French administrators than British officials in their colonies, who were more likely to replace recalcitrant traditional leaders with pliable servants and to reconstitute at will the authority and territory of their chiefs.

As France's empire in Africa expanded during the late nineteenth century the practicality of assimilation came to be questioned. By the end of the century several of the most famous French imperialists, Louis Faidherbe (1818–1889) in the Senegal, Joseph Gallieni (1849–1916) in Indochina and Madagascar, and Louis Lyautey (1854–1934) in Morocco, had realized that millions of Africans and Asians were not about to become Frenchmen. Moreover, France's vast colonial territories in Africa were too large to be ruled directly by European or assimilated bureaucrats, and the prospect of millions of Africans voting in French parliamentary elections frightened voters and politicians. At the end of the First World War, during which the public experienced the practical and racial problems of the presence of large numbers of Africans fighting on French soil, French officials embraced a policy of association. Law and order was now to be achieved at little expense by collaboration with the traditional authorities accompanied by respect for their language, customs, and institutions – in theory, not much different from British indirect rule.

Many French officials believed, however, that association was little more than assimilation disguised by the cloak of hypocrisy in which it was wrapped. French officials continued to maintain complete control of the administration of their colonies unchecked by the chiefs, who had been converted into convenient petty officials rather than representatives of their people. French administrators had no illusions about this contradiction but were quite content to ignore it in order to replace African customs, for which they had little more than contempt, with the relentless dissemination of the French language and culture. A greater percentage of French Africans learned to speak the language of their masters than did their neighbors in the British colonies. In the British territories district officers were encouraged – and often required – to learn and use the local language in their daily administrative duties; the French seldom did. During the 1930s when African leaders in the British colonies were agitating for greater political influence in government, their contemporaries in the French colonies were focused on the threat of cultural imperialism, and rather indifferent to demands for political reform. It is no coincidence that the political movement for pan-African unity was born and promulgated from the British colonies, while their counterparts in the French colonies debated the validity of a distinctly African identity, dubbed Negritude, to oppose the threat of French assimilation.

Like those of the British and the French, the Portuguese colonial empire in Africa at the end of the nineteenth century was established in territories

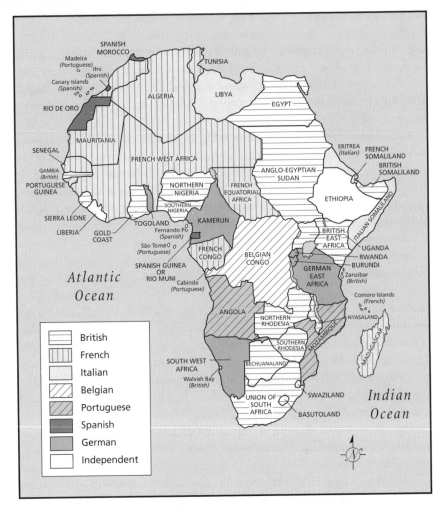

Map 20.1 *Africa in 1914.*

with which Portugal had for centuries had commercial relations, and by the end of their conquest of Africa the European powers had officially recognized Portuguese rule over the Atlantic islands of Cape Verde, São Tomé, and Príncipe, and the larger mainland colonies of Portuguese Guinea, Angola, and Mozambique. Portuguese colonial policy was governed more by this long commercial heritage of exploitation than by recognition of African traditional rulers or their culture. When the republicans gained power in Portugal in 1910, they were determined to revive their African empire by encouraging Portuguese to immigrate and settle in the colonies, where their presence as petty clerks, shopkeepers, and landowners gave them privileged opportunities but increased racial tensions and exacerbated old antagonisms. In Angola Portuguese policy after the First World War was driven by the need for the republican government to restore Portugal's finances by extracting its wealth. Under the dynamic administration of the high commissioner, Colonel Norton de Matos (1867–1955), Angola was transformed into a corporate satellite of Portugal. Africans were coerced to build roads, produce cotton and coffee, and work in the De Beers diamond mines. There was not even the pretense of including Africans in the administration, even by the appointment of token officials, and the few educational, medical, and welfare services were left largely to foreign missionaries.

Portuguese policy in Mozambique was quite different, but with much the same results as in Angola. In the past the Portuguese monarchy had never been able to raise the capital necessary to exploit the interior territories of Mozambique that surrounded the commercial enclaves on its eastern African coast except by granting royal charters of colonization to private companies. These charters included grants of land that created the prazo system of feudal land tenure in the Zambezi Valley and in the twentieth century franchises to private companies, such as the Witwatersrand Native Labour Association (WNLA), to recruit labor for the South African gold mines. The Africans of Mozambique were given the choice of leaving home on contract work or being pressed into the chain gangs that built and repaired the colonial roads. These charters granted wide powers to the concessionary firms, including the collection of taxes, the suppression of rebellions, and the forcible recruitment of farm labor for Rhodesian settlers. After the Second World War the postwar boom in commodity prices encouraged a substantial increase in the number of Portuguese immigrating to Mozambique. The new settlers took positions in the service industries previously held by Africans, and established coffee plantations on land expropriated from the African population. The legacy of 400 years of commercial exploitation as colonial policy resulted in rebellion, repression, and the ultimate independence of Mozambique from the Portuguese colonial empire.

Like the Portuguese empire the colonial policy of the Belgian Congo was deeply influenced by the commercial exploitation of its predecessor, the Congo Free State. In 1885 at the Berlin Conference other European states conferred upon King Leopold of the Belgians personal sovereignty over the Congo. At the time and thereafter the Belgian government wanted nothing to do with the administration of the Congo Free State, which, as Leopold's personal fief, was exploited by him for his profit and gratification. When the gross abuses of Africans by Leopold's agents were exposed in 1908, the aging king was forced to cede his authority over the Congo Free State to a very reluctant Belgium. Belgian colonial policy was formulated in the Carte Coloniale, which served as the constitutional statute of the Belgian Congo until independence in 1960. The apprehensive Belgians insisted that the administration of the Congo be completely separate from that of Belgium, however, and during the fifty years of Belgian rule neither suffrage nor citizenship was contemplated for the Congolese. Instead of emulating the French-style policy of assimilation or the indirect rule of the British, the Belgian Congo was to be administered by a trinity consisting of the colonial state apparatus, the Catholic Church, and big business.

In the wake of the world's horrified reaction to the wanton cruelty of King Leopold's agents in the Congo Free State, a Colonial Institute was set up in Antwerp to train Belgian Colonial officials. Graduates of the insititute were familiar with the principles of both association and indirect rule. They all had read *The Dual Mandate in British Tropical Africa*, but the Catholic hierarchy that controlled the missionary churches and schools was not about to dignify African chiefs with authority when their traditional positions were based on indigenous belief systems and not Christianity, preferably Catholicism. The chiefs were officially confirmed in their *chefferie* (French, "chieftaincies") but with little or no authority, and the actual administration was organized into arbitrary and distinctly nontraditional *secteurs* (French, "administrative units"), each with an appointed warrant chief who carried out the orders of Belgian officials. This policy of paternalism was most conspicuous in the organization of labor for large Belgian firms – particularly the Katanga mining industry controlled by Union Minière, which at first was modeled on the South African WNLA. The harsh practice of recruitment of single males was more reminiscent of the brutality of Leopold's Congo Free State, however, and under pressure from missionaries and officials who hated the egregious methods required of them to recruit labor, the mining companies introduced a paternal policy of "manpower stabilization" in the 1930s, which provided housing for families and trained Africans in skilled jobs, replacing expensive and demanding white employees. This reinforced the paternalism that characterized the state administration and its welfare system.

The philosophy of Belgian paternalism was based on the assumption that if Africans were assured of a standard of living above subsistence, they would not bother to seek political participation. Consequently, education was left to the missionaries, who were to provide literacy, vocational training, and spiritual sustenance; but during the fifty-two years of Belgian administration post-secondary education for Africans was systematically prohibited. As late as 1955 Belgium had no intention of including Africans in the political process. When in panic Belgium unilaterally declared the independence of the Congo in 1960, they reaped a violent harvest from their policy of neglect.

German and Italian colonialism in Africa was too short-lived to establish any coherent administrative policy. During the thirty years (1884–1914) of the German colonial experience in Kamerun, Togo, South West and East Africa less than 25,000 settlers were attracted to its million square miles that proved of little commercial value and was characterized by bloody African rebellions. South West Africa was essentially administered by a military bureaucracy on behalf of the repressive settler society which in 1904 accepted a deliberate policy of genocide advocated by Commander General Lothar von Trotha (1848–1920) to eliminate the Herero people, 80 percent of whom were killed and the remainder forced to labor. The German administration in Togo was more benign, largely because of the presence of German traders and missionaries who prevented the introduction of plantation agriculture, which would have destroyed the individual and productive African farmers. Kamerun was less fortunate, as the plantation owners and state railway company colluded in a brutal system of forced labor that was not exposed and reformed until 1906. Colonial administration in German East Africa at first was delegated to a chartered company, the German East Africa Company, whose harsh methods precipitated a rebellion in 1888, led by Abushire al-Harthi, which resulted in the intervention and direct rule by the German government. In order to make the colony pay for its administration African farmers were forced to labor on state cotton plantations and pay taxes collected by the hated African German agents, the *akida*s. This led to a massive rebellion known as Maji-Maji from 1905 to 1907, which was only suppressed by a scorched-earth policy in which more than 250,000 Africans were killed or died from starvation. Despite efforts at reform by the liberal banker and secretary of state for colonies Bernard Dernburg (1865–1937), the violent history of German colonialism in Africa was the principal justification for stripping Germany of her colonies at the end of the First World War.

Italy was the last European nation to acquire African colonies (*c.* 1890–1941), but its colonial policy was never coherent, and was characterized by bursts of expansion interspersed with military defeat. Italy had no colonial tradition, no cadre of colonial administrators, and a vacillating national policy. The rise to power of the fascist strongman Mussolini in 1922 resulted in a ruthless policy of law and order in Eritrea and Italian Somaliland, although this was often checked in Rome by a strong anti-colonial lobby of socialists, the Catholic Church, and even some commercial interests. In 1896 Italian imperial adventures in Ethiopia had ended in the disastrous defeat at the battle of Adua. Italy's massive second invasion of Ethiopia in 1935 was greeted by international opprobrium, and became a symbol of repressive European colonialism to the young nationalists in Africa. The final defeat of the Italians in 1943 by the allied forces and the restoration of the Ethiopian emperor Haile Selassie I (1892–1975) ended the dream of the "new Rome." Eritrea was given to Ethiopia, but after 1950 Somaliland continued to be administered by the Italians under a UN trusteeship until 1960, when Somalia became independent.

Whatever the colonial policy, or lack thereof, by the European powers – Britain, France, Portugal, Belgium, Germany, and Italy – all had some common objectives. They were all determined to keep the peace at whatever cost, as without it there could be no administration, exploitation, or development. They were all determined to raise revenue to pay for the administration of the colony, and perhaps a surplus for the national treasury. Revenue could only be generated by the production and export of cash crops, raw materials, or minerals, a process that was accomplished by private or state-controlled economic enterprise and the collaboration of Africa political leaders. All colonial governments condoned labor coerced or dubiously recruited in order to build the infrastructure required to extract the wealth of colonial Africa. In retrospect, the Europeans gained few benefits from their African colonies, and what little they received was at great cost to the Africans. When the Second World War destroyed the global power of Britain and France, neither of them could sustain the demands of empire, which vanished with the tunes of glory and the memories of the White Man's Burden.

Further reading

Brett, E. A., *Colonialism and Underdevelopment in East Africa: The Politics of Economic Change, 1919–1939*, London: Heinemann, 1973

Crowder, Michael, *The Story of Nigeria*, 4th ed., London: Faber, 1978

Crowder, Michael, *West Africa under Colonial Rule*, Evanston: Northwestern University Press, 1971

Daly, Martin, *Empire on the Nile: The Anglo-Egyptian Sudan, 1898–1934*, Cambridge: Cambridge University Press, 1986

Daly, Martin, *Imperial Sudan: The Anglo-Egyptian Condominium, 1934–1956*, Cambridge: Cambridge University Press, 1991

Gifford, Prosser and William Roger Louis (eds.), *France and Britain in Africa: Imperial Rivalry and Colonial Rule*, New Haven: Yale University Press, 1971

Hochschild, Adam, *King Leopold's Ghost: A Story of Greed, Terror, and Heroism in Colonial Africa*, Boston: Houghton Mifflin, 1998

Iliffe, John, *A Modern History of Tanganyika*, Cambridge: Cambridge University Press, 1979

Manning, Patrick, *Francophone Sub-Saharan Africa, 1880–1985*, Cambridge: Cambridge University Press, 1988

Newitt, M. D. D., *Portugal in Africa: The Last Hundred Years*, London: Hurst, 1981

Zwede, Bahru, *A Modern History of Ethiopia, 1855–1974*, London, Athens, and Addis Ababa: James Currey, Ohio University Press, and Addis Ababa University Press, 1991

21 The colonial legacy

The colonial enterprise in Africa has been condemned as exploitative and praised as constructive. The West Indian scholar Walter Rodney asserted that European pressure distorted African economic growth and led to the under-development of the continent. Rodney's critics counter that colonialism drew capital and investment into the continent that ultimately built an infrastructure which proved beneficial to the African peoples. At the beginning of the twenty-first century controversy continues without respite, but there are two aspects of European colonialism in Africa upon which the antagonists agree: European colonialism dramatically transformed Africa; and the Africans played a critical role in shaping the nature of colonialism and exposing its limitations.

The colonial experience in Africa can be roughly divided into two periods. At the end of the nineteenth century the beginning of European colonialism was characterized by the imposition of imperial administrations accompanied by violent economic expropriation which imposed tremendous hardships on their African subjects. By the end of the First World War most European states had indicated that the excessive abuse of Africans that had taken place during the preceding decades would no longer be tolerated, but during the interwar years the British and French found it difficult to maintain coherent colonial policies. Their efforts were complicated by the world economic depression of the 1930s and then the Second World War, which found them allied with the anti-imperialist powers of the United States and the Soviet Union. To respond to the growing criticism of colonial rule Britain in 1940 and France in 1946 launched programs for development that would mobilize African resources to restore their own economies but also provide employment and improved conditions for African wage laborers. When it became increasingly clear that these plans for economic revitalization drafted in London and Paris had failed to transform the colonial economic structure, European rulers were faced with the choice of either using massive force to suppress unrest or undertaking dramatic political reforms within their colonies. In most cases the colonial powers determined that the latter option was the lesser of two evils.

Colonial rule required the imposition of a new economic order, one that sought first and foremost to generate sufficient revenue to pay for its administration. This was achieved by compelling Africans to enter into wage labor

Box 21.1 Did Europe underdevelop Africa?

The early hopes for economic prosperity in post-colonial Africa ended in disappointment. As African economies faltered, scholars began to search for the roots of the continent's economic problems. Why had African economies failed to develop according to Western models? Why did African nations remain dependent on the export of a handful of commodities? Why had the continent experienced virtually none of the industrialization that had enriched North American, European, and even some Asian countries? These questions were answered forcefully in 1972 by the Guyanese scholar Walter Rodney in his book *How Europe Underdeveloped Africa.*[1] Rodney's explanation was simple – modern Africa's problems stem directly from its long connection with Europe. Beginning with the trans-Atlantic slave trade Europe had imposed unequal terms of trade on African states. The slave trade made Africa an exporter of human labor, and an importer of goods that were detrimental to future development. This lopsided economic relationship culminated in the colonial era, when European states wrested control of African economies from indigenous rulers, destroyed local industries, and broke up communities and commercial networks by introducing new and artificial boundaries. To Rodney, this was not accidental, but a calculated policy intended to strangle African development by denying the continent the machinery, markets, and expertise it needed to develop an industrial base.

The tone of Rodney's book was polemical, written for a popular audience, and intended to raise public awareness of the continued exploitation of Africans by colonial rulers. When his book appeared in 1972 Portugal remained firmly entrenched in its vast African empire, while white settler regimes in South Africa and Rhodesia dominated the continent's south. But despite the book's inflammatory tone its analysis influenced a generation of scholars who undertook local studies in support of his thesis.[2]

Not all scholars accepted Rodney's assertions. His criticisms of colonial rule were themselves a response to arguments by historians such as D. K. Fieldhouse,[3] who insisted that colonial empires had not enriched European nations, or the conservative scholars Gann and Duignan, whose work *Burden of Empire*[4] credits colonialism with invigorating African

[1] Washington: Howard University Press, 1972.
[2] See for example Edward A. Alpers, *Ivory and Slaves: Changing Patterns of International Trade in East Central Africa to the Later Nineteenth Century*, Berkeley: University of California Press, 1975 and Bade Onimode, *Imperialism and Underdevelopment in Nigeria: The Dialectics of Mass Poverty*, London: Zed Press, 1982.
[3] D. K. Fieldhouse, *The Colonial Empires: Comparative Survey from the Eighteenth Century*, New York: Delacorte Press, 1966.
[4] L. H. Gann and Peter Duignan, *Burden of Empire: An Appraisal of Western Colonialism in Africa South of the Sahara*, London: F. A. Praeger, 1967.

Box 21.1 (continued)

economies by supplying them with needed infrastructure, capital, and technological expertise. More recently, Rodney's contention that the trans-Atlantic slave trade underdeveloped African economies has been questioned by John Thornton in his book *Africa and Africans in the Making of the Atlantic World, 1400 to 1800*. Thornton's work, which synthesizes the conclusions of many other scholars, raises several questions regarding the degree to which African economies were underdeveloped by the slave trade. While Thornton recognized that the trade drew millions of laborers out of the continent, he contends that the population increases in Africa brought on by the introduction of New World crops compensated for the loss of population (at least in economic terms). Thornton also disagrees with the argument that African merchants irresponsibly exchanged objects of innate economic value (scarce human labor) for items that had little intrinsic value (such as cloth), undermined indigenous industries (such as iron goods), or were socially and economically destructive (such as alcohol and firearms). In Thornton's view, such imports brought status, wealth, and power to the Africans who exchanged them for slaves. Arguing that such imports undermined African economic institutions misses the central point that it profited the narrow interests of those involved in the commerce. While Thornton's analysis complicated Rodney's assertions about the impact of the slave trade, it did not specifically engage the subject of colonialism's influence in Africa, which formed the basis of Rodney's argument.

Recently the debate on underdevelopment has moved out of academia and into politics. Rodney's arguments continue to inspire activists who are campaigning to force nations that were involved in the trans-Atlantic slave trade to pay reparations to Africans and their descendants throughout the world. A conference on reparations in Nigeria in 1993 led to the proclamation of the Abuja Declaration, which demanded that the United Nations Security Council consider reparations for "African Enslavement, Colonization, and Neo-Colonization." A United Nations Conference on Racism, Racial Discrimination, and Xenophobia held in Durban, South Africa, in 2001 demanded that Western nations apologize for their role in the slave trade. Proponents of debt relief for African nations have similarly argued that European rule in Africa, as well as subsequent European and North American interference in the affairs of the continent, are at the root of modern Africa's poverty and indebtedness.

so that they could pay their new colonial taxes in cash, and by encouraging the production of cash crops which could be exported (and taxed). A second objective (which was far less pressing, but which dovetailed with the primary objective) was to provide foodstuffs and raw materials for European industries and their workers, and to encourage consumption of European manufactured goods. Initially colonial administrators could derive revenue from the staple crops of the pre-colonial export trade – palm oil from the Niger Delta, cloves from the plantations of Zanzibar. Such crops, however, were few, and many regions had no cash-crop agriculture before the colonial conquest. Heat, distance, and terrain discouraged many farmers from exporting their surplus crops. Not surprisingly, in many territories the colonial authorities, desperately in search of revenue, soon concentrated on the promotion of African cash crops best adapted to the specialized environments of individual colonies – cocoa in the Gold Coast and the Côte d'Ivoire, peanuts in Senegal and the Gambia, cotton in Tanganyika, Mozambique, Uganda, and the Anglo-Egyptian Sudan, rubber in King Leopold's Congo Free State. Minerals were in even greater demand – copper in the southern Congo and Northern Rhodesia (Zambia), tin from Nigeria, and the diamonds and gold of Southern Africa.

Although cotton was introduced into the Upper Niger Valley in pre-colonial times by the trans-Saharan caravan trade, it became the principal colonial crop much in demand by European and North American textile industries. It had long been grown in Egypt and proved readily adaptable to areas of southern and Central Africa. Unlike other tropical produce it was not perishable. African cultivators, however, were less enthusiastic, and their response was shaped by a combination of coercion, resistance, and initiative. Being forced to cultivate cotton severely limited the ability of African farmers to raise their essential foodstuffs. Also, cotton, being inedible, could not be consumed in times of economic depression, drought, or famine.

In Tanganyika the brutality of German efforts to enforce cotton cultivation precipitated the massive Maji-Maji rising in July 1905, which was not suppressed until 1907, at a cost of 250,000 African lives. In Mozambique compulsory cotton cultivation placed a burden on peasant farmers that was still resented long after the end of colonial rule. In some instances, however, cotton cultivation provided an opportunity that was embraced by African entrepreneurs. The initiative for the people of Uganda to grow cotton came from Baganda chiefs who, with assistance from colonial agronomists, had their people cultivate cotton, from which they derived a handsome profit. It became a popular crop in Uganda, and its export provided much of the revenue for the colonial and post-colonial administrations. After the First World War farmers in Northern Nigeria were growing cotton as a profitable export crop, and in 1923 the world's largest cotton plantation in the Gezira (Arabic, "island") between the Blue and White Nile Rivers south of Khartoum in the Anglo-Egyptian Sudan was worked by free tenants who profited from the large export revenues generated by the scheme.

Since the ownership of their modest holdings was now made secure by European colonial land laws and regulation, locally owned African family farms readily adapted to the cultivation of New World cash crops, particularly cocoa and peanuts (groundnuts). There soon followed an extraordinary

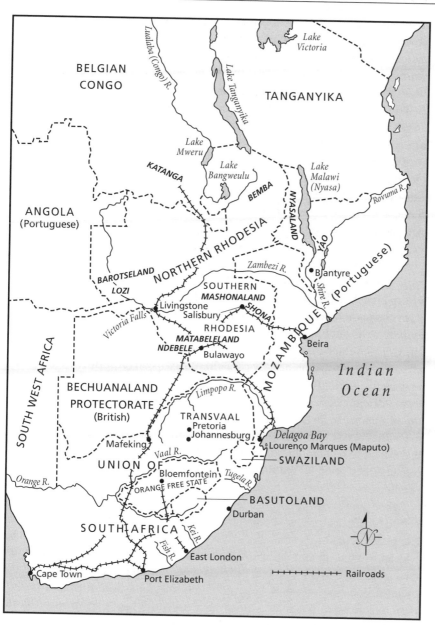

Map 21.1 *Central Africa under colonial rule.*

expansion of cocoa production in the Gold Coast, and by 1911 its farmers had became the world's leading exporters, generating considerable profits for themselves and greater revenue for the colony than gold. In the similar moist, forest environment of the West African coast individually owned African cocoa farms spread to Nigeria in the 1920s and the Côte d'Ivoire in the 1940s. Encouraged by French officials, peanut cultivation become popular with farmers in

Senegal, particularly those associated with the Mouridiyya an Islamic brotherhood. From Senegal it spread to the Gambia, where it became the colony's main export crop. The rise of African entrepreneurs was not always greeted with enthusiasm by white settlers, who feared competition, or colonial officials, who viewed them as politically dangerous.

In order to generate further revenues to support the colonial administration, and to stimulate the production of cash crops, European governments encouraged their citizens to emigrate to those colonies with an environment suitable for European settlement; the British in Kenya, Tanzania, and the Rhodesias; the French in the Côte d'Ivoire; the Portuguese in Angola and Mozambique. Most European settlers were not small farmers, but large plantation owners. Some arrived in Africa with their own considerable wealth to invest, others with only modest sums, but all were supported by the colonial state, which expropriated large tracts of land for commercial plantations and individual settler farms. Extensive land grants in Kenya, Tanzania, and Southern Rhodesia in particular were made or sold at a nominal price to white farmers, while much of the French and Belgian Congo was partitioned among well-funded European concession companies. Land grants in Angola and the *prazo* plantation system in Mozambique had been the fundamental economic policy of Portugal since the seventeenth century. Tea, tobacco, coffee, sisal, and sugar cane were all cash crops grown on heavily capitalized European farms that were worked by wage laborers. In many cases these white farmers faced stiff competition from African peasant farmers. Colonial authorities sometimes intervened to tilt the balance in favor of white producers by forbidding Africans to grow certain cash crops – tea in Southern Rhodesia, coffee in Kenya. Although settlers had access to technologies, credit, and coerced labor denied to African small farmers, they often lacked the latter's crucial knowledge about local growing conditions.

Labor, however, had been – and remained during the European colonial period – Africa's principal commodity. The Atlantic and Asian slave trades had been brought to an end, but slavery in its many manifestations remained widespread throughout Africa. Although European colonial policy was committed to end slavery, colonial officials were not prepared to precipitate the social dislocation that they believed would inevitably result from a sweeping emancipation. When an African slave asked for his freedom, a certificate of manumission would usually be granted, but most officials did little more to transform slaves into workers. In fact, the economic policy of the colonial state was dependent upon harnessing African labor, by force if necessary, to build the infrastructure for military and political control and obtaining cheap workers for export-oriented industries and settler farms. Africans needed to be prodded into productivity for the plantation, the mine, and the state. As the historian Walter Rodney explained, "It was rather coercion, either bare-faced or clothed by the laws of the new colonial regimes, which was principally responsible for bringing labour and cash crops to the market place."[1]

In the early years of colonization men were simply conscripted and, in King Leopold's Congo or French colonial Africa, impressed into the corvée where they were often victims of atrocities. Early scandals involving the exposure of forced labor in African colonies forced colonial officials to adopt more subtle tactics to pressure Africans into service, such as passing vagrancy laws and requiring the payment of taxes in cash. Convict labor was widely used, particularly in the salt mines in Senegal and the railways in northern Nigeria. Although forced labor was made illegal in French Africa by the Forced Labour Convention of 1930, there were numerous exceptions for military and penal service, civic improvements, and state-declared emergencies. Conscript labor was, therefore, common in every colony until after the Second World War, usually in the form of compulsory labor levies that worked for the state on a short-term basis and paid well below the market rate. Squatters, who were given rights to cultivate land, would be required to labor a number of days for their white landlords.

The most common form of labor was the migrant-labor system in which men were given temporary contracts for work in distant mines and on plantations. The system was based on a combination of the employers' need for cheap labor and the need of African labor to earn income, especially to pay taxes. Male labor was recruited by African chiefs, private European recruiters, and parastatal recruitment agencies. The incentives employed by recruiters included promises of food, blankets, and free transport, as well as unrealistic assurances of high wages and attractive working conditions. Coercion by armed recruiters was not uncommon. In many colonies the contract required the worker to be subject to a master-and-servant ordinance that enabled the employer to threaten penal sanctions for misbehavior or desertion. Housing and food on the mines were often inadequate; health care for the numerous diseases contracted in cramped living and working conditions and the injuries from a hazardous occupation was deficient, if it existed at all. The forgotten women who remained at home paid a heavy price by having to take on greater responsibilities to work the farm with no support. By the Second World War there was a growing realization in the mines that the mineworkers could become more efficient as a stable workforce of males permanently settled with their families in towns surrounding the mines rather than migrant labor confined in compounds.

Economic and political control by the colonial state could only be achieved by the construction of an elaborate infrastructure that European technology

---

[1] Walter Rodney, quoted in the UNESCO *General History of Africa*, vol. VII: *Africa under Colonial Domination, 1880–1935*, ed. A. A. Boahen, London and Berkeley: Heinemann and University of California Press, 1985, p. 155.

and capital alone could build. Although Africa had been involved in international trade for two millennia, the environment had imposed limitations on the nature of this trade. The tsetse fly prohibited the use of reliable pack animals, reducing transport to inefficient, labor-intensive human porters; the cataracts on the continent's great rivers prevented ready access to the interior; and the dearth of natural harbors had historically kept long-distance trade confined to relatively light, highly valued items such as gold, ivory, and slaves. The large-scale exportation of Africa's abundant but heavy agricultural and mineral commodities could only be made profitable from cheap transportation by railways, steamships, and roads.

Railways were the fashion of the Victorian age of steam and well suited to open the interior of Africa, but their construction could only be completed by tens of thousands of workers – often conscripted, convicts, or slave laborers. Over 127,000 Africans were forced to labor between 1921 and 1932 on the construction of the infamous Congo-Océan railway from Pointe Noire on the Atlantic to Brazzaville on the Congo River; 20,000 died on the job. The pattern of railroads was naturally designed to link the African interior with the coast, creating a transportation network that ultimately gave some logic to the arbitrary borders of the colonial states but ignored landlocked colonies such as French Equatorial and West Africa and Rwanda and Burundi. Railways in British Kenya and German East Africa (Tanganyika) followed the basic contours of pre-colonial trade routes and carried the goods that had hitherto been confined to the caravan trade. Other railways in Central and southern Africa formed a complex grid that stretched from the copper belt of Zambia (Northern Rhodesia) to Cape Town and whose branch lines opened new farmlands for commercial development. Colonial railways made possible the rapid circulation of people, goods, ideas, and microbes throughout the continent. They facilitated the dissemination of religions, musical traditions, dances, dialects, hairstyles, fashions, and innumerable other cultural practices. They connected sheltered enclaves to the popular culture of America, and the ravages of unknown epidemics. They provided employment to thousands of Africans, education for some skilled workers, and opportunities for African farmers and entrepreneurs to supply foodstuffs and transportation to the railways.

The expansion of colonial railways was coordinated with and complimentary to the fleets of steamers plying the inland waters of Africa's great rivers – Niger, Nile, Congo, Zambezi. Once beyond the cataracts on the edge of the great African plateau, these great rivers were navigable for over a thousand miles by steamers that could carry hundreds of passengers, officials, and tons of cargo. The Belgians established a very efficient steamer service on the Congo from Léopoldville (Kinshasa) to Stanleyville (Kisangani) that was similar to the British service from Khartoum to Juba on the White Nile. The development of mechanized transport and a road system to support it evolved very slowly. Heavy rains, blistering heat, and the clay soils made road construction difficult and expensive. Although lightweight trucks from the United States were used

Figure 21.1 *Railway workers, Broken Hill, Northern Rhodesia. African railways were often constructed with forced labor.*

increasingly by African entrepreneurs in West Africa from the 1920s, the first reliable motorized vehicle capable of negotiating the tracks that masqueraded as roads was the American Model A Ford in the 1930s. The development of an African road system did not effectively begin until after the Second World War, when the truck became the dominant means of transportation in the post-colonial decades.

Figure 21.2 *Women on chain gang, Tanganyika. Much of the infrastructure of colonial Africa was built by impressed laborers.*

The transformation of African economies produced dramatic changes in African societies. Demands for labor and the introduction of a cash economy created new responsibilities, opportunities, and lifestyles. Many men could only fulfill their new obligation to pay a head or hut tax by finding work in domestic service, agriculture, the mines, or in the colonial civil and military service. There were few workers who could perform such services while remaining in their villages, so that whole communities lost their male workforce for many months – and often years. In this new economic environment the young men engaged in wage labor now had the resources and the opportunities to challenge or ignore established hierarchies in their traditional societies. In most African communities the dominance of older men was based on their control of land, cattle, and women. The colonial economy made it possible for young men to circumvent this by acquiring capital and social advancement outside the authority of the elders, and with their new wealth came the prospect of land, cattle, and multiple marriages.

The participation by African men in the wage economy, which usually resulted in absence from the homestead, transformed the traditional gender roles – that which constituted appropriate masculine and feminine social practice – negotiated and renegotiated throughout time in pre-colonial societies. The economic and social policies imposed by the colonial state virtually excluded women from employment and, both consciously and unconsciously, inclined African gender roles to imitate European – and particularly Victorian – concepts of masculinity and femininity. This phenomenon manifested itself in many ways. Colonial bureaucracies exclusively hired men to serve as soldiers, clerks, and interpreters. Colonial schools catered mainly to boys. Mines hired men as wage laborers, giving them a monopoly on access to cash, which they used to purchase cattle and wives. Cash-crop agriculture also increased the dominant role of the African man. In most African societies women had been responsible for producing the food crops such as cassava and maize, which were the staples of rural life. Their labor and expertise made them the backbone of the rural economy. When colonial administrators sought to introduce new crops and modern European agricultural techniques, men rather than women received instruction and were more likely to receive the necessary financial credit to farm commercially.

In many instances these colonial views of gender enabled African men to increase their control over women. Male elders in Shona society, for example, were accepted by European officials as arbiters of tradition, a trust they often used to intensify their control over wives and daughters in the name of custom. This inflation of male prestige in African societies, assisted by the colonial authorities, was not without its contradictions, for the massive labor migrations set in motion by colonial economic policies inadvertently created greater burdens and responsibilities, but also new opportunities, for African women. Many colonial officials – and particularly their wives – thought that African women should play a greater role in the transformation of their societies as home-makers, like middle-class European women, in addition to their traditional role as the mainstay of agricultural production. Colonialism thus placed a double burden on African women by expecting them to embrace a European cult of respectability, while at the same time encouraging the construction of migratory labor industries that further increased the dependency for rural agricultural production upon them.

Colonial rule also introduced profound changes in the way African peoples identified themselves. Pre-colonial Africans defined their identity by the ties of family, clan, and lineage, but colonial rule encouraged them to embrace identities beyond those of lineage and village. For example, when European officials conducted a census within a colony, they invariably asked their new subjects to associate themselves with specific tribal communities. This system of classification was consistent with European ideas about biology and ethnicity that were accepted and popular in the late nineteenth century. The assumption that all Africans must belong to a tribe conditioned virtually every aspect by which colonial authorities administered their subjects. In the words of the historian John Iliffe, "The British wrongly believed that Tanganyikans belonged to tribes; Tanganyikans created tribes to function within the colonial framework."[2] In such circumstances, scattered peoples were now made aware of a common linguistic and cultural heritage that in the past had been less apparent. The Kikuyu in Kenya, for instance, who lived in scattered

---

[2] John Iliffe, *A History of Tanganyika*, Cambridge: Cambridge University Press, 1979, p. 324.

agricultural settlements with relatively few inhabitants, increasingly came to think of themselves during the colonial decades as a Kikuyu people.

Ethnic identity was further defined by the logistics of migrant labor. The passes issued to all migrant laborers in order to identify and control their movements gave an official imprimatur to a person's identity that encouraged a sense of belonging to a distinct tribe. The growth of tribal consciousness found fertile ground in the townships and mining compounds, where new migrants relied on tribal affiliations to help them find work, to provide a social network, and to maintain their ties to their rural homelands. It was in the new colonial cities that surrounded the diamond mines of Kimberley and the gold diggings on the Witwatersrand that the Shangaans and Zulu developed powerful and enduring associations with their tribal identity.

There were other, less obvious, ways by which colonial policies fostered notions of ethnic identity. The transcribing of African languages into Roman script inadvertently enhanced the importance of regional languages. The initiative for translating the languages of Africa came largely from Protestant missionaries, who, following Luther's belief that personal salvation came from reading the Bible, sought to make the text accessible to Africans in as many languages and dialects as possible. These translations had begun in the pre-colonial era, but in the need to understand and administer the Africans colonial authorities enrolled the Christian missionaries to translate and transcribe the multiplicity of African languages in return for exclusive rights to pursue their missionary activities in colonial territories. Hundreds of dictionaries and grammars were produced, but in the process of translating those into European languages, regional differences became standardized into the official tribal language, which often had little meaning to pre-colonial peoples of the same ethnic group and none to those whose languages faded into obscurity because they had not been selected for translation.

European colonial rule in Africa also fostered the spread of Christianity and Islam. Both religions had ancient roots in Africa, and both had witnessed dramatic expansion in the decades preceding the colonial conquest. However, they were able to spread more widely under the umbrella of patronage and protection of the colonial administrations, at the expense of traditional African religions. Not surprisingly, the Christian missionaries were favored and supported by European officials, except in those regions of the Western Sudan and the Nile Valley where Christian proselytizing among Muslims was regarded as a destabilizing threat to ordered administration, and was officially discouraged. Elsewhere in Africa Christian missions offered an alternative to traditional religious practices and escape for marginalized people. Christianity also connected converts to a wealthy and sophisticated Western tradition, whose political and technological dominance was everywhere apparent.

Christianity also proved sufficiently elastic for many Africans to include revered aspects of their indigenous religious traditions in the new rituals of the missionaries. While many African Christians joined the traditional European Catholic and Protestant religious hierarchies, many more followed

Figure 21.3 *Christian mission station, Belgian Congo (1930s).*

the teachings of African preachers who founded their own dissenting Christian denominations and who were largely responsible for the spread of Christianity among Africans. Their zealous converts concerned colonial officials, who saw them as a potentially destabilizing force. The Watchtower movement in Central Africa was but one of several Christian denominations viewed with suspicion by colonial authorities, particularly those like the Watchtower who refused to recognize secular authority.

Ironically, Islam expanded rapidly in the African territories lying on the periphery of the Islamic world under Christian colonial rulers. Europeans had a long history of conflict with Islam, and did not wish to jeopardize their fragile administrations by provoking the African Muslims. They recognized the Muslim rulers as traditional rulers, particularly in the Western Sudan, despite the fact that many of them had only come to power in the eighteenth and nineteenth centuries. These African Islamic authorities now had the tacit support of colonial officials to encourage the conversion of the non-Muslims. Moreover, Islam was untainted by any association with European colonialism, its historic adversary, and, unlike Christianity whose missionaries were largely European or American, virtually all Muslim missionaries were Africans. Islam, like Christianity, opened up membership for Africans in a powerful, global religious tradition, but it allowed them to retain important indigenous social and cultural practices, particularly polygyny. Islamic mysticism (Sufism), in particular, allowed the faithful to integrate aspects of traditional rituals into their worship. Sufism is almost as old as Islam itself and was spread throughout sub-Saharan Africa by fraternal brotherhoods (*tariqa*), whose followers sought

God, not through the legalistic liturgical interpretations of the Quran, but by mystical experiences defined by the ritual of the individual brotherhood. The two oldest orders in Africa, the Qadiriyya and the Shadhiliyya, date from the twelfth and thirteenth centuries, but in the Islamic renaissance of the nineteenth century a host of new orders appeared in Sudanic Africa – the Tijaniyya, Sanusiyya, and the Khatmiyya. These Sufi orders brought a new awareness of Islam to the rural Africans that was frequently taught in local languages rather than Arabic without regard to ethnicity, and often called popular Islam.

Colonial rule also introduced Africans to Western education, which was first propagated by Christian missionaries. Conversion to Christianity was largely dependent on literacy. After the establishment of a colonial administration there was little money for education, which was considered a marginal priority when its organization and expense were eagerly undertaken by the Christian missionary societies. At first mission schools produced a sufficient number of literate Africans who could do simple arithmetic and whom the colonial officials could afford to fulfill the needs of their administration. Mission schools attracted a variety of students, but in the early years they were mostly marginalized members of society – slaves, women, orphans, undesirables – who found opportunities in the mission stations denied to them in their own communities.

After the First World War colonial governments could no longer remain aloof from education. There had been increasing criticism of missionary education, which was concerned more with prayer than with reading, writing, and arithmetic, and African elites who at first had shunned Western education now perceived that it was an avenue to social and political advancement. Secular government elementary and secondary schools were established, to which the chiefs in service to the colonial state sent their sons, but only Great Britain established institutions of higher education that became colleges and, at the end of the colonial era, universities in such places as the Sudan, Nigeria, Ghana, Southern Rhodesia, and Uganda for the sons of the elite. There were no such opportunities in the Portuguese colonies and the Belgian Congo, and Africans seeking higher education in the French colonies were sent to France. Some in the British colonies had the opportunity to study at universities in the United Kingdom or the United States.

Colonial rule also had a powerful influence on African demography. Despite the massive destruction and dislocation that had accompanied the European conquest of Africa, the population began to experience an extraordinary increase after the First World War, from an estimated 120 million in 1885 to 142 million in 1920. Thereafter the population exploded, reaching 165 million by 1935 and 200 million after the Second World War. By 1960, the year of African independence, the estimated population had reached nearly 300 million. Some attribute this dramatic growth to African initiatives to abandon traditional constraints on births, the end of slavery, and better food, others to the introduction by the colonial authorities of the means to transport food to areas in need, and to the containment of epidemics and the improvement of African public health and personal hygiene made by colonial innovations in tropical medicine.

Colonial health authorities were now able to treat and contain many of Africa's devastating parasitic diseases – malaria, bilharzia, sleeping sickness, kala-azar, and river blindness – and viral diseases such as yellow fever. New drugs were able to cure infectious diseases – measles (one of the most common causes of infant mortality), pneumonia, tuberculosis, and a host of intestinal worms, guinea worm and loiasis, and skin diseases such as leprosy. Hospitals were built in the urban areas, though their patients were mostly colonial officials and the African elite. Networks of clinics and dispensaries were established in the rural countryside, but their numbers could never meet the need and they suffered from a chronic shortage of trained staff. In order to control the spread of epidemic diseases the colonial administration frequently employed all the powers of the state to enforce severe measures that the Africans often did not understand and consequently resented. Tropical medicine saved lives, but the rigor with which health officials applied it to the sick often symbolized and confirmed the authoritarian character of the colonial state.

The threat of epidemics was most prevalent in the growing colonial urban centers. While Africans had lived in towns throughout their history, most of the pre-colonial African cities were established between the sixteenth and the nineteenth centuries. The new urban areas of the twentieth century, however, dwarfed in size and complexity the old cities of trade and courts of African kings. The new settlements were the administrative headquarters of the colonial state, regional market towns, burgeoning communities surrounding the mines, and strategic towns created by railroad and river steamer transport. Moreover, the colonial state's emphasis on law and order – either accepted or imposed – enabled Africans to move from country to town in greater security. The town or city was the hub of mercantile activity, where the few industrial jobs were concentrated. The drift to the towns that characterized the period following the First World War was of deep concern to all colonial administrations, for it threatened to destabilize rural societies, and transform African peasants into an urban proletariat capable of challenging their authority. Migration to the towns was discouraged, pass laws were applied in many colonies to control the movements of rural Africans, and in many places families could not legally reside in the towns. When all restrictions on migration to the cities were removed after 1960, only 20 percent of the Africans lived in an urban environment; 80 percent remained in the rural countryside.

Modern Western media – motion pictures, phonographs, radios, and newspapers – also introduced urban Africans to the world beyond their borders. After the end of the First World War radios and phonographs became more widely available in cities and towns, where the influence of the American cinema among urban Africans was well established by the 1920s. At the end

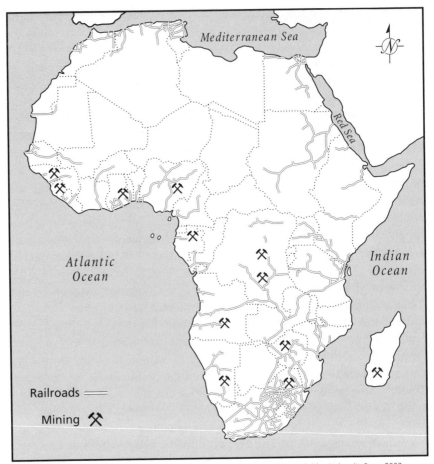

Source: Frederick Cooper, *Africa Since 1940: The Past of the Present.* Cambridge: Cambridge University Press, 2002

Map 21.2 *The infrastructure of colonial Africa.*

of the Second World War radio networks programmed for African audiences had spread throughout the continent. Over its airwaves American jazz became a staple of urban township life. The flood of Western media soon produced a synthesis of African and American musical traditions, and the development of new forms of African popular music. The development of highlife music in the Gold Coast was influenced by the ballroom music of Europe, *soukous* in the Congo by Afro-Cuban jazz, and *isicathamiya* music in South Africa by the Afro-American gospel traditions. The impact of these new forms of communication, creativity, and entertainment rapidly percolated into rural villages.

European colonial rule also influenced Africans in less conspicuous ways. Whether the intent was to tax, convert, prosecute, or educate, the colonial order treated Africans as individuals. The colonial authorities insisted that

Box 21.2 The media in colonial and independent Africa

The advent of the colonial era coincided with a period of remarkable technological innovation in electronic media. Motion pictures, the phonograph, and radio were all invented in the decades following the conquest of Africa. These media were soon established in the largest colonial cities; the first motion pictures premiered in South Africa in 1900, a scant five years after their world premier in Paris in 1895.

Many Europeans held high hopes for the future of electronic media in Africa. If machine guns, telegraph, and steamships were the tools of empire to conquer the African continent, many expected that radio and movies would facilitate their rule, but they were well aware that the new media could prove to be a double-edged sword. On the one hand, it presented the Europeans with a unique opportunity to communicate the blessings of colonial government to the African masses. On the other hand, it could just as easily be used to convey messages hostile to the colonial administration. Cinema presented the most immediate threat, because it was relatively easy for entrepreneurs to organize shows. Fear of what Africans might see on screen led to strict censorship in all colonies of any film that might undermine European prestige or encourage criminal behavior. Radio was less of a concern before the Second World War because broadcasting was in its infancy on the continent, and few Africans could afford receivers.

The heavy hand of colonial censorship did not prevent Africans from becoming avid movie-goers. During the 1920s and 1930s the cinema became a popular pastime for miners and workers on European commercial plantations and for the masses in the rapidly growing cities. The cinema served the interests of an array of colonial institutions – mining companies, tea-marketing associations, and missionary evangelists – all of which were among the earliest groups to sponsor free film shows for Africans in the rural areas. The first cinema houses on the continent catered to small settler communities, but the enthusiasm by the flood of laborers pouring into urban areas during the 1930s and 1940s spawned a host of entrepreneurs, often Coloured, Indian, Greek, or Lebanese, who began to establish movie theaters specifically for African audiences.

The Second World War was a watershed for electronic media in Africa. It inspired the British colonial office to mount an aggressive campaign to introduce cinema and broadcasting to their subjects as a way to mobilize support for the war effort. The British Colonial Film Unit began producing and screening propaganda films for African audiences in 1940. By 1948 there were colonial institutions making films expressly for Africans throughout British Africa and in the Belgian Congo. While the efforts of these government film-makers to influence African opinion had little

Box 21.2 (continued)

tangible effect, they did introduce the medium to people in rural areas, often with dramatic effect. Dull, amateurish movies about soil conservation were often interspersed with cartoons, classic shorts from the silent era, and, most often, American Westerns, which became the most popular movie genre on the continent.

Radio experienced a boom during the war which continued in the postwar period. One of the leading services was the Central African Broadcasting Service, which began broadcasting to African audiences in British Nyasaland, Southern Rhodesia, and Northern Rhodesia in 1948. Inexpensive radios became more widely available during the 1950s, dramatically expanding the audience for colonial broadcasting. It was over colonial air-waves and through the increased sale of phonograph records that American blues and jazz became popular on the continent, and new forms of African music, often influenced by European and American records, spread throughout the continent.

In the first decade of independence broadcasting and cinema production were taken over by African governments. Radio, which had been first and foremost a tool of propaganda under colonial rule, continued to play this role under the new African regimes, now joined by television, which became a part of African life from the early 1960s. In the post-colonial era radio and television have continued to play important roles in the lives of the African people. Cinema has declined in popularity, in part because urban infrastructures no longer support large cinema houses and in part because of the challenge of television and video. In Nigeria and several other West African countries the cinema halls have been replaced by video parlors that show locally produced soap-operas. This new genre of movie-making draws on Western and indigenous idioms to create dramas infused with supernatural elements.

individuals rather than kin-groups be held responsible for taxes, criminal and civil prosecution, debts, and job performance. This emphasis on individual responsibility was consistent with the acceptance of capitalism and Christianity, but perhaps the most intangible, enduring legacy of colonial rule was the psychological impact of the colonial experience, the colonization of the mind, which had a profound influence particularly on middle-class Africans. Every colony had a small but growing number of Africans who avidly adopted European dress, diet, and culture. They were the first in their communities to take European names, to speak European languages, and to dress in European clothing. Many accepted the European characterization of African culture as primitive and believed that eventually Africans would be assimilated by European beliefs, customs, and languages. Not all educated Africans adopted these views, but the influence of European culture indelibly shaped the class that would take power after independence.

In the 1950s and 1960s the Caribbean writer Frantz Fanon warned that colonialism was creating a bourgeois class of Africans in the image of their colonizers. It is difficult to argue with this assessment. The states that became independent during those decades were essentially run by Africans who had shared the values and goals of their colonial masters.

Further reading

Cooper, Frederick, *Africa since 1940: The Past of the Present*, New York: Cambridge University Press, 2002

Cooper, Frederick, *Decolonization and African Society: The Labor Question in French and British Africa*, Cambridge: Cambridge University Press, 1996

Fanon, Frantz, *The Wretched of the Earth*, New York: Grove Press, 2004

Hochschild, Adam, *King Leopold's Ghost: A Story of Greed, Terror, and Heroism in Colonial Africa*, Boston: Houghton Mifflin, 1998

Rodney, Walter, *How Europe Underdeveloped Africa*, London: Bogle-l'Ouverture Publications, 1988

PART IV

Independent Africa

22 Nationalism and the independence of colonial Africa

In 1915 a Baptist minister, John Chilembwe (*c.* 1871–1915), led an ill-fated insurrection against British rule in Nyasaland (Malawi). As a young man he had believed that colonial rule would "civilize" his native Nyasaland by introducing Christian values and British liberalism. In 1892 he came under the influence of the popular radical Baptist missionary Joseph Booth (1851–1932), whom he accompanied to the United States, where he studied at the black Baptist seminary in Lynchburg, Virginia. Upon his return in 1900 he established the Providence Industrial Mission where, inspired by Booker T. Washington, he preached the gospel of hard work, cleanliness, and respect for the colonial authorities. He became increasingly critical, however, of the harsh treatment and brutality of white settlers toward African laborers on their plantations and the indifference of British officials to these abuses. Convinced that his colonial government would never make good on the promise of social equality he found in English law and the Christian Bible, Chilembwe published a letter in the *Nyasaland Times* on November 26, 1914 that ran under the heading "The Voice of the African Natives in the Present War," in which he laid out his complaints against colonial policies. His message of African grievances and hopes was ignored, and two months later, on January 29, 1915, Chilembwe and 200 of his followers launched their uprising to establish an independent African state. The colonial authorities retaliated swiftly and ruthlessly. Two weeks later Chilembwe and many of his supporters were dead and their brick mission church razed to the ground.

Chilembwe's uprising failed to shake the foundations of British rule in Nyasaland, but it remains a watershed in the history of colonial Africa. Unlike the resistance movements of the late nineteenth and early twentieth centuries, which were organized along local, ethnic, or dynastic lines, Chilembwe's rebellion looked to new forms of identity – Christianity and the unity of Nyasaland – to build a modern nation-state on the foundation of colonial rule. This marked the beginnings of twentieth-century African nationalism, and foreshadowed the end of imperial rule. He represented a new generation of African leadership that would play a pivotal role in dismantling the European empires. These men were mission-educated Christians, many of whom had studied in Europe and the United States. They would channel the diffuse discontents of their African followers into the movement for independence and negotiate the end of empire in the language of nationalism and liberalism that they had learned from their European rulers. During the four decades that followed the Nyasa-land rebellion the pace and direction of this search for independence was often opaque, confused, and disunited, but it was inexorable. Indeed, few people at the time recognized the compelling significance of Chilembwe's desperate insurrection, and until the Second World War only a handful of visionaries dreamed of an Africa free from colonial rule.

Today, the movement for African independence appears to have been inevitable, but few of Chilembwe's contemporaries anticipated the course or the pace of events precipitated by the First World War that would lead to the end of European rule. Even before the war they had failed to recognize that the Europeans were inadvertently sowing the seeds of their own demise. They had introduced new ideologies and technologies that would ultimately undermine their domination in Africa. The condescension, brutality, racism, and despotism that characterized colonial rule inexorably alienated its subject peoples, nurturing a resentment that would become apparent during the upheavals of the First World War.

The First World War's impact was felt throughout the continent. The first British shots of the war were fired in the invasion of Togo in August 1914. Thereafter the war relentlessly dragged Africans into the European conflict, as colonial powers sought to occupy the territory of their imperial rivals. The war's insatiable appetite for raw materials to feed Europeans and their factories, and troops to fight on the Western Front placed unprecedented demands on the Africans. Forced labor and requisitioned foods brought privation to Africans, most of whom were subsistence farmers and herdsmen with little surplus for Africa, let alone Europe. One of the colonies most dramatically affected by the war was Nyasaland, where British requisitioning of foodstuffs inadvertently caused famine in parts of the colony, made all the more destructive by the British campaign in neighboring German Tanganyika, which claimed the lives of tens of thousands of Africans. Indeed, Chilembwe's revolt was in part a reflection of the bitter resentment felt by Nyasa men who were being pressed by unscrupulous colonial recruiters into service as carriers for the army. Thousands of Africans in the eastern Congo were forced to supply food, labor, and porterage for the Belgian armies in the German colonies of Rwanda and Burundi. Fighting was not confined to German East Africa. South Africa suppressed an internal revolt by German sympathizers and launched a military campaign on its northern border against German forces in South West Africa. In West Africa British and French troops defeated the Germans in Kamerun (Cameroon).

Even those colonies far removed from the actual fighting experienced the relentless demands of war. All of the colonial governments requisitioned men into service as soldiers and laborers. France was particularly aggressive and determined to recruit Africans to fight in Europe to compensate for the devastating losses suffered by the French army on the Western Front. Many villages in the Western Sudan lost most of their agricultural laborers, creating hardship for many communities that precipitated demonstrations, and in some cases open rebellion. Those soldiers and workers who survived the fierce fighting in Europe often returned to African village life no longer in awe of colonial rule. Many of them had witnessed Europeans killing other Europeans in France and in Africa; this inevitably undermined the aura of invincibility of their colonial rulers.

The end of the war and subsequent peace treaty introduced significant changes in the international order that altered the colonial composition of Africa. Germany's African colonies were transferred to France, Belgium, and Great Britain, and justified by the victors on the grounds that Germans had proved themselves unfit to rule Africans. Thus the subjects of German Africa would be governed with greater concern for their interests as a "trusteeship" administered by their French, Belgian, and British colonial neighbors on behalf of the newly created League of Nations. This established an important precedent because it granted oversight of a European colony to an international organization with the intention of ultimate independence.

The war also saw the emergence of two new great powers – the United States and the Soviet Union – that would come to dominate world affairs in the latter half of the twentieth century. Although both countries became ardent opponents of European imperialism for ideologically opposite reasons, the immediate impact on Africa of their anti-colonialism was limited. Although President Woodrow Wilson (1856–1924) was an enthusiastic supporter of the principle of self-determination of nations, which appeared to offer colonized peoples the promise of choosing their form of governance, the realities of the Treaty of Versailles did little for the prospects of African independence. The Soviet Union was a more active champion of colonial peoples, and such anti-colonial figures as Ho Chi Minh (1890–1969) of French Indochina (Vietnam) and I. T. A. Wallace-Johnson (1894–1965) of Sierra Leone were welcomed in Moscow for training in organizing opposition to colonial rule. Despite their confirmed hostility to colonialism, however, both the United States and the Soviet Union during the inter-war years were much too absorbed in their own internal affairs to demonstrate much interest in Africa. At the same time an increasing number of European intellectuals began to question the ideological justifications of imperialism. The First World War had deeply eroded public enthusiasm for many of the ideologies – including nationalism and social Darwinism – which had made the conquest of Africa seem morally acceptable. After the war a new generation of European intellectuals began to criticize colonial rule. In 1926 the French novelist André Gide (1869–1951) published an account of his travels in French Congo that described the harsh treatment of its people by the French regime. In the 1930s a few former colonial administrators, such as the English author George Orwell (1903–1950) and the Anglo-Irish writer Joyce Cary (1888–1957), published novels highlighting the brutality and hypocrisy of empire. Several members of the colonial administration in British Nigeria published critiques of indirect rule for supporting corrupt despots determined to prevent Africans from developing democratic institutions. These authors represented only a tiny minority of Western writers and administrators, and were advocates not of the end of empire but of its reform. At the same time, however, more vociferous African-American critics and West Indian intellectuals vigorously disputed the legitimacy of European rule in Africa. The most influential of these new voices was the Jamaican-born Marcus Garvey (1887–1940), whose vision for the continent's future was captured in the slogan "Africa for Africans." Garvey's United Negro Improvement Association, which sought to create a closer association of the peoples of the African diaspora, developed a global following during the two decades between the First and Second World Wars. His appeals for African liberation were echoed by other New World intellectuals, particularly the African-American W. E. B. Du Bois (1868–1963). Du Bois played a leading role in the Pan-African Congress held in London in 1900, which demanded that Africans and their descendants be given "their civil and political rights."

The demobilization of soldiers and laborers in 1918 produced high unemployment in Africa as well as Europe, and the painful transition from war to peace by the European economies contributed to postwar inflation and a shortage of basic European commodities imported to Africa. Disease combined with economic plight to exacerbate the misery of the Africans. In 1918 the worldwide influenza epidemic killed millions of Africans, whose colonial governments were ill prepared to respond to the epidemic. The immediate postwar economic problems, however, did not disappear like the influenza. During the 1920s numerous protests emerged among African workers in the growing urban areas. Strikes broke out in the mining towns of the Belgian Congo and British Northern Rhodesia, on the railways of Southern Rhodesia, and on the docks of Kenya and South Africa. In the rural areas tax collection, land expropriation, and labor conscription resulted in demonstrations and even insurrections. All these forms of protest were suppressed by the colonial authorities, for virtually all strikes were illegal, and punitive raids against rebellious rural subjects often resulted in the destruction of villages and the slaughter of their inhabitants. These outbursts of discontent did not threaten the domination of colonial government in Africa, but collectively they produced a smoldering resentment toward colonial rule that would be exploited by advocates of political reform.

During the 1930s a small group of educated Africans and trade union leaders began forming associations to lobby for a role in colonial governance. The most influential of these organizations were in the British West African colonies, for the British policy of indirect rule was predicated on the assumption that British colonies were politically separate from the national government in London. This distinction sharply contrasted with the policies of France and Portugal, who regarded their African possessions as overseas territories represented in the legislatures of Paris and Lisbon. Consequently, in British West Africa politicians could discuss political autonomy without fear of being arrested for sedition. In 1917 Great Britain had accepted the eventual independence of India, and thus British officials in the Gold Coast and Nigeria were prepared to tolerate a degree of political criticism. A key figure was the Nigerian journalist Benjamin Nnamdi Azikiwe (1904–1996, known as "Zik"), a mission-educated Christian who spent much of the 1920s in the United States, where he attended the University of Pennsylvania and was acquainted with Garveyism. He returned to West Africa in the early 1930s and worked as a journalist in Liberia and the Gold Coast before returning to his native Nigeria where he became the leading writer for the *West Africa Pilot*, advocating self-government for Nigeria within the British empire.

Zik's vision of Nigeria as an independent sovereign state would come to be challenged by an emerging African elite who sought to replace the colonial order with a pan-African union of all the former colonies. This political doctrine advocated by black intellectuals in the Americas and in Africa known as pan-Africanism had first appeared in the late nineteenth century. The pan-Africanists aspired to forge the former colonies into a "United States of Africa," a "homeland" for blacks throughout the world. It would be the instrument to end colonial rule and provide an alternative to the arbitrary divisions of ethnicities imposed by the boundaries of colonialism. W. E. B. Du Bois was one of its most enthusiastic spokesmen, and helped to organize a series of international meetings to protest colonial rule and promote pan-Africanism.

Pan-Africanism had its greatest following among English-speaking Africans. Within the French-speaking regions of the African diaspora, intellectuals focused on cultural rather than political liberation. When British colonial policies were giving English-speaking Africans limited political freedom, the French policy of assimilation was creating a dilemma for many intellectuals, who were concerned that their African cultural identity would be subsumed by language and culture into the larger Francophone world. Moreover, the French had been willing to admit a few of these assimilated intellectuals as representatives in the French Assembly in Paris. Although small in number, these influential African politicians were the living symbols that the French political system was willing to share – in the fullness of time – political equality with its colonial subjects. It was precisely this fear of assimilation that encouraged the African subjects of the French empire to focus on cultural rather than political liberation. The Caribbean poet Aimé Césaire (1913–2001) coined the term *négritude* to describe a unique identity shared by all peoples of the African diaspora. *Négritude* inverted social Darwinism by accepting the premise that humanity was divided into different "races," each of which had its own innate characteristics, but that the "Negro" identity possessed equal merit with that of "Caucasian" Europeans.

During the interwar era most of these debates took place in Europe and North America, and their influence in Africa was negligible. Of greater concern for most Africans was the beginning of the global depression in 1929, which quickly had a devastating impact on the fragile economies of the continent's colonies. Ironically, the arrival of the depression in Africa coincided with a time when the colonial authorities were finally establishing effective administration over their African subjects. By 1929 even the most isolated communities had become integrated into the colonial administrative system, and many villagers found themselves for the first time accountable to colonial tax collectors, police, and courts. In order to meet these new obligations of hut and poll tax traditional subsistence farmers had been pulled, usually with great reluctance, into the colonial economy as cash-crop farmers, miners, plantation laborers, and service workers in the rapidly expanding colonial cities. The increasing number of wage laborers resulted in the farmers becoming more dependent on foreign markets for their produce in return for imported commodities, often including essential foodstuffs. The incorporation of Africans into the money economy had produced thriving import, export, transport, and marketing services, as well as the expansion of the colonial bureaucracies that required African functionaries to protect and tax the new wealth. Thus when the depression struck, vast numbers of Africans dependent on the export economy for their livelihood were thrust into poverty. Farmers and herdsmen found international demand for their products drastically curtailed. With the export trade slackening dock workers became unemployed. Miners could no longer expect a steady demand for their labor. African clerks were the first to be laid off when colonial bureaucracies retrenched. Thus, at the time when members of the incipient African middle class were agitating for reform of colonial governance, their rural agrarian and urban industrial compatriots were becoming increasingly frustrated by the inability of their colonial rulers to improve their situation.

African peasants, workers, and elites expressed their grievances during the depression in many ways, but by the eve of the Second World War no coherent organization or movement emerged to channel this discontent into a common cause. Political associations, where they existed before 1940, were dominated by the few educated Africans who lobbied for some influence over state policy. Their demands were usually ignored by colonial officials, who dismissed these "de-tribalized" Africans as not representative of mainstream African opinion, unlike the loyal "traditional" chiefs, who were recognized as better qualified to know the legitimate interests of their people. If the colonial officials in Africa resisted reform, those in London and Paris were more sensitive to the events of the interwar years – the creation of the League of Nations and its trusteeships, the depression and its dislocations, the Italian invasion of independent Ethiopia in 1935, and the increasing criticism of colonialism by intellectuals. They abandoned the illusion that the colonies should be economically self-sufficient and had begun to invest in colonial development and contemplate minor political reforms, when the Second World War broke out. The war would transform colonial Africa.

The rapid defeat of France by Nazi Germany in 1940 placed her African colonies under the rule of the collaborationist Vichy regime, leaving French subjects in Africa to choose between a fascist, racist regime in Vichy or the Free French in London led by General Charles de Gaulle (1890–1970). Only one province, French Equatorial Africa, whose governor was Félix Eboué (1884–1944), a black West Indian, defied the Vichy administration, and supported de Gaulle, giving the Free French a crucial base in equatorial Africa. After the fall of France Great Britain mobilized all the resources of her empire to fight both Germany and Japan, and her African colonies instantly became a vital economic and strategic asset. Minerals from African mines, foods from African farms, and soldiers from African villages were desperately needed to make war, but the demands for men and materials were too many and too much to be requisitioned by coercion, as in the First World War. Although many of Africa's elites and chiefs rallied to support the empire, its farmers, laborers, and soldiers would have to be given incentives to support the allied cause. British propaganda, disseminated through colonial newspapers, radio, and cinemas, promised that victory would lead to better economic opportunities and improved political status for Africans.

Events seemed to give some truth to the propaganda. When Italy allied with Nazi Germany in 1940 the first substantial allied victory was the conquest of the Italian East African empire and the return to Ethiopia of Emperor Haile Selassie (1892–1975) in May 1941. In August the United States president Franklin Delano Roosevelt (1882–1945) and British prime minister Winston Churchill (1874–1965) signed the Atlantic Charter, which proclaimed that the war was being fought to liberate subject peoples. Churchill interpreted this declaration as applying only to the people of occupied Europe, but many Africans anticipated that the charter would bring important changes for Africa at the end of the war. Moreover, the demands of war revived the economic growth in Africa that had been interrupted by the depression. The allies invested in new roads, rail lines, and improved port facilities in an effort to speed the movement of men and material to the war zones. The people best poised to take advantage of the revived economic situation were white settlers, but African farmers and workers also found their produce and labor in greater demand. However, the wartime economy also brought hardships. Colonial governments fixed prices on export goods as a wartime expedient, limiting the profits of farmers and merchants. Imported goods were scarce and expensive. During the war most people accepted these problems as necessary. Afterwards they would become intolerable.

During the war large numbers of African men were recruited into the allied armies, often for service far from home and alongside black soldiers from the African diaspora. War service in the Second World War had a deeper and more widespread influence on African troops than that in the First World War, for they were far more likely to see combat. Indeed, British recruitment propaganda touted the achievements of a Nigerian officer in the Royal Air Force. Although such positions of responsibility were rare, the significance of this unprecedented recognition of ability was not lost on the African trooper.

Africans also served alongside soldiers from other parts of the empire, many of whom enjoyed greater political representation and economic opportunities. African troops also were exposed to African-American soldiers who, unlike them, received the same pay as their white compatriots. These experiences made them aware that the colonial system denied them political and economic opportunities that were taken for granted throughout the rest of the world.

When the war ended in 1945, the colonial powers had emerged victorious in no small part because of the contributions from their African empires. Although few observers in 1945 were prepared to accept an imminent end to colonial rule in Africa, there was general agreement that some transformation of colonialism was necessary. France had already sought to institute reform in 1944 when Charles de Gaulle held a conference in Brazzaville to discuss the political future of French Africa. No Africans were invited to participate, and the French delegates emphatically refused to contemplate independence for their African colonies. They did, however, abolish some of the more odious aspects of the colonial administration, particularly the hated *corvée*, or forced labor, and publicly acknowledged that Africans had earned the right to a reform of colonial administration. In the same year the government of Kenya appointed the first African to its legislative council, and during the next four years Britain introduced new constitutions into their West African colonies. These moderate constitutions did little to satisfy the rising expectations of African politicians, and although proclaimed with much fanfare as the harbingers of reform, they were more a symbol of British self-delusion than an acceptable response to the aspirations of their subjects.

The end of wartime controls unleashed a ferment of political activity in West Africa that was exacerbated by the slackening demand for African commodities and the scarcity of imported goods, neither of which could be satisfied by the wreckage of the European war-torn economies. Nnamdi Azikiwe, who had been advocating independence for Nigeria since the late 1930s, now found support from other African activists both within and outside Africa. In October 1945 the Pan-African Conference in Manchester, England, had called for the "complete and absolute independence of the people of West Africa." In Nigeria during the war Zik had organized a political party called the National Council of Nigeria and Cameroon (NCNC) to educate Nigerians about self-government. The task was formidable – Nigeria was a vast colony with significant geographical, cultural, religious, and ethnic differences – but by the end of the war Zik and politicians like him were determined to create political alliances across class and ethnic lines to work toward independence.

The other center of anti-colonial agitation in West Africa in the late 1940s was the Gold Coast colony. During the war a student from the Gold Coast named Kwame Nkrumah (1909–1972) had helped organize the Pan-African Conference in Manchester. Like Zik, Nkrumah had studied in the United States, where he had become an admirer of Marcus Garvey. After the war a small group of politicians in the Gold Coast created the United Gold Coast Convention

(UGCC) and invited Nkrumah to return from Britain to serve as its organizing secretary. His arrival in 1947 coincided with widespread discontent which culminated in an incident in which British troops fired on a crowd of protestors, killing several veterans. Nkrumah's outspoken condemnation of British handling of the ensuing riots thrust him into the leadership of the exuberant political scene.

Azikiwe and Nkrumah emerged as powerful spokesmen against colonialism at the same time that the relationship between Europe and Africa had reached a crossroads. Virtually everyone agreed that the war and its aftermath precluded any return to the colonialism of the past, but there was a deep division of opinion as to the nature of any new relationship between Europe and Africa. The British and French envisaged that change would come gradually by the combination of limited constitutional reforms and state-sponsored economic development that had been accepted by their governments even before the war. In the immediate postwar years the political and economic manifestations of these policies would be systematic steps toward self-government – a few even anticipated eventual independence – combined with significant funds for development. There was little altruism in these plans: they were designed to create political stability in the African colonies, on the one hand, and to produce cheap African commodities – oils, cocoa, rubber, cotton – for British and French consumers, on the other. To African nationalists this renewed commitment in London and Paris appeared little more than heavy-handed paternalism that did not address Africa's postwar problems, which included the continuation of the demographic boom that had been underway since the First World War. This placed increasing pressure on African cultivators, a situation that was exacerbated by the arrival of new white immigrants in Kenya, Southern Rhodesia, South Africa, and the Portuguese colonies. Land hunger in turn produced numerous problems for African farmers, including soil exhaustion and increased erosion. To combat this degradation of the land colonial officials introduced "scientific" farming techniques that were bitterly resented by African farmers and herdsmen, and often failed to improve the soils.

These policies drove many rural Africans into alliance with urban leaders who offered appealing and understandable solutions. Kwame Nkrumah was one of the first to recognize that the simple demand for independence could mobilize the African masses in the countryside as well as the city. While more moderate politicians and elites were agitating for greater influence over colonial policies, Nkrumah electrified crowds with the tantalizing prospect of an immediate end to British rule that would resolve all of the postwar grievances – the tyranny of "traditional" authorities, inflation, shortages, colonial marketing boards that paid cheap prices for farm produce, and unemployment. Nkrumah stoked unrealistic expectations, insisting that the many problems of the Gold Coast could be resolved by an independent African government. He would have to deal with their disappointments later, but at the time his demands for independence proved irresistible.

Before the Second World War most African politicians had thought in terms of reforming colonial rule, rather than overthrowing it, and of winning greater influence in colonial governance to secure economic and legal equality for at least some Africans. Early political movements focused on specific issues – improving wages, eliminating government price controls, and removing racist legal restrictions. After the war events moved quickly, however, and the most ambitious demands of the 1930s seemed hopelessly inadequate by 1951, when the first popular elections were held in the Gold Coast. The realization that African independence was no longer a vision but a reality mobilized elites, ethnic groups, and political organizations to become involved in a political debate in which they had previously demonstrated little interest. In the Gold Coast, the dramatic success of Nkrumah's Congress People's Party (CPP) in the elections of 1954 motivated anxious Asante activists to create a rival ethnically based party, the National Liberation Movement. In the Belgian Congo the government's abrupt announcement in 1957 of impending elections led to the precipitous birth of over a hundred ethnically based parties, the larger of which claimed to represent Bakongo, Luba, and Lunda interests. In neighbouring Congo-Brazzaville the generic names of early political parties such as the Congolese Progressive Party and the African Socialist Movement masked the predominantly ethnic basis of their membership. On the eve of independence for Uganda in 1961 the Bugandan-based Kabaka-Yakka Party was founded, dedicated to preserving the prerogatives of the monarchy.

The sudden appearance of these ethnically based parties was an inevitable response to the colonial administrators, who had made a fetish of customary law and their favouritism and support for rulers who could establish their legitimacy as tribal leaders. Not surprisingly, these "traditional" rulers felt threatened by the nationalists, who sought to subsume the power of royal institutions and ethnic minorities within a unitary state, just as the African urban politicians perceived these ethnically based parties and their "traditional" rulers as a threat to the integrity of the post-colonial state. They often viewed royal and ethnic parties as tools of the colonial authorities and as a potential impediment to national integration. They despised them as a retrograde form of tribalism that was antithetical to their modernizing agenda. They also suspected the leadership of these ethnic entities of defending narrow regional economic interests – petroleum in southern Nigeria, cocoa-farming among the Asante, or the mineral wealth of the Katanga region of the Belgian Congo dominated by the Luba. In the rush to independence nationalist leaders – Nkrumah in Ghana, Lumumba in Congo – outmaneuvered these popular ethnic parties, but the anxieties that spawned them did not diminish. By the late 1960s, when independent governments had failed to deliver on the promises that had swept them into office, the political aspirations of the tribally based parties, which had been marginalized in the race to independence, resurfaced to jeopardize the stability of the young nations.

The transformation of the Gold Coast from colony to the nation of Ghana in 1957 and the powerful example of European colonies in Asia becoming independent sovereign states launched the other African colonies on their own paths to independence. Once Ghana had become independent it became impossible for British and French negotiators to convince most African politicians to settle for anything less. In retrospect, the creation of dozens of separate, independent states on the ashes of the former colonial empires appears to have been almost inevitable, but in the 1950s several schemes were proposed to consolidate existing colonies into larger political units. The British proposed a federation of its East African territories, and in 1953 created the Central African Federation consisting of the colonies of Southern Rhodesia, Northern Rhodesia, and Nyasaland. The French in 1958 sought to cajole their Central and West African colonies into joining a federation that would leave France in control of their defense and foreign policy. Both proposals foundered on the resistance of African nationalists, who dismissed them as cynical attempts to maintain colonial influence.

In 1960 the British prime minister Harold Macmillan (1894–1986) delivered a speech in the South African parliament that warned of the "Winds of Change" sweeping the continent. In that same year France granted independence to all of her sub-Saharan possessions, and within five years Great Britain had relinquished control over all of her colonies. In those French and British territories that had insignificant white settler populations the transfer of power was relatively peaceful, the result of protracted negotiations throughout the decade following the war, culminating in elections to a parliament and concluding with a grand ceremony celebrating the passage from colony to independent sovereign state. Unfortunately, Africans living under other colonial regimes would experience a much more difficult road during their journey to independence.

In 1960 the declaration of independence for the Congo by Belgium precipitated a collapse of order upon the abrupt departure of the colonial government, necessitating the deployment of a peace-keeping force under the aegis of the United Nations. The violent disturbances that swept through the Congo were largely the result of Belgian colonial policies since the end of the war. Unlike Great Britain, Belgium had refused to consider any political reforms that would devolve real power into the hands of its African subjects. No effort was made to prepare Africans for leadership positions in the colonial administration. The few educated Africans in the Congo had received their education either in the colonial army or the mission schools of the Roman Catholic Church, as the colonial government had failed to provide any education beyond the primary school. The dearth of educated African leadership in the Congo was exacerbated by the sheer size and diversity of the colony, which made communication – and thereby administrative coordination by the state – very difficult. Consequently, in 1958, when the Belgian government, under international pressure, legalized political parties, over a hundred ethnically based associations appeared almost overnight. At independence two years later there were only a handful of college graduates available to administer one of the largest and potentially wealthiest states in Africa. The young government of Congo was plagued by the meddling of foreign governments – particularly Belgium and the United States, who were anxious to control the nation's substantial mineral wealth.

Belgium's precipitous withdrawal from the Congo was the result of a political calculation that all colonial powers were forced to make during the decade after the war. Would the benefits of clinging to power be greater than the costs? Each imperial power had a slightly different set of priorities. The businessmen and shopkeepers of Belgium were not prepared to bear the huge financial expense of a protracted military occupation of Congo. Since the motives for conquest of the Congo had been from the beginning to seize its rubber and mineral wealth, the decision to sever the imperial connection was a financial one that was made with little concern as to the effect of withdrawal on the African populace. Britain's liquidation of its empire in Africa was undertaken in part to curry favor with the United States, but Britain's rulers were also anxious to be relieved of the financial responsibility for the colonies, particularly if the new states could be persuaded to remain within the British Commonwealth. Moreover, the British could leave most of their colonies in the hands of bourgeois, mission-educated African leaders who had promised to protect private property and respect the rule of law. There was, however, a formidable obstacle to the transfer of power to the Africans: the resistance of white settlers in Kenya, Southern Rhodesia, and South Africa. In Kenya the Kikuyu Mau Mau conflict in the late 1940s, which resulted in the deaths of tens of thousands of Africans, had convinced British officials that white rule was unsustainable, and Kenya became an independent democracy in 1963. The white minority governments in Southern Rhodesia and South Africa, unwilling to cede power to an African majority, severed their connections to Great Britain in the 1960s.

Since Portugal considered her colonies to be overseas provinces, any discussion of independence was regarded as seditious, a fact which inexorably led to violent confrontations between the colonizer and the colonized. The Portuguese had been the first Europeans to arrive in Africa, in the fifteenth century. By the end of the 1960s Portugal, the first European state to establish a colony in Africa, was the only European empire remaining on the continent, and was fully determined to be the last to leave. Portuguese policy was particularly obdurate in part because of the nation's poverty and the fear that the loss of her tropical colonies would prove disastrous for her economy. Portugal was also ruled by a fascist regime whose claims to legitimacy were tied to the nation's long colonial history in Africa and Asia. There was also a significant number of poor white settlers in Mozambique and Angola, who were firmly against any kind of political reform. When the Portuguese government refused to negotiate any reform of the colonial government, the anti-colonial movement in Portuguese Africa became a guerrilla war for liberation.

Moreover, the Portuguese forces in Angola and Mozambique could rely on military and moral support from the white-dominated states of South Africa and Southern Rhodesia. Together these three powers formed a bloc in southern Africa that was committed to resisting any political reform that would challenge white privilege. The rebels could count on support from the socialist countries – Russia, China, and even Cuba – that turned the guerrilla war into an extension of cold war rivalry. Innovations in military technology worked to the advantage of mobile guerrilla armies, and international opposition to the racist policies of these states made them diplomatic pariahs. Portugal was the first to crack. As the guerrilla wars in Angola and Mozambique dragged on at great economic and human cost, disgruntled officers in Portugal staged a coup in 1974. Within a year the new regime had liquidated the African empire. With a new government in Mozambique that was hostile to neighboring Southern Rhodesia, African guerrillas in that country now had supply lines to the outside world and training camps for their soldiers. Within five years of the end of Portuguese rule in Africa, the settler regime in Southern Rhodesia had given up their opposition to democratic reform. New elections in 1980 created the Republic of Zimbabwe. The only remaining vestige of colonial rule on the continent was the settler state of South Africa.

Further reading

Birmingham, David, *The Decolonization of Africa*, London: University College of London Press, 1996

Cooper, Frederick, *Decolonization and African Society: The Labor Question in French and British Africa*, Cambridge: Cambridge University Press, 1996

Davidson, Basil, *The Black Man's Burden: Africa and the Curse of the Nation-State*, New York: Times Books, 1992

Manning, Patrick, *Francophone Sub-Saharan Africa, 1880–1985*, Cambridge: Cambridge University Press, 1988

Shepperson, George and Thomas Price, *Independent African: John Chilembwe and the Origins, Setting and Significance of the Nyasaland Native Rising of 1915*, Edinburgh: The University Press, 1987

23 The Union of South Africa and the apartheid state

The history of South Africa in the twentieth century, culminating in an independent, democratic republic, appears to have much in common with that of the white settler colonies in East and Central Africa. As in these colonies to the north, whites in South Africa dominated the land and government at the beginning of the twentieth century. At the same time a minority of mission-educated African men had begun to advocate the reform of colonial government in the language of European liberalism; this evolved into more radical demands that ultimately led to a democratic dispensation at the end of that century. These superficial similarities, however, cannot obscure the important differences between the history of South Africa during the twentieth century and that of its northern neighbors. White rule remained deeply entrenched in the country decades after most African colonies had become independent from white settler domination. A black South African born in 1957, the year the Gold Coast became the independent state of Ghana, would be nearly forty years old when he or she would, for the first time, be allowed to vote in a South African election. Unlike Africans in the other settler colonies, he or she would grow up in a sophisticated and wealthy industrial economy. This affluence would sustain the privileges and prosperity of a white minority whose standard of living was comparable to that of the wealthy citizens of the Western world.

In 1910 the Union of South Africa was founded, after several years of hard bargaining between the leaders of the Afrikaner republics and the British government which had defeated them in the South African War of 1899–1902. The settlement created a single state, a union, from the territories of Natal, the Cape Colony, the Orange Free State, and the South African Republic (usually referred to as the Transvaal). Like other political combinations being forged in Nigeria and Northern Rhodesia, the Union of South Africa embraced disparate communities differentiated by culture, ethnicity, and race into a geographical configuration defined by arbitrary boundaries and called a state. However, unlike Nigeria and Northern Rhodesia, South Africa included a large and diverse white settler population. The Union immediately became the wealthiest state on the African continent by a combination of political stability, guaranteed by Great Britain, and the gold industry of the Transvaal and the diamond mines of Kimberley, which secured economic prosperity. Mining attracted a steady flow of labor and investment, which stimulated the demand for imported foodstuffs, as well as cattle and sheep from the domestic farms, fruit from the

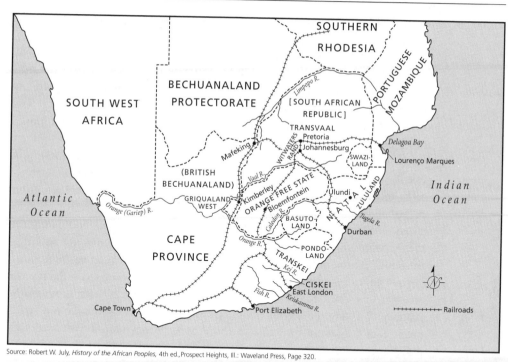

Source: Robert W. July, *History of the African Peoples*, 4th ed.,Prospect Heights, Ill.: Waveland Press, Page 320.

Map 23.1 *The unification of South Africa, 1910.*

orchards, and wine from the vineyards of the Cape. This vigorous combination of mining and farming (and, later, industrial manufacturing) endowed South Africa with a diverse and thriving internal and export economy.

During the protracted discussions over the Union, British negotiators had reluctantly agreed to give a large measure of autonomy to the white Afrikaans-speaking inhabitants of the Transvaal and the Orange Free State to avoid the possibility of the truculent Trekker republics taking up arms and renewing the war. Consequently the Union constitution permitted each territory to establish its own criteria as to who might vote. Before the Union all those in the Cape Colony of whatever "color" who satisfied a property qualification possessed the right to vote. In Natal the franchise was reserved only for whites – "non-whites," as in the Transvaal and Orange Free state, not being allowed to vote. This automatically assured the minority white settler population unassailable authority over a large and politically impotent black African majority. This constitutional discrimination deeply troubled British liberals who consoled themselves by predicting that the Union would encourage British citizens to immigrate to South Africa where their increasing numbers and liberal-ism would prevail in the future against the intransigent voting restrictions of the Afrikaner republics. This well-intentioned rationalization proved an illusion. The anticipated immigration from Britain never materialized on the scale envisaged by British liberals, and the English-speaking citizens of the Union failed to embrace liberal views of race.

Once established, the Union government began chipping away at the limited rights that Africans enjoyed in the different provinces. In 1911 the right of non-white workers to break labor contracts was prohibited and Africans were forbidden from holding skilled positions in the mining industry. Two years later the Union parliament passed the Native Land Act, which prohibited non-Europeans from owning land in most of South Africa, restricting them to the ownership of property in only some 7 percent of its landmass. The relentless passage of this repressive legislation did not go unchallenged. In 1912 the South African Native National Congress was founded by a group of mission-educated Africans who advocated political equality for all "civilized" men. Modeled on the Indian National Congress, this body, renamed the African National Congress (ANC) in 1923, initially did not aspire to rid South Africa of white rule, nor was it anxious to extend suffrage much beyond educated men in the Union. Its agenda was encapsulated in the famous aphorism by Cecil Rhodes: "Equal rights for all civilized men south of the Zambezi." Today the objectives of the ANC appear surprisingly moderate, but in fact they were the same as those expectations held by the emerging indigenous elites throughout the British empire. After all, it was only during the nineteenth century that men in Great Britain had been granted the vote by ascending degrees based on a property qualification, and no women were permitted to vote in British general elections until after the First World War.

Having no access to the public forum the ANC printed its own newspaper, *Abantu-Batho* (The People), to publish their views and platform in Setswana, isiXhosa, Sesotho, and isiZulu as well as English. As legislation against non-Europeans became ever more numerous and restrictive, the ANC began to be regarded as one of the more venerable but least effective of the nascent nationalist movements in Africa. During the First World War other organizations were founded that appealed to a much broader constituency than the relatively small numbers of the educated elite represented by the ANC. One was the Industrial and Commercial Union of Africa, popularly known as the Industrial and Commercial Union (ICU), founded by Clements Kadalie (*c.* 1896–1951) in 1918. Kadalie was born in Nyasaland (Malawi), where he received a mission education and taught for a year in a mission school before traveling through southern Africa and settling in Cape Town. Here he founded the ICU to demand practical benefits for black workers, rather than focusing on the broader political issues such as suffrage, which occupied the ANC. Initially the ICU was extraordinarily effective. In 1919 it won wage increases after strikes on the Cape Town docks and in 1920 on the Rand. By 1923, the same year the government passed legislation to expand segregation in the towns and deny blacks in South Africa the right of collective bargaining, the ICU had seventeen regional branches and over 100,000 members. The movement declined during the late 1920s, partly because Kadalie's relatively moderate way of dealing with white politicians and labor unions ultimately limited the movement's effectiveness. However, it was an important milestone in the history of South African politics, the first mass labor movement in South Africa's history, and an important symbol for future political organizations.

The years following the conclusion of the South African War saw other disenfranchised groups beginning to organize as well. In 1902 leaders of the Coloured community founded the African Political Organization (APO) under its president Dr. Abdullah Abdurahman (1872–1940). Substantial numbers of Indians and Malays had arrived in Natal during the nineteenth century as indentured servants to work on the sugar plantations. In the peace that followed the South African War these Asians decided to remain in Natal and the Transvaal rather than return to India after their terms of service had expired. They began to bring women over from India to raise families. White workers in Natal and the Transvaal felt threatened by the growing Indian population, and the governments of the two provinces passed legislation limiting Asian immigration. Indentured servants were now required to pay an onerous tax if they decided to remain in South Africa. South African Asians were required to carry identity cards, the humiliating passes, and their marriages could not be legally recorded with the registry office. The plight of the South African Asians was vigorously adopted by a young Indian lawyer named Mohandas K. Gandhi (1869–1948). His campaigns of non-violent protest, or satyagraha, launched in 1906 against these abuses filled the jails with his followers and forced the Union government to repeal its discriminatory legislation. Although his movement remained concerned with exclusively Indian interests, the Gandhi policy of non-violent protests continued after the founding of the South African Indian Congress (SAIC) in 1923 and impressed other groups seeking redress of their grievances.

During the negotiations that ended in the agreement of Union in 1910, the British had made considerable concessions to insure Afrikaner goodwill. When Great Britain declared war against Germany in August 1914, that policy received its first real test. The Union government was under the control of the South Africa Party led by Louis Botha (1862–1919) and Jan Christian Smuts (1870–1950), both of whom had been famous guerrillas and Boer generals during the South African War. Although Smuts and the majority of his followers supported the British government, there were many Afrikaners in the former republics who deeply resented the close association with Great Britain represented by the Union agreement. Although only a tiny minority – 10,000 Afrikaners – staged an armed rebellion, Smuts quickly and harshly suppressed it to add yet another grievance to Afrikaner resentment against British rule and another stimulus for Afrikaner nationalism. Among the paramount demands of the Afrikaners during the negotiations over the Union were cultural issues relating to the preservation of Afrikaner identity. Specifically, they insisted that Afrikaans be treated as equal to English. Another concern was the plight of landless farmers who had drifted into the growing urban areas, where they were competing for jobs with black and Coloured workers.

Like the rest of colonial Africa, South Africa was not immune to the economic depression at the end of the First World War. Demobilized soldiers flooded the job market, and shortages of imports produced spiraling inflation. Economic hardship had precipitated the dock workers' strike of 1919 and the rise of the ICU, and inflation, the low price of gold, and mining at great depths for low-grade ore had produced financial losses for the mine owners, which they resolved by replacing white workers, whose wages were fifteen times those of blacks, with lesser-paid Africans. To preserve their jobs the white miners of Johannesburg went on strike, effectively closing the gold mines. Smuts declared martial law and ordered the military to break the strike by force. Nearly 150 were killed, hundreds wounded, and four executed after their trial. The violence not only cost the Smuts government the elections of 1924, it convinced both Smuts and the mine owners to retain and eventually strengthen segregation in the mining industry.

The Rand Strike, as the disturbance came to be called, was symbolic of a larger problem facing postwar South Africa – the future of white privilege. The gold-mining industry was only profitable because of the vast reservoir of cheap African labor. The white miners had demonstrated in the Rand Strike that they were a powerful political force, and the population of poor white Afrikaners on farms and in the mines and urban industries continued to grow in the postwar era. Each represented a powerful constituency in the Union determined to preserve white privilege and political power. In the postwar era Afrikaner leaders took a series of steps intended to improve the position of their constituency. In 1926 Union politicians passed new legislation to reinforce segregation in the mines. A group of wealthy Afrikaner agriculturalists established a Land Bank for insurance and farm credits to help the poor white farmers to keep the farms they already possessed and purchase new ones. In the Cape Province white women were enfranchised; this lowered the proportion of black voters from 20 to 10 percent. A secret society called the Broederbond was formed to promote the interests of Afrikaners, and in 1934, in response to the National Party's cooperation with the more liberal South Africa Party led by Jan Smuts, Daniel F. Malan (1874–1959) organized a group of Afrikaner politicians into a *gesuiwerde* ("purified") National Party. The new party focused on the specific interests of Afrikaner workers, professionals, and businessmen, and was committed to a strict policy of racial segregation.

The great depression ravaged social and economic life throughout the world, but South Africa was less affected than many world regions. The gold industry actually prospered because the precious metal was in greater demand during the economic crisis. South Africa's economic situation improved in particular after the country went off of the gold standard in 1932, which made its export products more attractive to foreign buyers. From 1934 the high price of gold produced significant revenues. One beneficiary of the boom in gold profits was the newly formed United Party, a coalition of the National Party of James Hertzog and the South Africa Party of Jan Smuts. Under the United Party South Africa experienced a decade of spectacular economic growth. The government invested heavily in steel and electrical industries, and encouraged light manufacturing, whose products were South African substitutes for American and British imports. By 1940 manufacturing had replaced both mining and agriculture as the largest economic sector in South Africa.

The outbreak of the Second World War severely strained the political cooperation that had created the United Party. Although Smuts managed once again to muster the votes to support Great Britain and declare war on Germany in September 1939, Hertzog resigned and many Afrikaners openly sympathized with Germany. Many admired the Nazi Germany of Adolf Hitler and considered the ethnic purity advocated by his racist National Socialist Party as a model for South Africa. A paramilitary organization known as the Ossewa Brandwag (OB; Afrikaans, "Oxwagon Sentinel") was organized along the lines of the Nazi Brown Shirts. In 1938 the OB and other groups of Afrikaner nationalists staged a torchlight procession across the country commemorating the centennial of the Boer victory over the Zulus at Blood River in 1838. Several prominent Afrikaner politicians were interned during the war as Nazi sympathizers, including two future prime ministers. During the war South African combat troops fought in East and North Africa and in Italy, and as in the First World War the Coloured and African volunteers were confined to non-combat roles in labor battalions and as transport drivers.

The war further stimulated the buoyant South African economy, creating opportunities for entrepreneurs to invest in new industries, particularly in Natal and the Cape. South African factories produced steel and munitions, its mines coal and strategic minerals – gold, platinum, uranium – its farms foodstuffs to replenish the huge convoys making their way around the Cape of Good Hope to Asia and the Pacific. This rapid economic expansion drew half a million South Africans, black and white, to the growing industrial centers. Urban areas were soon beset with a host of problems. Swarms of squatters, unable to find housing, built shantytowns on the outskirts of cities. Workers organized new unions to protest the low wages and inflation that characterized the wartime economy. Most significantly, the African miners on the Witwatersrand created the African Mine Workers' Union in 1941 to fight against the poor wages and dangerous conditions of their work. Despite the best efforts of the mine owners and politicians to destroy the union, it had, by war's end, garnered enough support to organize a strike of nearly 100,000 miners. The pass system, which had been implemented to keep Africans in the rural areas, proved unenforceable in the face of this massive migration to the cities, and the burgeoning numbers of whites, blacks, and Coloureds now packed together in adjacent neighborhoods eroded the hitherto strict urban segregation. At the same time white farmers found it increasingly difficult to find cheap agricultural laborers in rural areas as black workers were drawn to better paying jobs in growing urban industries.

From the year of Union in 1910 to 1948 politics had been dominated by those leaders who were unabashedly pro-British or moderate Afrikaners determined to maintain South Africa as a member of the British Empire and Commonwealth. This meant that the British government maintained the right to insure that the Union's "native" policies were consistent with those of other African colonies. The economic and social upheavals caused by the war led many white voters to fear that segregation was dissolving in the turmoil of the booming cities. These fears were played upon by D. F. Malan's National Party, which advocated a policy called *apartheid* (Afrikaans, "apartness"). This was a concept developed by Afrikaner intellectuals after the First World War, which envisioned the total separation of South Africa's "racial" groups. It was a doctrine that maintained that racial populations had biologically determined cultures, characteristics, and historical destinies. The theory of apartheid held that to insure its given destiny, each race should be permitted to develop independently. As one Afrikaner intellectual put it:

> The preservation of the pure race tradition of the *Boerevolk* must be protected at all costs in all possible ways as a holy pledge entrusted to us by our ancestors as part of God's plan with our People. Any movement, school, or individual who sins against this must be dealt with as a racial criminal by the effective authorities.[1]

In 1948 the National Party defeated the ruling United Party of the moderate Jan Smuts. The result was as much a rejection of Smuts as a referendum on apartheid. Nevertheless, over the next two decades Malan's party effectively segregated all aspects of South African society into white and non-white – residential and rural land, education, public services. Pass laws were strictly enforced. Black trade unions were denied legal recognition. The Suppression of Communism Act of 1950 was used to intimidate African nationalists, socialists, and even liberals. Under Prime Minister Hendrik Verwoerd (1901–1966), apartheid reached its ultimate conclusion, the grand apartheid program, which designated ten zones of rural poverty as homelands or "Bantu nations" for the vast majority of black Africans. In the 1970s black Africans from the squatter camps that surrounded the urban areas were forcibly removed and dumped into overcrowded and environmentally degraded reserves, which were declared "independent Bantustans." The segregated conditions for the Indian and Coloured communities were little better. The introduction of a strictly segregated society dominated by white Afrikaner power was made largely possible by the continuing and extraordinary rate of economic growth of 6 percent per year during the high point of apartheid from 1963 to 1972. Very little of this economic expansion trickled down to black Africans as the chasm in the

---

[1] Quoted in Leonard Thompson, *A History of South Africa*, rev. ed., New Haven: Yale University Press, 1995, p. 184.

Figure 23.1 *Apartheid. Under apartheid, public services in South Africa, such as this railway platform, were racially segregated.*

standard of living between blacks and whites virtually eliminated the poor white problem which had haunted every Union government since the South African War of 1899–1902.

At the end of the Second World War the aging leaders of the ANC were challenged by members of the organization's Youth League, who viewed the old guard as too moderate. The election of the National Party convinced the radical faction of the ANC led by Walter Sisulu (1912–2003), Oliver Tambo (1917–1993), and Nelson Mandela (b. 1918) that reform was inadequate, and that fundamental changes were now imperative. These three young activists rose to prominence in the ANC after the 1948 election. Under their leadership the organization would be transformed from an elitist group into a mass movement, committed to ending white domination. Rejuvenated during the 1950s under Mandela and his close associates, the ANC allied with the South African Indian Congress in a campaign of passive resistance against racial discrimination. Working with the South African Indian Congress, the Coloured People's Congress, African unions, and some white sympathizers, the ANC built a coalition during the 1950s in opposition to apartheid. However, government crackdowns and dissension within the ranks sapped much of its momentum by the end of the decade.

The split in the anti-apartheid alliance was over the issue of cooperation with sympathetic white supporters. The main opponent of such an alliance

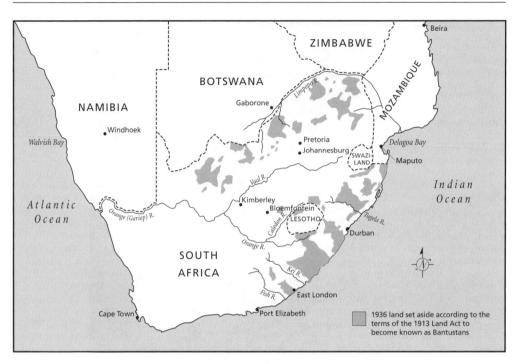

Map 23.2 *"Bantustans" in South Africa.*

was Robert Sobukwe (1924–1978), who broke with the ANC over this issue, and formed the Pan-Africanist Congress (PAC). The PAC platform required its followers to liberate themselves without assistance from white or Western influences, and to refuse any cooperation with white liberals and communists. The PAC attracted younger rural black migrants to the cities, who had been largely ignored by the ANC. In March 1960 the PAC launched a campaign of civil disobedience against the pass laws. In Sharpeville, in Orlando township, near Johannesburg, several thousand PAC members marched to the police station without their passes. The police met the crowd with a hail of gunfire, killing 69 and wounding 186, most of whom were shot in the back. In retrospect Sharpeville was the turning-point for the liberation movements and a watershed in the history of South Africa. The leaderships of both the ANC and PAC realized that civil disobedience would no longer achieve their objectives. The ANC created Umkhonto we Sizwe (MK; isiXhosa/isiZulu, "the Spear of the Nation") to fight apartheid by sabotage. The PAC had its own militant arm, called Poqo (isiXhosa, "Pure"), and the African Resistance Movement – a multiracial militant movement of young professionals and students – launched hundreds of bomb attacks on government buildings, railways, and industrial centers. The government retaliated fiercely. The ANC and PAC activists and their leaders were arrested, convicted of treason, and imprisoned on Robben Island in Cape Town's Table Bay. By the end of 1963 violent resistance was over, and South Africa remained quiet, enabling its white citizens to enjoy the country's unprecedented prosperity and contemplate the country's fate as a pariah state.

By the early 1970s the pace of economic growth began to slacken. The international recession precipitated by the dramatic rise in the price of oil after 1973 quickly depressed the South African economic boom. Without sustainable reserves of fuel, the increased cost of manufacturing, compounded by government subsidies to white enterprises, made South African goods less competitive in the world market, and increased the country's dependence on imported technology and capital. The determination of the National Party to prevent the emergence of a black skilled labor force made South Africa increasingly dependent upon black semi-skilled and unskilled workers. Their grievances, stoked by inflation and unemployment, exploded into a wave of strikes, which signaled a resurgence of black trade unionism.

The growing activism of the black labor force soon came to be felt in the government's tightly controlled public education system. Black schools were the most deprived institutions of the state, and yet the only ones that offered any prospects – no matter how bleak – for students and their parents to break the cycle of poverty. With the ANC leadership in exile or in prison, the leadership of the agitated students was taken up by the South African Students' Organization, which was founded in 1968 by a twenty-two-year-old student named Steve Biko (1946–1977). Biko was an advocate of Black Consciousness, which he defined in his 1971 book *I Write What I Like*:

> Black Consciousness is an attitude of mind and a way of life, the most positive call to emanate from the black world for a long time. Its essence is the realization by the black man of the need to rally together with his brothers around the cause of their oppression – the blackness of their skin – and to operate as a group to rid themselves of the shackles that bind them to perpetual servitude. It is based on a self-examination which has ultimately led them to believe that by seeking to run away from themselves and emulate the white man, they are insulting the intelligence of whoever created them black. The philosophy of Black Consciousness therefore expresses group pride and the determination of the black to rise and attain the envisaged self.[2]

Black Consciousness soon permeated into the urban schools where it was eagerly adopted by black students. On June 16, 1976 thousands of black schoolchildren in Soweto demonstrated against instruction in Afrikaans, a language they viewed as a tool of their subjugation. The student protests swept through the nation, only to be brutally suppressed. By February 1977 nearly 575 Africans had been killed, 137 under the age of eighteen. Steve Biko was arrested and subsequently murdered by the police.

Under increasing international and domestic pressure the new prime minister, P. W. Botha (1916–2006) devised a desperate dual policy called the Total

[2] Steve Biko, "Black Consciousness and the Quest for True Humanity," in *I Write What I Like*, ed. Aelred Stubbs, San Francisco: Harper & Row, 1986, p. 88.

Strategy to save apartheid by the creation of a black middle class whose education, housing, and jobs would be subsidized by the state, while the police, whose powers were already overwhelming, would be coordinated with the army and intelligence agencies under a central command. Defense spending was doubled to combat the increasing support from the successful liberation movements that had won independence in neighboring Mozambique and Angola in 1975 and Rhodesia in 1980 and were ready to assist in the liberation of South Africa. The South African Defence Force found itself bogged down in a war in southern Angola against the Cuban and Namibian forces which would ultimately lead to the independence of Namibia in 1990. On every front the Total Strategy proved a total failure. The South African government was confronted by growing activism within black civil society – organizations that mobilized the youth and women, as well as civic associations in black townships, conducted constant campaigns of civil disobedience. The ANC returned to the center of domestic politics, its exiled leaders regarded as a government-in-waiting, and its MK guerrillas carrying out acts of sabotage. In 1983 black militant students and workers formed the United Democratic Front (UDF). Several smaller political parties emerged, such as the Azanian People's Organization (AZAPO), which had ties to the PAC, and the Inkatha Freedom Party (IFP), a Zulu nationalist organization originally founded in 1928. In 1990 a Zulu politician, Chief Mangosuthu Gatsha Buthelezi (b. 1928), who had been head of the so-called homeland of KwaZulu since 1975, disingenuously claimed that Inkatha was a national organization – although few believed him – and when confronted with the growing popularity and influence of the ANC in Natal, he made alliances of convenience with the National Party and several extremist white supremacist organizations.

The government of President Botha met the escalation of violence with even greater force. A state of emergency was declared on July 20, 1985 followed by massive repression – arrests, detentions, torture, and the assassination of anti-apartheid activists – which momentarily gave the illusion of peace, but at great cost. Capital fled, the rand collapsed, and international bankers refused credit. Leading businessmen, African academics, and church leaders were meeting with the exiled leaders of the ANC in Lusaka, London, and Paris, and the monolithic façade of the National Party cracked. An ailing President Botha was replaced by F. W. de Klerk (b. 1936). Although confronted by protracted economic decline the National Party government still commanded the formidable military and security forces of the state, but it was constantly challenged by the mass mobilization capacity of the ANC and the UDF. The ANC was also ready to negotiate. The movement enjoyed massive popular support within South Africa, and its leadership had effectively harnessed international opinion against apartheid. Moreover, by the mid-1980s it had produced two figures of international stature – Bishop Desmond Tutu, the black Anglican clergyman who won the 1984 Nobel Peace Prize, and Nelson Mandela, whose incarceration on Robben Island since the 1960s had made him a world renowned prisoner of conscience. However, the ANC was also under intense pressure from the

South African government, which had infiltrated its ranks and assassinated many of its members. It had also lost key bases in Mozambique in 1984 and Angola in 1988, thereby limiting its ability to mount operations within South Africa. The winding down of the cold war after 1989 also diminished the amount of support the movement could expect from the Eastern Bloc. The time had come to break the stalemate.

On February 2, 1990 President de Klerk delivered a historic speech in parliament, announcing the unbanning of the ANC, PAC, and the South African Communist Party, the removal of restrictions on suspect organizations and trade unions, and the release of political prisoners – including Nelson Mandela, who from prison had recently proposed negotiations between the ANC and the government. Negotiations began a year later in December 1991, when 228 delegates from most political parties gathered near Johannesburg as the Convention for a Democratic South Africa (CODESA). Complex and protracted negotiations continued amidst escalating violence, mainly between supporters of the ANC led by Nelson Mandela and the Inkatha Freedom Party of Mangosuthu Buthelezi who, with hardline Afrikaners, were opposed to the interim constitution agreed upon by the negotiating forum in December 1993. This created a multiparty democracy based on universal suffrage, proportional representation, a separation of powers, and a bill of rights. When elections were finally held in April 1994 after Buthelezi reluctantly agreed to participate, the ANC gained 62.7 percent of the vote, followed by 20.4 percent for the National Party, 10.5 percent for the IFP, and the remainder to the other lesser parties. The ANC's popularity was largely attributable to its leadership. Men such as Nelson Mandela and Govan Mbeki (1910–2001) had made great personal sacrifices on behalf of the freedom struggle that had earned them enormous credibility among a wide spectrum of the diverse South African electorate. On May 10, 1994, 342 years after the Dutch East India Company had established its settlement at the Cape of Good Hope, Nelson Mandela took the presidential oath of office and addressed the dignitaries from all over the world: "Out of the experience of an extraordinary human disaster that lasted too long, must be born a society of which all humanity will be proud."[3]

The ANC formed a government of national unity, in an atmosphere of euphoria. The extraordinary success of the ANC against formidable opponents was not solely the result of African insurrection within South Africa. Indeed, the powerful state security apparatus had effectively demonstrated its ability to contain internal and external enemies of the regime. There is no question that the moral justification to end the inequalities of apartheid had a profound impact within Africa and around the world. White South Africans had been particularly frustrated when their athletes were unwelcome at international sporting events, and Western entertainers increasingly refused to perform for South African audiences. Moral persuasion, however, could not have

---

[3] Nelson Mandela, *Long Walk to Freedom: The Autobiography of Nelson Mandela*, Boston: Little, Brown & Co., 1994, p. 154.

triumphed without the financial boycotts that dried up foreign investment and, by the late 1980s, caused serious economic problems for the apartheid state. Foreign companies and individuals could no longer justify to their shareholders or their own consciences financial support for a regime based on racial injustice. After the demise of the cold war Western governments found it increasingly difficult to justify support for the regime in the name of national security. Moreover, after nearly a half century the South African white electorate had grown weary of being citizens of a pariah state.

The 1994 election that brought Nelson Mandela to power was the culmination of the long march of African independence throughout the continent in the twentieth century. Although it was almost four decades after the independence of the Gold Coast, the whites who conceded power to the African majority in 1994 did so on terms that would have seemed familiar to colonial officials during the 1950s and early 1960s. Mandela was a mission-educated African nationalist who promised to respect the rule of law and protect private property. He was yet another in a long line of African leaders who could articulate his arguments for democracy and social equality in a way that spoke to Western leaders. However, despite the euphoria that greeted Mandela's election, South Africa in 1994 was a traumatized society. The bitterness bred by years of state-sponsored violence and internecine conflict would not dissipate quickly. In an effort to heal the divisions engendered by apartheid, the new government established a Truth and Reconciliation Commission, which offered amnesty to persons willing to testify fully and publicly about politically motivated crimes they had committed under apartheid.

Apartheid had bequeathed a host of social problems to the new South Africa. More than a decade after the 1994 elections the country remains plagued by stark economic inequalities. The HIV/AIDS epidemic, which took root in black townships under apartheid and spread to rural areas, continues to strain the country's health-care system and creates thousands of orphans each year. However, since 1994 the government has made significant strides towards developing the infrastructure of communities that were neglected under apartheid. And while there remain radicals – both black and white – opposed to the democratic process, since 1994 South Africa has held several more successful elections.

Further reading

Mandela, Nelson, *Long Walk to Freedom: The Autobiography of Nelson Mandela*, Boston: Little, Brown & Co., 1994

Waldmeir, Patti, *Anatomy of a Miracle: The End of Apartheid and the Birth of the New South Africa*, New York: W. W. Norton & Co., 1997

Worger, William H. and Nancy L. Clark, *South Africa : The Rise and Fall of Apartheid*, New York: Longman, 2004

24 A decade of hope

There are few more bittersweet scenes in the history of modern African than the newsreel films taken on the night of March 6, 1957 to record the transfer of authority from British officials in the colony of the Gold Coast to the leadership of the independent Republic of Ghana. When the Union Jack of Great Britain was lowered and the Black Star flag of the Republic of Ghana was raised, President Kwame Nkrumah was accompanied by British dignitaries amidst rejoicing and jubilant throngs dancing in the streets. It is a scene of African hope and triumph over European colonialism, but also one of reconciliation between the ruler and the ruled that symbolized the contemporary optimism of a peaceful and prosperous future for Ghana and the other European colonies of Africa that would soon follow down the road to independence.

Twenty-three years after the independence of Ghana every colony on the continent had become independent, as the vast empires of Belgium, Great Britain, France, and Portugal were transformed into a checkerboard of sovereign states. These new nations were dramatically different one from another in size, population, economic development, and natural environments. Giant states such as the Congo and Sudan dwarfed the tiny territories of Togo, Benin, and Equatorial Guinea. The population of Nigeria alone accounted for nearly 20 percent of the continent, but the inhabitants of the kingdom of Swaziland amounted to less than 1 percent. Economically there was little industrial development outside South Africa. The Congo and Zambia had extensive mining industries, but the economies of the remaining new states of Africa were predominantly agricultural. Some such as Ghana, Senegal, Kenya, and Uganda possessed pockets of fertile agricultural land that supported a vibrant export economy. Other new states survived more on subsistence than cash crops, and had little to offer from their regional economies apart from the export of human labor. Many straddled diverse ecological and geographical zones. Niger and Mauritania lay along the arid border between savanna and the sahel and the Sahara of western Africa. Nigeria stretched from the rainforests of the Niger Delta to the shores of the slowly evaporating Lake Chad. The Sudan extended from the sands of its Nubian desert in the north to savanna, swamp, and mountains in the south. Yet despite all these many differences the leaders of these new states shared a common goal to assert their authority as sovereign, independent nations.

The celebrations of independence in Accra, Ghana, in 1957 symbolized that the transfer of power from imperial Great Britain to the Republic of Ghana could be accomplished without the level of violence that accompanied many independence movements in other world regions. There had been outbursts of discontent in the past, but the transfer of power from Britain to Ghana proceeded with relative peace, followed by the equally tranquil decolonization of the French colonies three years later. There were several significant exceptions. The British in Kenya had fought a brutal war against the Mau Mau insurgency in the decade preceding independence and the Belgians had supported the Hutu in a bloody civil war on the eve of independence in Rwanda. But compared to the conflict associated with anti-colonialism in South-East Asia, the decolonization of Africa south of the Sahara between 1957 and 1964 was remarkably free from violence.

The men who came to power after 1957 were towering figures whose shadows continue to sprawl across the African landscape today. They were charismatic, intelligent, often inspiring leaders. Many of them had spent time in colonial prisons for their nationalist activities. Almost all were products of a Western education. Kwame Nkrumah of Ghana, Nnamdi Azikiwe of Nigeria, Léopold Senghor of Senegal, and Jomo Kenyatta of Kenya were among the new heads of state who had attended universities overseas. Others were the graduates of mission schools within their home colonies. All were proficient in the languages of their colonial masters, all had justified their independence struggle in the language of liberalism and nationalism, and all took power as the heads of parliamentary democracies. As a group, however, they ultimately proved more proficient at organizing revolution than ruling a nation. One by one the leaders of the liberation struggle were cast aside by less glamorous but often more practical and astute soldiers and politicians. The very traits and training that had allowed them to negotiate effectively with colonial officials and European diplomats ultimately alienated them from their African supporters.

Léopold Senghor of Senegal was the prototype of these African leaders from two different worlds. He was fluent in French and a devout Catholic in a predominantly Islamic state, and much more comfortable in the intellectual circles of Paris than among the ceddo aristocracy or the Muslim marabouts in the countryside of his native Senegal. As a writer, poet, and philosopher, he remains one of the most significant intellectuals of the twentieth century, yet he ultimately had little in common with the people he ruled. He never resolved his ambivalent attitude as to the relationship between Africa and Europe, between Senegal and France. As a writer he warned of the dangers of Africans becoming assimilated into French culture; as a politician he was resistant to the idea of complete independence from France. When events forced Senegal to become a sovereign state in 1960, he became its first elected president, yet within two years he had abolished democracy and declared Senegal a one-party state.

Independence for these new African leaders meant taking over the colonial state rather than revolutionizing it. When Kwame Nkrumah instructed his supporters "Seek ye first the political kingdom," his vision was of blacks replacing whites in the corridors of power, the first objective of all the contemporary African leaders. Thus, after their electoral victories many of the new presidents and prime ministers simply slipped into the autocratic roles played by their former colonial masters. Most demonstrated an enthusiasm for the modernizing initiatives of the socialist governments of the West that had characterized the late colonial era. Since the end of the Second World War the industrial nations of the world – in North America, Western Europe, and behind the Iron Curtain – had increasingly perceived the state as the primary engine of economic development. Socialist ideology combined with political self-interest in postwar Europe dominated the colonial policies of France and Great Britain, leading to more direct intervention in the economies of their African colonies. They introduced scientific schemes to modernize traditional African agricultural practices and promoted the expansion of mining and cash-crop production. Virtually every African educated overseas had embraced socialism, and often Marxism, whose doctrines placed the state at the very center of economic development. Not surprisingly, the new African leaders continued and reinforced these interventionist policies that had been a major source of African discontent in the postwar years leading to independence. Ironically, African socialism now became the cornerstone of the economic policies of the new national governments.

All of these new leaders were conscious that whatever personal talents they possessed could not have been developed without the opportunity for a Western education. Thus public education became a priority to their administrations. However promises for universal education as well as for better jobs, hospitals, and roads created unrealistic expectations for the new regimes. Africa had been colonized in an era in which governments were not held responsible to feed, educate, or employ their citizens. In the colonies, however, white officials and settlers were accustomed to a more benevolent administration that provided them with education for their children, hospitals, and often land and loans in return for their services. Not surprisingly, the Africans assumed that the end of white rule would mean that these amenities would now be forthcoming to all Africans. The colonial state with the revenues generated by its African subjects had the means to provide a high standard of living for its tiny white minority, but the economies of even the wealthiest colonial states were hopelessly inadequate to provide basic services and employment for the vast majority of Africans. The unrealistic nature of these expectations soon became apparent throughout independent Africa, and when a new state could not immediately provide promised services, the disappointment by most of its people became all the more bitter when they realized there was little prospect of any future improvement in their standard of living.

Discontent against the new ruling elite, who seemed indifferent to the concerns of the average African, became widespread, and certainly contributed to the rapid demise of democracy in post-colonial Africa. Since the army was the only multi-ethnic, national institution in most African states, its officers, often educated and professional, became increasingly exasperated by the failure of the democratically elected leaders to govern. Some of these officers were self-seeking, ruthless thugs, but others were motivated by a sense of responsibility and a desire to rectify the mistakes of incompetent politicians. All the new independent African states had inherited from their imperial patrons well-trained armies with modern equipment. During the colonial era they had been used largely for internal policing, and although the salaries for soldiers were meager, the quality of discipline and training far surpassed that of the civil servants in the colonial bureaucracy. In fact, governments of most of the newly independent states relied heavily on their armies to bolster their political authority.

Consequently, during the first decade of independent Africa there was a spate of military coups d'état beginning in 1958, when General Ibrahim Abboud (1958–1964) seized control of the Republic of the Sudan, followed by Colonel Christophe Soglo (1963–1964) taking over the government of Benin (Dahomey) and Sergeant (later General) Etienne Eyadema that of Togo in 1963. In the former Belgian Congo Joseph Mobutu, a client of the United States government and former soldier in the notorious Belgian Force Publique, set himself up as a virtual dictator in 1965 with the title of President Mobutu Sese Seko (1965–1997) of the Republic of Zaire (now the Democratic Republic of the Congo). Even President Kwame Nkrumah was not immune to a coup d'état by Lieutenant-Colonel Joseph Ankrah (1966–1969) in 1966, the same year that Lieutenant Colonel Yakubu Gowan (1966–1975) seized power in Nigeria. The following year Brigadier David Lansana (1967–1968) led a brief military government in Sierra Leone, and in 1968 Major Marien Ngouabi (1968–1977) took over the government of the People's Republic of Congo and Colonel Moussa Traoré (1969–1991) in Mali overthrew the government of President Modibo Keita. In 1969 Major General Mohammed Siad Barre (1969–1991) seized the government of the Somali Democratic Republic. Military coups continued with less frequency during the 1970s in Rwanda (1973) and Chad (1975), for there were now few states without military governments or authoritarian single-party states.

Governments democratically elected at independence were also threatened by their own civilian rulers who, when confronted by internal opposition, proved as willing as the military to subvert the electoral process. Some were influenced by the success of the Soviet Communist Party, which had forged the many ethnicities of Eastern Europe and Central Asia into a one-party state. Others justified their autocracy by arguing that "tribalism," made multiparty politics innately unstable. The fact that Africans were slow to transfer their loyalty from clan and lineage to the new nation gave many rulers a ready excuse to silence internal opposition. When Sékou Turé (1958–1984) defied President Charles de Gaulle and rejected the French Community in favor of independence in 1958, he consolidated his autocratic authority by the Parti Démocratique de Guinée (PDG) and tolerated no opposition until his death in 1984. Immediately upon independence in 1960 President Ahmadou Ahidjo (1960–1982) of the Republic of Cameroon declared his Cameroon National Union (CNU) the single legal party, and for the next twenty years tolerated no opposition. His neighbor, President Léon Mba (1961–1964) of the Gabonese Republic, did the same, and he and his successor, Albert-Bernard (later El Hadj Omar) Bongo (1967–1990), and the Parti Démocratique Gabonais (PDG) imposed autocratic rule on Gabon for the next twenty years. The longest political opposition was carried against Hastings Kamuzu Banda and his Malawi Congress Party (MCP) after independence in July 1964. During the next thirty years he methodically crushed all dissent, vocal and violent, amidst accusations of gross human rights violations. During this same period President Hamani Diori (1960–1974) of Niger suppressed all opposition to his Parti Populaire Nigérien (PPN), and in the tiny Republic of Guinea-Bissau President João Bernardo Vieira (1974–1991) and his Party of Guinea and Cape Verde (PAIGC) ruled for seventeen years as a single-party state. Even under the relatively benign and paternal government of President Félix Houphouët-Boigny (1960–1993) in the République de Côte d'Ivoire (Republic of the Ivory Coast) all the members of the National Assembly until 1990 were required to be members of the Parti Démocratique de la Côte d'Ivoire to make certain that no opposition political party could take root in Ivorian society.

The rapid disintegration of democratic institutions in Africa during the 1960s was not inevitable. Some states – Botswana, Kenya, Sudan, Tanzania – tolerated opposition parties, but throughout Africa loyalty to the new nation-state was fragile at best. There was a demonstrable popular enthusiasm for the end of colonial rule, but these arbitrary configurations of the past had little relevance for the future after the colonizers had packed up and gone home. Personal loyalties for most Africans were intricately woven in a network of connections – kinship groups, religious and fraternal organizations, local clients, patrons – all of which transcended the remote and recently invented nation-state. Moreover, colonial governments had provided Africans with little experience in parliamentary democracy. The indirect rule of the British had embraced the autocratic institution of the chief and the monarchical authority of the king as traditional and thus legitimate. The assimilation of the French had permitted Africans to participate in democratic elections, but their numbers were few and their influence greater in France than in Africa. Despite the appeals of socialist policies at the end of the Second World War the imperialists had never been democrats, and least of all in Africa.

Cold war competition between the West, specifically the United States, and the Eastern Bloc, particularly the Soviet Union, certainly did not encourage the development of democracy. Despite the anti-colonial and democratic rhetoric propagated throughout Africa by both the Americans and Russians, each was more concerned with securing loyal clients to protect their own national interests. Some of Africa's new leaders were motivated by ideological principles of socialism and Marxism; others sought to use cold war rivalries to secure power for their own personal advantage. Many found themselves reduced to pawns in the larger global struggle between the two super-powers and their allies.

Fearful of growing Soviet influence in the newly independent and mineral-rich Congo in 1960, the United States contrived to have its president, Patrice Lumumba (1925–1961), assassinated shortly after his election. When Guinea broke with France in 1958 to become independent rather than a member of the French Community, President Sékou Touré and the Marxist rhetoric of his PDG closely associated Guinea with Eastern Europe and the Soviet Union, who were eager to develop the rich deposits of bauxite for aluminum production. Russia financed the Kindia Office of Bauxite in direct competition to the American-controlled Compagnie des Bauxites de Boké. The government of Mali under President Modibo Keita cut most of its ties with France amidst a flood of Marxist rhetoric to become an economic satellite of the East European countries. Perhaps the most contentious cold war battleground was Angola. When the nation became independent of Portugal in 1975, President Agostinho Neto (1975–1979) used Soviet military advisers and Cuban soldiers to gain control of most of the oil-rich state.

Ambitious economic policies adopted by some of the new regimes did little to encourage political democracy. In the past African leaders had denounced many of the colonial economic policies such as marketing boards, but after independence the large development projects managed by the state and its principal source of revenue were expanded more for the benefit of the government than its citizens. In a fit of nationalism a few states – Ghana, Sudan, Zaire – expropriated foreign-owned businesses. Although the confiscation of foreign firms produced instant employment, the new owners simply did not have the education, experience or capital to manage them. Corruption became the means to get things done, and gained a measure of acceptance as it became ever more rampant. In 1960 the economies of the African colonial states were overwhelmingly agricultural, and remain so to this day; but in the heady days of independence, some of the new leaders educated in the West aspired to implement their own industrial revolution. They believed that Africa as simply a supplier of primary agricultural produce was vulnerable to the volatile prices fixed by manufacturing nations. The desire to emulate the industrial nations was irresistible, particularly when heavy industry was a source of employment, revenue, and a visible symbol of national vigor and economic independence. The creation of mines, dams, ports, and factories also provided important opportunities to reward regions or ethnic groups loyal to the government; such considerations often made the decision to finance and implement development schemes more political than economic.

The Sudan embarked upon the Managil Extension of the vast Gezira cotton-growing scheme that solidified support for the government in the heartland of the country and its capital, Khartoum, at the expense of those Sudanese on the periphery. Nigeria in the 1960s launched the drilling of the rich oil deposits in the Niger Delta and offshore, but the enormous wealth generated by oil development proved of little benefit for the Nigerians in the region. In Ghana the construction of the Volta River Dam had been proposed by the British but was immediately endorsed as his own by Prime Minister Kwame Nkrumah upon independence. It was hoped that the great dam would produce sufficient hydro-electric power for the industrial development of Ghana which would be inaugurated by an aluminum industry to consume – rather than export – bauxite from its rich mines. Nkrumah's vision of an economically self-sufficient Ghana proved an illusion. The dam displaced thousands of people and failed to provide sufficient power for even domestic use. Ghana's experiment with heavy industry was one of many similar, expensive, and ultimately unprofitable projects that were brought to life by political ambition rather than economic pragmatism during this first decade of independence.

If state-sponsored industry proved economically inefficient, the socialist state management and organization of peasant agriculture was equally unproductive. Scientific and often stern measures to improve peasant farming during the postwar colonial years had little economic success and considerable political cost for more than any other colonial policy it mobilized conservative rural farmers to vehemently protest against colonial rule. Draconian methods to contain disease among livestock and the digging of contour ridges to curb erosion reminiscent of the hated prewar *corvée* were among the least popular initiatives of the colonial state. Nevertheless, the new governments in the spirit of African socialism proved equally enthusiastic about imposing a revolution in agriculture introduced and managed by the state from the capital as a spur to development.

The emphasis on the role of the state in economic life made access to the corridors of power essential in obtaining a share of the limited resources available to the newly independent governments. Those Africans with access to the president and his ministers would be the most likely beneficiaries of highways, hospitals, schools, and foreign monetary and humanitarian assistance and private foreign investment. Most every aspect of the new African state was controlled by the central government. The men with the political authority – for there were few women – regulated the revenues from exports, imports, taxes, and customs. They decided who was permitted to travel and study abroad. Thus, African politicians controlled both the national purse and access to the world beyond the borders and jurisdiction of the state. In this environment systems of patronage developed to reward friends, relatives, and followers guided the apportionment of development projects – usually to the regions where the patrons and their supporters lived. Leaders who had been elected on a national platform now found themselves reverting to positions of tribal chiefs, responsible not to the nation, but to their own ethnic and regional allies. They did not command the authority of their colonial predecessors, whose confidence had been assured by the military and economic power of their imperial governments. They did not possess the power to govern without the more devious means of corruption, bribery, intimidation, and, frequently, violence. These methods became increasingly accepted, both within Africa and in the eyes of foreign donors, and were effective so long as members of their personal entourages maintained control of the resources flowing in from foreign nations, humanitarian organizations, and international corporations.

During this decade of hope the armies of Africa were much too involved in local coups d'état to attack their neighbors. Virtually every African leader, civilian or military, realized that any attempt to redraw the arbitrary and often irrational borders delineated by the colonial powers during the partition of Africa would end in chaos. There were appeals that Africa should overcome its colonial dismemberment by forging associations larger than the new independent states. Nkrumah was a passionate pan-Africanist, and Senghor had tried in vain to create a federation of Francophone nations from the pieces of the vast French West African empire. However these made little impact, and the commitment to recognize the political boundaries inherited from the colonial powers was ratified by the Organization of African Unity (OAU). Founded by thirty-two leaders of independent African states on May 25, 1963, the OAU was the visible manifestation of the pan-Africanism of W. E. B. Du Bois in the early decades of the twentieth century. Now, during the decade of independence and hope, it was to promote the unity and solidarity of the African states, to eradicate all forms of colonialism in Africa, to encourage continental cooperation, and to defend the sovereignty and territorial integrity of each independent state. With its headquarters in Addis Ababa the OAU has had only modest success in carrying out its mission when trying to reconcile the competing claims and ambitions today of its fifty-two member states, despite the reform of the organization into the African Union (AU) in 2002.

By the late 1960s the enthusiasm and optimism of the decade of hope was ebbing like a receding tide. In addition to the military coups d'état there were three bloody internal secessionist movements in Sudan, Nigeria, and the Congo. In 1955 the southern Sudanese started an insurrection against the domination of the Arabic-speaking northerners in control of the national government. By the time peace was finally concluded by the signing of the Comprehensive Peace Agreement (CPA) in January 2005, after twenty-two years of violent conflict, over 2 million southern Sudanese were dead and another 4 million displaced refugees, and the southern Sudan had been reduced to a devastated and impoverished region. In 1966 Odumegwu Ojukwu (b. 1933) and his Igbo followers in eastern Nigeria seceded to proclaim the short-lived Republic of Biafra from 1967 to 1970, which was forcefully reunited with Nigeria at a cost of over a million lives. After the assassination of Patrice Lumumba in 1961 the Congo disintegrated and the copper-rich province of Katanga seceded under Moïse Tshombe (1917–1969), supported by the United States. The chaos allowed a former officer of the Belgian Force Publique, Joseph Mobutu, to seize power. With the support of the United States, he would remain the dictator of the Congo for the next three decades.

Although these secessionist struggles riveted the bewildered attention of the outside world, the dramatic decline of the economy of African states attracted less attention. International economic conditions had devalued many African agricultural exports. State bureaucracies, which had become bloated by politicians handing out jobs to supporters, were imposing a heavy burden on fragile revenues. African economies plunged dramatically with the onset of the global recession in 1973. In that year the Arab–Israeli war provided the opportunity for the Organization of Petroleum Exporting Countries (OPEC) to monopolize the price and production of crude oil, dramatically increasing the cost of oil and creating a shortage that had a particularly devastating effect on the economies of the African states which did not produce their own petroleum. African agricultural exports faced a shrinking demand at a time when African states had to import petroleum at greatly inflated prices. The economic crisis that ensued after 1973 fully revealed the fundamental limitations of the African states that had attained independence during the 1960s. In every state, democracy had been abandoned in favor of autocracy, justified by the demon of tribalism. Foreign patrons and businessmen evaluated African nations based on stability and the malleability of the ruling class, often secured by grotesque human rights violations. When a second wave of African independence movements arose in the mid-1970s, it came in a context that was far removed from the optimism, confidence, and jubilation captured by the newsreel cameraman at the celebrations in Accra in 1957. The decade of hope had become the decade of disillusion.

25 Cold war Africa

The decade of hope in Africa gave way to two decades of crisis. Much of the optimism that had greeted independence evaporated as economic development stalled, people began to experience a steady decline in their standard of living, and African states faced new challenges to their stability. There had been warnings of the coming crises almost from the moment colonial flags were run down their poles. The appearance of a one-party state in Ghana, the bloody and failed secession movements in the Katanga (Congo) and Biafra (Nigeria), and the massacre of ethnic minorities shortly after independence in Rwanda were all the harbingers of future political conflict and humanitarian disasters elsewhere in the continent. During the 1970s most African states were racked by some form of insurrection, coup d'état, or civil war. These internal conflicts continued in the 1980s, often accompanied by drought, epidemic, and famine. During these two decades a second era of decolonization developed in southern Africa, as white rule in Portuguese Africa, Rhodesia, and eventually in South Africa came to an end. At the same time the states that had achieved independence during the 1950s and 1960s were overwhelmed by a bewildering array of political and economic problems in which ethnic – or "tribal" – identities emerged to challenge national unity. When governments proved incapable, or unwilling, to deal effectively with these challenges, opposition to political ineptitude, tyranny, and corruption coalesced along ethnic lines. The specter of tribal separatism hung over many African states from their inception, and some leaders used the threat as an excuse to dismantle democratic institutions and suppress dissent. Minorities that could not be suborned or coopted by the ruling party frequently faced discrimination, persecution, and, in some cases, ethnic cleansing.

During the two decades after 1973 many governments proved incapable or unwilling to provide good government for their subjects, and opposition to the political ineptitude, corruption, and tyranny divided many of the independent states along ethnic lines. Ethnic identities were invoked as a means of resisting government policies, insuring security in ethnic cohesion, or even mobilizing a community for secession. The specter of separatist movements spread rapidly throughout Africa after independence, and in response those politicians who had most benefited from the system left by the colonial powers denounced tribalism as the enemy of the nation, as a means of justifying their dismantling democratic institutions in order to mold competing ethnicities into one-party states. Those ethnic minorities they could not suborn were subject to discrimination which was justified in the name of combating tribal resistance to national sovereignty.

Because Westerners – Americans and Europeans alike – saw Africans as living in timeless "tribal" groupings, they tended to turn a blind eye to the excesses of African rulers undertaken in the name of national unity. The ethnic hostilities of the 1970s and 1980s, however, developed in a new environment. During these decades Africa experienced a severe depression in its export products, spiraling inflation, unprecedented population growth, new epidemic diseases, political corruption, and the destabilizing influences of cold war politics. In the cauldron of these crises, tribal solidarity offered the individual reliable and familiar allies in the competition for dwindling resources and communal security.

These ethnic identities often had deep roots in African history, but they had been accentuated and made concrete under European rule. Colonial scholars identified hundreds of discrete "tribes," each of which was ascribed distinctive characteristics. Colonial administrative and educational policies turned these tribal identities into realities which live on in Africa today. However, tribalism is a form of identity, like nationalism, whose relevance in most African communities is a product of the colonial and post-colonial eras.

During Africa's first decade of independence, few observers anticipated the coming crises. Their optimism was informed by a boom in the world economy that appeared to promise prosperity to the new nations. In Zambia, a decade of rising copper prices filled the coffers of the new state. In the Ivory Coast global demand for cocoa produced steady economic growth from independence until the mid-1970s. In much of southern Africa growing demand for maize and other food crops encouraged the expansion of indigenous agricultural production, enabling farmers to command a price worth growing a surplus. This economic bubble, however, was very fragile, as future prosperity depended on continued demand for these commodities. Many governments invested the profits from the boom in large-scale development projects, many of which proved to be poorly planned and ultimately unprofitable. Zaire (now the Democratic Republic of Congo) and Ghana used the revenues from commodity exports to invest in heavy industry. In Zaire state funds were poured into the creation of a steel industry that proved economically unsustainable and was eventually shut down. Ghana invested heavily in hydro-electric power and an aluminum-processing industry that proved economically uncompetitive. Zambia spent the revenues from copper sales on unproductive extensive social programs and infrastructure. All over Africa independent governments plowed revenues into modernizing projects that emulated the levels of infrastructure and industrial development of their former colonial masters. They were ambitious – indeed, visionary – plans that could not be supported solely by an agriculture whose development was studiously ignored.

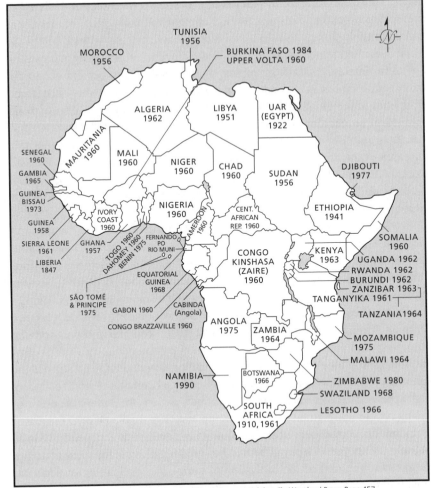

Source: Robert W. July, *History of the African Peoples,* 4th ed., Prospect Heights, Ill.: Waveland Press, Page 457.

Map 25.1 *Independent Africa.*

Virtually all the independent African states failed to invest in agriculture despite the fact that it was practiced by the vast majority of their citizens, and was the major source of state revenues and the pillar of their economies. The ruling African elite viewed industry and heavily capitalized farming as the key to economic growth, a bias that they had inherited from the colonial rulers. In their estimation, peasant farming was traditional and backward, and though small-scale agriculture was the backbone of most African economies, it did not feature prominently in most economic planning. Consequently, politicians and civil servants sought to extract revenues from agriculture through price controls, a revival of the unpopular colonial marketing boards. This allowed governments to pay artificially low prices to farmers and export the crop at the highest possible price. In the short term this provided governments with much-needed revenue, though the long-term effect was to discourage farmers from expanding production.

Not all the new independent African states neglected agricultural development. Having no mineral resources, Kenya and the Ivory Coast recognized that agriculture was the driving force of their economies and could best be developed by intensive capitalist agriculture – large, scientifically organized plantations that would be more productive and profitable. Under the leadership of President Julius Nyerere Tanzania adopted economic policies that sought to support peasant farmers while stimulating agricultural production by creating planned villages called *ujamaa vijijini* (Kiswahili, "familyhood of villages").

Whether capitalist, collective, or peasant, the farmers of independent Africa found themselves increasingly dependent upon new, imported seeds and fertilizers which promised to produce greater and more profitable yields on the same amount of land. In the declining decades of the colonial state, particularly after the Second World War, European agricultural officials had sought to introduce scientific techniques into traditional agricultural practices – with mixed success, and often in the face of local hostility. After 1960 the Green Revolution had begun to transform global agricultural productivity. New strains of genetically improved seeds and the application of synthetic fertilizers combined with increased mechanization to dramatically expand agricultural productivity in Asia and the Americas. Despite much optimism the Green Revolution failed to dramatically expand the output of African agriculture. Differences in soil, climate, and plant disease combined with the dearth of capital and technological expertise to thwart the widespread adoption of these innovations. Thus in Africa the chief effect of the Green Revolution was to lower the cost of imported foodstuffs. This benefited the state treasury, selling African export crops at high prices, but it gradually transformed self-sufficient farmers into cash-crop producers vulnerable to a fickle world market.

In retrospect, it appears that African politicians, the African elite, and foreign experts, both in and out of Africa, learned the wrong lesson from the first decade of independence. African leaders expected capital earned from foreign exports to stimulate the creation of an industrial economy that would insure genuine political and economic independence from the West. Ironically, this strategy not only failed to generate increasing autonomy but dragged the African economies into greater dependency on Western investment and expertise. This enthusiasm for industrial development was a logical response to the colonial experience. African leaders perceived, quite correctly, that the conquest of Africa by Europe, the subsequent half century of colonial rule, and the dominant role of Western influence in post-independent Africa was made possible to a great extent by their vibrant industrial economies. What they failed to realize was that the chimerical attempt to produce similar economies in Africa would ultimately increase the reliance of Africa on Western imports, assistance, and skills.

The year 1973 was a turning-point in world economic history, and particularly for independent Africa. When the Arab members of the Organization of Petroleum Exporting Countries (OPEC) suspended oil shipments to certain Western countries in retaliation for their support for Israel during the Arab–Israel War of October 1973, most African states firmly supported the embargo. The economies of Europe and the United States were sufficiently resilient to accommodate the loss of Arab oil. The African states were not, forty of them being net importers of oil. The price quadrupled, making the price of African exports no longer competitive in the world market and the cost of imported food, upon which most of the Africans had become dependent, increasingly prohibitive. Moreover, the Arab exporting countries did little to assist their African brothers who supported the embargo. The Arab states half-heartedly offered some financial assistance, mostly to countries with Muslim majorities, but that did little to assuage the bitter sense of betrayal felt by many African leaders and their citizens.

The oil embargo soon produced worldwide inflation, to which the economies of the African states were particularly vulnerable. They were dependent on a handful of exported cash crops or mineral resources whose sale was exposed to the fluctuating prices on the world market. In good years this gave the illusion of sustained growth; in bad years it could plunge the economy into a severe recession. As the world price for export crops such as cocoa and coffee plummeted and the price of transportation drove the costs of imported foods higher, many Africans could no longer afford imported food. Destitute farmers soon gravitated to the cities to swell the ranks of the unemployed, creating social problems that strained the resources of local and state governments. There were some commodities that remained profitable during the oil crisis, such as gold and copper, but revenues from these exports did little to alleviate the plight of rural farmers.

Not all African countries had to import oil. Shortly after independence large fields of petroleum were discovered in Angola, Nigeria, and Gabon. Although Angola and Nigeria had their own state-owned firms, oil production throughout the subcontinent was in the hands of foreign companies – French, British, Dutch, and American – and petroleum proved to be a lucrative export commodity; but it failed to bring sustainable or equitable economic development to any of these African countries. It contributed to the collapse of the agricultural-export economy as resources were transferred from that sector to those producing an international commodity. Declining agricultural exports drastically reduced the income of the small farmers; oil revenues went directly to the government for public spending and private pillage, creating a massive redistribution of income. Nor could the unemployed be absorbed into the petroleum industry, for it requires relatively few employees. Moreover, the urban elites who profited from oil were not about to divert its revenue into the traditional agricultural economy. Finally, petroleum revenues failed to stimulate significant economic growth in oil-producing countries. In the twentieth century the discovery of oil was regarded as an unmitigated blessing; many in the twenty-first century now regard it as a curse.

If Africans and non-Africans could manipulate, for better or for worse, their national economies, nature imperiously controlled climate. During the period of decolonization and the first decade of independence Africa enjoyed above-average rainfall. This decade of expanding agricultural production culminated in the onset of a multi-year drought that blistered Africa for twenty years during the 1970s and 1980s. Drought begins when the rains fail in successive years so that the seed corn is eaten, leaving only death by starvation and disease that ravages those too weak to resist. Drought contributed to desertification, but this did not become a major subject of environmental concern until the droughts of the 1970s as the need for firewood and cultivation in marginal lands with now little rain destroyed a landscape that could not be easily restored. Acute famines and several million deaths were experienced in Ethiopia (1984–1985), Mali (1970–1974; 1984–1985), Mauritania (1980s), and Mozambique (1984–1985). The effects of the two decades of drought, particularly in 1984–1985, were certainly aggravated by the increasing growth of population that had pushed African cultivators into marginal lands made vulnerable by the lack of rain. The specter of famine produced massive amounts of international assistance, and the establishment of agencies in Europe and the United States to investigate drought and its impact on the rural African population. Africa's droughts also stoked fierce debates over global warming and the political economy of underdevelopment. In the meantime African rulers struggled to combat drought with their limited resources or, in countries such as Sudan, ignored its presence altogether.

The central role of the state in economic life – a holdover from the colonial era – posed additional problems for fragile economies. Economic life in the colonial world had been dominated by the European administration. The distribution of land and labor, the pricing of commodities, and the import and export of goods all passed through the hands of colonial officials and the African civil servants who succeeded them after independence. Since African countries inherited little capital upon independence, most financial investment came from abroad. With all investment being funneled through the state, it was much easier to enrich oneself through a career in the civil service than as an entrepreneur exposed to considerable risk in the private sector. Consequently, the wealthiest and most powerful figures in Africa since independence have been those civil servants known as "gate-keepers" who occupied positions that gave them the authority to approve private investment, foreign aid, and humanitarian assistance and channel it to favored communities, industries, and regions. The opportunities to augment a minimal government salary were innumerable and often proved irresistible.

African armies also provided a further drag on economic development. In the multi-ethnic composition of the independent African states the army was the only visible national institution. Not surprisingly, most of the coups d'état in Africa during the turbulent 1970s and 1980s were carried out by army officers on the pretext of bringing an end to the misgovernment of incompetent politicians. They, rather than political parties, religious brotherhoods, or tribes, could speak for the nation. Since their seizure of power had been carried out at the point of a gun, however, it could only be continued by the support of the troops to sustain the new military rulers. This was accomplished in the old-fashioned way by looting the national treasury to enlarge the armed forces, reward the troops, and bestow privileges of land and concessions on their officers. Historically, civil servants and soldiers are the least productive members of society. They contribute virtually nothing to the economic livelihood of the state and are a drag on investment for education, health, and social welfare by consuming a huge portion of the limited national revenue.

The unique positions of the gate-keeper class and the soldiers explains in large part why African states have found themselves plagued by what Western observers call corruption. In some cases the theft of the public purse was particularly egregious, such as the billions stolen from Zaire by the dictator Mobutu Sese Seko (1930–1997). Many more bureaucrats and politicians used their positions to steer foreign aid into pet projects as a reward to their ethnic or regional followers. Undoubtedly despoiling public treasuries demonstrated a venality that was unconscionable by any standard, but much of the corruption identified by Western observers occurred because of the failure to establish a national identity that could claim a greater fidelity than lineage, or "tribe." The Western concept of loyalty to the state over all other associations and institutions evolved through many centuries. Historians have associated the process by which the peoples of European and American states came to recognize the primacy of national identities with a series of significant developments; religious reformation, the rise of print capitalism, literacy, and the nationalist struggles of the nineteenth century following the French Revolution were all unknown to Africa except for the transformation of exuberant European nationalism into imperialism and colonialism. The process of nation-building in African states was telescoped into the four decades following the First World War. This was hardly sufficient time for African leaders, let alone their peoples, to accept a national loyalty greater than the personal and psychological security of clan, lineage, and tribe. Labeling the distribution of spoils of decolonization to these deep-seated identities as corruption obscures the important African historical roots of that phenomenon.

In southern Africa the economic crises of the early 1970s were exacerbated by the liberation struggles against the governments of states ruled by intransigent white minorities. In Rhodesia in 1965 white settlers led by Ian Smith (b. 1919) had severed their ties with Great Britain by a Unilateral Declaration of Independence (UDI) rather than implement democratic reforms. During the next fifteen years Rhodesia would remain an international pariah, recognized only by South Africa and Portugal. In Mozambique and Angola Portugal desperately clung to power, fearing that the loss of its African colonies would further impoverish what was already one of the poorest nations in Europe. In South Africa control of the government by the white supremacist National Party showed no signs of faltering. All these white settler regimes readily cooperated with one another to combat the growing internal threat to their security and the gathering criticisms against them by the international community. Landlocked Rhodesia evaded international sanctions with the assistance of its neighbor Mozambique, which provided much-needed petroleum by rail from its Indian Ocean port at Beira. South Africa could count on the Rhodesian Front government to suppress the activities of the African National Congress (ANC) on its northern border, and Portugal received military and logistical support from both the Rhodesian and South African governments. These regimes also benefited to some extent from tacit support from the United States, which preferred the capitalist, anti-communist settler leadership to the socialism espoused by African nationalists like Samora Machel (1933–1986), Nelson Mandela (b. 1918), and Robert Mugabe (b. 1924).

The first cracks in this edifice appeared in 1974 when events in Europe precipitated the sudden dissolution of Portugal's ancient African empire. Led by incompetent generals, ill-equipped, and hopelessly demoralized, the Portuguese army realized they were fighting a losing war against the nationalist guerrillas – in Angola the Popular Movement for the Liberation of Angola (MPLA), the National Front for the Liberation of Angola (FNLA), and the National Union for the Total Independence of Angola (UNITA); in Mozambique the Frente de Libertação de Moçambique (FRELIMO). In Portugal in April 1974 the Armed Forces Movement of young officers, determined to restore democracy to Portugal, overthrew the fascist government in Lisbon and granted independence to Mozambique in September 1974 and Angola in November 1975.

Independence left Angola and Mozambique in a far more precarious position than those African states that had become independent in the 1950s and 1960s. The Sudan, Ghana, Nigeria, and even some of the former French African colonies had had the better part of a decade to prepare for independence and could rely on the expertise of Western technocrats and financial credits from their governments to help them through the transition to independence. Angola and Mozambique could expect little assistance from their sullen former colonial ruler, and certainly none from the white settler governments of neighboring Rhodesia and South Africa, to restore their war-ravaged countryside and resettle vast numbers of refugees. The sudden decision by Portugal to leave Angola and Mozambique, similar to the abrupt departure of Belgium from the Congo in 1960, left behind rival armed liberation movements that proved incapable of resolving their ideological and ethnic differences.

When the Portuguese withdrew, Angola erupted into a three-cornered civil war among the MPLA, FLNA, and UNITA, each of which sought to exploit the cold war rivalries of the United States and the Soviet Union for weapons, financing, and even at times troops. The withdrawal of American aid in December

1975 soon marginalized the FNLA and the solicitation of South African troops discredited UNITA, enabling the MPLA, supported by the Soviet Union and Cuba, to secure its traditional base of power in the strategic capital of Luanda. The MPLA government was soon recognized by most African and European countries, and President Agostinho Neto (1922–1979) sought to implement the Marxist-Leninist principles of the MPLA and its patrons and to instill a sense of Angolan national identity. His optimism was premature, for Angola was turned into a cold war battleground when the United States provided extensive aid to UNITA, the South Africans occupied the southern borderlands, and 50,000 Cuban mercenaries arrived to reorganize the Angolan (MPLA) army and air force. After long and acrimonious negotiations a peace agreement was finally reached among all the parties in 1988, based on the withdrawal of Cuban troops in return for South Africa accepting the independence of Namibia.

The independent FRELIMO government of Samora Machel in Mozambique was similarly challenged by an opposition movement, the Mozambique National Resistance Movement (RENAMO). At first armed and supported by the white Rhodesian Front, RENAMO became a client of South Africa when Rhodesia became Zimbabwe in 1980. The civil war between these rivals dragged on for several years, against a backdrop of economic collapse and devastating drought. Exhausted and without patrons, the two sides were forced to enter into negotiations in 1990, and ultimately signed a peace accord in 1992. The People's Republic of Mozambique peacefully became, simply, the Republic of Mozambique.

The independence of the Portuguese colonies had immediately threatened settler rule in neighboring Rhodesia. No longer having access to the Indian Ocean and exposed on its eastern and western borders to hostile neighbors willing to harbor insurgent guerrilla armies, the Rhodesian Front could no longer sustain itself. The insurgency in Rhodesia had become ever more militant after 1973 when the Zimbabwe African National Union (ZANU) launched a full-scale war of liberation, a second Chimurenga, against white rule from their bases in Mozambique and Zambia. In 1976 ZANU allied with its rival, the Zimbabwe African People's Union (ZAPU), to form the Patriotic Front (PF) and waged a bitter guerrilla war, mostly in the rural areas, until September 1979 when Great Britain brokered a ceasefire that led to negotiations and an independent Zimbabwe in 1980. The subsequent democratic elections exposed the old ethnic rivalries that divided the colony and now independent state. ZANU, led by Robert Mugabe and representing a majority of Zimbabwe's Africans, was predominantly a Shona organization. ZAPU, led by Joshua Nkomo (1918–1999), was mainly composed of the Ndebele who had invaded and conquered much of the region in the mid-nineteenth century. Democratic elections in 1980 swept Mugabe to power, but Zimbabweans came to view ZANU as committed only to the interests of the Shona-speaking majority. State resources were channeled into the eastern regions where the Shona population was concentrated. Criticism that this strategy neglected the poorer western regions dominated by ZAPU's Ndebele minority precipitated brutal government reprisals that led to the intimidation, torture, and murder of thousands of Ndebele speakers in the name of "national unity."

In states racked by ethnic tensions, political corruption, and deteriorating economic conditions, many of the governments of Africa fell prey to new military coups. Many of the resulting military regimes soon proved dysfunctional and unstable, and between 1960 and 1979 a total of fifty-nine African rulers were either toppled or assassinated.[1] These who avoided this fate often did so through the influence of powerful foreign patrons. The United States helped to sustain President Jaafar Numayri's regime (1969–1985) in the Sudan and the kleptocracy of Mobutu Sese Seko in Zaire (1960–1997). France had supported the 1966–1979 regime of the self-styled emperor of the Central African Republic, Jean-Bédel Bokassa (1921–1996), until his blatant atrocities, including the arrest, torture, and killing of women and children, could no longer be ignored by the French, whose troops forced him into exile. Great Britain at first assisted Uganda's notorious dictator Idi Amin Dada (1925–2003), who was a veteran of the British King's African Rifles, until he expelled and seized the property of Uganda's relatively affluent community of 50,000 Asians, most of whom held British passports. Not all military dictators were consumed by the avarice of Mobutu, the megalomania of Bokassa, or the mental instability of Idi Amin. Flight Lieutenant Jerry Rawlings (b. 1947) of Ghana undertook two coups, one in 1979 of a few months that purged the army before peacefully handing over the government to an elected civilian, and another in 1981. Although accused by his opponents of extensive human rights abuses, he remained sufficiently popular to win a free presidential election in 1992 and reelection in 1996.

Cold war patrons also proved eager to aid those who promised to further their economic or ideological interests. Those African leaders who were staunchly conservative, such as Félix Houphouët-Boigny (1905–1993) of the Ivory Coast, could depend on Paris and Washington to ignore their autocratic tendencies. States that turned to Moscow or the capitals of the Eastern Bloc – such as Guinea or Congo-Brazzaville – could count on their assistance against the opposition movements supported by the West. Ethiopia became a prominent example of cold war rivalries transported to Africa. There Western powers, and particularly the United States, had long provided assistance and strongly supported the early efforts at modernization by the autocratic but aging emperor Haile Selassie (1892–1975). Exacerbated by a dynamic rebellion in Eritrea, the collapse of the economy precipitated by the OPEC oil crisis of 1973, and drought and famine in the overpopulated north that the government largely ignored, the growing dissent against the emperor culminated in the coup of 1974 carried out by a Coordinating Committee of the Armed Forces, known as the Derg (Amharic, "committee"), led by Major Haile Mariam Mengistu (b. 1942). By 1977 in order to transform Ethiopia from its backwardness Mengistu and the Derg had embraced a Marxist-Leninist ideology and had

[1] "A Survey of Sub-Saharan Africa," *Economist*, Jan. 17–14, 2004, p. 5.

become a client of the Soviet Union. Ethiopia remained a staunch ally of the Eastern Bloc and the recipient of generous aid and arms until the final defeat of the Ethiopian army by the Ethiopian People's Revolutionary Democratic Front (EPRDF) and Mengistu's flight on May 21, 1991 into exile in Zimbabwe.

At the end of the 1980s Africa remained a pawn in the aggressive game between cold war rivals. Most of its governments were burdened with massive foreign debt, and most of its people were experiencing a depressing and steady decline in their standard of living. Nigeria and Zaire, two of the wealthiest and most populous states on the continent, were also among the most corrupt and autocratic. South Africa, the third economic giant in Africa, remained in the control of its white elite, which showed little interest in sharing its economic and political power. Few Africans participated in politics in any kind of meaningful way. Famine stalked the Horn of Africa, drought threatened the Sahel and southern Africa, and the HIV/AIDS pandemic was just beginning to be the major new addition to Africa's long list of disease. In the world beyond Africa, Afro-pessimism had eclipsed the decade of hope. The shocking climax to the cold war era in Africa came in 1994 when 800,000 Rwandans were murdered in a paroxysm of ethnically motivated violence. This catastrophe had deep roots in the region's history (see chapter 8). But it was equally the result of colonial manipulation of tribal identity, interference by foreign powers, and the unraveling of the old cold war order.

However, with the end of the cold war, there were tentative signs that change was once again in the wind. The horrors of the Rwandan genocide transpired in the same year that Nelson Mandela became South Africa's first democratically elected president. With the end of the cold war aging dictators could no longer rely on their foreign patrons to turn a blind eye to their human rights abuses and corruption for ideological reasons. The 1990s fostered a cautious optimism that the worst had passed, and that the change of the decade would usher in a new era in the history of Africa.

Further reading

Cooper, Frederick, *Africa since 1940: The Past and Present*, Cambridge: Cambridge University Press, 2002

Gourevitch, Philip, *We Wish to Inform you that Tomorrow we will be Killed with our Families: Stories from Rwanda*, London: Picador, 1999

Legum, Colin, *Africa since Independence*, Bloomington: Indiana University Press, 1999

Meredith, Martin, *The Fate of Africa: From the Hopes of Freedom to the Heart of Despair*, London: Free Press, 2005

Nugent, Paul, *Africa since Independence: A Comparative History*, London: Palgrave Macmillan, 2004

26 Africa at the beginning of the twenty-first century

After traversing more than three millennia of the African past it is time to pause and take stock, to look back in history as well as forward, at the beginning of the twenty-first century. Over the past half-century scholars have scoured archaeological sites, colonial archives, published works, and oral traditions, utilized social science methodologies – anthropology, linguistics, and demography – and developed an appreciation of African art, music, and literature, to construct a new paradigm for understanding the continent's past. Readers of this text will hopefully have recognized the themes in the last several thousand years of the African past that thread their way through the text into the twenty-first century. They are indeed the themes of this book, and they will most certainly reappear – in different forms, to be sure – in the twenty-first century.

Environment continues to shape the lives of the African peoples. As seen in the previous pages, population has long been tied to the interaction between humans and the unique African environment. In relation to its landmass Africa has, historically, been underpopulated. Two thousand years ago Africa south of the Sahara had only an estimated population one-fifth that of China or the Roman empire. During the next 1,500 years this ratio continued to decline so that by 1500 Africa contained less than an estimated 15 percent of the world's human beings. At the beginning of the twentieth century the population of Africa accounted for only about 1 percent of the 2 billion people inhabiting the earth. The reasons for this low rate of growth remain unclear to this day. Was this creeping rate of reproduction caused by a harsh climate, disease, poor soils, conflict, and slavery? One can only reflect, and suggest that the reasons lie in the complex interaction between humanity and nature in Africa.

Over the last century the demographic trajectory of Africa has changed dramatically. Though the early colonial era encouraged dramatic population loss in some regions, between 1900 and 1960, the year of independence from colonial rule, the African population grew at an unheard-of rate of 2.3 percent, from an estimated 142 million to 300 million. This pace continued after independence, as between 1960 and 2000 the African population more than doubled to over an estimated 600 million people, and is expected to more than double again in the first half of the twenty-first century. Today sub-Saharan Africa has the highest birth and growth rates of any continent, and people of sub-Saharan Africa represent approximately 10 percent of the world's population. When the global population growth is predicted to come to a virtual

Box 26.1 African history and the academy

The rush to decolonization in the late 1950s ushered in a new era in the academic study of Africa's past. Under colonial rule African history had been for the most part confined to the study of Europeans on the continent. Academic works that focused on the African experience – written by curious European administrators and Western-educated Africans – were for the most part ethnographic descriptions of contemporary societies. Within the mainstream of academia Africa was believed to be a region which had no history, or at least had no history that could be reclaimed. This position was stated forcefully by the English historian Hugh Trevor-Roper, who wrote of Africans in 1965: "To study their history would be to amuse ourselves with the unrewarding gyrations of barbarous tribes in picturesque but irrelevant corners of the globe."[1] Although intellectuals throughout the African diaspora had pioneered the study of African history in the nineteenth century, the doors of the academic establishment remained closed to them until the final decades of the colonial era.

After the Second World War a handful of scholars in Europe and the United States began to treat African history as a subject of intellectual inquiry that was no less feasible or valid than that of any other world region. In 1948 Northwestern University in Illinois established the first interdisciplinary African studies program. In the 1950s philanthropic organizations began funding the growth of African studies programs at several American universities. Having emerged from the Second World War as a superpower with a growing interest in international affairs, the United States government began funding African studies centers in the 1950s as well. The passage of the National Defense Education Act of 1958 included a provision (Title VI) for the funding of African studies at Howard University, UCLA, and Michigan State. The Act was later expanded to support programs at other large research institutions, including the University of Florida, the University of Wisconsin-Madison, and Indiana University. The growth of interest in African studies in the United States is reflected in the establishment of the African Studies Association in 1957, an academic organization which held its first meeting in 1958. While this expanded institutional support proved a boon for the broader field of African studies, it ignored the historically black colleges, which had been in the vanguard of establishing African studies curricula.

Great Britain, with its long imperial history, had several universities which taught African languages, geography, and culture by the 1930s. The most famous was the School of Oriental and African Studies (SOAS), which had been founded during the First World War. After the Second

---

[1] Hugh Trevor-Roper, *The Rise of Christian Europe*, New York: Harcourt, Brace & World, 1965, p. 9.

Box 26.1 (continued)

World War African studies at British institutions expanded the number of faculty positions focused on studying African – as opposed to colonial – history. The appointment of Roland Oliver as a lecturer in Tribal East Africa in 1948 was a watershed in the history of SOAS, and pointed to growth in positions in African history that would continue at British universities into the 1960s. A crucial moment in the emergence of the field was the founding of the *Journal of African History* in 1959 by Cambridge University Press.

Today much of the study of Africa's past takes place on the campuses of large American research universities. Students interested in African history require support for language training and travel to the continent that only well-funded programs can provide. Economic crises in African countries over the past several decades have driven many African students to Europe, Canada, and the United States to receive graduate training in African history and archaeology. In recent years African history in Great Britain has suffered from the cost-cutting that has plagued higher education throughout the country. Though African studies in the United States has experienced some of the challenges of British institutions, federal funding remains relatively strong. African history has become a 'mainstream' field of history, and is taught at virtually all of the top institutions of higher education in the United States.

halt at the end of the twenty-first century, Africa will account for one-fifth of its people – ironically, the same percentage of the world's population it possessed 2,000 years ago. Was this explosion the result of advances in tropical medicine, personal hygiene, public health, the relative stability of the colonial state, the cultural and economic need to have ever more children, or the limited but demonstrable development of the colonial and independent African economies? Just as one can reflect and suggest the reasons for near-stagnant growth in 2,000 years, this extraordinary surge in the number of Africans since 1900 has been a theme that has confronted the reader during the latter chapters of this history, and presents today one of the numerous challenges for Africa in the twenty-first century. Despite its economic and political problems Africa will remain demographically vibrant well into the twenty-first century.

Demography has been closely connected to disease, which retains a demonstrable influence on contemporary Africa. When one is sick, it is extremely difficult to provide for oneself or one's family, or contribute to the society in which one lives, and throughout the millennia Africans have been afflicted with a variety of deadly diseases. Undoubtedly, advancements in the field of tropical medicine over the last century have permitted the successful diagnosis of the sources and transmission of the four deadly parasitical diseases – sleeping sickness, bilharzia, kala azar, and malaria – and have discovered ways to prevent numerous viral diseases. These cures have been accompanied by campaigns of inoculation and eradication in which individuals, non-governmental organizations, and the World Health Organization (WHO) of the United Nations have played a major role. Some formerly devastating diseases – yellow fever, onchoceriasis (river blindness), and polio – have been drastically reduced or virtually eradicated. Nevertheless, the largest killer disease in Africa, malaria, has defied through its many mutations the massive attempts to find a vaccine like that which has controlled yellow fever. However, recent breakthroughs in malaria research, in part funded by billionaire Bill Gates, provide hope of introducing a malaria vaccine within the next decade.

The struggle against disease in Africa has been made more complicated by the appearance of a new and deadly disease in the last decades of the twentieth century, the virus known as the human immunodeficiency virus (HIV), which causes the acquired immune deficiency syndrome (AIDS). The first reports of the HI virus emerged in North America in 1981, and it was first isolated in France in 1983. The two HI viruses causing AIDS are believed to have their origin among non-human primates in Africa, from where they spread throughout the world. By the beginning of the twenty-first century there were an estimated 25 to 28 million Africans infected with the HI virus. Its rapid spread throughout the continent – some 3 to 4 million Africans are infected annually – has resulted in death from AIDS of an estimated two-and-a-half million Africans in 2003, and the prediction of a steady annual increase in that number. Since the incubation period of AIDS is long, the disease lives, and is spread, among seemingly healthy populations where the presence of the HI viruses is very high, particularly in the cities of Africa – Kinshasa, Nairobi, Cape Town, Lusaka, and Dar es-Salaam. In some regions of eastern and southern Africa an estimated one-quarter to one-third of the population are considered to be HIV positive. Here the HI viruses are rapidly circulated among the emerging young and middle-aged elite – the teachers, doctors, civil servants – whose skills are essential to the development of the state. In an ever more mobile Africa HIV/AIDS has spread inexorably into the more rural areas where hunger and famine go hand in hand with AIDS, each reinforcing the other. Hungry people deprived of their immunity to disease become vulnerable to Africa's infectious killer diseases such as tuberculosis and a wide variety of intestinal fungal infections, and sick people cannot grow food. Moreover, AIDS is unrelenting, for it kills slowly, draining the limited resources of those who must care for its victims. The control of AIDS and its cure have become the principal health challenge for Africa in the twenty-first century, and although at first slow to recognize the extent of HIV/AIDS, African states and the international community are now beginning to mount major campaigns to combat the pandemic.

Though urbanization is an important theme in twentieth-century Africa, agriculture has dominated life in the continent over the past several thousand years, and in the twenty-first century it will certainly continue to do so. Despite the river of migrants that flowed into the cities of the colonial states becoming a flood after independence in 1960, Africa remains agrarian and rural, and 80 percent of the people till the soil and pasture their herds. The economies of African states are and will undoubtedly continue to be dependent upon agriculture in the twenty-first century. Historically this has been the consistent theme of development from the beginning of the domestication of crops and animals that spread throughout Africa before the Christian era. Millet, rice, yams, and particularly sorghum became the principal food crops of Africa, supplementing wheat, barley, and lentils from the Fertile Crescent. Their cultivation was made more productive by the iron hoe and the domestication of cattle, goats, and sheep in areas free from the tsetse fly. The revolution in African agriculture came from the New World in the sixteenth century, when the Portuguese carried maize (corn) and cassava (manioc) to Africa where it rapidly spread – maize in the savanna lands, cassava in the tropical rainforests – to become the principal food crops today. After the Second World War the Green Revolution attempted to improve crop yields throughout Asia and Africa through the introduction of new hybrid crops, chemically based synthetic fertilizers, and greater application of motorized agricultural equipment. Though it had a dramatic effect on agriculture in some world regions (such as India), it ultimately failed to revolutionize African agriculture. The failure of the Green Revolution – which required technical expertise, capital, and transportation infrastructure that most African states lacked – reflects the challenges that face agriculture on the continent in the twenty-first century. Recent studies by international organizations tell a grim story of exhausted soils and declining agricultural productivity. As African populations grow they will place increasing pressure on the continent's depleted agricultural infrastructure.

Africa's mineral wealth will also continue to be an important theme in the twenty-first century. Mining is an ancient art in Africa, dating back to the gold of Pharaonic Egypt, to the copper of the savanna kingdoms, and the gold of the Akan forests and of Great Zimbabwe. The rich resources of Africa's mines will continue to produce, but their labor demands will only employ a small proportion of the population. They will also continue to draw the avarice of outsiders, as foreign governments, bandits, and war-lords will continue to bring instability to the diamond-rich countries of the Democratic Republic of Congo, Angola, and Sierra Leone. Since the 1950s petroleum has become a major source of revenue for some African countries, and new oil fields are discovered on the West African coast almost annually. However, like the mineral wealth of other nations, the petroleum windfall has, and will continue to create many internal problems over the sharing of this resource. Nor will the petroleum industry bring much-needed employment, as once wells are drilled and productive, the industry requires relatively few workers to maintain its facilities.

The most vital and scarce resource, however, is not petroleum, but water. There can be no life on land without fresh water, and consequently no agriculture or animals to sustain the human race. Moreover, if control of fresh water, insures control of the land that depends upon it and the people who derive their livelihood from it. Theoretically, Africans should have ample water from the vast reservoir of the South Atlantic whose moisture is carried diagonally across Africa to create the tropical rainforests of West Africa, the Congo Basin, the northern savanna, and the well-watered uplands of the Lake Plateau and the highlands of Ethiopia. The coasts of East Africa and southern Africa receive their rainfall from the Indian Ocean, which is much more irregular than that from the Atlantic. The Africans, however, have yet to construct the schemes required to keep the rainfall on the land before it flows to the sea, carrying with it the thin, precious layer of topsoil. In the past the modest number of people in relation to the continent's landmass largely offset the loss of their water, but no longer. Since there appears no prospect that the total amount of available water from the oceans will increase, there will simply be insufficient water for domestic, agricultural, or pastoral use. In the great basin of the River Nile its waters will remain relatively constant while its population will increase from 265 million in 2001 to 405 million in 2025. In the twenty-first century water has become a scarce resource, and the greatest and most neglected challenge Africa must face in its future.

Africa has felt the effects of its commerce with other continents for millennia, and it will continue to do so into the twenty-first century. From its inception, ocean-borne trade with Europe and Asia brought manufactured products to Africa's shores, which were exchanged for raw materials. For most of the history of this trade, Africans were importing goods that they already produced, such as pottery from Asia, alcohol and cloth from Europe. However, with the rise of industrialization – first in Europe, later in North America and parts of Asia – Africans have increasingly exported raw materials for products that they do not produce themselves. During the colonial era European powers had little interest in cultivating indigenous African industries, such as the production of cloth or iron, or protecting them from foreign competition. Nor were they interested in encouraging new industrial activity. In some cases colonial authorities actively deterred manufacturing initiatives in Africa, such as when the British discouraged their Gold Coast colony from utilizing their cocoa production to manufacture candy bars. With independence came an enthusiasm for industrial production to wean Africa's fledgling economies away from reliance on individual commodities, but little came of these efforts. Today Africa's industrial base forms a negligible component of the continent's economy. While there are exceptions to this rule in contemporary Africa (for example, South Africa assembles some Japanese and German automobiles), the continent continues to export raw materials for electronics, transportation equipment, and other sophisticated manufactured goods which are not produced on the continent.

Foreign economies continue to exert a powerful influence on African affairs. Historically cheap imports from European manufacturers have choked off the production of goods in Africa. Today African economies continue to feel the pressure of foreign influence. In the past the economic policies imposed upon African governments by the international community to promote growth have been less than successful. Known as "Structural Adjustment," these policies assumed that independent African states had become economically inefficient because of bloated bureaucracies, state-guided economic policies, subsidies for food and fuel prices, and economic policies they had been encouraged to implement by Western "experts" during the 1960s. International lending institutions such as the International Monetary Fund and the World Bank insisted that future economic aid would be dependent upon African states embracing aggressive policies of retrenchment modeled on Western principles of classical, capitalist economics. Although these policies may have long-term benefits for economic growth, their short-term results can prove disastrous for poverty-stricken Africans forced into unemployment without the safety net of subsidies for basic goods. Structural adjustment programs placed a tremendous stress on social systems in Africa, and encouraged a backlash among politicians whose followers had to bear the brunt of these reforms.

In 1998 two economists at the World Bank revealed in a new study that African countries whose economic policies maintained low inflation, budget surpluses, free trade, and functioning institutions – had a growing individual and national income even with little aid, and that a larger amount of aid would create an even higher rate of growth in contrast to those states with unsustainable policies and stagnant institutions. The policy that development aid should favor well-governed poor countries has become conventional wisdom that has opened a new era for African economic growth in the twenty-first century. This is the logic that has stimulated the Millennium Challenge Account (MCA) by the United States to fund African development projects with an increase of 50 percent by 2006 to complement a similar independent African initiative, the New Partnership for Africa's Development (NEPAD). These similar schemes are based on the principle of major assistance in return for transparency in business, a verifiable standard of political conduct, and military reform. Those countries, such as Ghana and Uganda, that meet certain criteria, whether it is Freedom House standards of democracy or IMF development rules, will receive greater aid. These African and Western initiatives are being joined by private philanthropic organizations. Less ideologically driven than foreign donors, these organizations demand accountability for the projects they support, and insist that the use of their donations be assiduously monitored. These new economic policies are not without controversy, but they are bold and creative efforts to encourage economic growth.

African societies retain many of the political, class, and gender inequalities that have existed for millennia. The most conspicuous of these anomalies is slavery, which continues today in pockets of the continent. The most egregious examples have been in the Sudan during its long and debilitating civil war, where the capture and sale of slaves from among the people of the

Figure 26.1 *Johannesburg, South Africa. Less than 150 years ago Johannesburg was an uninhabited field: today it is Africa's fifth largest city.*

southern Sudan by those from the north has ignited international condemnation. There are also recorded instances of slavery in West Africa; some are the result of conflicts, while other slaves – such as those in the Sahelian country of Mauritania – are the victims of ancient dependent relationships. International intervention, largely organized by the United Nations, has resolved and contained some of these internal conflicts and helped to disrupt this new slave trade. Other African governments are firmly committed by international agreements to prevent the practice of slavery. With the increasing settlement of Africa's civil wars, the slave trade and slavery in Africa will diminish to illegal contraband or be redefined, as in the West and Asia, to those imprisoned by the economic poverty of the sweat shop, the picking fields, or servitude to the wealthy.

Gender inequalities continue to plague many African societies. Though gender equality was promised in the constitutions of many African states, the deeply rooted patriarchal social systems in many communities continue to limit the economic opportunities of women. Studies indicate that women do 80 percent of the work in contemporary African societies. However, in many countries their legal rights are limited, and they remain subject to the domination of fathers, husbands, and brothers. The problem is particularly acute in communities where cattle-keeping has historically dominated social and economic life, as male control of livestock has given men greater authority over women. Lack of education, economic opportunities, and legal equality has made rural women in southern Africa particularly vulnerable to infection with HIV. On a national scale, women continue to play a limited role in governance or in electoral politics Africa. There have been some signs of slow movement to rectify these discrepancies in the past two decades. In 1991 it was public protests by women in Bamako that brought down the dictatorship in Mali. In 1993 Agathe Uwilingiyimana (1953–1994) was appointed prime minister of Rwanda, only to be assassinated at the beginning of the genocide in 1994. In 2004 Mozambique appointed Luis Diogo (b. 1958) as its first female prime minister. And in 2006 Liberian voters elected Ellen Johnson Sirleaf (b. 1938) as the continent's first elected female president. Despite the success of these remarkable women, the twenty-first century will surely continue to witness a struggle to bring gender equality to African communities.

Women are not alone in being disenfranchised from contemporary African politics. In 2006, many African states are ruled by an old-guard elite that has resisted political opposition, often ruthlessly. Elections in Zimbabwe and Kenya, to choose but two examples, are consistently criticized by international observers for their lack of transparency. States that have been racked by civil war – such as Angola and the Democratic Republic of Congo – have no infrastructure for operating representative elections. However, here again there are promising signs for the twenty-first century. The patrons of many of Africa's old-guard despots have, since the end of the cold war, proven more willing to pressure their allies to reform the political process. The collapse of the Mobutu dictatorship in Zaire (now the Democratic Republic of Congo) in 1997 came about in part because his Western allies were no longer willing to prop him up at all costs. And democratically elected regimes are beginning to emerge in several African states. South Africa's first-ever democratic elections in 1994, though marred by political violence, gave legitimacy to the ANC as the democratically elected leadership of the continent's greatest economic power. And the Democratic Republic of Congo, after almost a decade of civil war, held national elections in October 2006.

Africa continues to feel the influences of the world's two great monotheist religions, Christianity and Islam. Both religions have deep roots in Africa's history, and both continue to expand their influence on the continent, though as the new millennium dawned, scholars debated which of the two was spreading more rapidly. European missionaries have been seeking African converts since the Portuguese first made contact with the kingdom of Kongo in the fifteenth century. Today a wide array of European and American mission groups blanket the continent, and their efforts are expanding annually. Some estimates hold that fully 40 percent of the peoples of Africa converted to Christianity during the twentieth century. While many became affiliated with European and American Christian organizations, others gravitated toward indigenous Christian groups. In 1899 Mary Kingsley observed that Christianity in Africa would be challenged and integrated with African traditional religions. She was correct, and this trend is set to continue. With a Christian population of over 300 million, the continent has become a new Christian heartland. African apostolic Christianity has divested itself of much Western cultural and political baggage, adopting Evangelical voluntary forms of Christian independence expressed as a mass movement fluent in the vernacular, which responds to local spiritual needs and values.

Like Christianity, Islam has adapted itself to African circumstances. In the past Sufism provided a major ingredient in the practice of Islam that continues to flourish throughout the African Muslim world and beyond. Much thought and debate by African Muslims in the past as to the relation of Islam and the secular state and its interaction with Christianity and traditional religions will accompany the spread of Islam in Africa in the twenty-first century. There is a growing belief among African Muslims that Islam has returned to the center of society in the individual search for identity in Africa and the wider Islamic world. Islamic conversion gathered momentum under colonial rule, and continues to exert a powerful sway over West and coastal East African communities. The simultaneous explosions at the US embassies in Tanzania and Kenya in 1998, carried out by terrorists associated with the international terrorist group al-Qaeda, reflects the connections between radical Islamists in northeast Africa and the Middle East, and the coastal Islamic communities.

In the nineteenth century the world's strongest nations sought to impose a political order onto the continent. These same countries granted African nations their independence in the expectation that they would continue to influence their affairs, and continued to meddle in the affairs of independent African nations. The end of the cold war in the 1990s appeared to change this dynamic, as Western interference was replaced by a policy of neglect, to the point that during the 2000 American presidential election, presidential candidate George W. Bush maintained that Africa "doesn't fit into the national strategic interests." In a post-cold war era, foreign powers would continue to intervene in Africa, but the reasons, nature, and scope of their intervention was much changed. The disastrous United States mission to Somalia in the early 1990s foundered because it was justified as a humanitarian mission. When the American public recoiled at images of the bodies of American servicemen being mutilated in the streets of Mogadishu, there was little incentive for politicians to maintain a presence in the region. In the years since the US withdrawal, Somalia has remained a "collapsed" state, with no effective government, under the sway of militant Islamist groups and warlords.

The failure of foreign intervention in Somalia discouraged the USA and its allies from intervening two years later when a genocidal civil war broke out in the Great Lakes nation of Rwanda. When it became apparent to the international community that Rwanda was experiencing a human rights catastrophe on a scale unprecedented since the Second World War, the Western powers were hesitant to support intervention. With no perceived national security interests in Rwanda, the United States declined to take decisive action to avert the slaughter of 800,000 Tutsi and moderate Hutu. In 2001, however, when British prime minister Tony Blair sent troops to Sierra Leone and encouraged his American allies to do the same in Liberia, he argued on behalf of historic responsibility, not Great Britain's national self-interest.

But if the West's growing indifference to African affairs allowed civil war in Somalia and genocide in Rwanda to go unchecked, it also made some of Africa's elderly dictators vulnerable to internal opposition. Ethnic and political violence during the 1990s reflected the death knell of a generation of despotic regimes that had dominated cold war Africa. In Zaire the West turned its back on the crumbling regime of Mobutu Sese Seko, allowing insurgents supported by neighboring Uganda to topple him in 1997. However, the demise of Mobutu was a mixed blessing for the people of the re-named Democratic Republic of Congo, as his departure ushered in nearly a decade of civil war and humanitarian catastrophe. In a similar vein, the death in 1993 of strongman Félix Houphouët-Boigny after three decades in power in Ivory Coast set in train a series of coups and ultimately a civil war in 2002.

The war that ended Mobutu's long reign was part of a wave of violence that swept the Great Lakes region during the 1990s. Uganda for its part has had to contend with an insurgency from the Lord's Resistance Army (LRA), led by a reclusive mystic named Joseph Kony (b. 1964), who draws his support from the Acholi of northern Uganda. The LRA claims it aims to overthrow the Ugandan government and install a regime based on the Ten Commandments. For the last couple of decades it has successfully defied all attempts by the Ugandan army to crush it, and continues to terrorize northern Uganda, massacring civilians and abducting children for use as soldiers and slaves. Kony and several of his followers have been indicted by the United Nations International Criminal Court for crimes against humanity.

Across Uganda's northern border in southern Sudan, Africa's longest-running conflict (1955–1972, 1983–2004), in which the southern Sudanese Sudan People's Liberation Movement/Army (SPLM/A) has been trying to win independence for southern Sudan from the Islamist government in Khartoum, took on a renewed intensity during the 1990s. The regime in Khartoum has also earned international condemnation since 2003 for supporting the mounted militias, or Janjawid, in the western province of Darfur, in their campaign to terrorize and drive off farmers.

In West Africa the 1990s witnessed several protracted and related civil conflicts. At the center of much of the violence was the Liberian leader Charles Taylor, who toppled Samuel Doe from power in 1989 (who had himself carried out a coup in 1980) and embarked on an invasion of neighboring Sierra Leone in 1991. Taylor's supporters forced children into the army and carried out horrible mutilations against civilians. The civil conflicts in Sierra Leone and Liberia plunged both states into anarchy until a United Nations peacekeeping force helped reestablish a national government in Liberia in 2002. Taylor went into exile in Nigeria before being turned over to a United Nations tribunal in 2006 to face prosecution for war crimes and crimes against humanity.

Not all of Africa's strongmen were pushed aside during the tumultuous decade that followed the end of the cold war. In Equatorial Guinea, Spain's lone former colony south of the Sahara, Teodoro Obiang Nguema Mbasogo (b. 1942) has terrorized political opponents and made himself one of the world's richest people since seizing power in a 1979 coup. In Zimbabwe, President Robert Mugabe, popularly elected in 1980, and a leader of the nation's liberation struggle, has become increasingly autocratic, persecuting political opponents and limiting the freedom of the press. The rule of Africa's longest-serving leader, El Hadj Omar Bongo Ondimba (b. 1935) of Gabon, has been criticized as corrupt and despotic since he seized power in a 1967 coup.

If the end of the cold war left African affairs largely neglected by the Western powers, it also strengthened the position of reformers in the continent who have demanded political and economic change – democracy and economic restructuring. The political reforms were welcomed and encouraged by the West. At the beginning of the 1990s there were no more than four or five states that could reasonably claim to have democratic governments. By the beginning of the twenty-first century there are more than twenty whose stable and popular governments have little attraction for the international media – who prefer to seek the sensational disaster – but have quietly and purposefully improved the lives of their citizens. No where has the triumph of democracy drawn greater attention than in South Africa. In 1994 South Africa ended its long march to democracy when Nelson Mandela was elected president in the first multiracial elections. Although the campaign was marred by violence among supporters of various political parties, white South Africa ceded power peacefully to a democratically elected regime, in the greatest triumph for democracy in post-independent Africa. Recent elections in Kenya, Zimbabwe, and Gabon have been dogged by charges of intimidation and vote-rigging. But even such contests reflect the pressure African regimes are facing as enthusiasm for democracy spreads.

The gradual spread of democracy has also been accompanied by a growing realization of a greater need for regional and continental cooperation hitherto inhibited by the old arbitrary colonial boundaries. The increasing recognition and demand for inter-state arrangements has its roots in the pan-African vision of Kwame Nkrumah and other nationalists who saw the unity of African states as a bulwark against Western influence. These dreams of continental or regional unity disappeared during the dying days of colonialism, as the new rulers of independent states, having won sovereignty, were not about to abandon it to leaders of a larger and more amorphous union, a principle that was cemented in the charter that established the Organization of African Unity on May 25, 1963. Twenty years later new African leaders began to realize that more could be gained by cooperating with their neighbors than by insular sovereignty. The series of violent conflicts that broke out in West Africa during the 1980s and early 1990s, threatening to destabilize neighboring states, led to greater regional cooperation. In May 1975 sixteen Anglophone and Francophone states of West Africa had formed a single economic community, the Economic Community of West African States (ECOWAS), to coordinate economic policies and to liberalize trade and commerce within West Africa. In 1990 ECOWAS expanded its regional authority by forming the Economic

Community Ceasefire Monitor Group (ECOMOG), a regional peacekeeping force that has deployed troops to intervene in civil wars in Liberia, Côte d'Ivoire, and Sierra Leone.

In southern Africa Botswana took the lead in developing a regional trade zone in 1992 by which regional production and marketing would influence national economic planning. By 2000 the Southern African Development Community (SADC) was coordinating the closer integration of the economies of its thirteen member states, which included South Africa and the Democratic Republic of Congo. Its leaders did not limit themselves solely to economic affairs, for Nelson Mandela (South Africa), Robert Mugabe (Zimbabwe), and Sir Ketumile Masire (Botswana, b. 1925) have played an important role in supporting peace, reconciliation, and democracy in Angola. In eastern Africa a similar regional association, the Inter-Governmental Authority on Drought and Development (IGADD, after 1996 the Inter-Governmental Authority on Development, IGAD), consisting of Kenya, Ethiopia, Somalia, Djibouti, Sudan, and Uganda, was founded in 1986 to coordinate relief in drought-stricken northeast Africa. It has since been the chief mediator in conflict resolution between Ethiopia and Somalia in 1986 and 1988 and since the 1990s has played the principal role in ending Africa's longest civil war in the Sudan.

The widespread recognition that African states need to work together to resolve common problems was recognized by the transformation of the Organization of African Unity (OAU) to the African Union (AU) in 1999. The venerable OAU had been established in 1963 to safeguard the sovereignty of new African nations, and to coordinate the movement against the last vestiges of colonialism on the continent. However, by the 1990s the OAU had become widely regarded as a "dictators' club" of aging African leaders. The creation of the AU symbolized the need for an institution that could mobilize its members to work together on issues and problems that are continental rather than local or even regional. In 2002 the organization drafted the New Economic Partnership for Africa's Development, a blueprint for coordinating economic development throughout the continent. In 2004 the AU sponsored a "peer governance" board to encourage political reforms and democracy in Africa by having participating nations grade the quality of governance in member states. The AU has also established its own human rights court, an All-African Parliament, and a Council of African Leaders. It has framed the necessary requirements for the organizations of a continental peacekeeping force by 2010. Although these initiatives remain in their early stages, they symbolize a new spirit of cooperation and a greater realization among African states that is unprecedented in the post-independence era and a demonstration of optimism for the future of Africa in the twenty-first century.

Index